Ana Moreira Serge Demeyer (Eds.)

Object-Oriented Technology

ECOOP'99 Workshop Reader

ECOOP'99 Workshops, Panels, and Posters
Lisbon, Portugal, June 14-18, 1999
Proceedings

Springer

Volume Editors

Ana Moreira
Departamento de Informática
Faculdade de Ciências e Tecnologia
Universidade Nova de Lisboa
2825-114 Monte da Caparica, Portugal
E-mail: amm@di.fct.unl.pt

Serge Demeyer
University of Berne
Neubruckstr. 10, 3012 Bern, Switzerland
E-mail: demeyer@iam.unibe.ch

Cataloging-in-Publication data applied for

Die Deutsche Bibliothek - CIP-Einheitsaufnahme

Object oriented technology : workshop reader, wokshops, panels, and posters ; proceedings / ECOOP '99, Lisbon, Portugal, June 14 - 18, 1999. Ana Moreira ; Serge Demeyer (ed.). - Berlin ; Heidelberg ; New York ; Barcelona ; Hong Kong ; London ; Milan ; Paris ; Singapore ; Tokyo : Springer, 1999
(Lecture notes in computer science ; Vol. 1743)
ISBN 3-540-66954-X

CR Subject Classification (1998): D.1-3, H.2, F.3, C.2, K.4

ISSN 0302-9743
ISBN 3-540-66954-X Springer-Verlag Berlin Heidelberg New York

Typesetting: Camera-ready by author
SPIN: 10749981 06/3142 – 5 4 3 2 1 0 Printed on acid-free paper

Lecture Notes in Computer Science 1743

Edited by G. Goos, J. Hartmanis and J. van Leeuwen

Springer

Berlin
Heidelberg
New York
Barcelona
Hong Kong
London
Milan
Paris
Singapore
Tokyo

Preface

The 13th European Conference on Object-Oriented Programming (ECOOP'99) brought some 500 participants to Lisbon from June 14th to June 18th, 1999. As usual, the workshops took place during the first two days of the conference and gave authors and participants an opportunity to present and discuss the most topical and innovative ideas in object-oriented technology. The importance of the workshops within the context of ECOOP is becoming increasingly recognised; for the first time in the history of the conference, the number of workshop proposals for ECOOP'99 actually exceeded the slots available and some had to be refused.

In addition to the usual conference proceedings, Springer-Verlag has also undertaken, for the past two years, the publication of a Workshop Reader, which brings together the results of the workshops, panels, and posters held during the conference.

This book, the 4th ECOOP Workshop Reader, differs from previous editions in two significant ways. Firstly, instead of simply reproducing the position papers, it presents an overview of the main points made by the authors as well as a summary of the discussions that took place. Secondly, to make the text more uniform and readable, all chapters have been written in a common format (using LaTeX lncs style files).

This book was only possible thanks to the effort of each workshop organiser in particular, and each workshop, poster, and panel participant in general. The innovations introduced in this book implied additional work for the workshop organisers in terms of recording and summarising the discussions as well as adapting the written presentations to a common format. This extra effort will certainly be appreciated by the readers.

The workshop proposals initially submitted covered a wide range of topics, too diverse and specialised for any single person to evaluate adequately. The proposals were distributed for evaluation to colleagues in the computer science department of the Universidade Nova de Lisboa, and their assistance in this regard is gratefully acknowledged.

Organising the workshops and this book proved to be very stimulating and instructive; we wish our readers an equally fruitful experience.

October 1999

Ana Moreira
Serge Demeyer

Table of Contents

Object Interoperability

Antonio Vallecillo[1], Juan Hernández[2], and José M. Troya[1]

[1] Universidad de Málaga, Spain
{av,troya}@lcc.uma.es
[2] Universidad de Extremadura, Spain
juanher@unex.es

Abstract. This report summarizes the presentations, discussions and outcomes of the ECOOP'99 Workshop on Object Interoperability, held in Lisbon on Monday, June 14, 1999. Divided into four main sessions, the workshop covered some of the most important issues related to object interoperability at different levels (such as protocols, semantics, or mediated architectures). Two are the main goals of this report. First, it tries to provide a snapshot of some of the current research being carried out within the object-oriented community in these areas. And second, it summarizes some of the open questions and issues related to object interoperability, in order to set the basis for further research activities.

1. Introduction

Interoperability is one of the key aspects related to the construction of large object-oriented systems, and can be defined as the ability of two or more entities to communicate and cooperate despite differences in the implementation language, the execution environment or the model abstraction. Basically, three main levels of interoperability between objects can be distinguished: the *signature level* (names and signatures of operations), the *protocol level* (partial ordering between exchanged messages and blocking conditions), and the *semantic level* (the "meaning" of the operations).

Interoperability is now well defined and understood at the signature level, for which middleware architects and vendors are currently trying to establish different interoperational standards (e.g. CORBA, JavaBeans or DCOM), as well as bridges among them. Nevertheless, all parties are starting to recognise that this sort of interoperability is not sufficient for ensuring the correct development of applications in open systems. Typical interface definition languages (IDLs) provide just the syntactic descriptions of the objects' public methods, i.e. their signatures. However, nothing is said about the ordering in which the objects expect their methods to be called, or their blocking conditions, or what the objects really perform. Basically, current IDLs do not describe the usage and the capabilities of the objects. We have lately seen some partial advances at the protocol and semantic levels, but we are still far from reaching any satisfactory solution because special problems appear when objects have to interoperate in open and independently extensible systems, in which components can dynamically evolve.

A. Moreira and S. Demeyer (Eds.): ECOOP'99 Workshops, LNCS 1743, pp. 1–21, 1999.

Apart from this, object interoperability can also embrace aspects besides and beyond components. Although often confused, components and objects can be really seen as orthogonal concepts, each one having its own specific and distinguishing features. In general, component interoperability can be seen as a particular case of the object interoperability problem.

Another interesting issue and closely related to object interoperability is replaceability, i.e. the polymorphic substitutability of objects in clients, or how to guarantee that the behaviour of subclass instances is consistent with that of superclass instances. Interoperability and replaceability are the two flip sides of the *object compatibility* coin.

All those are currently hot issues for international standardisation bodies, like ISO and OMG. In particular, RM-ODP is one of the standards that is now trying to incorporate semantic interoperability between objects. However, the study and usage of those levels currently present serious challenges to the object-oriented community, from both the theoretical and practical points of view. This marked the starting point of our workshop.

2. The WOI'99 Workshop

The first ECOOP Workshop on Object Interoperability (WOI'99) was held in Lisbon, Portugal, on Monday, June 14, 1999. The main aim of the workshop was to provide a venue where researchers and practitioners concerned with all aspects of interoperability and replaceability between objects could meet, disseminate and exchange ideas and problems, identify some of the key issues related to these topics, and explore together possible solutions.

As stated in the call for papers, the workshop aimed to promote research concerned with all aspects of interoperability and replaceability between objects, specially at the protocol and semantics levels. In particular, topics of interest included:

- Enabling models, technologies and architectures for object interoperability.
- Interface and protocol matching.
- Mediated architectures and automated construction of mediators.
- Resource discovery based on semantic matching.
- Extensions to object interfaces and IDLs to deal with protocol or semantic interoperability.
- Formal aspects of interoperability.
- Object replacement and correct subclassing.
- Using coordination to achieve interoperability.

All papers submitted to WOI'99 were formally reviewed by at least two referees, and nine papers were finally accepted for presentation at the workshop. Contributions were divided into three groups, according to the main subjects of the workshop and providing new research directions with regard to questions mentioned above:

- First, the contributions focusing on object interoperability at the *protocol level*, addressing both IDL extensions to deal with protocol interoperability and interface and protocol matching.
- In the second group we find the contributions focusing on object interoperability at the *semantic level*, including IDL extensions to cope with semantic interoperability, resource discovery based on semantic matching and formal aspects of interoperability at this level.
- And finally, there were three contributions proposing enabling models, technologies and mediated architectures for object interoperability.

The workshop was organized in 4 sessions. The first three were devoted to the aforementioned topics (protocols, semantics, and mediated architectures), where the ideas and issues related to the selected papers were presented and discussed. In the last session some issues of special interest to the participants were identified, and attendees split into four working groups to discuss them in detail. The conclusions reached by each group were presented and debated during a final wrap-up session.

The workshop gathered 19 people from 12 different countries, who actively participated in very lively discussions, in which quite a few new and consolidated ideas were presented and analyzed. Names and affiliations of participants are as follows:

- Rick van Rein (`vanrein@cs.utwente.nl`), Univ. of Twente, The Netherlands.
- Jun Han (`jhan@monash.edu.au`), Monash Univ., Australia.
- Sotirios Terzis (`Sotirios.Terzis@cs.tcd.ie`), Univ. of Dublin, Ireland.
- Mauro Gaspari (`gaspari@cs.unibo.it`), Univ. of Bologna, Italy.
- Twittie Senivongse (`stwittie@chula.ac.th`), Chulalongkorn Univ., Thailand.
- Jaime Gómez (`jaime@dlsi.ua.es`), Univ. of Alicante, Spain.
- Juan M. Corchado and P. Cuesta (`{corchado,pcuesta}@uvigo.es`), Univ. of Vigo, Spain.
- Elena Rodríguez (`malena@lsi.upc.es`), Technical Univ. of Barcelona, Spain.
- Markku Sakkinen (`sakkinen@cs.jyu.fi`), Univ. of Jyväskylä, Finland.
- Miguel P. Correia (`mpc@di.fc.ul.pt`), Univ. of Lisboa, Portugal.
- Edi Ray Zavaleta (`ediray@pollux.ipn.mx`), Instituto Politécnico Nacional, Mexico.
- Ulf Schünemann (`ulf@cs.mun.ca`), Memorial Univ. of Newfoundland, Canada.
- Augustin Prodan (`aprodan@umfcluy.ro`), Iulin Hatieganu Univ., Romania.
- Holger Riedel (`Holger.Riedel@uni-konstanz.de`), Univ. of Konstanz, Germany.
- Richmond Cooper (`rich@dcs.gla.ac.uk`), Univ. of Glasgow, Scotland.
- Juan Hernández (`juanher@unex.es`), Univ. of Extremadura, Spain.
- Carlos Canal and Antonio Vallecillo (`{av,canal}@lcc.uma.es`), Univ. of Málaga, Spain.

This report summarizes the workshop presentations, discussions and results, and has been put together with the help of all the workshop participants. After this introduction, sections 3, 4 and 5 describe the outcomes of the first three sessions, where the selected papers were presented and debated. Each section starts with a brief outline of the session, together with the extended abstract of the presented papers as prepared by their own authors. Section 6 is dedicated to the last session, in which four main topics were identified for discussion in small groups, and their outcomes debated at the end by all participants. Finally, section 7 draws some conclusions and also raises some interesting questions about the topics being discussed during the workshop. Some of the discussions that happened during the initial three sessions have been shortened or left out in the summary of the sessions as they became part of the final conclusions presented at the end of the report.

In addition to this report, a book with the Proceedings of the workshop has been produced [23]. The book, entitled "Object Interoperability", has been published by the University of Málaga and contains the full-length version of all selected papers. More information about the workshop and its participants is also available at the Web page of the workshop: www.lcc.uma.es/~av/ecoop99/ws.

3. Session 1: "Protocols"

The first session was dedicated to the introduction of the workshop and the discussion of interoperability issues at the *protocol* level. In our context, a protocol is a restriction on the ordering of incoming and/or outgoing messages.

Two papers were presented at this initial session. The first one, by Rick van Rein, showed how protocol information can be used for checking workflow processes among objects. Protocols of incoming messages are used to specify how an object should access the services exported by another object(s). Workflows are encapsulated into classes, roles are defined to model the behaviour of objects, and protocols are checked using a protocol checking tool called Paul. Protocols can be used for the automatic checking of workflow processes, allowing the discovery of some workflow flaws in the early stages of the system design.

The work by Carlos Canal, Lidia Fuentes and Antonio Vallecillo proposes an IDL extension that uses a subset of π-calculus for describing objects service protocols. In their proposal, the IDL specifies not only the services that objects offer but also the services that objects require from other objects in order to accomplish their tasks. Besides, the IDL provides protocol information for specifying the ordering in which the objects call other methods and in which they expect their methods to be called, and their blocking conditions.

3.1. Protocol-Safe Workflow Support for Santa Claus

Rick van Rein. University of Twente (vanrein@cs.utwente.nl).

During object oriented analysis, objects can be partially modelled using any state diagram formalism [10, 6]. This facilitates the understanding of the order in which objects may participate in operations. With a few exceptions [19, 13] including our own work on the protocol checker Paul [18], it is not customary to exploit this form of process information in consistency checks.

On the other hand, during workflow analysis business processes are captured in workflow charts. It is common for workflow systems to perform consistency checks, exploiting formal process notions such as Petri nets [1] or Spin [11]. Workflow processes often act as clients of a set of implementation objects, and if the process knowledge of both notions is brought together, it is possible to check whether they are compatible or not. We perform a process check, by translating workflow processes into our protocol assuring universal language Paul. Although several other process aspects are interesting to consider, we limit our current presentation to checking just protocols, i.e. the order of invocations.

Our work introduces a kind of Petri nets to describe workflow processes. In addition to standard Petri net concepts, we also allow communication between workflows. A workflow model can in general refer to multiple implementation objects, and this matches well with the notion of multiple import roles in Paul. To perform protocol checking, we map each workflow process onto a class in Paul, with one import role for each object accessed. The imported protocol for an object is the projection of the workflow process on that object. We assume that implementation objects are already described in terms of Paul objects. It is not hard [18] to generate Paul classes from state diagrams (or our extended Petri nets). We assume that different workflows each access a different export role of a Paul class.

Our last modelling step is to associate the workflow classes' imported roles with the corresponding implementation objects' exported roles and let Paul search for protocol inconsistencies. For each discovered protocol error, Paul generates a helpful error message, including the trace that led to the error. It has been our experience (and our full paper demonstrates this point) that this feedback is very helpful in debugging the protocol aspects of software.

The full version of our paper [17] walks through a case study demonstrating this process of workflow/implementation verification. The paper, plus case study files and the the protocol checker Paul can be downloaded from the following URL `ftp://ftp.cs.utwente.nl/pub/doc/Quantum/Paul/Santa-1.0-2.tar.gz`.

3.2. Extending IDLs with π-Calculus for Protocol Compatibility

Carlos Canal, Lidia Fuentes, and Antonio Vallecillo. University of Málaga. ({canal,lff,av}@lcc.uma.es).

Traditional object *Interface Description Languages* (IDLs) were meant for describing object interfaces in closed client-server applications, and therefore they present some limitations when used in open component-based applications:

1. IDLs describe the services that objects offer, but not the services that they require from other objects in order to accomplish their tasks.

2. Typical IDLs provide just the *syntactic* descriptions of the objects public methods, i.e. their signatures. However, nothing is said about the ordering in which the objects expect their methods to be called, or their blocking conditions.
3. IDLs are mainly used during compilation time but not during object execution, where other mechanisms need to be in place for dynamically knowing about the object interfaces and for checking their compatibility at run time.

On the other hand, component models are supported by middleware platforms. Distributed component platforms usually offer the common services and the communication mechanisms needed to dynamically assemble applications. By finding out the components currently connected and their IDLs, the platforms may be able to keep track of the dynamic attachments among components, check thier compatibility, and even manage some of the exceptions that arise during system execution (e.g. deadlock conditions).

The main aim of our work is to cover the three requirements mentioned above, namely describing at the IDL level the services that objects require during their execution, providing protocol information beyond the signature of their methods, and making all this information available at run time.

As the base IDL we have used CDL [22], an IDL which contains information about the incoming and outgoing messages of the components it describes. CDL has been extended in this work to contain protocol information, specified in textual π-calculus following the work by Canal et al. in [5]. MultiTEL [9] is a framework for building Web-based multimedia and collaborative applications that provides an ideal environment for building real applications, and that uses the latest component-based technology. MultiTEL serves as the platform in which our proposal can be experimented and validated. As major benefits of our proposal, the information needed for object reuse is now available as part of their interfaces, and also more precise interoperability checks can be done when building up applications, both static and dynamic (run-time) checks.

In our paper we also point out some of the limitations we have discovered when implementing our approach, and some of the problems encountered. For instance, checking π-calculus specifications is in general an NP-hard problem, which makes it impractical for real heavy-weighed applications (which is, by the way, one of the most unavoidable drawbacks of checking object compatibility at the protocol or semantic levels during run time). One way of overcoming this problem is by doing it on the fly as the platform captures the messages exchanged by the components, checking the conformance to a given protocol message by message. This method has the advantage of making it tractable from a practical point of view, and it also allows the management of dynamic attachments in open environments in a natural way. The disadvantage is that detection of deadlock and other undesirable conditions is also delayed until just before they happen, which may be unacceptable in some specific situations.

In summary, we have found that protocol information can be easily added to objet interface descriptions, but that some unavoidable problems do occur when this information is used for building applications in open systems.

4. Session 2: "Semantics"

The second session covered some of the semantics aspects of object interoperability, with the presentation of four selected papers. It is sometimes difficult to separate the protocol and semantic information (see section 6.5), and therefore the allocation of papers to sessions is always questionable. In this report we have maintained the order in which the papers were presented at the workshop.

In the first place, Jun Han proposed an IDL extension which accounts not only for the syntactic aspects of the objects (components) interfaces (i.e. the signatures of their methods), but also includes semantic information (constraints, roles of interactions, etc.) for improving the selection and usage processes in component-based software development.

The paper by Sotirios Terzis and Paddy Nixon presented a semantic trading architecture for tackling interoperability problems at the semantic level in open systems. In order to provide a common vocabulary between the components (traders), the authors propose the construction of an ontology about the system's domain. This ontology may be built extracting information either at system design phase or by reverse knowledge engineering.

On the other hand, Anna Mikhajlova described an approach for reasoning about object interaction in distributed systems. By knowing the precise behaviour of client objects, it is possible to analyze the effect that object substitution will have on the clients, design the appropriate object interfaces, etc. The mathematical foundation for reasoning about this sort of interacting systems is based on the idea of contracts between the servers and their clients, uses proxy objects on both sides (the client and the server) for making distribution transparent, and defines a formal specification language for specifying behaviours.

Finally, Mauro Gaspari, Enrico Motta and Dieter Fensel introduced an automatic approach for selecting problem solving libraries based on semantic matching, using description logic. The proposed solution uses a formal basis and provides a decidable solution for the semantic matching problem in certain scenarios. One of the main advantages of their proposal is that in certain circumstances, resource discovery can be automatically achieved.

4.1. Semantic and Usage Packaging for Software Components

Jun Han. Monash University (`jhan@monash.edu.au`).

Interface specification provides a basis for the development, management and use of software components. As shown in Figure 1, our framework for software component packaging aimed at comprehensive component specification, especially its support for semantic and usage specification. It has the following aspects: signature, configurations, behavioural semantics, interaction constraints, and quality properties.

At the bottom level of the interface specification, there is the *signature* of the component, which forms the basis for the component's interaction with the

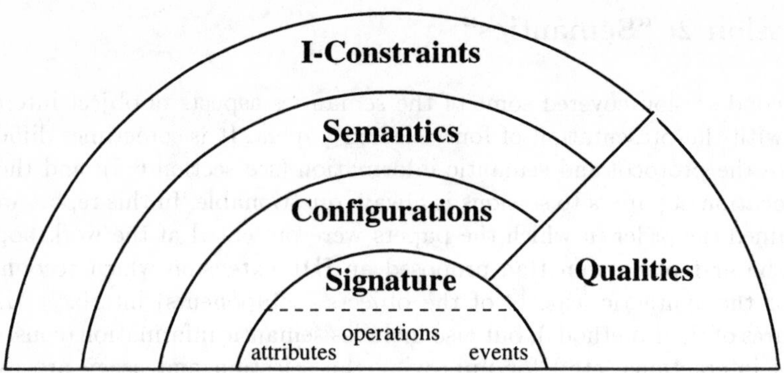

Fig. 1. Structure of Component Interface Specification

outside world and includes all the necessary mechanisms or elements for such interaction (i.e., attributes, operations and events).

The next level up is about the structural organisation of the interface in terms of component's roles in given contexts of use, i.e., *configurations.* As such, the component interface may have different *configurations* depending on the use contexts, each configuration may consist of a number of ports reflecting the roles that the component plays relative to neighbouring components, and a port has a number of associated interface elements. The interface configurations do not necessarily reflect the overall functional capability of the component. Rather, they capture the characteristics of the component relative to the respective use contexts, but behave within the overall capability of the component possibly with further restrictions.

The third level of the interface specification concerns the *semantics* of the individual signature elements, capturing their precise behaviour.

The fourth level up is the *interaction constraints* defining the interaction protocols of the component. Observing these constraints is necessary to ensure the proper use of the component in a given context.

The fifth aspect of the interface specification is about the characterisation of the component's *non-functional* or *quality properties*, such as performance, reliability and security. In general, each of the quality attributes requires its own model of characterisation and corresponding specification scheme in the interface.

The interface signature and behavioural semantics define the overall functional capability of the component, which should be conformed to by any use of the component. The interface configurations and interaction constraints concern the proper use of the component in perceived application contexts. The quality properties provide the basis for assessing the usability of the component (relative to given application contexts).

4.2. Semantic Trading: Tackling Interoperability Problems During System Integration

Sotirios Terzis and Paddy Nixon. University of Dublin.
({Sotirios.Terzis,Paddy.Nixon}@cs.tcd.ie).

The development of new enterprise systems is a process of dynamically selecting the appropriate components, and composing them into a new configuration. During this process severe interoperability problems arise since different systems were developed using different languages and protocols, on different platforms, under different models. A community of traders with the support of a composition service could tackle interoperability problems by selecting "compatible" components and plugging them together.

Currently, a trader with the support of an object request broker (ORB) could solve interoperability problems by locating all the compatible components (compatibility is translated into type conformance, which guarantees through interface matching that no unexpected input or output requirements or operation termination conditions will emerge) and allowing the ORB to plug them together by forwarding messages (method calls). But, limiting the matching process to the interface of the component means that information, such as message ordering or behaviour semantics, cannot be captured. So, although current trading is sufficient for solving interoperability problems at the signature level is unable to tackle problems at the protocol or the semantic level. What is needed is a new kind of semantically rich trading, which we call semantic trading, that shifts focus from the syntax (interface) to the behaviour (semantics) of the component.

Semantic trading differs from current trading in a number of aspects. First, the basis of semantic trading is a Component Description Language (CDL) instead of an Interface Description Language (IDL). CDL along side the interface is also able to capture behavioural characteristics (invariants and pre post-conditions), context dependencies (the interface of consumed and produced events) and relationships between components. Second, the matching process in semantic trading is based on the notion of component compatibility instead of type conformance, which is determined by substitutability according to the different reuse patterns. Finally, the trading process is supported by an ontology of concepts, which captures semantic relations identified either during system design or through reverse knowledge engineering, instead of a type hierarchy.

So, semantic trading could be used during system integration to tackle interoperability problems at all levels: at the semantic level by providing a common ontology for the expression of behaviour and relationships between components; at the signature level by maintaining interface conformance through the creation of a container and wiring of the retrieved components; and at the protocol level by making component dependencies explicit through the use of the ontology and CDL constructs. Finally, there are a number of open issues: how do we construct the ontology from design information, what are the component composition rules, what is the scripting language for the composition phase like, and how do we annotate components in order to expose their interoperability constraints.

4.3. Reasoning about Object Clients and Distributed Object Interaction

Anna Mikhajlova. Turku Centre for Computer Science, Åbo Akademi University (`Anna.Mikhajlova@abo.fi`).

Object-oriented systems consist of collaborating or interacting objects. To be able to ensure the correctness of an object-oriented system in its entirety, it is first necessary to capture the behaviour of the system in a precise specification. Although various standard methods can be used for specifying separate objects, specifying all possible clients of a given object presents a challenge. The ability to model and reason about object clients is critical for reasoning about systems consisting of interacting objects. The developer of a class should be aware of the behaviour of clients that will use instances of the class. Knowing the precise behaviour of the clients, it is possible to analyze the effect that substituting subclass instances for superclass instances will have on the clients, design the appropriate object interface, etc.

We show how to specify client objects using the mathematical foundation for reasoning about interactive systems, based on the idea of contracts [2] to support contracts between objects and their clients. In particular, we demonstrate how our approach can be used for reasoning about objects interacting with other objects possibly residing in different address spaces across the network. Such *distributed objects* can issue and receive *remote method calls* with the object issuing the call referred to as *client* and the object receiving the call referred to as *server*. To bridge the conceptual gap between local and remote method calls, objects known as *client-sides proxies* and *server-side proxies* are usually used.

We show how our model of object clients can be used to specify proxies and how one can reason about their properties. In particular, we focus on the issue of behavioural conformance of subclasses to their superclasses, and show how to reason about the behaviour of clients using subclass objects instead of superclass objects. We argue that in order for clients to benefit from using subclass objects, the subclass has to be a *refinement* of the corresponding superclass. The details of *class refinement* are, however, outside the scope of the paper and can be found in [15, 14].

As future work we would like to test the applicability of our approach to modeling other architectural solutions such as the *implicit invocation* mechanism.

4.4. Automatic Selection of Problem Solving Libraries Based on Competence Matching

Mauro Gaspari. University of Bologna (`gaspari@cs.unibo.it`).
Enrico Motta. The Open University (`e.motta@open.ac.uk`).
Dieter Fensel. University of Karlsruhe (`dfe@aifb.uni-karlsruhe.de`).

One of the main goals of the knowledge engineering research community is to develop methods and mechanisms which facilitate the reuse and the sharing of the knowledge that has been already formalised and embedded in specific applications [16]. An essential aspect of this knowledge concerns the problem solving method that have to be adopted to compute the solution in a knowledge based system (KBS). A problem solving method (PSM) decompose the reasoning task of a KBS in a number of subtasks and inference actions that are connected by knowledge roles. In this way a PSM describes the complex architecture implementing the reasoning part of a knowledge-based system.

The aim of the IBROW3 project [3] is to produce a software broker able to configure semi-automatically an intelligent problem solver out of reusable components. In order to identify the components relevant to an application the broker needs to understand their functionality and relate them to a problem specification. IBROW3 supports the development of reusable specifications by means of the UPML language [7]: the Unified Problem-solving Method description Language. UPML provides a general framework for specifying PSM which includes components, adapters, architectural constraints, informal guidelines and tools. The components are used to specify generic ontologies, tasks, PSMs and domain models: an ontology defines the terminology used in the specification; a task formalises a problem to be solved; and a domain model represents the knowledge which characterise a given application. Adapters instantiate these generic components in particular application domains. The UPML components include mechanisms to specify the competence of PSMs and tasks: these mechanisms express the semantics of PSM and are essential to understand if a PSM can be used to solve a given problem (task). This operation is realized by a competence matching rule.

The current version of the IBROW3 broker supports a semi-automatic competence matching rule. More precisely, the broker tries to select a PSM such that the PSM competence matches a given goal and, if it does not succeed, it asks the user. However, if certain conditions hold in the UPML specification, the problem of matching the goal with the PSM competence can be made fully automatic. In this paper we investigate this issue. We try to individuate a subset of UPML where competence matching is decidable. UPML specifications are translated in LOOM [4] an efficient theorem prover based on a description logic and competence matching is performed exploiting concept subsumption in LOOM. Since concept subsumption is decidable in LOOM (this holds for at least a well defined subset of its description logic), our matching rule is also decidable. Of course to obtain this result the UPML competence specification must be translated into the subset of LOOM descriptions which guarantees a decidable subsumption algorithm. Thus we need to restrict UPML which is based on first order logic, individuating a decidable subset. Although, this subset of UPML has still not been defined (it will be source of future research), the advantage of this approach is that we can apply results which have been achieved concerning concept subsumption in description logic (this issues has been investigated deeply in the literature) to our specific context of competence matching in UPML and in general in knowledge based systems. The reader interested to the details of our work can refer to the full paper which appears in the workshop proceedings [23].

5. Session 3: "Mediated Architectures for Object Interoperability"

The last session of the workshop was dedicated to enabling technologies and mediated architectures for object interoperability.

In the first place, Twittie Senivongse presented an approach for handling interface versioning in open systems, where component interfaces can dynamically evolve. In her approach two interfaces are considered equivalent if there exists a "mapping function" that transforms calls to one of them to equivalent calls to the other (and vice versa). Service substitutability can also be achieved with this function. Analogously, interface signatures can be changed at will as long as the evolver is able to define a mapping function to it. The paper also introduces the figure of a "mapping operator object", an entity that implements the actual diversion of method calls between different (substitutable) versions of a service.

Secondly, Jaime Gómez and Oscar Pastor extend a conceptual modelling approach (called OO-method) for developing distributed object-oriented applications using different component models.

The last of the presented papers, by Juan M. Corchado and Pedro Cuesta, introduced a multi-agent architecture for an advisory system where students can interact with teachers in order to get tutorial advice, i.e. to help them choosing the optional subjects more appropriate for them to enroll in depending on different criteria. Teachers and students are modelled as agents that interact by means of what the authors call "facilitators".

5.1. Behavioural Mapping for Service Substitutability

Twittie Senivongse. Chulalongkorn University (`stwittie@chula.ac.th`).

This work introduces the use of mappings that can map the behaviour of two services to create an illusion of one service for its clients, while in fact the clients' requests are processed by the other service. These mappings will enable substitutability between two service types that may not be related to each other by inheritance but are somehow functionally equivalent.

The mechanism consists of a mapping operator, a set of mapping functions, and a mapping information base. If a service type B can create an illusion of a service type A, a mapping operator object will intercept a request from a client of A, transform the request into that of B using the mapping functions that describe how the request is mapped, and forward the request to an instance of the service B. The result of the request will also be intercepted and transformed from the format of B into the format of A for the client. The mapping functions are stored in the mapping information base and it is required that they are defined by a human user who knows how B's functionality can be made equivalent to A's. In this mechanism, the most difficult part is defining the mapping functions. This work only presents a way to make use of the mapping functions once they are defined; it does not guide how to define them.

At present, the mechanism is used to support evolution transparency for clients of an old service such that their requests can be processed by a new-version service, and thus their programs need not be changed even though the new-version service has a changed interface that is not compatible with the old one. The mechanism allows a more flexible kind of service relationships, but its practicality is still questionable. Many times, when there is a version conflict, we simply throw away the old software version and start over with a new version with a new set of programs and hardware. The coercion of one software version into another as described here is useful only for systems that are not easily disposable where change of existing clients cannot be conducted immediately. Still, this mechanism may not be appropriate for critical systems as it introduces indirection into a normal invocation. There is also an issue on how different the interfaces of the two services can be to maintain functional equivalence. This is hard to say as there is no metrics to measure the differences and functional equivalence is semantics-related. We might require more description on the behaviour of the services to decide whether it is possible to define mappings. In this work, the definitions of the two interfaces can be different in an arbitrary way as long as the mappings for their behaviour can be defined.

Service substitutability can be extended to any two services that are not necessarily versions of each other, but have equivalent semantics. The mapping information base should then be integrated with the type repository of the supporting distributed architecture [20] so that the trading service can also select a service that has can-be-mapped behaviour, apart from that of the requested type or a subtype.

5.2. Conceptual Design and Development of Applications Based on Object Interoperability

Jaime Gómez. University of Alicante (jgomez@dlsi.ua.es).
Oscar Pastor. University of Valencia (opastor@dsic.upv.es).

In the field of OO methodologies, the move towards the object interoperability paradigm (OIP) requires existing approaches to be reconsidered. In particular, any method supporting OIP is required to exhibit at least the following 4 key principles: (1) a clear separation of object specification from its design and implementation, (2) an interface-focused design approach, (3) more formally recorded object semantics, (4) a rigorously recorded refinement process.

Our contribution to this state of the art is the OO-Method approach, which is basically built on a formal object-oriented model (OASIS) and whose main feature is that developers's efforts are focused on the conceptual modelling step. In OO-Method, when the designer is specifying the system, what he is really doing is capturing "on the fly" a formal specification of the system, according to the OASIS formal specification language. System requirements are captured according to a predefined, finite set of what we call conceptual modelling patterns because they are a representation of relevant concepts at the problem-knowledge space level. This way of capturing the requirements is concentrated on the object specification instead of their design and implementation. In consequence, the use of such a formal specification permits to capture formally the object semantics, based on the OASIS model.

Once the conceptual modelling step has been completed, the full OO implementation is obtained in an automated way following an abstract execution model (including structure and behaviour). This execution model establishes the corresponding mappings between conceptual model constructs and their representation in a particular software development environment.

In this way, the OO-Method can be seen as a CARE environment (Computed-Aided Requirements Engineering) where to face the whole software production process. We focus on how to properly capture the system requirements. The resultant conceptual model specifies what the system is (the problem space). Then, an abstract execution model is provided to guide the representation of these requirements in a specific software development environment (the solution space, which is centered on how the system will be implemented).

The abstract execution model is based on the concept of Conceptual Modelling Patterns. The OO-Method provides a well-defined software representation of these patterns in the solution space. A concrete execution model based on a component-based architecture is introduced to deal with the peculiarities of interoperability-based software (i.e. CORBA and Java RMI). The implementation of these mappings from problem space concepts to solution space representations opens the door to the generation of executable software components in an automated way. These software components together constitute a software product that is functionally equivalent to the requirements specification collected in the conceptual modelling step.

These ideas are being applied in the context of a component-based development tool that has been called JEM. JEM is a Java-based implementation for the OO-Method Execution Model. The basic purpose of JEM is to animate conceptual models captured with the OO-Method, over distributed internet/intranet environments. JEM fulfills all the requirements with respect to the model and the architecture proposed in this paper for the execution model.

5.3. Improving the Interoperability in Multi-agent Systems

Juan M. Corchado and Pedro Cuesta. University of Vigo.
({corchado,pcuesta}@uvigo.es).

This work introduces a multi-agent system architecture that facilitates the communication and co-operation of heterogeneous components. Multi-agent systems represent a new way of analysing, designing and implementing complex software systems. These systems are composed of several interacting agents. The flexibility and high-level nature of these interactions provide the power of this paradigm.

An agent is a computer system, situated in some environment, which is capable of flexible autonomous action in order to meet its design objectives [12]. The term agent is used to denote a computer system that enjoys the following properties [12, 24]: Autonomy, Social ability, Reactivity and Pro-activeness. In addition to having these properties, agents could be modelled using concepts that are more usually applied to humans. Shoham describes agents as entities with mental states such as believes, capabilities, choice and commitments. These states determine the actions that the agents perform and which can be affected by the information that they receive [21].

Multi-agent systems could be composed of agents implemented in different programming languages and which could be running in different execution environment. Our work is based in the use of communication agents or "facilitators" [8] to guarantee the interoperability between their components. Facilitators contain information about the rest of the agents of the system, including their location, low level communication protocol, and the KQML performative [8] subset used by the system. The facilitators are in charge of searching for the most adequate path to send the information to other facilitators or agents.

Agents are a new approach to guarantee the interoperability between heterogeneous components at conceptual or semantical level. Currently we are working on models for analysing, designing and building multi-agent systems using object oriented techniques with the intention of facilitating the implementation of such systems.

6. Session 4: Working Session

Once all presented works were debated, the last session was dedicated to the identification of several important issues related to object interoperability, and its discussion in small groups. The idea was not to solve them completely (impossible in just one hour and a half), but to define them in detail, identify the key problems behind them, and try to agree on possible research directions to overcome them.

As in a brainstorm, raised issues were written down in the blackboard. The following list of issues was obtained:

- **Protocol issues**
  - How do we transfer the protocol information into the program implementations?
  - Who checks the protocols at run-time? (needed in open systems)
  - Protocols can be seen as restrictions (constraints) on the behaviour of objects. But so are coordination constraints and rules . How does protocol interoperability relate to *coordination*? Are they both similar things?
- **Object (component) IDLs**:
  - What sort of information should they contain?
  - What sort of mechanisms should they allow (e.g. inheritance, type definitions, polymorphism, ...)?
  - How to incorporate all this information to existing commercial IDLs (CORBA, COM,...)?

- **Semantic issues**
  - Is it possible to analyze the system behaviour (e.g. safety and progress properties) just from the IDL descriptions of its constituent components? What additional information should be provided? And, by whom?
  - What needs to be checked at this level? What can be really checked and when?
- **Mediated architectures**
  - Metrics for object interfaces. Can we define a "distance" about how different two interfaces are?
  - Is interface versioning the same thing as subtyping?
  - When does a change in an interface result in a new interface version, or in a completely new interface?
  - Can we somehow automate the creation of "mediators" (mapping functions, facilitators, etc.)? When is it feasible?

From all those, the following questions were selected, and the attendees divided into 4 groups to discuss them:

- **Group 1** (moderated by Jun Han):
  - IDL contents and mechanisms
  - What to check and when to check it
- **Group 2** (moderated by Antonio Vallecillo):
  - What is an interface change?
  - How do we measure it?
- **Group 3** (moderated by Markku Sakkinen):
  - "Automatic" creation of mediators. Is it feasible?
  - What is a good "matching" rule?
- **Group 4** (moderated by Juan Hernández):
  - Component interoperability and application architectures

The conclusions reached by each group were presented by their moderators at the end of the session:

6.1. Group 1: IDL Information and Checking

The information that needs to appear in an object IDL will depend on the kind of checks we need to make, and on the usage information we want to know from the components. At least three different levels were identified:

- Signature information (currently available in all IDLs).
- Protocol information: expressed using process algebras (such as CSP or π-calculus), or temporal logic (basic TL, PSL, ...).
- Semantic information:
  - Operational semantics (i.e. object functionality):
    * Using state-based approaches (i.e. pre- and post-conditions),
    * Using algebraic approaches (but... is it really useful?),

    * Using pre- and post-conditions of *services* that are the composition of operations.
- Quality properties, e.g. performance, security or reliability. However, they are very tough to describe!

Regarding the second issue, what to check and when to do it, it depends on the level of information we want to use:

- We can have type checking using the signature information included in current IDLs. This sort of checks are usually static, although dynamic checks can be easily implemented for dynamic invocations.
- Protocol checks should be static as much as we can. However, the boundary between dynamic and static protocol checks in open systems should be defined. An important point here is the use of checking tools, currently available for most formal notations.
- In the third place, semantic checks are usually carried out using theorem proving or model checking techniques. Their complexity forces these checks to be static.
- Finally, quality checks (performance, security, reliability,...) cannot be usually done for individual components, but for applications as a whole: these checks are at the system (architectural) level. An important problem in this approach is how to characterize the information of individual components, to infer from them some of the desired system's properties.

6.2. Group 2: Metrics, Versions, and Interface Changes

Do we really need interface metrics? We tried to identify some scenarios that support the need of metrics, or their uselessness. One scenario where metrics are needed is in case of system re-design, when interfaces can (or have to) be redefined, combined or merged in order to fulfill some specific requirements. In those cases we need to know how *close* a given interface matches a given requirement, and how *far* it is from what we need. However, if components are black-box, immutable entities and we have only 0-1 choices for building with them our application (e.g. in a Windows environment), there is no need for metrics: interfaces either match our requirements or not, and that's all that matters.

An issue raised about interface metrics was about the need for heuristics when defining them. Some subjective information is always required for that, which seriously difficulties the definition of this sort of metrics.

On the other hand, the issue "versioning (vs.) subtyping" was also raised. At the end, we concluded that interface versioning is defined in each component model depending on the *rules* for deriving interfaces they use (i.e. the 'subtyping' rules that the model allows). For instance, COM does not allow interface changes, hence forbidding interface versioning. CORBA uses inheritance as the mechanism for deriving interfaces from existing ones, while in SOM special rules are defined for interface versioning.

In general, we concluded that if we decide to use 'standard' behavioural subtyping ($\sqsubseteq$), we can then define that A is a *new version* of B iff $B \sqsubseteq A$, and that A and B are *not comparable* iff $B \not\sqsubseteq A$ and $A \not\sqsubseteq B$.

6.3. Group 3: Automatic Creation of Mediators + Competence Matching Rule

Mediators are one of the keys for dealing with heterogeneity in open applications (e.g. in heterogeneous distributed databases). However, after the discussion it was agreed that they can hardly be generated automatically. Nevertheless, it was also pointed out that well-designed and implemented generic mediators are of special interest and that they can be widely and successfully used.

The second topic discussed was the competence matching rule defined in the paper presented by Mauro Gaspari. Here the problem is how to take into account the fact that problem solving methods may not be able to fulfill the goal of the tasks in all cases. No conclusions were reached on this issue, apart from realizing that this looks like a non-trivial problem.

6.4. Group 4: Mediated Architectures

Due to the background of the participants in this group, discussions were centered about software agents, and how they can be used for dealing with some of the semantic aspects of interoperability.

In the first place, in agent architectures the role of each agent is well-defined and known, and each agent maintains its own knowledge base. Furthermore, through the knowledge of the system domain, agents can identify the requirements and intentions of other agents. Hence, agent-based technology appears to offer some important benefits to the construction of open applications based on semantic (knowledge-based) requirements.

6.5. Final Discussions and Further Issues

Apart from the issues debated here, some further questions and interesting comparisons among the presented approaches were raised during the post-workshop discussions and preparation of this report. The e-mail discussions greatly helped to refine some of the common concepts and to define the exact terminology to be used (special thanks to Ulf Schünemann, Rick van Rein and Mauro Gaspari for their valuable inputs on this):

- The *signature* level was originally called the *syntactic* level. However, the separation between 'syntactical' and 'semantical' issues is hardly objective and certainly not absolute. For instance, what is semantical to one person (e.g. λ-calculus to model a functional programming language) can be considered as syntactical to another person (Barendregt). Also, in the programming languages community the type information is considered as semantic. The term 'signature' was agreed to be more accurate for this first level of interoperability.

- Similarly, the term and contents of the *semantic* level also triggered some interesting discussions. As Ulf Schünemann put it, semantic information may be already present on the signature level (types) and on the protocol level (c.f. trace semantics). So is this "semantic" level only concerned with the semantics not captured by signatures and protocols? Definitely the computed functions are located on this level, maybe they *are* the level?
- Protocols are one essential aspect of interoperability. However, do all presented approaches support them? Is "protocol" the ordering of invoked messages (as in Paul), the ordering of incoming and outgoing messages (as in CDL or in Han's proposal), or the ordering of messages going out from a method (as defined by Mikhajlova, although she does not explicitly call it "protocol").
- In the same sense, many of the presented approaches talk of *roles* of objects. But do they all mean the same thing?
- In most approaches (at least in CDL, Han's packaging, and Mikhajlova's formalism) the specification of behaviour relevant to interoperability is structured object-wise (component-wise). Only van-Rein's Paul has workflow-wise structured specifications additionally to object-wise ones. These two (orthogonal?) perspectives on behaviour are then checked for consistency.
- Pre-post conditions and invariants can have an important role in defining the interoperability of objects, although not necessarily at the semantic level: they can also be used to define protocols (e.g. blocking conditions, some semantic constraints on the dynamic behaviour of objects, or coordination constraints in exogenous coordination languages). At the semantic level we need mechanisms to express the fact that a given object can be used in a certain context, no matter whether these mechanisms are at the signature, protocol or semantic level.
- Concerning semantic information, an open point is to establish if there exists semantic information which is neither protocol or type information, and that can be effectively used to represent "competence" of libraries. Furthermore, given that it is possible to encode significant semantic information about objects, could the semantic matching be decidable or not?
- Finally, run-time (protocol and semantic) checks are sometimes needed. However, when it comes to real applications either their cost is too high or their results are obtained too late. Are they really practical?

7. Conclusions

A distinctive characteristic of any emerging research area is that the number of questions and open issues is bigger than the number of well established and widely agreed results. This is exactly what we saw at WOI'99.

Several are the conclusions that we would like to point out here. In the first place, the number of attendees and their participation showed the interest raised by the subject, bigger than initially expected. On the other hand, the variety of the topics covered during the workshop revealed the wide range of problems and issues that the study of object interoperability brings out. And finally, the list of open questions is still too long and unstructured for addressing them in a comprehensive way.

In this sense, WOI'99 contributed to gather some of the current researchers on object interoperability, and let them start building a common understanding of the different problems and unexplored areas yet to be investigated. Several points were finally agreed, and the workshop helped identifying many important problems that need to be addressed by the object-orientation community to cope with the interoperability issues in open systems. Much work remains to be done, but we hope that WOI'99 has provided the basis for concrete research activities, and that following WOI's serve as a stable forum for discussion on these topics.

Acknowledgements. First of all, we would like to thank the ECOOP'99 organization for giving us the opportunity to organize the workshop, especially to the Workshops Chair, Ana Moreira, for her kindliness, assistance, and continuous support. Many thanks to all those that submitted papers, have they been finally accepted or not, and to the referees who helped in choosing and improving the selected papers. Finally, we want to especially thank all WOI'99 attendees for their active and enthusiastic participation in the workshop, and for their contributions to this report. Many thanks to all for making of WOI'99 a very enjoyable and productive experience.

References

[1] W.M.P. van der Aalst and K. van Hee. *Workflow management: modellen, methoden en systemen.* Academic Service, 1997.

[2] R. Back, A. Mikhajlova, and J. von Wright. Reasoning about interactive systems. In *Proceedings of the World Congress on Formal Methods (FM'99)*, LNCS. Springer-Verlag, 1999. Previous version appeared as Technical Report No. 200, TUCS. `http://www.tucs.abo.fi/publications/techreports/TR200`.

[3] V.R. Benjamins, E. Plaza, E. Motta, D. Fensel, R. Studer, B. Wielinga, G. Schreiber, and Z. Zdrahal. An intelligent brokering service for knowledge-component reuse on the World-Wide-Web. In *Proceedings of the 11th Banff Knowledge Acquisition for Knowledge-Based System Workshop (KAW'98)*, pages 18–23, Banff, Canada, April 1998.

[4] D. Brill. The LOOM reference manual. Technical report, University of Southern California, 1993.

[5] C. Canal, E. Pimentel, and J.M. Troya. Specification and refinement of dynamic software architectures. In Patrick Donohoe, editor, *Software Architecture (Proc. of WICSA'99)*, pages 107–125. Kluwer Academic Publishers, February 1999.

[6] Rational Software Corp. *UML Semantics.* Rational Software Corp., 1997.

[7] D. Fensel, V.R. Benjamins, S. Decker, M. Gaspari, R. Groenboon, W. Grosso, E. Motta, E. Plaza, G. Schreiber, R. Studer, and B. Wielinga. The unified problem-solving method description language UPML. In *IBROW-3 Esprit Project 27169. Project Deliverable 1.1*, 1998.

[8] T. Finin, Y. Labrou, and J. Mayfield. KQML as an agent communication language. In Jeff Bradshaw, editor, *Software Agents*, Cambridge, 1997. MIT Press.

[9] L. Fuentes and J.M. Troya. A java framework for web-based multimedia and collaborative applications. *IEEE Internet Computing*, 3(2):52–61, March/April 1999.

[10] D. Harel. Statecharts: A visual formalism for complex systems. *Science of Computer Programming*, 8:231–274, 1987.

[11] G.J. Holzmann. The model checker Spin. *IEEE Transactions on Software Engineering*, 23(5), May 1997.

[12] N. R. Jennings, K. Sycara, and M. Wooldridge. A roadmap of agent research and development. *Autonomous Agents and Multi-Agent Systems*, 1(1):7–38, 1998.

[13] G. Kristen. *Object Orientation: The KISS Method: From Information Architecture to Information System.* Addison-Wesley, 1994.

[14] A. Mikhajlova. *Ensuring Correctness of Object and Component Systems.* PhD thesis, Åbo Akademi University, October 1999.

[15] A. Mikhajlova and E. Sekerinski. Class refinement and interface refinement in object-oriented programs. In *Proceedings of 4th International Formal Methods Europe Symposium (FME'97)*, number 1313 in LNCS, pages 82–101. Springer-Verlag, 1997.

[16] E. Motta, D. Fensel, M. Gaspari, and R. Benjamin. Specification of knowledge components for reuse. In *Proceedings of SEKE'99*, 1999.

[17] R. van Rein. Protocol-safe workflow support for Santa Claus. In Vallecillo et al. [23], pages 3–11.

[18] R. van Rein and M. Fokkinga. Protocol assuring universal language. In *Formal Methods for Open Object-Based Distributed Systems*, pages 241–258. Kluwer Academic Publishers, 1999.

[19] B. Selic, G. Geullekson, and P.T. Ward. *Real-time Object-Oriented Modeling.* John Wiley & Sons, Inc., 1994.

[20] T. Senivongse. An approach to making CORBA support equivalence relationships. In *Proceedings of the 3rd Intl. Enterprise Distributed Object Computing Conference (EDOC'99)*, Germany, 1999.

[21] Y. Shoham. Agent-oriented programming. *Artificial Intelligence*, 60(1):51–52, 1993.

[22] J.M. Troya and A. Vallecillo. Software development from reusable components and controllers. In *Proc. of ASOO'98*, pages 47–58, Argentina, 1998.

[23] A. Vallecillo, J. Hernández, and J. M. Troya, editors. *Object Interoperability.* Universidad de Málaga, Dept. Lenguajes y Ciencias de la Computación, 1999.

[24] M. Wooldridge and N. R. Jennings. Intelligent agents: Theory and practice. *The Knowledge Engineering Review*, 10(2):115–152, 1995.

Object-Orientation and Operating Systems

Lutz Wohlrab[1], Francisco Ballesteros[2], Frank Schubert[1], Henning Schmidt[3], and Ashish Singhai[4]

[1] Chemnitz University of Technology, Germany
{lwo,fsc}@informatik.tu-chemnitz.de - http://www.tu-chemnitz.de/~{luwo,fsc}/
[2] Universidad Carlos III Madrid, Spain
nemo@gsyc.inf.uc3m.es - http://www.gsyc.inf.uc3m.es/~nemo/
[3] Potsdam University, Germany
hesch@haiti.cs.uni-potsdam.de - http://www.haiti.cs.uni-potsdam.de/~hesch/
[4] University of Illinois at Urbana-Champaign, United States of America
ashish.singhai@acm.org - http://choices.cs.uiuc.edu/singhai/home.html

Abstract. ECOOP Workshop on Object-Orientation and Operating Systems (ECOOP-OOOSWS) workshops aim to bring together researchers and developers working on object-oriented operating systems and to provide a platform for discussing problems arising from the application of object-orientation to operating systems and solutions for them. This paper summarizes ECOOP-OOOSWS'99 with its invited talk, eleven paper presentations and lively discussions between and after them. It gives a fairly distinct idea of where research in object-oriented operating systems is going to, according to the opinions of the participants.

1. Introduction

1.1. ECOOP-OOOSWS Scope and History

The first ECOOP Workshop on Object-Orientation and Operating Systems was held at ECOOP'97 in Jyväskylä, Finland [11]. It was organized by Frank Schubert, Lutz Wohlrab, and Henning Schmidt.

Since it provided a good forum for interesting discussions, the participants suggested that this workshop be periodically organized. At the same time, it was decided that the 2nd ECOOP-OOOSWS would be organized at ECOOP'99. At ECOOP'98 Francisco Ballesteros and Ashish Singhai joined the organizing team. The scope of ECOOP-OOOSWS workshops includes topics like:

- adaptable and adaptive OOOS,
- frameworks for OOOS,
- architecture of OOOS,
- distributed OOOS and middleware (e.g. CORBA),
- what are the penalties of OO in OS and how to avoid them,
- reflective OOOS,
- OOOS tools,
- reusability and interoperability of OOOS components,

A. Moreira and S. Demeyer (Eds.): ECOOP'99 Workshops, LNCS 1743, pp. 22–32, 1999.

- OOOS configurability, maintenance, tuning, and optimization,
- OOOS for embedded systems,
- real-time OOOS.

Prospective participants submit a position paper. Submitted papers are reviewed by the organizers. Participation is by invitation only, the number of participants is limited to facilitate lively discussions.

A distinguished member of the OOOS community is asked to give an invited talk. Authors of accepted papers give either a full talk or a short position statement. Discussion happens between the presentations and at the end of the workshop.

1.2. ECOOP-OOOSWS'99

The invited speech was given by Roy H. Campbell, leader of the Choices and 2K projects. ECOOP-OOOSWS'99 was attended by 15 participants from different parts of the world, who presented 11 papers. The participants were:

- Roy H. Campbell, Fabio Kon, and Ashish Singhai from University of Illinois at Urbana-Champaign, USA;
- Olaf Spinczyk from Otto von Guericke University Magdeburg, Germany;
- Darío Álvarez Gutiérrez and María Ángeles Díaz Fondón from University of Oviedo, Spain;
- Frank Schubert and Lutz Wohlrab from Chemnitz University of Technology, Germany;
- Markus Hof from Johannes Kepler University of Linz, Austria;
- Reinhard Meyer and Henning Schmidt from Potsdam University, Germany;
- Christophe Gransart from Lille University of Sciences and Technologies, France;
- Francisco Ballesteros from University Carlos III, Madrid, Spain,
- Antônio Augusto Fröhlich from GMD, Germany;
- Michael Clarke from Lancaster University, United Kingdom.

The paper presentations were structured into three sessions:

1. "Dynamic System Configuration and Adaptation",
2. "System Construction and Experiences", and
3. "Virtual Machines and Meta".

The rest of this report is structured as follows. Section 1 sketches the invited talk. Section 1 gives an account of each paper presentation given. Section 1 summarizes the discussions and is followed by the conclusion of the report.

2. Keynote Speech: 2K: An OS for the New Millennium

Keynote speech and summary by Roy H. Campbell
roy@cs.uiuc.edu

As we end this millennium, the characteristics of the environments for which we build operating systems are radically changing, leading to a new set of operating system requirements involving the management of change, mobility, quality of service and configuration. These requirements are driven by the inventions of the Internet, streaming multimedia, portable low-powered computing devices, wireless networks, visualization, smart rooms, and smart devices. Future operating systems should support anytime/anywhere computer usage. We propose that network-centric operating systems should be constructed as systems that manage distributed objects and that exploit the current trends in middleware and interpretive languages that support interoperability, to focus on the management of change.

New approaches to the management of dynamically changing resources are needed for the intelligent information spaces of the coming decades that exploit smart mobile devices, clothing, and vehicles and create smart offices, homes, and cities. Our approach is to leverage object-oriented research on building adaptive and customizable systems to create an infrastructure that supports change. New generations of hardware rapidly replace older ones and current users often use multiple computers. Thus, we look to interface standards produced by organizations like OMG to simplify the organization of changing systems. A middleware layer like DCOM, CORBA, or Java RMI abstracts platform dependencies. In a software architecture that supports dynamic, mobile devices, computers, and users, we propose modeling all entities of interest as distributed objects. To help overcome the issues of dynamic configuration, the distributed objects are collected into configurable components and any dependencies between components are modeled as objects. Services are used to manage the placement, configuration, change, persistence, reliability, and migration of objects. To achieve efficiency, the middleware layer, services, and distributed components may be optimized through customization and adaptation controlled through dynamic configuration. Thin layers of middleware support the interconnection of dedicated devices into the fabric of the distributed system. Within this kernel of object-oriented support, we build a new form of operating system that manages the resources within intelligent information spaces.

The new operating system architectures must accommodate a mobile user and multiple networked mobile computing devices. We assume that the computing environment is a dynamic collection of services and objects that is associated with a network-centric, distributed representation of the user. Individual pieces of the environment are cached and used on appropriate computing devices according to the needs and locality of the user and the availability of the devices. The system employs an object-oriented representation of its components and activity that we have come to term *architectural awareness* and this data representation drives dynamic resource management and configuration. The

2K Project (http://choices.cs.uiuc.edu/2K) is building an experimental system based on these principles.

3. Paper Presentations

3.1. Session "Dynamic System Configuration and Adaptation"

This session included paper presentations and discussions related to how to handle reconfiguration and dynamic adaptation. Mechanisms to handle adaptation and to address issues of how to adapt, when to adapt and what to adapt were the main topic of the talks.

Fabio Kon (`f-kon@cs.uiuc.edu`) presented:
Fabio Kon, Dulcineia Carvalho, and Roy H. Campbell:
Automatic Configuration in the 2K Operating System [8]

As the variety in computer hardware and user requirements increases, it becomes more difficult to provide customized operating systems for each different situation. Users need an operating system that is capable of configuring itself in order to adapt to a given hardware architecture and to user- and application-specific requirements. An architectural framework for automatic configuration was proposed and its implementation in the 2K operating system discussed. Automatic configuration is achieved by representing component prerequisites and runtime inter-component dependence explicitly. The implementation is based on distributed CORBA objects and standard CORBA services, which makes it extremely portable and accessible to a large community.

Lutz Wohlrab (`lwo@informatik.tu-chemnitz.de`) presented:
Lutz Wohlrab:
Adaptation Manager: Continued Story [12]

With large operating systems a major practical concern is ease of administration and dynamic adaptation. The introduction of the adaptation manager was proposed, an inherent component of the operating system, responsible for ensuring that it is properly configured and not subjected to erroneous adaptations. A Linux prototype implementation and its advantages and drawbacks were discussed.

Michael Clarke (`mwc@comp.lancs.ac.uk`) presented:
Michael Clarke and Geoff Coulson:
An Explicit Binding Model for Runtime Extensible Operating Systems [3]

Operating system design has traditionally followed a philosophy in which the system is structured as a fixed set of abstractions and mechanisms. This approach, however, is showing its limitations in the face of new application areas; particularly those which demand extensibility and configurability. Aspects of the design of a runtime extensible operating system called DEIMOS were discussed. DEIMOS is unique in that it does not define a kernel entity. Instead, both traditional kernel abstractions (i.e. memory model, concurrency model and inter process communication) and application specific services (e.g. file systems and device drivers) are encapsulated as objects which can be loaded, configured and unloaded on demand (i.e. at run time) under the jurisdiction of a base system component called the Configuration Manager.

Christophe Gransart (`christophe.gransart@lifl.fr`) presented in a short position statement:
Christophe Gransart, Phillippe Merle, and Jean-Marc Geib:
GoodeWatch: Supervision of CORBA Applications [5]

The GoodeWatch project is developing a solution to observe applications and/or component behavior using transparent grabbing of events from the CORBA ORB so that feedback about and control of applications can be provided to the users. Events generated by applications are propagated by middleware and stored into repositories to be used by exploitation tools. This offers opportunities for easier design, deployment, administration, and reconfiguration of large-scale CORBA applications.

3.2. Session "System Construction and Experiences"

This session addressed practical issues of the creation of object-oriented kernels. It was focused on system construction, as well as on experiences made by re-engineering procedural designs in an object-oriented way.

Olaf Spinczyk (`olaf@ivs.cs.uni-magdeburg.de`) presented:
Danilo Beuche, Abdelaziz Guerrouat, Holger Papajewski, Wolfgang Schröder-Preikschat, Olaf Spinczyk, and Ute Spinczyk:
On the Development of Object-Oriented Operating Systems for Deeply Embedded Systems – The PURE Project [2]

The PURE project aims at providing a portable, universal runtime executive for deeply embedded parallel/distributed systems. The phrase "deeply embedded" refers to systems forced to operate under extreme resource constraints in terms of memory, CPU, and power consumption. The notion "parallel/distributed" relates to the growing architectural complexity of today's embedded systems. Olaf discussed design issues and implementation results of the family-based, object-oriented operating system PURE targeting the area of embedded systems in the above-mentioned sense. The results show that a highly modular system consisting of a large number of reusable abstractions (i.e. C++ classes) still can be compiled to a fairly small and compact entity.

Reinhard Meyer (`rm@haiti.cs.uni-potsdam.de`) presented:
Reinhard Meyer and Henning Schmidt:
Scalable Adaptation Based on Decomposition – A Modest Subset of Family-Oriented Adaptation Schemes [9]

Reinhard raised the question whether the pure circumstance of *dynamics* is in fact a good reason for applying *high level, meta concepts*, covering the needs for a broad range of configurational problems in a single "fitting all" manner. He discussed the adaptation scheme SABOD (Scalable Adaptation based on Decomposition), that tries to found a modest scheme for handling (dynamic) configuration, scalable and extensible to semantically richer schemes in a family-oriented sense.

Antônio Augusto Fröhlich (`guto@first.gmd.de`) presented:
Antônio Augusto Fröhlich and Wolfgang Schröder-Preikschat:
EPOS: An Object-Oriented Operating System [4]

Antônio reported about the current development stage of the EPOS project. EPOS aims to deliver, whenever possible automatically, a customized run-time support system for each (high performance) parallel application. In order to achieve this, EPOS introduces the concepts of adaptable, scenario independent system abstractions, scenario adapters and inflated interfaces. An application designed and implemented following the guidelines behind these concepts can be submitted to a tool that will perform syntactical and data flow analysis to extract an operating system blueprint. This blueprint can, in turn, be submitted to another tool that will tailor the operating system to the given application.

Frank Schubert(`fsc@informatik.tu-chemnitz.de`) presented:
Frank Schubert and Kevin Brem:
An Object-Oriented, Dynamically Adaptable, Virtual File System for CHEOPS [10]

Frank presented some of the recent results of the CHEOPS operating system project. He discussed practical experiences about restructuring traditional operating system components in an object-oriented manner. Furthermore, he explained how fine-grained dynamic adaptability can be achieved by means of the CHEOPS class-object architecture. As a vehicle for this discussion served a newly designed, dynamically adaptable VFS implementation for the CHEOPS operating system.

Francisco Ballesteros (`nemo@gsyc.inf.uc3m.es`) presented:
Francisco Ballesteros, Christopher Hess, Fabio Kon, Sergio Arevalo, and Roy H. Campbell:
Object-Orientation in Off++ – A Distributed Adaptable Microkernel [1]

Off++ is is a object-oriented, distributed, adaptable microkernel whose task is to export distributed hardware resources to the 2K operating system. 2K builds on those resources to provide a network-centric, adaptable computing environment. The kernel is an object-oriented redesign of an initial non-OO prototype, named Off. It includes new features that provide basic architectural-awareness support for 2K. Off and Off++ were compared, the experienced benefits and drawbacks of using object-oriented methodology discussed. It was described how design patterns were used for Off++, and how new patterns have emerged during the development process. The impact of using OO and design patterns on the performance of the system were discussed.

3.3. Session "Virtual Machines and Meta"

Finally, the third session addressed issues related to the design of systems based on virtual machines and meta-level architectures.

Darío Álvarez Gutiérrez (`darioa@pinon.ccu.uniovi.es`) presented:
Darío Álvarez Gutiérrez, María Ángeles Díaz Fondón, Fernando Álvarez García, and Lourdes Tajes Martínez:
Eliminating Garbage Collection by Using Virtual Memory Techniques to Implement Complete Object Persistence [6]

Persistence is a key property for future Integral Object-Oriented Systems (IOOS) based solely on the object-oriented paradigm, which stores objects in an instance area. Complete persistence makes all objects persistent without distinctions. Implementing complete persistence by applying virtual memory techniques to the management of the instance area of an IOOS has the added benefit of eliminating main memory garbage collection. Adding another level of storage to the persistence system makes garbage collection not necessary at all.

Markus Hof (`hof@ssw.uni-linz.ac.at`) presented in a short position statement:
Markus Hof:
Object Model with Exchangeable Invocation Semantics [7]

Common object oriented systems have a fixed invocation semantics (synchronous procedure call). Some systems extend this concept with a fixed amount of additional semantics (RPC, best effort, asynchronous...). Markus went a step further and introduced invocation semantics as first class abstractions. This offers the possibility to write or compose completely new invocation semantics. The implementation of a distributed object system which introduces new invocation semantics to forward invocations across a network was sketched. A second application, the decoration of local objects with additional semantics, e.g. transparent invocation logging, synchronization semantics, was discussed. By putting the framework into an operating system, a highly increased flexibility in the system's object model can be achieved. Markus claimed that the delay introduced by exchangeable invocation semantics is constant and therefore neglectable.

4. Summary of the Discussions

A distinct movement from bigger universal computers to smaller, networked computer systems is perceived. This is reflected by the increasing focus of OS research to frameworks for the construction of operating systems for these devices.

For advanced networking with dedicated devices, flexible CORBA-based middleware layers are used and investigated. These are lean adaptive systems with an ORB as a central building block. One of the problems is that the ORB itself can be big. It was mentioned during the discussion, that the image of TAO (from Washington University at St. Louis) is two megabytes. On the other hand, it is feasible to build small ORBs.

While two years back adaptability and adaptivity in their own right were a major topic, the focus has shifted. Now, mastering adaptability, providing tools for this purpose, (at least partly) automating adaptation decisions, and scaling adaptability are hot topics of the day. Current research in this direction covers either stand-alone systems or very limited areas of operating system adaptation.

The first session of the workshop consisted of talks about adaptability and mastering it. Knowledge based systems are seen as the way to help system administrators to harness highly adaptable systems, leading also to new systems with a higher degree of adaptivity.

An important question for building knowledge bases fit for this job is the selection of the appropriate tools and representation language. Lutz chose Prolog for knowledge representation while Fabio constructed his own mini-language and is thinking of switching to a language commonly used for formulating QoS demands and constraints. Both agreed that for real-world problems and systems, using a powerful and sufficiently abstract, high-level language is essential. However, experts fluent in both operating systems and languages widely used for knowledge-based systems and the underlying concepts is not common. The question whether we should better use an AI language like Prolog or a powerful language more geared for usage by OS programmers could not be resolved. A possible solution might be the combination of simple and low-power language for the common name value pair type of knowledge, and a full-fledged one for the more complicated issues.

Another problem discussed in relation with these knowledge bases is the step for going from a local system to a distributed system. Where to put knowledge about distribution issues? How to instrument it and make decisions? Lutz pointed out that this should be handled depending on the structure of the network. If the network has the structure of a star with a central server, a single knowledge base for the distribution issues should be located there. Decision-making requests on distribution issues are to be forwarded to this server. If the network has redundant servers, each of them should carry this knowledge base. Contradictory decisions of multiple servers can be overcome, for instance, by voting.

In his talk, Lutz pointed out that there are basically three sources for instrumentable knowledge, in order of importance: knowledge engineering (studying sources, comments, documentation, interviewing administrators and putting the results into rules by hand), system structure and tools deriving rules from it (e. g. extracting the class hierarchy from the source code of an object-oriented system) and observation of the system at runtime. The latter is the hardest: grabbing runtime events without disturbing the base system and deriving rules from sequences of runtime events. As Christophe´s short presentation showed, we can expect more research in this direction in middle and long term future.

During the second session of the workshop, static tailoring of kernels was the main topic. It showed that the pros and cons of object-orientation for this purpose is still something to have hot discussions about. C++ compilers have not yet reached the level of quality common for C compilers. Further, template-based genericity consumes inherently more space than genericity based on C-like pointer manipulation. Francisco stated similar issues about using variants of off-the-shelf design patterns: the implementation of an object-oriented redesign of Off using design patterns is twice as large as the C-based Off implementation, and slower. However, PURE shows that extremely lean object-oriented systems are feasible by using special build techniques such as inlining.

During the discussion, we agreed that special care has to be taken when using C++ compilers. Otherwise, the resulting code can be both big and inefficient.

Another discussed topic was whether object-orientation could be an overkill for really tiny systems (e.g. like when we *force* our students to use a particular OO technique, even if it is not strictly necessary for toy, academic, examples). Francisco pointed out that in many cases, for a *really small* OS kernel, the OO implementation can be more complex than a non-OO equivalent. We agreed that the complexity comes from the need to learn complex frameworks and because "more interfaces" means "more complexity".

The subtleties of meta-programming represent a vast field of research. It is very important for stable reliable future systems to arrive at simpler meta programming concepts. Aspect-Orientation seems to be a way widely investigated now to achieve this goal.

Darío proposed eliminating garbage collection by including tertiary storage in the storage hierarchy. Several related problems were discussed, including what to do with those systems without tertiary storage and how that would affect latency.

Both the vision of a multitude of small computers sourrounding people and the discussion about Darío's paper showed that we need to re-think established concepts such as the distinction between transient and persistent storage and PC-centric computing. The network is already more important than the computer, and a lot of old resource constraints ceased to be an issue.

5. Conclusion

There is still a lot to be done in the field of object-oriented operating systems. A lack of tools to support adaptability from static tailoring of kernels up to adaptivity has to be overcome. An appropriate tool chain is needed to provide the operating systems for the devices and computers of the future, numerous and diverse as they will be.

The majority of small systems will soon run kernels tailored using frameworks rather than written from scratch. Object-oriented frameworks geared for this purpose can already very well compete with their procedural counterparts.

Middleware infrastructure software on lean systems to build flexible networked information spaces is a major topic soon to hit the markets. The vision is easy network-centric and mobile computing where nobody needs to worry about system configuration, adaptation, or location, where most computers are not perceptible as such.

ECOOP-OOOSWS'99 [13] featured lively discussions giving a distict idea where the train of OOOS research is moving to. As ECOOP-OOOSWS proved a successful platform for bringing OOOS researchers together and ECOOP-OOOSWS'98 was badly missed, the participants decided that the next ECOOP-OOOSWS will be organized in conjunction with ECOOP'00 in France.

References

[1] Francisco Ballesteros, Christopher Hess, Fabio Kon, Sergio Arevalo, and Roy H. Campbell. Object-orientation in Off++ – a distributed adaptable microkernel. In *Proceedings of the 2nd ECOOP Workshop on Object-Orientation and Operating Systems (ECOOP-OOOSWS'99)*, pages 49–53, 1999. See [13].

[2] Danilo Beuche, Abdelaziz Guerrouat, Wolfgang Schröder-Preikschat Holger Papajewski, Olaf Spinczyk, and Ute Spinczyk. On the development of object-oriented operating systems for deeply embedded systems – the PURE project. In *Proceedings of the 2nd ECOOP Workshop on Object-Orientation and Operating Systems (ECOOP-OOOSWS'99)*, pages 27–31, 1999. See [13].

[3] Michael Clarke and Geoff Coulson. An explicit binding model for runtime extensible operating systems. In *Proceedings of the 2nd ECOOP Workshop on Object-Orientation and Operating Systems (ECOOP-OOOSWS'99)*, pages 20–25, 1999. See [13].

[4] Antônio Augusto Fröhlich and Wolfgang Schröder-Preikschat. EPOS: an object-oriented operating system. In *Proceedings of the 2nd ECOOP Workshop on Object-Orientation and Operating Systems (ECOOP-OOOSWS'99)*, pages 38–43, 1999. See [13].

[5] Christophe Gransart, Phillippe Merle, and Jean-Marc Geib. GoodeWatch: supervision of CORBA applications. In *Proceedings of the 2nd ECOOP Workshop on Object-Orientation and Operating Systems (ECOOP-OOOSWS'99)*, page 26, 1999. See [13].

[6] Darío Álvarez Gutiérrez, María Ángeles Díaz Fondón, Fernando Álvarez García, and Lourdes Tajes Martínez. Eliminating garbage collection by using virtual memory techniques to implement complete object persistence. In *Proceedings of the 2nd ECOOP Workshop on Object-Orientation and Operating Systems (ECOOP-OOOSWS'99)*, pages 54–58, 1999. See [13].

[7] Markus Hof. Object model with exchangeable invocation semantics. In *Proceedings of the 2nd ECOOP Workshop on Object-Orientation and Operating Systems (ECOOP-OOOSWS'99)*, page 59, 1999. See [13].

[8] Fabio Kon, Dulcineia Carvalho, and Roy H. Campbell. Automatic configuration in the 2K operating system. In *Proceedings of the 2nd ECOOP Workshop on Object-Orientation and Operating Systems (ECOOP-OOOSWS'99)*, pages 10–14, 1999. See [13].
[9] Reinhard Meyer and Henning Schmidt. Scalable adaptation based on decomposition – a modest subset of family-oriented adaptation schemes. In *Proceedings of the 2nd ECOOP Workshop on Object-Orientation and Operating Systems (ECOOP-OOOSWS'99)*, pages 32–37, 1999. See [13].
[10] Frank Schubert and Kevin Brem. An object-oriented, dynamically adaptable, virtual file system for CHEOPS. In *Proceedings of the 2nd ECOOP Workshop on Object-Orientation and Operating Systems (ECOOP-OOOSWS'99)*, pages 44–48, 1999. See [13].
[11] Frank Schubert, Lutz Wohlrab, and Henning Schmidt. ECOOP workshop on object-orientation and operating systems. In Jan Bosch and Stuart Mitchell, editors, *Object-Oriented Technology: ECOOP'97 Workshop Reader*, number 1357 in Lecture Notes in Computer Science, pages 497–552, Jyväskylä, Finland, June 9–13 1997. Springer Verlag.
[12] Lutz Wohlrab. Adaptation manager – continued story. In *Proceedings of the 2nd ECOOP Workshop on Object-Orientation and Operating Systems (ECOOP-OOOSWS'99)*, pages 15–19, 1999. See [13].
[13] Lutz Wohlrab, Frank Schubert, Francisco Ballesteros, Henning Schmidt, and Ashish Singhai, editors. *Proceedings of the 2nd ECOOP Workshop on Object-Orientation and Operating Systems (ECOOP-OOOSWS'99), Lisbon, Portugal, June 14th, 1999.* Number CSR-99-04 in Chemnitzer Informatik-Berichte. Chemnitz University of Technology, 09107 Chemnitz, Germany, 1999.

UML Semantics FAQ

Stuart Kent, Andy Evans, and Bernhard Rumpe*

pUML@york.cs.ac.uk
WWW home page: http://www.cs.york.ac.uk/puml

Abstract. This paper reports the results of a workshop held at ECOOP'99. The workshop was set up to find answers to questions fundamental to the definition of a semantics for the Unified Modelling Language. Questions examined the meaning of the term *semantics* in the context of UML; approaches to defining the semantics, including the feasibility of the meta-modelling approach; whether a single semantics is desirable and, if not, how to set up a framework for defining multiple, interlinked semantics; and some of the outstanding problems for defining a semantics for all of UML.

Introduction

This paper describes the results of a workshop held at ECOOP 1999, in Lisbon. The aim of the workshop was to identify and answer key questions concerning the semantics of the Unified Modelling Language (UML [8]). A list of the questions discussed here is given below:

1. What does the term *semantics* mean in the context of UML?
2. Why is it desirable to make semantics for UML explicit? What are the different ways in which a UML semantics might be made explicit?
3. Is a precise semantics desirable? For what purpose?
4. What is the current status of UML semantics? What are the reference documents?
5. Should UML have a single semantics? Should UML have a single *core* semantics?
6. Is it possible to express a semantics of UML in UML (the meta-modelling approach)?
7. Is it feasible to construct a semantics for all of UML? What are the main outstanding issues?

Specific aspects of UML were explored in attempting to answer these questions. There was broad agreement on questions 1-4; it was generally felt that individual contributions submitted before the workshop could be polished in answer to these questions. Participants broke out into groups to discuss the remaining three questions. Two groups considered the last question by exploring two specific areas of UML, respectively: concurrency, events, and dynamic behaviour in general; and aggregation.

* Editors on behalf of the pUML group

A. Moreira and S. Demeyer (Eds.): ECOOP'99 Workshops, LNCS 1743, pp. 33–56, 1999.

This report is a snapshot of the state of affairs at the time. The UML Semantics FAQ will continue to be maintained by the pUML group, who encourage contributions from practitioners and academics interested in the UML as a standard modelling language. To this aim we are continuing to organise workshops at major conferences such as ECOOP and OOPSLA. However, this does not preclude other forms of contribution: it is always possible to improve current statements or add new topics. If you have any comments, or would like to offer alternative answers or suggest clarifications to existing ones, then please visit the website of the precise UML group (pUML), located at

http://www.cs.york.ac.uk/puml
where an updated FAQ will be maintained.

Q1. What Does the Term *Semantics* Mean in the Context of UML?

Bernhard Rumpe, Technische Universität München, Germany
Stuart Kent, University of Kent at Canterbury, UK
Andy Evans, University of York, UK
Robert France, Colorado State University, USA

Q1.1. What Does the Term *Semantics* Mean at All?

Today, a lot of confusion arises from the fact that the word "*semantics*" itself has many different semantics! Developers tend to use the word "*semantics*" when they talk about the behaviour of a system they develop. This kind of usage is almost contradictory to the *semantics* in scientific areas like Mathematics or Logic. There, "semantics" is a synonym for "meaning" of a notation – this is regardless of whether this notation deals with structure or behaviour.

Basically, a semantics is needed if a notation (syntax) is given or newly developed, and its meaning needs to be defined. Almost all approaches define the semantics of its elements by relating it to another already well understood language.

This is comparable to natural languages. For example Chinese can be (roughly) understood if a Chinese-English dictionary is available. Of course grammar, or the definition of how elements of a language are modified and grouped together, also need to be mapped.

In computer science, the pattern is similar. A new language is given a meaning in three steps:

1. define precisely the *syntax* of the new language, which characterises all the possible expressions of that language
2. identify a well understood language, herein called the *semantics language*, and
3. define a mapping from expressions in the syntax of the new language to the semantics language.

The semantics language is often called the *semantics domain*. The mapping from syntax to semantics is usually intensional rather than extensional, which means that the mapping is not explicit, but by example. If a language is to be automatically processed and/or be unambiguous then the syntax, the semantics language, and mapping from one to the other must be completely, precisely and unambiguously defined.

Q1.2. What Is Special about UML *Semantics*?

UML does have some specific characteristics, which makes the task of semantics definition interesting:

1. a substantial part of UML is visual/diagrammatic.
2. UML is not for execution, but for modeling, thus incorporating abstraction and underspecification techniques.
3. UML is combined of a set of partially overlapping subnotations.
4. UML is of widespread interest.

Whereas the last issue leads to the sociologically interesting question, how to reach agreement for a semantics definition, the other three topics lead to problems of a technical nature.

The fact that a large part of UML is diagrammatic makes it somewhat more difficult to deal with its semantics, but it is no problem in principle. Currently, its semantics is explained in English: UML semantics is ambiguous and imprecise. We speak of a *formal* or *precise* semantics for UML if the semantics domain of this translation is a formal language and – very important – the translation itself is precisely defined. This goal can be achieved, as several graphic formalisms, like Statecharts, Petri-Nets, or dataflow-diagrams have shown. The first step for UML is to precisely define its syntax. In the standard, this has been done by using the meta-model approach, which in the UML documents is mainly used to describe the abstract syntax of the UML [8] itself. Thus a meta-model for diagrams replaces the abstract syntax tree of textual notations.

The usage of UML as a modeling language and not as a programming language has an important impact that is often poorly recognised. A UML model is an *abstraction* of the real system to be developed. The model is used to capture important properties, but to disregard unimportant ones. As an effect, a UML model typically has a set of more than one possible implementation. A semantics definition must reflect this by making the *underspecification* of the model explicit.

Third, the UML is composed of a set of notations that partially overlap. For example [4] shows how (a subset of) the state diagram notation can be used to express the same information that could be expressed in terms of pre/post conditions on operations in a class diagram; but there are other aspects of state diagrams which can not. This adds an extra problem, as semantics definitions for each of the UML notations need to be consistent with each other. Only then will an integrated use of these notations be feasible. To check the consistency of semantics definitions, it is necessary either to have a common semantic domain for all of them, or to establish precise mappings between different semantic domains.

A more detailed discussion of these topics can be found in [13].

Q1.3. What Is a UML Semantics Good for?

Semantics of UML is a means to understand how UML should be used, and to ensure that when UML models are communicated there is a common shared understanding of what they mean. On the other hand, the actual practice of applying UML is necessary to get a *feeling* for it. A semantics definition is a necessary prerequisite, but certainly not sufficient. Furthermore, it is not necessary to understand the complete language to start using it.

Semantics is a vehicle for people who speak the same semantic language $\mathbb{D}$ (formal or informal) to discuss certain UML subtleties and improve the notation and use of UML in terms of $\mathbb{D}$.

Semantics can be for automating certain tasks by machine: for example, tools which can do more than simply process syntax, such as simulating or (partially) executing models, checking models are consistent, etc.

It is important to clarify the purpose of a semantics definition. There may be different semantics definitions to suit different purposes: the definition for explaining semantics to users of the notation may be different to that required to perform sophisticated automatic processing tasks, and both may be different to a semantics definition whose purpose is to demonstrate properties about the language, such as a measure of how expressive it is compared to other languages.

Q1.4. Common Misunderstandings about Semantics

The UML documents contain a paper called the "*Semantics of UML*". However, this paper does not focus much on semantics, but mainly on syntactic issues. The meta-model of UML gives a precise notion of what the abstract syntax is. However, it currently does not cope with semantics. Analogously, the semantics of C++ can not be understood from the context free grammar (without knowledge of similarly structured languages).

Furthermore, context conditions are by no means *semantic conditions*, but purely constrain the syntax. They give well-formedness rules, e.g. each variable must be defined before use, without telling you what a variable is. In the UML case, context conditions are usually explained using OCL. A context condition tells us what is constrained, not why it is constrained. The latter is a task of the semantics definition.

As explained earlier: semantics is not behaviour. A structural description technique, like class diagrams, need an adequate semantics in the same way as do behaviour description techniques.

Q2. Is a Precise Semantics Desirable? For What Purpose?

Stuart Kent, University of Kent at Canterbury, UK
Bernhard Rumpe, Technische Universität München, Germany
Andy Evans, University of York, UK
Robert France, Colarado State University, USA

Q2.1. Degrees of Precision

A semantics definition consists of three parts:

1. define the syntax,
2. define the semantics domain, and
3. define the semantics mapping, as a relationship between syntax and semantics domain.

The degree to which each of these three parts is made explicit and/or precise may vary. Whenever a natural language, like English, is involved, we speak of an informal semantics definition.

The semantics definition gains much on precision, if at least its syntax is precisely defined. One can distinguish between a *concrete* and an *abstract* syntax. A concrete syntax provides the rules for stating exactly how the language will appear when written; the abstract syntax identifies the main concepts onto which the concrete syntax maps. These concepts are then given a semantics. For example, the following equations define the *concrete* syntax for numerals:

$$Character \supseteq Digit = \{'0','1','2','3','4','5','6','7','8','9'\}$$
$$String \supseteq Numeral = Digit \cup \{d \frown n \mid d \in Digit \wedge n \in Numeral\}$$

The concrete syntax talks about concrete things: digits are characters, numerals are strings. In an abstract syntax we would just assume that we have a set *Numeral* of arbitrary tokens. The semantics would map members of this set uniquely to the natural numbers in the (well understood) mathematical language of arithmetic.

For UML, and other diagrammatic languages, the trend has been to define an abstract syntax. So, rather than, say, talk about boxes and lines between them (the equivalent of digits and strings) the syntax talks about class and association.

For textual languages, a context free grammar (BNF) is used, though this can be viewed as just a short hand for set theory. There is no reason why similar techniques could not be used to describe both the concrete and abstract syntax for diagrammatic languages such as UML. The UML standard has chosen to use a meta-modelling approach based on class diagrams to characterise the abstract syntax of the language. The concrete syntax seems only to be defined by example.

A precise definition of the semantics domain is usually given either by explicitly defining the notion of "system" using mathematical terms, or by using a formal language, like Z or Object Z, as the semantics language. However, precision does not require the language to be mathematical in the traditional sense.

Finally, to get a fully precise semantics, the semantics definition must also be represented precisely. This is feasible using mathematics, as done many times for other notations. The mappings can also be encoded in a meta-model — see FAQ 5 for details.

An alternative way to write down the mapping is algorithmically — a recipe for converting expressions in the (abstract) syntax to expressions in the semantics language. This would be useful where it is intended that the mapping is to be automated, for example where the semantics domain is an OOPL such as Java, and the mapping corresponds to code generation. Unfortunately, using a programming language as a semantics domain leads to a severe problem which needs to be considered: any model defined in an executable language can only describe one implementation and therefore cannot exhibit any form of underspecification. As discussed earlier, modeling languages like UML need to allow underspecification. Thus code generation necessarily involves a selection of one of the possible implementations – possibly a wrong one.

Q2.2. Abstraction versus Precision versus Detailedness

In the UML reference book [12] there is a detailed definition of the nature and purpose of models given. Abstraction is mentioned there as a key concept to yield understandable models, conveying the essentials of a view.

Different levels of abstraction allow information to be revealed about the systems on different levels of detailedness. So abstraction and detailedness are complementary – adding details makes a model less abstract. However, the word "precision" is ambiguous in that context. Sometimes it refers to the amount of details a model has and sometimes it is used as the degree of formality the modeling notation has. These two kinds of "precision" need to be distinguished. "Precision of a notation" refers to the precision of the definition of its syntax and semantics and is the same for all models, not to the amount of detail included in the model.

Physics gives us a good example. "About 42" is a vague definition for a number, it is neither very detailed nor precise. One cannot exactly determine whether 41.7 is included or not. "About 41.34" is more detailed, but still not precise. It seems likely that 41.7 is excluded, but we cannot be sure, if we don't precisely know what "about" means. Physics gives us a precise technique: "42.0" determines the exact interval $[41.95, 42.05]$. The notation is fully precise, but we can make it more detailed: "42.010" is a specialisation conveying $[42.0095, 42.0105]$.

Of course this example is simple compared to the situation with UML. However, it is important to recognise that with the UML we can specify precisely, but still in an abstract manner, using underspecification wherever appropriate.

Q2.3. Why Is Precision Important? What Do You Lose?

A Benchmark. A precise semantics provides an unambiguous benchmark against which a developer's understanding or a tool's performance can be measured: Does the developer use the notation in ways which are consistent with the semantics? Does a tool generate code as the semantics would predict, or does it check the consistency of a model in accordance with the semantics?

Machine Processing. For a machine to process a language, that language must be defined precisely. If it is to perform semantics-oriented tasks, then its semantics must be defined precisely. Examples of semantics-oriented tasks are: model simulation or (partial) execution; checking that different views on a model (class diagrams, invariants, state diagrams, sequence diagrams, etc.) are consistent with one another; checking that the behaviour of a superclass is preserved in a subclass; and so on.

Establishing Properties of the Syntactic Language. Some important, but nevertheless largely neglected, issues in defining semantics are wrapped up in the question: Is the semantics mapping appropriate? Let us assume we denote the syntactic notation by $\mathbb{N}$, the semantics domain $\mathbb{D}$ and the semantics mapping as function

$$\mathbb{S} : \mathbb{N} \rightarrow \mathbb{D}.$$

By defining $\mathbb{S}$ precisely, we can use mathematics to prove properties about the syntactic language. For example, let us assume $\emptyset \in \mathbb{D}$ describes the invalid (or non-implementable) system, then it is an important result if we can show the following property:

$$\text{for all models } m \in \mathbb{N} \text{ it holds that } \mathbb{S}(m) \neq \emptyset$$

Another test of the appropriateness of a semantics definition is the question regarding what it distinguishes and what it identifies. Is the following possible:

$$\text{there are models } m_1, m_2 \in \mathbb{N} \text{ with } m_1 \neq m_2, \text{ but } \mathbb{S}(m_1) = \mathbb{S}(m_2)$$

Models that only differ in local variables should indeed have identical semantics, as the semantics should not rely on hidden or local properties. On the other hand, does the semantics distinguish models that are inherently different in nature?

Of greatest interest is the transfer of refinement, abstraction, composition and similar techniques from the semantic domain to the syntactic domain. Assume $\rightsquigarrow$ denotes a refinement relation on the semantics domain. Then it would be interesting to define transformation techniques $T : \mathbb{N} \rightarrow \mathbb{N}$ on the syntax with the following property:

$$\text{for all models } m \in \mathbb{N} \text{ it holds that } \mathbb{S}(m) \rightsquigarrow \mathbb{S}(T(m))$$

If this property is ensured once and for all models, then the transformation T can be applied, and we can be sure to get a refinement as a result, without dealing explicitly with the semantics anymore.

Thus representing the semantics mapping $\mathbb{S}$ precisely allows the notation developer to prove properties on his/her notation and associated development techniques, such that the user of the notation later need not explicitly deal with the semantics anymore. The syntactic transformations may also be built into automated tools to support the developer.

Having a Chinese-English translation at hand, I begin to learn Chinese words, but also how to build useful Chinese sentences. When I have learnt to do this I can directly deal with Chinese, without any translation to English anymore. This is the ultimate goal of a semantics definition.

Losses. Defining a precise semantics is hard work and time consuming. If the only purpose of the semantics is to show developers (roughly) how to use the notation, it could be argued that a precise semantics is not necessary. This is probably not (or will not be in the near future) the case with UML.

A precise semantics can also be hard to read, especially if it is written in a hard to understand mathematical language. We believe this can be mitigated in three ways: (1) develop a precise, yet rather widely agreed, semantics; (2) develop a reference implementation of that semantics that can be used actively by developers and tool builders to gain a deep understanding, rather like how a programmer gets to understand a programming language by writing programs, compiling them (checks that their programs are syntactically and type correct) and observing the effects when they are executed (checks their understanding of the semantics against what actually happens); and (3) write an informal semantics to complement, not replace, the precise one. It is important to stress that (3) is an exercise in *explaining* the semantics, it is not that effective in defining the semantics.

Q3. What Is the Current Status of UML Semantics? What Are the Reference Documents?

Martin Gogolla, Mark Richters, and Oliver Radfelder
University of Bremen, Germany

The current status of the UML semantics is that it is described in an informal manner. The 'UML Notation Guide' document gives an overview on the concepts, and the 'UML Semantics' document presents the abstract syntax together with context-sensitive conditions in form of class diagrams and OCL expressions. Both documents as well as the semi-official books by Booch, Rumbaugh, and Jacobson do not use formal techniques for explaining the semantics.

Concerning the reference documents, when studying the UML and especially the UML semantics, one has to take into account the official OMG UML definition, especially the 'UML Notation Guide' and 'UML Semantics' documents. But the problem is that the UML is an evolving language. Therefore many versions of these documents exist. The current version is version 1.3 [8] but there is already a call for contributions for version 2.0. In addition, there are also many books and papers on the subject, including the semi-official ones by Booch, Rumbaugh, and Jacobson, especially the 'UML Reference Manual'. Because of publication lead times, laziness of researchers and so on, one has to be very careful when reading a paper or book to identify on exactly which version of the UML it is based.

For example, one is likely to come up with a very different semantics for signals, depending on whether you read the UML standard or the three amigos reference guide:

- *Signals ... have no operations.*
  UML Notation Guide, Version 1.3, page 3-138, line -4..-2.
- *A signal ... may have operations.*
  UML Reference Manual, page 428, line 3.

In our view, semantics work must only use the official UML definition, which can be obtained from the OMG pages at http://www.omg.org, must try to use the latest version possible, and must make it clear which version has been used. And, as an aside, the author for this document is the OMG, not Booch, Jacobson and Rumbaugh.

Finally, anyone working on UML semantics should look up existing work in this area. An up-to-date bibliography is maintained at

http://www.db.informatik.uni-bremen.de/umlbib/.

Also see the pUML web pages.

Q4. Should UML Have a Single Semantics? Should UML Have a Single *Core* Semantics?

John Howse, University of Brighton, UK
Shusaku Iida, Japan Advanced Institute of Science and Technology (JAIST)
Richard Mitchell, InferData Corp, USA and University of Brighton, UK
Bernhard Rumpe, Technische Universität München, Germany

The advantage of having a single, standard semantics for UML is that it is easier for one person to understand another person's UML models. The advantage of having a variety of semantics is that you can choose what works best in your current project. We believe it is possible to support both standardisation and variation. Therefore, we answer 'no' to the question 'should UML have a single semantics?' The following sections elaborate on this answer. First, we explore a world in which variety is allowed. Then we explore how it could be actively supported.

Q4.1. Who Can Give UML a Semantics?

In practice, there are many individuals and groups who can contribute to discussions on the semantics of UML, and many ways for them to disseminate their proposals. Here are some:

Who?	**Disseminate how?**
OMG task groups	UML documents
The three amigos	Books
Tool vendors	Tools
Methodologists	Books, Research papers
Development teams	Shared experience

As long as no single group or individual has control of the semantics of UML, there will be a variety of semantics for UML. Some will be more popular than others, meaning that more people understand them and use them. Popularity would be influenced by a number of factors, including:

- the fame and power of those proposing a particular semantics (for example, you might pay particular attention to proposals from an OMG group)
- strengths and weaknesses of a particular semantics as highlighted by scientific research (for example, a semantics with proven flaws might become less popular)
- strengths and weaknesses of a particular semantics as highlighted by practical experience (for example, you might be influenced by favourable reports from several large projects)
- the effectiveness of tool support (the availability and quality of tools might influence your choice).

In practice, if variation was supported, we would expect there to be parts of UML for which there is widespread (but not universal) agreement on the semantics, and other parts for which there is less agreement.

And finally in this section, it is appropriate to note that UML is extensible, through such mechanisms as stereotypes. Modellers who introduce their own stereotypes must define the semantics of their models. Therefore, the problem we address in the next section must be addressed even if the UML community opts for central control of semantics.

Q 4.2. How Can We Support Variation?

There are two parts to our answer to the question of how can we provide support for a variety of semantics for UML. The first concerns a style of writing semantics. The second concerns a way of organising shared semantic models. For us, supporting variation includes both supporting the sharing of parts of UML, when that is appropriate, and supporting different variants of UML, when that is helpful.

A semantics for a language, L, maps elements of L to some other language, S, using a semantic function. The language S describes a semantic domain. A semantic function could map elements of L to elements of S. Alternatively, a semantic function could map each element of L to a set of elements of S, yielding a set-based semantics, illustrated in Fig. 1.

A set based approach to defining semantics has a number of advantages. First, it helps to make any underspecification in a UML model explicit. The

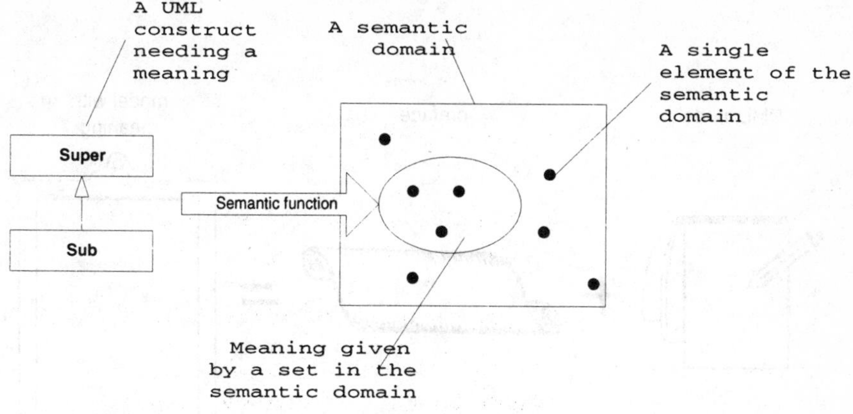

Fig. 1. Set-based Semantics for UML

more abstract (i.e., underspecified) a UML model is, the more elements (implementable systems) can be found in the set. The more detailed a model is, the fewer elements can be found.

Secondly, a set based approach allows us to have variants of semantic definitions. For example, we could build two different semantic mappings such that the second is a specialisation of the first: for each model, the semantics given by the second mapping is a subset of the semantics given by the first mapping.

Thus, a hierarchy of semantics definitions can be built, having a very general standard semantics (which has a lot of possible implementations), and very specialised semantics for particular projects.

We do expect that it will be possible to get large groups of people to agree on a semantics for many parts of UML. How might such agreement be conveyed, whilst still allowing variation? We suggest that every UML model has no meaning until someone prefaces it with a definition of the semantics of the modeling language (see Fig. 2). Think of the preface as being a semantic definition of the UML (chosen to be appropriate for your project) that conceptually comes before the model your project is building.

Prefaces will be large documents. They could be organised into a hierarchy of packages. Then a project team could begin with a popular package agreed by the OMG that defines a core of UML, and tailor it with a package from the vendor of the tool they plan to use, then with a package that defines company-specific meanings to certain parts of UML, and finally with a package that defines the project's own variations.

Further details of how packages might be used in this way can be found in [2] from which the illustrative diagram in Fig. 3 is taken.

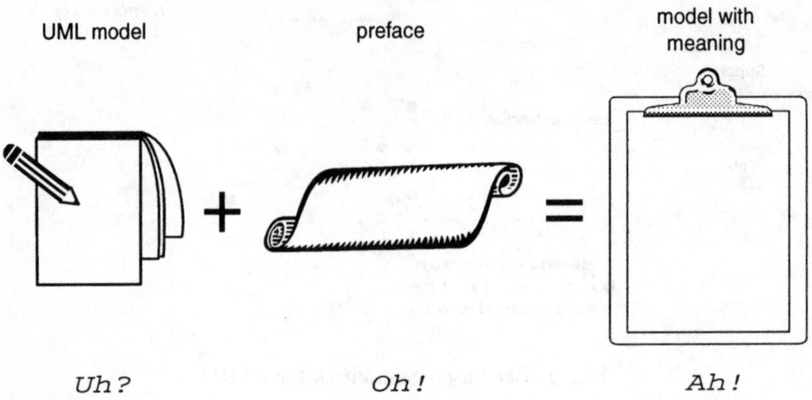

Fig. 2. Prefaces

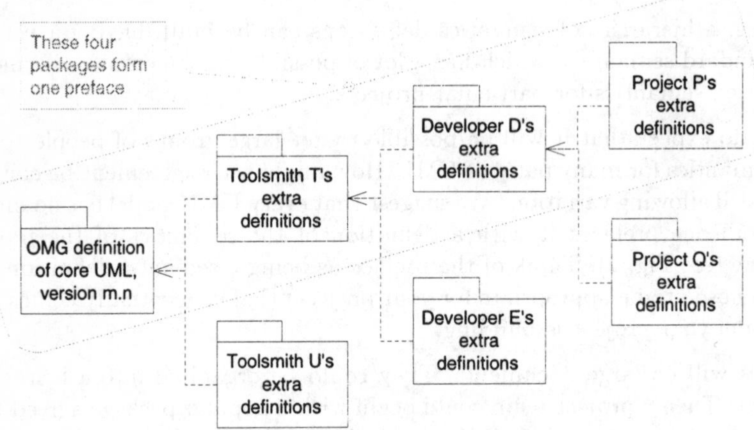

Fig. 3. A Hierarchy of Semantics Packages

Q5. Is It Possible to Express a Semantics of UML in UML (The Meta-modelling Approach)?

Martin Gogolla, University of Bremen, Germany
Stuart Kent, University of Kent at Canterbury, UK
Tom Mens, Vrije Universiteit Brussel, Belgium
Mark Richters and Oliver Radfelder, University of Bremen, Germany

Our answer to this question is: Yes, this is possible for a large part of UML. We call this approach to define the UML semantics the meta-modeling approach.

Q5.1. Why Use UML to Explain UML?

Before we show the details of this approach, we explain why we think it it useful to express UML in terms of UML itself. If one wants to describe the semantics of a language L_{start}, then one has to deal with at least one other language L_{target}, which is the language in which the semantics is to be given. Thus in order to understand the semantics one has to know both languages L_{start} and L_{target}.

The main advantage we see in the meta-modeling approach is that people wanting to understand the semantics of UML do not have to learn another language L_{target}. They just see the language whose features they want to see explained and use it for the translation. Proceeding this way, people who are not experts in formal semantics or formal specification languages will be given the chance to reason about UML without the burden of learning another language L_{target}.

The main danger of this approach, however, lies in the question of whether the expressive power of UML is suitable to express its semantics. We argue that a large part of UML can be expressed in this way but we currently do not know whether all UML features can be treated. On the other hand, it is also a demanding and interesting question for us to see which parts of UML can be transformed into UML and which parts not. Another danger of the approach is the possibility that confusion may arise because there is only one single language: one has to point out very clearly whether one is speaking of (1) a UML element which is currently being translated or (2) a UML element which occurs as the result of the translation.

Q5.2. Central Steps of the Approach

We now show the main steps to be taken for our meta-modeling approach. The general idea is presented in Fig. 4.

1. The first step to be taken is to develop the syntax of the core meta-modelling language, which is akin to what has been dubbed the *MOF*, essentially a diagrammatic modelling language for defining other languages (though we note that the current MOF is not as precise as it should be, and much larger than it needs to be). It is described in some detail below. This language will

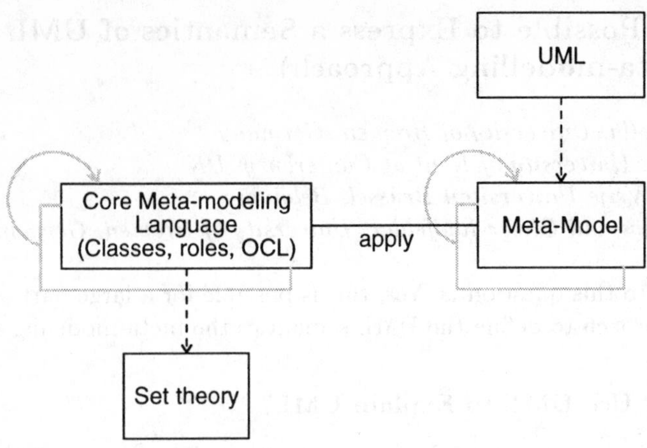

Fig. 4. General Approach to Answer Q5

for sure include class diagrams in which classes and binary associations are allowed. As a central description vehicle we will also use the Object Constraint Language OCL. Important restrictions on models must be expressed by using OCL for class invariants.

2. The second step is to develop the semantics of this core. As Fig. 4 shows, we propose to use set theory as the basis for the semantics. For us, set theory is the most natural choice here, because it is a widely accepted and the most popular formal foundation. Of course there are other approaches around (like temporal and dynamic logic, algebraic specification, streams, process theory, etc.) with advanced properties, but the drawback of these approaches are that they are hard to learn or that there is at least an additional learning effort for the average UML modeler. It is also important to note that the core should be kept as small as possible. It should be possible to gain an intuitive, yet unambiguous, understanding of the language without having to read its precise, set theoretic definition.

   With reference to FAQ 4, the core meta-modeling language and its semantics constitute a preface.

3. The third step is to produce a meta-model description of the set theoretic semantics of the UML core, using the UML core itself. This will include concepts such as *object configuration* or *snapshot*, which will contain objects and links, etc.
4. The fourth step of the meta-modeling approach is to transform the syntax of the complete UML language along the lines presented in the UML semantics document into the UML meta-model, i.e. into an abstract syntax. This step converts each concrete syntactic element into an element of the UML meta-model.

5. The last step is to relate the meta-model description of the syntax to the meta-model description of the semantics. This can be done directly (e.g. as is done for the UML core) or indirectly.

Directly Syntactic concepts are associated with semantic concepts. Thus models are associated with snapshots and traces (sequences of snapshots, interspersed with action invocations), and OCL constraints are written to ensure that all the semantic mapping rules are in place, e.g. that, in a snapshot, the number of links from an object of class A to objects of class B via association ab, must lie between the cardinality bounds imposed on ab. Or that the ordering of action invocations in a trace match the ordering of actions in sequence diagrams, that the transformation in snapshots through a trace satisfy the pre and post conditions of the actions involved, and so on. More detailed descriptions of this approach can be found in [6, 5].

Indirectly Features of the meta-model characterization of the UML abstract syntax are mapped into the meta-modeling core developed before. A very simple example for a transformation of UML language features into the meta-modeling core is given by Fig. 5. This shows how explicitly notated multiplicities in class diagrams can be transformed equivalently into a more basic class diagram without the multiplicities but with an additional restricting OCL invariant. The OCL formula (using a slight generalization of <=) requires that all instances of class A are connected to at least low and at most high objects of class B. An example of defining aspects of UML within UML can be found in [7]

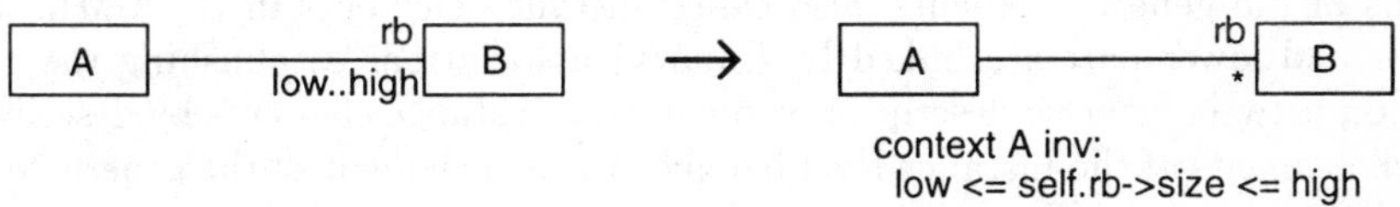

Fig. 5. Transformation of Multiplicities into OCL Invariant

The grey rectangles and the grey arrows in Fig. 4 indicate that both the core meta-model and the UML meta-model could be extended in a bottom-up manner so that more advanced features become available for meta-modeling. Such extensions could even be iterated, i.e. there could be extensions relying on already defined extensions.

Q5.3. Features of the Meta-modeling Core

In Fig. 6 we have displayed the main features of the meta-modeling core in some detail as a class diagram. Roughly speaking, the upper part shows classes responsible for a generic description of UML language elements, also called descriptor

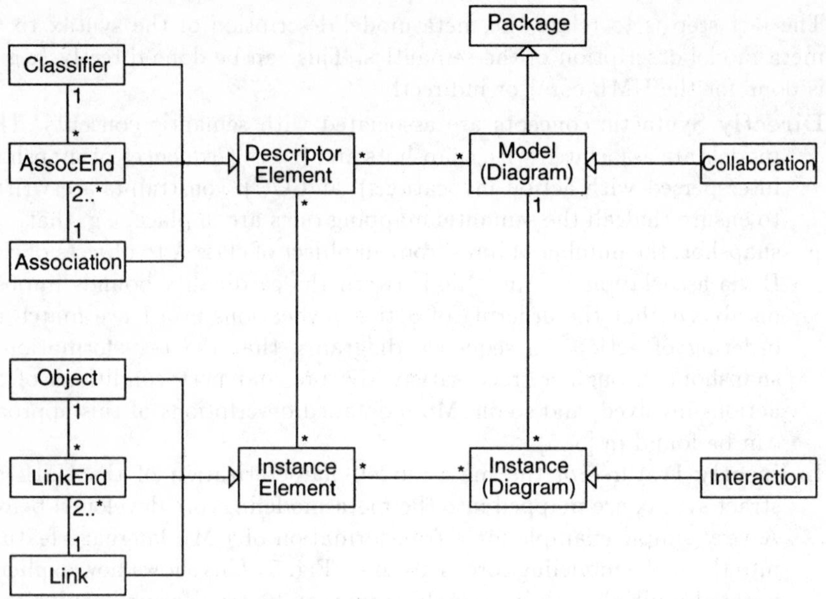

Fig. 6. The basis of the meta-modeling Core

elements in the UML. The lower part describes classes responsible for instantiations of the generic elements, also called instance elements in the UML. The upper and lower part are linked by (binary) associations establishing the connection between generic descriptor elements and instance elements by describing which elements of the instance level belong to which element of the generic level. (Note that concepts of descriptor and instance element do not currently appear in the standard UML meta-model – we believe they must.)

For example, the upper part mentions classifiers (i.e. in particular classes) and the lower part mentions objects. One class in an application domain (e.g. the class Person) will be described by one object of class Classifier. For a concrete system state, each Person instance, i.e. each Person object, will be represented by an object of class Object. The information that an instance in a concrete system state belongs to class Person will be provided by a link belonging to the association between InstanceElement and DescriptorElement.

Note that the meta-modeling core only includes very basic modeling features (i.e. classes, binary associations and the Object Constraint Language). The core does not include UML class diagram language features currently in controversial discussion (controversial at least from the formal semantics point of view – see FAQ 6) such as aggregation and composition.

Q5.4. What Can Be Treated Nicely? Where Are the Problems?

The ideas presented above can be applied to a variety of UML diagram forms. In general, we have the feeling that the approach works well for static and basic dynamic aspects in UML, but we are unsure about the advanced dynamic aspects. The approach works for:

- Language features of the UML core language,
- Pre- and postconditions formulated in OCL as part of class diagrams,
- Advanced class diagram features like aggregation and composition,
- A subset of statechart diagrams,
- Combinations of certain actions in statechart diagrams like parallel composition and concatenation, and
- A subset of sequence and collaboration diagrams.
- Model (package) extension and refinement (at least partially).

Areas with UML diagram features where problems are expected and further intensive research must take place are:

- Concurrency,
- Events and triggering,
- Active objects,
- Full treatment of refinement, and
- Deployment.

Q6. Is It Feasible to Construct a Semantics for All of UML? What Are the Outstanding Issues?

The first of these questions can only be answered constructively: the answer will be unknown until a semantics for all of UML is constructed. However, the more that is constructed the more confident we can be of a positive answer. The best that can be done, then, at this stage, is to examine the current state of affairs [8], and identify the places where it is incomplete, ambiguous or inconsistent. Improvements have been suggested where possible.

Q6.1. Dynamic Behaviour and Concurrency

Roel Wieringa, University of Twente, The Netherlands
Egidio Astesiano and Gianna Reggio, Universita' de Genova, Italy
Alain Le Guennec, IRISA, France
Heinrich Hussman, TU Dresden, Germany
Klaas van den Berg and Pim van den Broek, University of Twente

The issues discussed below rely upon an understanding of the distinction between active and passive (classes) objects. An active object is defined as one that has its own thread of control, a passive object is defined as one that has not. This means, roughly, that an active object has its own flow of control to dispatch requests sent to it. A passive object only performs a computation within the thread of control of an active object. State machines can be defined for active as well as passive objects, that constrain the order in which events can be handled by the object.

Objects communicate by means of call events and signal events, in which, respectively, an operation is called or an asynchronous signal is received. In an *operation call*, the caller calls an operation of another object, the callee. Control passes to the callee and returns when the callee has finished performing the body of the called operation. This is called *run-to-completion* (RTC) semantics. A *shape signal* is a message sent by one object to one or more other objects. Communication by means of signals is asynchronous: The caller can continue processing when the signal is sent. Each active object has a queue of events that have been received but not yet processed.

Event Queue on Active Objects. The event queue of an active object may be emptied in any order. This opens the possibility that an event in the "queue" is *never* processed by the receiving object. A similar problem exists for the so called change events, which are changes in a condition of the model: these too may be handled any time after their occurrence, or they may never be handled. The concept of event queue should therefore be made more precise by including a fairness requirement, which says that every event in the queue will be handled in a finite time after it entered the queue.

Concurrency Semantics of Operations. An object may receive several operation calls simultaneously. The UML allows the definition of several concurrency semantics for each operation. One of these is the sequential semantics, which does not guarantee the integrity of the object if several calls to this operation occur simultaneously; another is the concurrent semantics, which guarantees the integrity of the object under any number of simultaneous calls of the operation. But consider two operations of an object, one of which is sequential and the other concurrent, that both update the same variable. What happens if both are called simultaneously? Can the concurrent operation still maintain its guarantee if the sequential operation messes up the object? This suggests that the concurrency semantics should not be a property of each operation, but of the object as a whole, that applies to all its operations. This is confirmed by one remark in the UML documentation that seems to suggest that a passive object could be implemented by a monitor (page 2-149); but nevertheless, concurrency semantics is declared for operations rather than for the complete object.

Activity States. An activity state of an object is a state in which the object performs a non-atomic computation. It is defined by entering "do: activity" in the statechart node of that state. Activity states open a can of worms:

- Can a passive object have activity states? We think not. Since a passive object returns control after performing a transition, the activity of such a state would never be performed. For non-basic states in a passive object, however, activities can be defined: During an inter-level transition in a state hierarchy, activities of non-basic states may be started, and when control leaves the passive object, these activities are terminated.
- A state of an active object may have an activity. When is this activity performed? If, after a step, the object has another event in its queue, it will immediately proceed processing this event. But then the activity has no time to run.
- When an object is in an activity state, it will perform the activity defined for the state. But this activity may update local variables (attributes). Does this mean that some active objects may never be in a stable state?
- What happens if two concurrent basic states of an active object are both running activities? Can they update the same attributes? But then activities should have sequential, guarded or concurrency semantics just as operations of passive objects have.
- Suppose a state machine enters a hierarchy of nested states, for all of which activities are defined. A thread can only do one thing at a time. Is the activity of the superstate interleaved with that of the substates? Should it terminate before the activities of the substates commence?

Managing Redundant and/or Conflicting Descriptions of Dynamic Behaviour. The behaviour of an operation can be specified in many overlapping ways: Transitions on State Machines, Collaborations and associated Interactions, ActivityCharts, pre/post conditions, via Methods, and so on. For example, one can implement an operation by both a method and a state machine transition. The UML does not prohibit this. The method body may involve updates to state variables that conflict with actions triggered by the transition. And even if the method and the transition actions do not conflict, in which order are the actions in the method body and along the transition executed? Are they interleaved? The description on page 2.101 of the semantics document is extremely vague on this.

Further, a class may have a state machine but still have an operation that is defined by a method rather than by a state transition in the machine. In that case, the state machine does not specify the set of all possible behaviours of the class instances, *contra* what is said about state machines on page 2.136, namely that each state machine specifies *all* possible behaviours of the model element to which it is attached.

The previous observation is compounded by the fact that one object may have several state machines (page 2.136). Again, what happens if these two state machines have conflicting behaviours?

The Query Attribute. A query operation is an operation that does not update its owning object when called. However, the operation may be realised by a method that nevertheless modifies the state. An obvious fix to this inconsistency is to require the method to be read-only with respect to the owning object. This cannot be statically checked, but we can deal with this similarly to what has been done in the Ada semantics definition, namely by calling models that violate this constraint "erroneous" and leaving tools free to handle these errors in whatever way.

However, this addition is not enough, for the operation can also (even additionally) be realised by a transition in the state machine of the object; and even if no update actions are triggered by the transition, the transition causes a change of state and this itself is an update. A query operation should not be defined by a state transition.

Q6.2. Refinement and Extension

Tom Mens, Vrije Universiteit Brussel, Belgium

Intuitively, *refinement* is a mechanism that allows us to gradually add more detail to an arbitrary software artifact. In the case of UML, these software artifacts could be single model elements, parts of a diagram, an entire diagram, or even combinations of (parts of) several diagrams.

Unfortunately, there is some confusion about the exact meaning of the term refinement. Some researchers specifically mean the relationship between model elements at different semantics levels, such as analysis and design. Other researchers only use stepwise refinement to gradually add detail to software artifacts within the same phase. Sometimes, a combination of both is allowed as well. Regardless of the exact definition, a well-defined notion of refinement is crucial in the software engineering process, e.g., to provide better automated tool support for forward engineering as well as reverse engineering.

In [8], there are essentially four different Relationships that can be used as a refinement mechanism: Extend, Include, Generalization and Abstraction.

- The first two relationships are only meaningful in the context of use case diagrams. A UseCase can be an extension of another one, which is represented by an Extend relationship, requiring an ExtensionPoint in the UseCase that is being extended. A UseCase can also be included in another one, which is represented by an Include relationship.
- Another important relationship for expressing some kind of refinement is Generalization, which is defined between two GeneralizableElements (the child and the parent). Examples of GeneralizableElements are Classifiers, Associations, Stereotypes, and Packages. A Generalization is a taxonomic relationship between a more general element and a more specific element. The more specific element is fully consistent with the more general element (it has all of its properties, members, and relationships) and may contain additional information. Generalization is a *subtyping mechanism*, i.e., an Instance of the more general GeneralizableElement may be substituted by an Instance of the more specific GeneralizableElement. Generalization also

serves as an *incremental modification* or *inheritance mechanism*. The complete description of a GeneralizableElement is obtained incrementally by combining the descriptions of all its ancestors.
- Finally, an Abstraction is a special kind of Dependency relationship that relates two (sets of) elements that represent the same concept at different levels of abstraction or from different viewpoints. If the stereotype ≪refine≫ is attached to the Abstraction, it specifies a Refinement relationship between model elements at different semantic levels, such as analysis and design. The exact mapping between these different levels, however, is outside the scope of the UML semantics. Alternatively, a ≪realise≫ stereotype can be attached to the Abstraction to model stepwise refinement. Again, the exact mapping of such a Realisation is not specified by the UML.

Many problems can be identified with the way in which UML deals with refinement:

Unclear Distinction between Refinement and Realisation. While the definition of Refinement seems to indicate that Refinement serves specifically as a relation between different semantic levels, parts of [8] contradict this view. For example, there is a detailed description of state machine refinement that specifies how a state machine can be refined stepwise by gradually adding more detail. On the other hand, Realisation seems to overlap with Refinement, since it also addresses the link between different semantic levels (specification and implementation). To avoid this confusion, a clear distinction should be made between the two kinds of Abstraction. For example, Refinement could be reserved to express the relation between elements at the same semantics level but at different levels of detail, while Realisation could be reserved to express the relation between elements at different semantics levels.

One of the reasons for the above confusion is that the semantics of both Refinement and Realisation are not specified by the UML. This task is left entirely to the user or CASE tool developer. To find a commonly accepted definition for refinement and realisation, it might be useful to look at existing proposals in the literature. For example, an automatic link between sequence diagrams and statecharts is proposed in [15]. Similarly, in the research community of message sequence charts [11] (a more sophisticated variant of sequence diagrams), attempts are being undertaken to semantically link them to use case diagrams.

Undesired Interaction between Subtyping and Incremental Modification. Because the Generalization relationship is actually used for two completely different purposes, subtyping and incremental modification, it suffers from a lack of orthogonality. This leads to the problem that a GeneralizableElement can only be incrementally modified by adding items to it, but not by deleting items from it. Otherwise, the modification will not be substitutable anymore for the more general element. Nevertheless, in many situations it would also be useful to incrementally remove items from a Generalizable Element.

The main reason for the above problem is that the UML has chosen for a specific variant of inheritance, namely subtype inheritance. As a result, other interesting variants such as implementation inheritance are excluded. In [3], some strong evidence against subtype inheritance is provided. A possible solution would be to separate the orthogonal aspects of Generalization (subtyping and inheritance) into two different relationships.

Lack of Orthogonality between Refinement and Generalization. Generalization could be regarded as a specific kind of Refinement. They are both used to incrementally add more detail to a given element. The main difference is that Generalization imposes an extra substitutability requirement. In the meta-model, this commonality should be reflected by defining Generalization as a special kind of Refinement.

Extend and Include versus Generalization. While Extend and Include are used as refinement mechanisms for use cases, these use cases can also be connected by means of a Generalization relationship. The question arises whether such a Generalization relationship is still necessary between use cases. As an answer to this question: the subtyping aspect of Generalization is probably still useful for use cases, but maybe the incremental modification aspect is not, since it can be alternatively achieved via Extend and Include. In any case, the overlap in functionality between Generalization, Extend and Include leads to a lot of confusion.

Unclear Definition of Generalization. While it is more or less clear how Generalization is defined for classes and interfaces (it is described in natural language in [8]), the same is not true for other GeneralizableElements such as Nodes, Components, Associations and Packages. [8] does not specify how Generalization should be defined for these elements.

Scaleability of Generalization. The basic notion of Generalization is fairly primitive, because it can only be applied to single GeneralizableElements. However, by using a Generalization relationship between Packages it becomes possible to define a refinement of more complex software artefacts, since Packages can be used to group arbitrarily complex sets of ModelElements. The question arises whether a general meaningful and useful definition can be given to the notion of Generalization between Packages.

Refinement of UML Diagrams. UML does not specify how entire diagrams can be refined or realised. For example, when is a class diagram a refinement of another class diagram? The same question holds for all other UML diagrams. Part of the problem is that the UML meta-model does not have an explicit representation for each kind of UML diagram. The meta-classes Collaboration,

Interaction, StateMachine and ActivityGraph can be used for representing collaboration diagrams, sequence diagrams, statechart and activity diagrams, respectively. However, there is no corresponding meta-class for representing a class diagram, object diagram, use case diagram, etc ... Another problem is that the existing meta-classes that represent entire UML diagrams are defined as direct subclasses of ModelElement. To be able to refine diagrams through Generalization, they should at least be subclasses of GeneralizableElement. An even better idea would be to define them as subclasses of Model (a subclass of Package that is intended to describe the modeled system at a certain level of abstraction and from a specific viewpoint). An important open problem that remains is how Generalization (or refinement) should be defined for each kind of diagram. For different UML diagrams, refinement needs to be defined in a different way. State machine refinement will be defined in a completely different way than, say, collaboration refinement or use case diagram refinement. For most kinds of UML diagrams, there is currently no clear or commonly accepted idea of what refinement should look like. It might be useful to look at other approaches (formal as well as informal) where refinement has already been investigated. Especially in the area of theoretical computer science, there is a significant number of people working on formal refinement techniques for many different kinds of models, and using many different kinds of underlying formalisms. Many of these ideas might be relevant to the UML.

Q6.3. Aggregation

Andy Evans, University of York, UK
Robert France, Colorado State University, USA
Guy Genilloud, Swiss Federal Institute of Technology
Brian Henderson-Sellers, University of Technology, Sydney, Australia
Perdita Stevens, University of Edinburgh, UK

Aggregation has long been a thorny issue; the problem is that there seem to be so many subtle nuances to the concept. In UML things appear to be more clear cut at first: there are, essentially, two forms, represented by the black diamond and white diamonds. The intention would be to partition *all* whole-part relationships into two distinct, non-overlapping and exhaustive kinds. Furthermore, examination of the standard suggests that the black diamond *was intended* to have precise semantics, whilst the white one was probably intended to cover all the other cases (of whole-part).

Although the semantics of the black diamond should not be difficult to provide (the UML standard suggests a *deletion* semantics, where, if the whole is copied or destroyed, the parts are as well), a semantics for the white diamond will open the same can of worms that have been opened in the past, which, in turn, may raise questions about whether the black diamond is a useful or appropriate concept to treat as a special case. Problems with the definitions of UML's black and white diamonds are discussed further in [9]. Attempts to tease out the various subtle aspects of whole-part are provided in e.g. [1, 16, 9]. Attempts to formalise such analyses are provided in e.g. [14, 10].

References

[1] F. Civello. Roles for composite objects in object-oriented analysis and design. In *OOPSLA'93 Conference Proceedings*, ACM SIGPLAN Notices 23:10, October 1993.

[2] S. Cook, A. Kleppe, R. Mitchell, B. Rumpe, J. Warmer, and A. Wills. Defining uml family members using prefaces. In C. Mingins and B. Meyer, editors, *Proceedings of TOOLS Pacific 99*. IEEE Press, 1999.

[3] W.R. Cook, W.R. Hill, and P.S. Canning. Inheritance is not subtyping. *ACM Transactions on Programming Languages and Systems*, pages 125–135, 1999.

[4] Desmond D'Souza and Alan Wills. *Objects, Components and Frameworks With UML: The Catalysis Approach*. Addison-Wesley, 1998.

[5] A.S. Evans and S. Kent. Meta-modelling semantics of UML: the pUML approach. In B. Rumpe and R.B. France, editors, *2nd International Conference on the Unified Modeling Language*, 1999.

[6] Robert Geisler. Precise UML semantics through formal metamodeling. In Luis Andrade, Ana Moreira, Akash Deshpande, and Stuart Kent, editors, *Proceedings of the OOPSLA'98 Workshop on Formalizing UML. Why? How?*, 1998.

[7] Martin Gogolla and Mark Richters. Equivalence rules for UML class diagrams. In Pierre-Alain Muller and Jean Bézivin, editors, *Proceedings of UML'98 International Workshop, Mulhouse, France, June 3 - 4, 1998*, pages 87–96. ESSAIM, Mulhouse, France, 1998.

[8] Object Management Group. UML specification version 1.3. Technical Report ad/99-06-08, June 1999.

[9] B. Henderson-Sellers and F. Barbier. Black and white diamonds. In B. Rumpe and R.B. France, editors, *2nd International Conference on the Unified Modeling Language*, 1999.

[10] B. Henderson-Sellers and F. Barbier. What is this thing called aggregation? In R. Mitchell, A.C. Wills, J. Bosch, and B. Meyer, editors, *TOOLS29*, pages 216–230. IEEE Computer Society Press, 1999.

[11] E. Rudolph, J. Grabowski, and P. Graubmann. Tutorial on message sequence charts (msc'96). Tutorials at First Joint Conference FORTE/PSTV'96, Kaiserslautern, Germany, October 1996.

[12] James Rumbaugh, Ivar Jacobson, and Grady Booch. *The Unified Modeling Language Reference Guide*. Addison-Wesley, 1998.

[13] Bernhard Rumpe. A note on semantics (with an emphasis on UML). In Haim Kilov and Bernhard Rumpe, editors, *Proceedings Second ECOOP Workshop on Precise Behavioral Semantics (with an Emphasis on OO Business Specifications)*, pages 177–197. Technische Universität München, TUM-I9813, 1998.

[14] Monika Saksena, Robert France, and Maria Larrondo-Petri. A characterization of aggregation. In C. Rolland and G. Grosz, editors, *Proceedings of OOIS98*, pages 11–19. Springer, 1998.

[15] S. Sch÷nnberger and R.K. Keller. Algorithmic support for model transformation in object-oriented development. Publications of DIRO, August 1997.

[16] M. Snoeck and G. Dedene. Existence dependency: the key to semantic integrity between structural and behavioural aspects of object types. *IEEE Trans. Software Eng.*, 24(4):233–251, 1998.

Object-Oriented Architectural Evolution

Isabelle Borne[1], Serge Demeyer[2], and Galal Hassan Galal[3]

[1] Ecole des Mines de Nantes
Isabelle.Borne@emn.fr - http://www.emn.fr/borne/
[2] University of Berne
demeyer@iam.unibe.ch - http://www.iam.unibe.ch/~demeyer/
[3] University College London
G.Galal@cs.ucl.ac.uk - http://www.cs.ucl.ac.uk/staff/G.Galal/

Abstract. Software Architecture has become an established area of study within the software engineering community for a considerable time now. Recently, Software Architecture has become a topic of interest within the object-oriented community as well. The quality of an object-oriented architecture can be described by a set of characteristics, such as modularity, extensibility, flexibility, adaptability, understandability, testability and reusability, which are recognized to facilitate the evolution and the maintenance of software systems. Architecture represents the highest level of design decisions about a system and evolution aspects have to be considered at this level. Moreover, the ever-changing world makes evolvability a strong quality requirement for the majority of software architectures. The main objective of this workshop was to establish a working dialogue about the effective use of techniques, formalisms and tools, as well as their combinations in order to address the architectural evolution of object oriented software systems, either in their initial development or in their later redesign. The workshop also did aim to highlight outstanding issues that should form a part of the forthcoming research agenda in the evolvability of object-oriented software architectures.

1. Introduction (Aim, Organization)

The workshop aimed at distilling the views of participants from industry and academia on the issue that should become part of any future research agenda into the evolution of object-oriented system and software architectures.

A total of 19 position papers and presentation were received. All were deemed of a reasonable quality and scope. Requests for participation in workshop without a position paper or statement were turned down. A total of 28 people participated in the workshop. In preparation for the workshop, all participants were instructed:

- to skim through the papers, made available at:
  http://www.emn.fr/borne/ECOOP99/W4-ListOfPapers.html
- to read the last year workshop summary
  (http://www.emn.fr/borne/ECOOP98/W02-Synthesis.html);
  also available in [4]

A. Moreira and S. Demeyer (Eds.): ECOOP'99 Workshops, LNCS 1743, pp. 57–79, 1999.

Three participants were selected to give presentations on their respective papers. The organising committee felt that these papers had the potential to trigger discussions that are highly aligned to the objectives of the workshop and how the organisers felt it should go. Presenters were required not to try to present all the points in their respective papers. We asked every participant to read all the papers before the workshop, and explained that the goal of the oral presentations is to generate discussions and to help settle the scope of the day. We also asked that presentations should show the presenter's approach and particular points of view of software architectural evolution, and strongly suggest that every presentation is ended with some points of discussions and issues. Below are the papers selected and the reasons for selecting them:

- *Software Architectural Evolution in the Dragon Project (Michael Christensen, Christian Heide Damm, Klaus Marius Hansen, Elmer Sandvad, Michael Thomsen – University of Aarhus, Denmark).*
  The organisers thought that this paper contained a real good experience report on how architecture helps during iterative design. So it was felt that this paper is good in guiding the scope of the discussion.
  In the presentation, the following suggestions were made to the participants:
  - The problem domain objects should be isolated from the solution domain objects.
  - The problem domain model is never stable.
  - Architecture should be defined iteratively and bottom-up.
  - Tools cannot detect the need for architectural evolution, but they can help with re-structuring (manually).
- *Using Recovered Views to Track Architectural Evolution (Tamar Richner – University of Bern Switzerland).*
  The organisers felt that tracking how your architecture evolves is something that was particularly well-covered in this paper, this is especially so since architecture is very likely to evolve in ways other than what the designers intended. Thinking about architectural drift is particularly important, so this paper should broaden the perspective of the ensuing discussion. The presentation raised the following issues:
  - Change: what changes in architecture?; what has changed and why?; can we predict what will change next?; can we separate what should be changed from what should remain stable?
  - Architectural change: what is it?, how can it be detected?; how can architectural evolution be specified and documented?; when can an architecture be regarded as "stable"?; how can we build evolvable software?; how can we evaluate relative architectural quality?
- *Evolution of Layered Object-Oriented Models (Michel Dao – France Telecom, France).*
  This paper tries to address different rates of change in a (layered) architecture. And that is really the core issue of this whole workshop. This presentation ended with numerous statements and questions, from these we select:

- Can any class hierarchy be divided into layers or does it depend on the application domain?
- Assuming a layered architecture: is there an optimal number of layers?
- How can we characterise different types of evolution: intra-layer, inter-layer, and integration?
- What type of structuration may help software evolution?
- Organising class hierarchies into layers makes their evolution easier.
- One can organise class hierarchies into semantically coherent layers.
- Class hierarchies organised into layers can offer multiple 'access points'
- Working on only one layer is useful with respect to the complexity of evolution algorithms.
- Two types of evolution may be suggested: Semantic evolution (coarse-grain): inter-layer and integration, and technical evolution (fine-grain): intra-layer.

2. Workshop Discussions

On the basis of the range of papers submitted to the workshop and the presentations made, the organisers distilled the following questions as bases for more focused track discussions in smaller groups:

- What concepts of architecture and design are useful in supporting architectural evolution?
- What methods and techniques for modelling the evolution, architectural drift, recovery and detection of architecture should be investigated further?
- How can we evaluate the evolvability of a software architecture?

Participants selected tracks to join, and every group was asked to select a discussion chair and a reporter. A member of the organising committee joined each of the three tracks. After having worked on answering these questions in smaller groups, the workshop came together in a final plenary session where all the results of the different track discussions were presented and discussed. The members of the organising committee have written the following reports on the respective tracks.

2.1. What Concepts of Architecture and Design Are Useful in Supporting Architectural Evolution?

In order to answer this broad question, the group tried to break it down into some manageable pieces. First we addressed *what exactly characterizes software architectures* (i.e., what makes it different from design) and *how that does relate to system evolution ?* The discussion resulted in the following list of five characteristic properties.

1. *Repeated Abstraction.* A software architecture is an abstraction that is repeated across several software systems, so that people know where to look for certain functionality when facing the system. This is similar to building architecture, in the sense that people know where to look for the elevators and toilets when entering a public building, yet do not expect this functionality when entering a cathedral. The fact that an architecture is a repeated abstraction has implications on a system's evolution because it dictates what should remain consistent when the system changes.
2. *Robust.* An architecture emphasises robustness by separating more permanent from more adaptable functionality. Again, this is similar to building architecture, where well architected buildings can gracefully adapt to changing circumstances (people adapt a children's room when they grow to become teenagers), but where other changes are less easy to accommodate (adapting a church to become a concert hall is possible but costly; adapting a concert hall to become a church is nearly impossible). Consequently, an architecture has impact on a system's evolution because it helps in assessing the impact of a change, especially relevant when negotiating with end-users.
3. *Simple.* An architecture is inherently simple so that people can memorise and recognise it easily. Ideally, it is a drawing that fits on one page and that developers can reconstruct without having to consult the system's documentation or source code. Here as well there are similarities with building architecture, as good architects give a building some kind of identity that people recognise and reproduce at will. Keeping an architecture simple supports system evolution, because it may prevent problems like architectural drift.
4. *Difficult to Trace.* An architecture is ubiquitous yet intangible, i.e. it is present in the overall system yet difficult to lay your hands on. This brings up the issue of architecture as "art" versus "engineering", a tension also present in traditional building architecture. Indeed, architecture is not only concerned about constructing houses that do not fall apart, but also about houses which have an aesthetic appeal. Moreover, because a system's architecture ubiquitous yet intangible, it is very difficult to trace the architecture in the source code, thus it is hard to evolve an architecture once a system is up and running.
5. *Maps Function on Form.* A software architecture is a mapping between the requirements and the functioning software system, thus between functionality and form. This view is shared with building architecture, where it is the architecture that maps the required functionality on a spatial structure. Just like it is the case with buildings, the successful architectures are the ones that survive several functional changes, hence a good mapping is quite relevant for a system's evolution.

What makes all of these properties characteristic for architecture, i.e. why do they distinguish architecture from design ? Well, revising each of them, we observed that

- An architecture is *inherently reusable* because it has been repeated in several software systems. In contrast, design reuse is desirable but not inherent to the notion of design per se.
- All architectures implicitly impose *which functionality is to remain permanent.* In contrast, there exist designs that do not impose permanent functionality because their main purpose is to make things dynamically adaptable. See for instance the "Prototype", "Adapter", "Proxy", "Command" design patterns [8].
- At first glance, it may appear that there is a fundamental conflict between the inherent simplicity of an architecture and the typical complexity of a software system. One way to deal with this conflict is to allow multiple architectural views, just like architects have several blueprints to describe a house (see also the discussion in section 2.2). However, here as well there is a distinction between architecture and design, in the sense that *the number of architectural views is limited* while the number of design views is unrestricted.
- As far as traceability concerns, the distinction between architecture and design is less clear. Due to the intangible nature of architecture, it seems that traceability is a bit more difficult for architecture than it is for design. Yet, depending on the system's implementation platform, it is likely that the design is untraceable as well.
- Mapping function onto form is also something that is shared between architecture and design, so here as well the distinction is less prominent. We tried to see whether the functionality is more explicit in the design or in the architecture, but could not reach a satisfying conclusion.

After this discussion we focused our attention on which of these characteristic properties may be useful in typical system evolution scenarios by answering some of the questions raised by the three introductory presentations. Below are the questions and corresponding answers.

- *Does the process of architecture creation have an impact on its future evolution?* The answer to this question is clearly yes, because by specifying an architecture for a system you inherently state which functionality you expect to remain permanent and which you expect to vary (i.e., Robustness). As such you make a clear but implicit statement on how the system may evolve in the future.
- *Does the separation of problem domain objects and solution domain objects have an impact on software architecture evolution?* Here as well, the answer is clearly yes, as this separation of concerns is an abstraction that is often repeated in software systems (i.e., Repeated Abstraction). Moreover, this separation represents a successful mapping from function on form, as resulting systems will be able to survive typical functional changes (i.e., Maps Function on Form).
- *Can we model problem domain objects into layers and is it useful with respect to architectural evolution?* Concerning the first half of the question, we felt that it depends mainly on the problem domain at hand. However, concerning

the second half the answer is again yes, because layers have proven to be a good abstraction (i.e., Repeated Abstraction) that separate more permanent from more adaptable functionality (i.e., Robustness).

2.2. What Methods and Techniques for Modelling the Evolution, Architectural Drift, Recovery, and Detection of Architecture Should Be Investigated Further?

Before trying to answer this question, the group started by shortly looking at software architecture definitions. We conclude that, although generally stated as the overall structure of the system in terms of constituting components and interactions, we need views on software architecture rather than one single architecture. Indeed, the architecture imposes constraints on structure and behaviour, and the invariants (or constraints) depend on the view.

The discussion went on addressing the main question: *How to detect and deal with architectural drift ?* and considering some related problems :

- Version proliferation
- Iterative development of architectures
- Separation between problem and solution domain
- Role of tool support
- Architecture representation

How to detect and deal with architectural drift ? An architectural drift can be detected by version control systems as well as metrics that can point out "what changed?". Other techniques such as tagging systems [9] can answer both questions "what changed?" and "why it changed?". Further investigations are needed to detect architectural drifts more precisely, and to consider the case of a break of layering in a layered architecture, or a change propagation.

Once an architectural drift is detected, the problem is now "how to deal with it?" Based on its experience the group proposes several techniques that address software evolution and can be applied to software architecture and architectural drift:

- reuse contracts [17];
- refactoring or restructuring techniques [7];
- impact analysis techniques to deal with change propagation [1].

Version proliferation This problem can arise when a framework (v1) used to develop different systems for customers results in various customised systems (v2, v3,...) of the original framework. These customisations should then be merged at a certain time to take into account the improvements. Two open questions are "How can this merging be done? What about backward compatibility issues?"

Iterative development of architectures When you iterate architecture design, architectural reviews are necessary. The development process implies specific roles: the customer (final user) is client of the whole development team, whereas developers of the development team are client of the architects.

Separation between problem and solution domain The problem domain model is between the business logic and the solution domain model. In an iterative design if the problem domain is clear and well understood, its concepts are less subject to changes, i.e. remain more stable. Therefore it seems better to adopt a top down approach, and evolution is more likely to occur in the solution domain. In the opposite if the problem domain is vague, a bottom up approach is recommended and new requirements may imply changes in the domain model. To conclude on this point the group agrees that a separation between these domains is useful.

Tool support Current tools are good for detection of changes or conflicts, but not for re-architecting (i.e. evolving architectures). You have to decide manually what to do in that case. The investigation and the design of new tool supports, that can link architectural descriptions to design and source code, have to be explored.

Architecture representation How should architectures be represented in order to adequately deal with architectural evolution? is a key question. Architectural description notations exist but they only describe architectures statically without taking evolution into account. Some approaches do provide support for evolution but only at run-time or for dynamic reconfiguration. Current approaches provide no support for design time evolution. Reuse contracts are a good candidate. Other possible candidates must be investigated. A related issue concerns the representation of architectural invariants. It should be left up to architects to determine these invariants. Then, how do we encode invariants? What about architectural description languages, domain-specific languages? The representation problem in the context or architectural evolution addresses several research domains for which the group agrees on the needs of further invastigation.

Partial conclusions of the group are:

- Architectural description notations exist but they provide no support for design time evolution. Some exceptions are reuse contracts and formal description languages.
- Research is needed on architectural notation that can express evolution, and on tool support to aid in detecting and dealing with evolution.

2.3. How Can We Evaluate the Evolvability of a Software Architecture?

Premise Stability can be of at least two types: structural and behavioural. The structural stability of systems is what concerns us here.

A good architecture allows the system defined by it to evolve. Robust architecture is therefore one that accommodates a suitably wide range of adaptations to the software system based on it. This means that architectures should, by definition, be stable, but applications should be evolvable. The prime subject of evolution should thus be the application, rather than the architecture.

We distinguish between:

- Product-line architecture: where architectures evolve from one another. This is because one product's architecture is based on a previous one. This is where an architecture evolves from another, so as to underpin a new product in the same line.
- (single) product architecture: where the single system or product evolves. Here, the system itself evolves to accommodate new requirements. Ideally, the change to underlying architecture should be minimal: the architecture should be stable.

We need to

- Be able to predict or measure the evolvability of various architectures with respect to the particular problem domain under investigation. This means that a process should be instated in any software engineering activity to evaluate alternative architectures. Such process should be explicit in the process plan adopted and be open.
- Separate technical evaluation from semantic evaluation. Technical evaluation is about the correctness of the technical content (are we building the system right?); semantic evaluation addresses problem/architecture fit (are we building the right system?). Both types of evaluation are important when looking at the evolvability of architectures. However, a large part of the evaluation criteria is likely to come from the domain (semantic criteria).
- Be able to produce domain-specific interpretations, as no single general evaluation framework or techniques will be sufficient. It must be noted that both quantitative and qualitative evaluation techniques have their relevance here.
- Be able to construct a useful ***evaluation framework*** for evaluating architectures. We believe this to be the crux of the issue of producing robust and stable architectures.

We recognise that

- Both structure and architecture contribute to the non-functional attributes of software. However, architecture contributes to such attributes to a greater extent at the early stages of engineering, and structure contributes to such attributes to a greater extent at the later stages of engineering.
- Another source of architectural change is the solution domain itself (the actual technologies used to build the system).
- Sources that give rise to architectural change must be investigated and analysed.

A first stab at a framework for architectural evaluation Below we give an organising matrix with sources of change (column headings), and objects of evolution that such sources may dictate (row headings). We give examples of concrete changes in the respective cells of intersection.

	DOMAIN	BUSINESS	TECHNOLOGY
Content	new/changing concepts	new functions	platform changes
Context	standards	regulations markets	tools and programming environments
Process and learning	past domain changes and implications for these	past products; past market successes and failures	design knowledge and expertise

In each architecting situation, research should be conducting into the possible causes of architectural change. Sources that dictate such changes may be the narrow problem domain itself, the wider business context with its business decisions and strategies, or the technological context that normally lies beyond the immediate stakeholders. Brainstorming as well as studying precedent (past systems and causes and types of their change) should aid this process. The object of change can be the software system itself, its context-bound attributes (e.g. required response time), or the lessons learned from effecting changes to it. A corollary to this last point is that a log of changes, their rational and context, and their degree of success need to be captured to add to the "knowledge asset" about architectural changes.

3. Abstracts of the Submitted Position Papers

Participants' contributions can be categorized in four types of research or experience in the area of architectural evolution. The first set proposes ideas on the concepts of software architecture and some methodological points of view to design evolvable architecture. The second set studies the evolution of specific software architectures (i.e. family architecture, layered model). The third set discusses architecture assessment environments (i.e metrics and program visualisation). Finally the last set concerns tools and techniques that help to deal with architectural evolution and changes (visualization tool, reuse contracts, patterns).

3.1. Concept and Design of Software Architectures

3.1.1. Software Architecture: How Are the Boundaries Defined (Jean-Pierre Kuilboer and Noushin Ashrafi – UMASS Boston)? As software are built to address more complex problems projects often fail or are over- budget, over- time, and of low quality. Modern tools, languages, or even the latest crop of development methodologies has not alleviated the software development crisis. In order to find a lasting solution one needs to identify the problem first: is the problem due to a faulty architecture, deficient implementation, or perhaps unrealistic expectations of existing tools and methodologies ?

Today, after years of focusing on software development process and methodologies, the attention has switched to software architecture. The concept is not new, the definitions are not uniform, and there is a major confusion in the existing literature between system and software architecture. One of the biggest challenges to software architecture is the evolving structure of a software product or product line. To apply an architectural style, the scope and the boundary of the software artifact should be identified as well as its context. Intellectual contributions of movements such as general systems theory, which dealt with the concept of systems and subsystems, are often ignored. The heterogeneity or homogeneity of the software component is correlated with its size, and together they dictate what type of architectural style is to be used. A system may encompass different styles of software architecture (for example object-oriented for the presentation, client-server for the data, and main-program and sub-routine for some control mechanism). A heterogeneous software system could be partitioned into homogeneous components, each with its own architecture.

We need software architecture for many reasons. As in the building architecture, it is a means of communicating the structure of the software before its construction. It also offers guidelines and documentation of the structure for future improvements. In addition, careful planning can foresee future changes and specify an adaptive and robust infrastructure. In the presence of radical innovation or changes in the environment, initial performance is not always a clear indicator of future achievement.

Faced with many contentious factors, the role and responsibilities of the software architect are very critical. He/she has to consider not only the changing environment and time and cost constraints but has to evaluate the features, evolution path, and integrative abilities of many heterogeneous parts. A wise software architect should leverage existing taxonomies and frameworks, taking into account the data, process, actors, location, and timing. While the latest fashion for object orientation can bring partial solutions, keeping an investigative mind for the past (e.g. existing architectural proposal) and the future with an interdisciplinary slant should serve the developer best.

3.1.2. Interacting Components — A Conceptual Architecture Model (Palle Nowack – Maersk Institute, University of Southern Denmark). When considering the evolution of software, the information available concerning the software to be evolved is crucial. We need good descriptions of software systems in order to understand and communicate the design and the architecture. This implies that we need to find the proper set of abstractions and the right way to express them in order to support such descriptions.

Any software architecture model is described from a certain perspective. The perspective is given by the choice of component concept (the entities), structure concept (the relations), and abstraction level (the considered properties of the entities and the relations). We propose one such perspective: interaction architecture. We consider the design of the interaction architecture for the hardest part of any development effort, and thus it is desirable to reuse and adapt such architectures. Furthermore, as we argue below, we believe that for an object-oriented system, interactions are a much more feasible architectural abstraction than components.

An object-oriented software system consists of set of objects that interacts through a set of messages or method invocations. Throughout a system's lifetime objects gets created and garbage collected, thus a system is very dynamic in both its behavior and configuration. Even with small or medium sized systems the complexity caused by the number of objects and method invocations makes it hard to describe and reason about the system. Especially it gets hard to understand how the different objects are related at run-time: the structures and collaboration patterns they participate in. On the other hand these structures and collaborations are considered the hardest parts to get right when designing new systems, hence it is desirable to reuse successful examples. The required interactions between a set of objects effectively determines the required interface of the involved objects. Thus a lot more effort should be devoted to the design of object interactions: principles guiding the design, conceptual models for understanding the design, and proper notations for expressing the design. Design patterns, meta patterns and frameworks are examples of object-oriented techniques that have been proposed to counter these problems. In our approach we seek alternatives, prompted by the fact that both patterns and frameworks describe much more than just architecture.

Research within software architecture has given great attention to the notion of components; both implementation components and components as a software artifact concept. The latter implies that components are considered useful abstractions over the software domain. In our approach we try to develop a similar abstraction over the software domain, focusing on the interaction between objects. Concretely we try to obtain this abstraction by grouping sets of related method invocations into an interaction instance. Similar interaction instances are categorized into interaction classes. The interaction classes can be reused in descriptions of other interaction classes through specialization and aggregation of interaction classes. This form of interaction reuse aims to support evolution of object-oriented software architectures.

3.1.3. Searching Basic Notions for Software Architecture Design (Jorge L. Ortega-Arjona and Graham Roberts – University College London). Software Architecture is founded on the belief that software design can make use of practices and techniques of design in general, expected to generate software quality products. However, to achieve this, Software Architecture design should be based on a set of notions for design, which allows software architects to think about, understand and communicate their design knowledge. In this paper we search in the fields of design and problem-solving to find an initial set of basic notions for Software Architecture design.

3.1.4. A Note on Scenarios in Software Architecting (Galal Hassan Galal – University College London, United Kingdom). Our position is an extension of that we put forward in last year's workshop (ECOOP'98) in the same area, where we argued that much of what is currently being referred to as "software architecture" (such as pipes and filters, event-based systems etc.) should in fact be more appropriately be discussed under different headings such as structures, interactivity types, and so on. Our view is that a proper use of the term architecture should, and more beneficially, refer to a high-level, coarse-grain categorisation of components, exactly as it tends to be used in its home discipline: the architecture of buildings.

Referring to the philosophical discussions of the nature of Architecture in its home discipline, we find that it is used to refer to both product and process. That is, to produce an architecture, one has to architect. If one simply copies the design of a building onto another site, one cannot claim to have architected anything. Similarly, following any particular description of an architecting process is no guarantee that a structure will result that many people would wish to call architecture.

We argue that the two concomitant concepts of product and process are equally, and necessarily, applicable to software and systems architecting. For any given problem, it is quite likely that many architectures (or even architectural styles) may be devised. As all valid architectures for a given problem must be computationally equivalent, then the differences largely lie in their non-functional (or quality) and long term attributes, such as robustness and evolvability. This brings to the fore the criticality of an evaluation activity where competing architectures are compared against each other with reference to the domain under study. This is the central argument that we wish to put forward here: that most of the criteria by which valid architectures can be evaluated come from the problem domain. The domain is the central source that provides the architect with the attributes that need to be realised in a system. This is especially so since an architecture's main contribution is in the area of the non-functional qualities of the system being built.

This is why in this paper we suggest the use of system-wide scenarios to desk-test and evaluate competing architectures. For any given domain, a number of alternative scenarios that describe aspects of the evolution of the domain itself should be defined. The scenarios should be defined in conjunction with the domain's stakeholders, and given degrees of likelihood of occurrence, which may be expressed qualitatively. Such scenarios should be run through the various proposed architectures to assess the likely behaviour if each scenario is realised. The exercise should lead to more grounded evaluation of software and system architectures, it should also involve the domains stakeholders in a non-trivial manner to benefit the architecting process. Note that our proposal differs from others that involve the use of scenarios to evaluate software architectures, in that we evaluate global strategies for combining categories of software and coarse-grained system elements rather than individual elements at the component and interconnection level.

3.1.5. Towards Systematically Designing Evolvable Software Architectures (Lodewijk Bergmans – University of Twente, The Netherlands). We have developed and applied an —as yet largely informal— method for designing software architectures in a systematic, top-down manner. Its basic principles are:

- (1a) The structure of software architectures should be derived from domain knowledge.
  This principle nicely matches past experience: in the reuse community, the necessity of performing domain analysis is a known and proven concept. Common software engineering wisdom (in particular articulated by Brooks [5]) suggests that 'conceptual integrity' is the most important property of a software system. And in practice, software engineers are usually assigned based on their experience in a certain domain.
- (1b) and this structure must be retained within the software artifacts throughout the product life-cycle.

Otherwise most benefits of architecture-driven development, such as conceptual integrity and maintainability, are lost. In other words, this is a vital property to support evolution of software architectures.

An important consequence of the first principle is that the requirements specification (e.g. documents, scenarios, use cases, UI prototypes) are not sufficient input to the design of any system. The second principle refines our notion of domain knowledge:

- (2) Domain knowledge = application domain knowledge + solution domain knowledge
  The intuitive notion behind this principle is that a software system is more than just a simulation of the application domain; it should motivate its existence by solving problems.

In addition, the practical implementation of requirements in software that runs on a particular platform imposes many problems that require -usually already invented- solutions as well. We can summarize domain knowledge as follows:

- the essential structure of an application can be found by investigating application (domain) knowledge.
- the chosen solutions come from a solution domain.

Solution-related knowledge is usually more stable and reusable because it is not application-specific. This supports evolvability of the resulting architectures and implementations.

Note that most architecture work focuses on (computer-science) solution domains, for instance the work by Shaw & Garlan [16], Buschmann et.al. [6], while most software development methods drive the analysis and design products directly from requirements. The input from solution domains others than the computer science and mathematical domains are generally ignored or implicit.

The previous two principles provide an indication of what to model, the last principle discussed here provides an indication how to model:

- (3) Model knowledge by focusing on concepts from domain knowledge. The motivation behind this is that these concepts are usually the stable parts of a software system: the various tasks that a software system implements may vary substantially over its life-cycle, but the domain concepts will remain, or are refined. We use is-a and aggregation as basic knowledge structuring relations (it is known from the AI community that this is a suitable approach). In the design phase, the notion of concepts may, or may not, map to ADTs or objects. Again it is essential, however, to keep different concepts separated during the remaining design process.

We can briefly summarize our architecture development method by the following four steps:

1. Application domain modeling (e.g. car dealer administration)
2. Add domain solutions (e.g. task modeling & workflow of car dealer administration)
3. Create a software architecture (e.g. generic control flow mechanism)
4. From architecture to design (e.g. transform into OO design)

3.2. Evolution of Specific Software Architectures

3.2.1. Dealing with Evolution in Family Architectures (Pierre America and William van der Sterren – Philips Research, The Netherlands). The use of family architectures is becoming more and more important in the world of high volume electronics and professional systems. By developing new products from a common product platform instead of developing them from scratch, both time-to-market and development costs can be reduced. While products are created from the common family architecture, the family architecture is to be maintained and extended as well. Component technology and component based development are important enabling technologies for family architectures for software intensive systems. In Philips Electronics, there is an increasing need for a development process supporting family architecture construction and evolution, as well as component based development.

Within Philips Research, we are studying methods for family architecture and for (the corresponding) component based development. The currently available methods and processes for system development do not provide sufficient support to design, develop, and maintain family architectures. To support current product family construction, we are defining and implementing our own process and methods, reusing as much as possible from existing (OO) processes and methods.

3.2.2. Evolution of Layered Object-Oriented Models (Michel Dao – France Telecom). Class hierarchies constitute an important aspect of object-oriented software architecture: choosing the right architecture of classes is most of the time a key point to efficiency and easy future evolution. This is particularly true for classes modelling a business domain. Regarding evolution, we argue that in a given hierarchy classes fall into different categories with respect to their frequency of evolution. Our proposition is to organize class hierarchies into different layers of classes, each layer having a homogeneous pace of evolution; the only relationship between the layers being inheritance links. In our experience of telecommunication networks, layers may be obtained on a semantic basis: each layer having a common semantics from the more general to the more specific. For instance, in our case the layers are: set theory (elements and ensembles), graph theory, generic networks, telecommunication networks.

We further argue that layering class hierarchies makes their evolution easier because each layer may be modified somewhat independently from the others. We have identified different levels of evolution: intralayer evolution and evolutions involving two layers. Intralayer evolutions may be realized with the help of reorganizing algorithms (see Leblanc et al.) which efficiency may be greatly enhanced by the limitation to one layer. Those evolutions may be considered as "technical" evolutions. Evolutions involving two layers must be made on a semantics basis and may be of two types. On the one hand, the borders of the layers may evolve: in our case, some classes from the telecommunication network layer may be shifted to the generic network layer. On the other hand, two applications using the class hierarchy may have developped identical classes that may be integrated into the more specific layer (telecommunication network layer in our case).

As a summary, we strongly believe that class hierarchies must be structured according to the semantics of the domain involved in order to ensure easier further evolution. In our case, structuring into inheritance dependent layers have proven to be a good structuration but other choices may be more relevant for different application domains.

3.2.3. Architectural Evolution: A Multi-level Perspective (Huw Evans – The University of Glasgow, UK). In "Software Architecture" by Shaw and Garlan [[16], pg. 160] the authors state that *"[Architectural descriptions] focus on the components, leaving the description of interactions among these components implicit, distributed and difficult to identify. ... This view of software architecture organises information around the components and ignores the significance of interactions and connections among the modules."*

The DRASTIC project has provided a run-time platform and supporting framework to allow a software engineer to build a distributed, persistent system that is amenable to change at run-time. DRASTIC focusses on the interaction of components in the presence of evolving types. This is addressed by the application of zones, contracts and change absorbers and by providing a change methodology so that the software engineer is guided when updating their system.

Components in DRASTIC are used in a different way to that usually described in the software architecture literature. They have more in common with the megamodules reported in Wiederhold et al's Communication of the ACM paper from 1992. DRASTIC components (zones) encapsulate changes to code, restricting them to an identifiable part of the system. Interactions between components are made explicit and are recorded in terms of the types and objects that may be exchanged (contracts). Within a component, processes can have their types and instances changed without affecting code in other components (by using change absorbers). Papers on the support system outlined here can be found at http://www.dcs.gla.ac.uk/huw.

Zones, Contracts and Change Absorbers. Zones in DRASTIC provide a means to encapsulate processes, objects and types at design-time and run-time. A zone is a logical collection of 100s of processes, it is the unit of evolution and is defined at design-time becoming a concrete, identifiable part of the overall run-time system. Objects in DRASTIC may hold references to any other object. Therefore, references between objects can lead between zones.

Contracts are pair-wise agreements between two zones. A contract contains a description of the types that may be exchanged between two zones and the transformations that should be applied to an object if it moves from one zone to another. Contracts are present at design-time and they become an identifiable part of the run-time system.

Change absorbers are described in the contracts. They are used to perform the transformations of objects at the zone boundary and they transform calls made on a pre-evolution type from outside the zone into a call onto the evolved type. The software engineer is key to any evolution of a system. Please see the papers for more information.

DRASTIC takes a lower-level approach to that of the software architectures literature by allowing types and instances to be replaced within a component, without affecting code outside it. In addition to this, higher-level concerns are addressed by the partioning mechanism of zones and the explicit description of zone inter-dependencies by contracts. By providing a solution that works at both the design level and the run-time level, DRASTIC provides an effective run-time platform and support framework for the evolution of large, distributed, persistent system.

3.3. Architectural Metrics and Assessment Environment

3.3.1. Evolution Characteristics of an Industrial Application Framework (Michael Mattsson – University of Karskrona/Ronneby, Sweden). Frameworks generally evolve through a number of iterations due to the incorporation of new requirements and better domain understanding. We present experiences from a proprietary black-box application framework in the telecommunication domain. During six years four major version of the application framework has been developed and over 30 installations at customer sites has been done. Effort data for the framework development as well as framework-specific data for a set of object-oriented architectural metrics has been collected. The effort data gives quantitative support for the claim that framework technology delivers reduced application development efforts and the architectural metrics are used for formulating four hypotheses about framework stability.

The Mediation Framework The Mediation framework is developed by Ericsson Software Technology. The framework provides functionality for mediation between network elements, i.e., telecommunication switches, and billing systems (or other administrative post-processing systems) for mobile telecommunication. Typically, the mediation framework collects call information from mobile switches, processes the call information and distributes it to a billing processing systems. The driving quality requirements in this domain are reliability, availability, portability, efficiency and maintainability.

The Stability Hypotheses We present six of the metrics studied and four hypotheses about framework stability. For a more detailed description see [13]. The metrics are DSC (Design Size in Classes), NOH (Number of Hierarchies), NSI (Number of Single Inheritance), ADI (Average Depth of Inheritance), AWI (Average Width of Inheritance), ADCC (Average number of distinct classes that a class may collaborate with) and the Normalized-Extent-of-Change metric (an aggregated metric described in [13]) The four hypotheses about framework stability are based on analysis of collected metrics data from the Billing Gateway, Microsoft Foundation Classes and Borlands Object Windows Library frameworks.

- Hypothesis 1: Stable frameworks tend to have narrow and deeply inherited class hierarchy structures, characterized by high values for the ADI metric (above 2.1) of classes and low values for the AWI metric (below 0,85).
- Hypothesis 2: A stable framework has an NSI/DSC ratio just above 0.8 if multiple inheritance is seldom used in the framework. (the number of subclasses in a stable framework is just above 80 percent.)
- Hypothesis 3: The normalized ADCC metrics is going towards 1.0 or just below for stable frameworks.
- Hypothesis 4: The Normalized-Extent-of-Change metric is below 0.4 for a stable framework.

The Effort Distribution We only present the framework customization/ development ratios for all 31 customizations in total. Data for individual framework versions can be found in [12]. The average framework customization/development ratio is 1:58, which meant that half of the customizations made required an effort less than 1,8 percent of the framework development effort for a framework version. The upper fourth customization/development ratio is 1:44, which means that 75 percent of the customization made required an effort less than 2,3 percent of the total development effort.

3.3.2. Environment for Software Assessment (Claudio Riva, Michael Przybilski, and Kai Koskimies – Nokia Research Center, Finland). Many development units at Nokia require software developers to evaluate the quality of their software products. The evaluation should determine if the software system meets organization's quality requirements or the reasons why they are not reached. The evaluation is valuable to the developers all along the development life cycle. The architects have to choose among different design alternatives and need to evaluate how a software architecture satisfies quality levels. Detecting architectural shortcomings or unreliable architectures early in the life cycle is of vital importance for the organization and for the long evolution of the system. To our knowledge, these decisions often are based only on expert judgement, without making use of precise data or special tools for the basis of the analysis. As architecture changes with time, developers need also to reverse engineer parts of the system. This task includes extracting information from existing code and recovering design models. We have outlined a software assessment environment to support these tasks. The environment contains components developed in different research projects: analyzers for different languages, a UML-based visualizer and a metric tool. The FAMOOS Information Exchange Model (FAMIX model) is used for exchanging data among the tools. The environment aims to provide automated support for UML-based visualization and metrics-based assessment of existing object oriented software. In the context of architectural evolution, the environment can be the basis for the following two tasks:

- Recovering the design models of an existing software system for different releases. Tracking the changes of system designs can reveal how the architecture is evolving.
- Calculating software measures on an existing system. Some architectural characteristics and problems become manifested in the examination of software measures. Examining their variation trends can provide insights on the evolution of the architecture.

3.4. Techniques to Deal with Architectural Evolution

3.4.1. Using Recovered Views to Track Architectural Evolution (Tamar Richner – Universität Bern, Switzerland). Tracking the evolution of a software system through time gives us valuable information. It suggests which parts are likely to remain stable and which 'problem' aspects are likely to change, and it gives us insight into some of the design choices made. We are interested in comparing the recovered architecture of successive versions of an application, for its descriptive (what changed?), explanatory (why did it change?), predictive (what will likely change?) and prescriptive (what should change?) value. But comparing software architectures is not a straighforward matter - a software system has no one single architecture. Just as in forward engineering there is a recognized need for a variety of modeling techniques, or architectural views [10, 3], so in architectural recovery we need to be able to generate a range of views, depending on the questions we pose and maintenance task we undertake.

We have developed a tool prototype for recovering architectural views of an application. The tool makes use of both static and dynamic information, represented as Prolog facts, and analyzes this information using Prolog rules in order to create views which show the invocation behavior of the application at different levels of granularity. The views desired are specified declaratively by the user, and so can be tailored to the maintenance task at hand. A detailed description of our approach can be found in [15].

We used our tool to extract a range of views for two versions of the HotDraw framework [2], then compared these views to track changes between the two versions. This experiment raised a number of issues in the tracking of architectural evolution. In particular, it illustrated that different aspects of a software application evolve at different rates. For a well-understood domain, such as the HotDraw framework, the domain concepts and their roles remained the most stable, while the design patterns used changed faster; algorithmic aspects were even more volatile. This suggests a layered view of the software, with a more stable base level at the bottom and faster evolving layers on top. In tracking architectural evolution we must then decide which kinds of changes we are interested in (which views are appropriate) and we require a notation which can express both variant and invariant aspects of the software at these different levels. We are currently working on expressing collaborations of components as architectural invariants, and on extracting such collaborations using our tool.

3.4.2 Managing Unanticipated Evolution of Software Architectures (Kim Mens, Tom Mens, Bart Wouters, and Roel Wuyts – Vrije Universiteit Brussel). It is essential to evolve the architecture of a successful software system continually, because when the quality of the architecture degrades, software modifications become more difficult. Design decisions at the architectural level have far reaching consequences on the resultant code. These problems are often referred to as software aging, architectural erosion and architectural drift.

Architects may try to anticipate possible future modifications to the architecture, and design the architecture in such a way that it can be adapted to take these modifications into account. However, more often than not, architects are not able to predict adequately where and which changes to the architecture may possibly occur. So the problem remains what to do when "unanticipated" changes to the software architecture are required. Approaches to evolution of software architectures can be subdivided in "design-time" evolution, where changes are made to the architecture at design time, and "run-time" or "dynamic" evolution, where the architecture is dynamically modified while the software is running, without compromising application integrity.

Approaches for run-time evolution usually allow only a very restricted form of unanticipated evolution. Some approaches do not restrict or prohibit unanticipated evolution, but provide no support for it. The software architect is allowed to make unanticipated changes, but has to face the possible consequences of these modifications. We did not find an example of a run-time approach where unanticipated evolution is alloby, and fully supported.

For design-time evolution, the ability to manage unanticipated evolution of software architectures is even more important, because changes are almost always unpredictable. Even when architects have provided hooks for future evolution, these hooks are seldom what is needed when the system needs to change. Very few architects have sufficient foresight to anticipate where these changes are going to come from. Unfortunately, very little research has been done on the topic of unanticipated design-time evolution of software architectures.

We propose to deal with this problem by making use of the "reuse contract" model [17, 11, 14], which has been conceived specifically to reason about unanticipated evolution of software artifacts. Reuse contracts have already proven useful to deal with evolution conflicts at the implementation and design level, and the underlying ideas are sufficiently general to be applied to other levels, such as software architectures, as well [14].

Reuse contracts allob to assess the impact of changes, and detect potential evolution conflicts when merging independent evolutions of the same software architecture. Because design-time evolution is inherently unanticipated, it is not always as easy to know whether a conflict occurs or not. Therefore, reuse contracts take a "worst case" scenario by generating conflict warnings for every potentially undesired situation. The more information about the particular evolution, the better the approximation of the evolution conflicts will be.

3.4.3. Architectural Evolution Support Using Architectural Contracts (Bart Wydaeghe and Bart Michiels – Vrije Universiteit Brussel, Belgium). Current component description techniques are limited to a clear interface (API) and often a free text describing the intended use. There is no support to allob the automatic verification of the composition between two or more components against their intended collaboration. Quite often, components can be plugged together but they do not play at all. We state that architectural patterns are good candidates to solve this problem. We envision a component configuration tool where components are connected using suitable (and reusable) connection patterns.

Architectural patterns and components are documented in an extended UML-like collaboration diagram. As patterns and components differ in generality, we use another set of terms in these diagrams. Patterns are specified using general primitives, as they act on several component interactions. Components on the other hand, are expressed in implementation specific terms. In order to link the component documentation terms with the generic pattern primitives, every component term should be mapped to the generic primitives of the pattern documentation. Furthermore, we augment this documentation with contractual obligations. These contracts allob us to specify design invariants and interaction constraints.

We use this documentation to specify the overall architecture of an application. As this documentation allows automatic verification, we can prevent or at least warn for unanticipated architectural mismatch or drift. This is done be rechecking the documentation in every evolution step.

3.4.4. Pattern-Based Software Evolution (Takashi Kobayashi and Saeki Motoshi – Tokyo Institute of Technology, Japan). Software development can be considered as the evolution of the artifacts and the essential point of this evolution is the structural change of the artifacts that are being produced. Although the way of evolving the artifacts greatly depends on the application domain and on the steps of software development processes, we can have the styles of artifact evolution that frequently appear and that are reusable for the other development processes. Software patterns such as Analysis Patterns for requirements analysis step (modeling systems) and GOF's Design Patterns for design step are general structures that frequently appear in the artifacts.

Suppose that a developer used an Analysis Pattern to model the system and then designed it by applying Design Patterns. We can consider that this process as an evolution of the Analysis Pattern into the Design Patterns and that the patterns are also being evolved as the artifacts are being done in the process. This example suggests to us that there are some guidelines or ways how to evolve the usage of Analysis Patterns into that of Design Patterns.

We formalize and specify software patterns and this kind of evolution guidelines as manipulation operations to change the structure of the patterns. By specifying how to evolve software patterns as software processes progress, we can get a support for developing an artifact from the artifacts that were produced in the previous steps.

In our approach, we consider that a software pattern consists of a pattern structure (a class diagram and/or an object diagram) and manipulation operations on the pattern structure. These operations are divided into two categories; one is pattern instantiation (applying a pattern to an actual problem) and the other one is pattern evolution (evolving the artifacts of the previous steps into a new one). We model them with object-oriented technique encapsulating these operations into patterns. Patterns are defined as classes and the operations are methods. The operations are defined as the compositions of basic operations on class and object diagrams such as "adding a subclass" and "add a method to a class". To model large and complicated patterns, we can have a hierarchical decomposition technique by generalization and aggregation relationships of OO technique. In this technique, a pattern comprises the combination of smaller patterns. We have specified a couple of case studies of patterns and their evolutions.

3.4.5 An Environment for Building and Maintaining Class Hierarchies (Nathalie Chevaliera and Michel Dao – France Telecom, France; Christophe Dony, Marianne Huchard, Hervé Leblanc, and Thérèse Libourel – LIRMM, France). A crucial problem of object-oriented software development is the production and maintenance of "good" class hierarchies, which we consider as important parts in object-oriented software architectures. The goal of this project is to design and implement a high level environment for building and maintaining (reorganizing, merging, etc.) class hierarchies having formal properties ensured by the Galois sub-hierarchy that underlies the structure used to constrain them. Our goals are both to build well structured hierarchies from any kind of existing ones and to allow programmers or designers to perform basic as well as complex manipulations on their hierarchies in a safe way, with the insurance that they will not damage them. This project is held in conjunction with an industrial partner in the telecommunication domain.

One of the criteria used to evaluate class hierarchies is property factorization. The Galois lattice is a mathematical structure allobing to constrain class hierarchies having the maximal factorization property. The interactive environment we want to build is devoted to the controlled manipulation of these hierarchies.

4. Conclusions

The main remarks on object-oriented architectural evolution resulting from the workshop are the following:

- The process of architecture creation has an impact on its future evolution. The separation of problem domain objects and solution domain objects is useful and has an impact on software architecture evolution.
- Modelling the problem domain objects into layers is useful with respect to architectural evolution: layers have proven to be a good abstraction that separate more permanent from more adaptable functionality.
- Research is needed on architectural notation that can express evolution, as well as on tool support to aid in detecting and dealing with evolution.
- Sources that give rise to architectural change must be investigated and analysed (solution domain, business context, technological context).

The software architecture community is rather large, we believe that future meetings on object-oriented architectural evolution should take place in object-oriented conferences. This worskhop was organized around three main aspects to support evolution: concepts, methods and techniques, and evaluation. Now, we need to concentrate on more specific topics that emerged from the discussions: descriptions (models, languages and notations), process (architecture development and evolution), and sources as mentioned before.

References

[1] Robert Arnold and Shawn Bohner, editors. *Software Change Impact Analysis.* IEEE, 1998.

[2] Kent Beck and Ralph Johnson. Patterns generate architectures. In *Proceedings ECOOP'94*, LNCS 821, pages 139–149. Springer-Verlag, July 1994.

[3] Grady Booch, James Rumbaugh, and Ivar Jacobson. *The Unified Modeling Language User Guide*. Addison-Wesley, 1999.
[4] Isabelle Borne, Fernando Brito a Abreu, Wolfgang De Meuter, and Galal Hassan Galal. Techniques, tools and formalisms for capturing and assessing the architectural quality in object-oriented software. In Serge Demeyer and Jan Bosch, editors, *Object-Oriented Technology (ECOOP'98 Workshop Reader)*, LNCS 1543. Springer-Verlag, 1998.
[5] Frederick P. Brooks. No silver bullet. *IEEE Computer*, 20(4):10–19, April 1987.
[6] Frank Buschmann, Regine Meunier, Hans Rohnert, Peter Sommerlad, and Michael Stad. *Pattern-Oriented Software Architecture – A System of Patterns*. John Wiley, 1996.
[7] Martin Fowler, Kent Beck, John Brant, William Opdyke, and Don Roberts. *Refactoring : Improving the Design of Existing Code*. Addison-Wesley, 1999.
[8] Erich Gamma, Richard Helm, Ralph Johnson, and John Vlissides. *Design Patterns*. Addison-Wesley, Reading, MA, 1995.
[9] Koen De Hondt. *A Novel Approach to Architectural Recovery in Evolving Object-Oriented Systems*. PhD thesis, Department of Computer Science, Vrije Universiteit Brussel, 1998.
[10] Philippe Kruchten. The 4+1 view model of architecture. *IEEE Software*, 12(6):42–50, November 1995.
[11] Carine Lucas. *Documenting Reuse and Evolution with Reuse Contracts*. PhD thesis, Departement of Computer Science, Vrije Universiteit Brussel, September 1997.
[12] Michael Mattsson. Effort distribution in a six year industrial application framework project. In *Proceedings Internation Conference on Software Maintenance*, Oxford, UK, August 1999.
[13] Michael Mattsson and Jan Bosch. Characterizing stability in evolving frameworks. In *Proceedings TOOLS'99*, Nancy, France, 1999.
[14] Tom Mens. *A Formal Foundation for Object-Oriented Software Evolution*. PhD thesis, Departement of Computer Science, Vrije Universiteit Brussel, (in prepartation), 1999.
[15] Tamar Richner and Stéphane Ducasse. Recovering high-level views of object-oriented applications from static and dynamic information. In Hongji Yang and Lee White, editors, *Proceedings ICSM'99 (International Conference on Software Maintenance)*. IEEE, September 1999.
[16] Mary Shaw and David Garlan. *Software Architecture: Perspectives on an Emerging Discipline*. Prentice-Hall, 1996.
[17] Patrick Steyaert, Carine Lucas, Kim Mens, and Theo D'Hondt. Reuse contracts: Managing the evolution of reusable assets. In *Proceedings of OOPSLA '96 Conference*, pages 268–285. ACM Press, 1996.

Multi-user Object-Oriented Environments

Ivan Tomek[1], Alicia Diaz[2], Ronald Melster[3], António Rito Silva[4], Miguel Antunes[4], Vinny Cahill[5], Zièd Choukair[6], Alexandro Fernandez[2], Mads Haahr[5], Eric Jul[7], Atsushi Ohnishi[8], Luís Rodrigues[9], Erich R. Schmidt[10], Cristian Ţăpuş[10], Waldemar Wieczerzycki[11], and Daniel M. Zimmerman[10]

[1] Acadia University, Canada
[2] Lifia - UNLP, La Plata - Argentina
[3] GMD FIRST, Berlin, Germany
[4] INESC - Technical University of Lisbon, Portugal
[5] Trinity College Dublin, Ireland
[6] ENST Bretagne, France
[7] University of Copenhagen, Denmark
[8] Ritsumeikan University, Japan
[9] University of Lisbon, Portugal
[10] California Institute of Technology, USA
[11] Posnan University of Economics, Poland

1. Introduction

Network-based computer environments emulating selected aspects of the physical world and allowing interaction among their human users first appeared in the late 1970s. These environments implemented a networked version of a role-playing fantasy game known as Dungeons and Dragons, hence their acronym MUD (Multi-user Dungeons). When it became obvious that many MUD users use the environment mainly to meet virtually with other users rather than to play games, new forms of MUDs and other types of emulated universes were developed and the term Virtual Environment (VE) was introduced to refer to all of them.

Since their inception, VEs evolved in several interesting directions, including environments with new types of user interfaces, for example emulating visual aspects of physical reality via VRML and other means [8], and object-oriented environments known as MOOs (MUD Object-Oriented) allowing their users to extend the environment and communicate with it via a programming language [22]. As virtual environments became better known and more sophisticated, their user populations reached hundreds of thousands. At present, VEs are used for recreation, education [16], particularly distance education, and in work, particularly for collaboration among physically separated team members [6, 26, 36, 15, 45]. There is also a large and growing body of research on existing and potential VE uses, and several meetings similar to this workshop are held every year to address both the usage and the technical aspects of VEs. Collaborative work is, of course, an area of major interest to software developers and we will thus address this issue further.

A. Moreira and S. Demeyer (Eds.): ECOOP'99 Workshops, LNCS 1743, pp. 80–96, 1999.

Collaboration is emerging as a major application of computer networks and the use of MOO-based virtual environments based for this purpose is gaining interest. This is because of the growing pervasiveness of computer networks, and because MOOs perfectly satisfy collaboration needs. They are persistent (thus capable of maintaining history), allow user proxies and software agents to inhabit and create separate scopes for private and group communication in both synchronous and asynchronous forms, let them posses and hold on to objects and tools, and enable navigation and porting of tools and objects from one internal scope to another. Most importantly, MOOs are extendible without limits both in terms of instantiation of existing types of entities and creation of new ones.

Because of their extendibility and persistence, MOOs can support such CSCW features as knowledge management, role-based control of access to tools and control of their usage policy, objects, or places, workflow definition, separation of projects and teams from one another, history, and others. The fact that MOOs are based on a very natural metaphor and are easy and fun to use is critical for their usability.

Besides the fact that virtual environments offer a powerful paradigm for collaboration, VEs also have a great technical interest as well. Traditional MOOs are client-server Internet-based applications. The typical server holds the universe and implements an interpreter of MOO commands coming from the client. Commands often use a special-purpose language developed just for this purpose. Until very recently, the client was typically a Telnet-based textual interface used to enter commands interpreted on the server, and to display messages from the server. Recently, new approaches addressed the implementation of more user-friendly clients, mainly aimed at replacing the primitive text-based user interface with HTML or Java applets. Some implementations use VRML-based virtual reality as an alternative to textual input. In spite of the increased interest in usability and implementation, the server remains essentially unchanged and its further development opens many possibilities.

In view of their nature and their potential as a communication environment serving many users, MOOs present many technical challenges and provide a very interesting environment for addressing various OO issues. Evans identifies the building blocks of text-based virtual environments [17]. Associated with each of these building blocks we can identify some of the open object-orientation technical problems.

- *Locations with defined scopes*: "A user can sense events and objects within this scope, such as seeing and using objects within the room or hearing a conversation". Scope definition is an object composition problem, since each composition layer defines a scope and visibility constraints between scopes. It is also an object naming problem, because naming policies may be needed according to scope semantics.
- *Persistent objects*: Players holding objects upon leaving will still hold them when they return after having exited the environment. Moreover, the environment itself is persistent, and should survive system crashes. Persistence

should be supported in the wider context of object life cycle, as defined for instance by the OMG CORBA standard.

- *Transportation and Navigation*: Constructs must be provided to allow users to move between scopes. These constructs must allow moving between rooms via exits, allow teleporting directly to another room, or joining someone in a room. Transportation and navigation are related to object migration when the scopes are located at different sites, and to functionality reconfiguration, because object change scope on the fly.
- *Communication*: Users must be able to communicate. Communication can be synchronous or asynchronous. Synchronous communication can use scopes as in talking to other users in the same room or defining a "radio" with different frequencies. Asynchronous communication can use electronic mail or newsgroups. Distributed communication can be supported by infrastructure technology, such as CORBA and JAVA RMI. Which technology is best suited for the open requirements of MOOs?
- *Ownership and levels of control*: Users can own objects, pick them and move them between rooms. These and other features require the definition of levels of control. For instance, an object's owner can pick and move it but other users only can read its properties. Levels of control are supported by synchronization policies. Which synchronization policies are required by the MOO domain? How can MOOers specify their own synchronization policies?
- *Flexibility*: The environment should provide online creation of objects and online definition of their behavior. The definition of new objects should not require restarting the server. Behavior can be defined in terms of verbs and an object is defined by its properties and a set of verbs. Verb code is written in the MOO programming language and executed using some form of interpretation. How does the object model support online definition of object behavior? Which reflection properties should the object model and the MOO programming language possess?

Besides these functional building blocks Evans also identifies non-functional aspects of text-based virtual environments. These aspects raise additional interesting questions:

- *Server Requirements*: Object verbs execute in a server. This server should have database support, persistency, and robustness. How can we define a scalable server, particularly one that dynamically adjusts to its load?
- *Efficiency*: The MOO designer needs to decide whether functionality should be hard-coded into built-in functions for efficiency, or written in an online programming language for flexibility. Which MOO-specific languages should be defined? What should be the expressive power of such MOOspecific languages?

After outlining the general principles and listing some of the questions, the rest of this report contains brief summaries of workshop presentations, stressing the aspects and problems just mentioned. This is followed by concluding remarks and a list of selected references.

2. MUM - A Multi-universe MOO (Ivan Tomek)

It was already noted above that although MOOs have recently undergone some evolution, innovation has largely been restricted to improved user interfaces on the client side. In our experimental project called MUM (Multi-universe MOO), we have gone beyond these extensions in several ways and the following paragraphs briefly summarize some of them.

On the client side, MUM provides the user with a GUI-based interface that does not require typing (and remembering) commands. As much processing as possible is moved to the client to minimize the load on the server and the network, and to make the client freely user-extendible via downloading of 'tools' from the server.

On the server side, the universe is fully aware of all events, allowing users to subscribe to them. This is required by one of the basic requirements of collaboration - the need for awareness of relevant activities anywhere in the universe. MUM also allows any number of interconnected universes residing on arbitrary host machines to co-exist. When a host machine with a running universe is connected to Internet, other users can be transported to it, with their possessions. This is implemented via metaservers that keep track of running universes and provide access to them. The fact that users can run universes on their own machines means that they can work either on- or off-line and transport objects between off-line and on-line universes.

The workshop presentation of MUM focused on the implementation of event-based operation, which presents some interesting issues. Since everything in MUM occurs in terms of subscribable events passed among universe entities, event execution generally consists of a sequence of operations accompanied by event sends. While many events are broadcast without requiring feedback, some events sent to other objects may require response, and their further execution must be blocked until a 'confirmation event' is received. Further execution of the suspended event may depend on the nature of the received confirmation, and a description of event execution requires a branching path represented by a state diagram. Our implementation of events thus uses a finite state automaton interpreting an inter-linked structure called an event descriptor. Suspension of event execution that occurs during a wait for a confirmation event is accompanied by the creation of an event marker, which is stored in a collection of incomplete events. When sufficient confirmations have been received, the marker is retrieved and the confirmation event used to determine further course of execution.

MUM currently implements the features described above and provides a few basic tools and objects. Our immediate goals are to clean up the implementation and its documentation, add tools and objects, and make MUM available to the general public. We are hoping that this will generate interest and feedback, and that users will start adding new features such as new objects and tools. We also hope to obtain feedback on MUM's usability, performance, general philosophy, and design. A number of details that have not been addressed will have to be resolved. These include questions related to agents and objects traveling from one universe to another, modes of confirmation events and policies for dealing with them, forms of access control, and others.

3. Collaborative Requirements Definition with VRDL (Atsushi Ohnishi)

This section describes a collaborative tool for visual software requirements specification (SRS) and data flow and object-oriented modeling. The method provides describers for defining both the shape and semantics of icons for use in object model diagrams.

The method also allows description of a sequence of events corresponding to a data flow via a scenario description, enabling animation of the SRS. A describer can confirm his requirements by checking the animation. Scenarios can be transformed into sequence diagrams and vice versa. We also describe a supporting method of collaborative visual software requirements definition.

Our visual software requirements definition environment includes (1) a visual requirements language, VRDL (2) an icon manager, (3) a visual software requirements editor, (4) a visual scenario writer, (5) a visual software requirements executor and, (6) a collaborative requirements definition supporter [29].

The features of VRDL are

1. A requirements describer can define icons
2. A describer can specify data/control flow requirements with icons and arrows
3. A visual SRS can be specified structurally
4. A visual SRS can be executed by giving icons' movement descriptions (scenario)
5. Multiple describers can define a visual SRS via a network

Our plans are to improve our visual SRS environment [28] to support MOOR (Multi-user Object Oriented Requirements definition). Users will be able to define a visual SRS collaboratively and confirm the SRS with animation. By regarding icons in visual SRS as objects and flows among icons as associations among objects, a visual SRS can be transformed into an object diagram. Since a sequence of events is represented in a scenario, such a scenario can be transformed into a sequence diagram.

We are now developing the transformers from visual diagrams into Object-Oriented diagrams. These transformers will contribute to the MOOR.

4. Interfacing Real and Virtual Environments (Mads Haahr, Vinny Cahill, and Eric Jul)

Event-based communications has been used successfully in several graphically-oriented virtual world support systems [27]. Events are a useful concept in this context because they embody the notion of something happening in a world, be it real or virtual. We claim that the notion of events is not only a suitable communications paradigm to model purely virtual worlds but that it can also be used to *interface* one or more areas in the real world with a corresponding area in a virtual world by relaying events in both directions.

Essentially, the text-based interface adopted in MOOs is the simplest possible mapping between the virtual and the real world. (We use the term 'mapping' to denote translation of events from the virtual to the real environment or vice versa.) Events happening in the virtual environment are transformed into a kind of real world event (visible to the user) by means of text. Similarly, real world events (actions performed by the user) are mapped to virtual events by the means of a command line parser.

We have designed and are implementing a virtual representation of a real environment with support for mapping one type of event, called a *sighting event*, in both directions. The real environment is a series of research laboratories at the University of Cambridge equipped with an *active badge system*. In each room is an infrared sensor which picks up signals emitted by battery-driven badges worn by research personnel. The badge system is described in detail in [23].

The virtual environment is implemented using a generic event model called ECO (described in [44, 21]) and consists of a collection of objects interacting via events. For each badge in the real environment, there is a user object in the virtual environment. For each sensor in the real environment, there is an object in the virtual environment which raises a *sighting event* every time its real world counterpart detects a badge. Other objects represent rooms in the virtual world and monitor these events to keep track of users. All this effectively constitutes a mapping from the real to the virtual environment.

In addition to user objects representing badges, the virtual environment can also contain users without badges, i.e., purely virtual users. These users can move around in the virtual environment as a result of MOO-style text commands. The presence of a purely virtual user in a virtual location is mapped to the real environment by printing a text message in a window on a terminal in the corresponding real location. This lets real users register the presence of virtual users and therefore constitutes a (very simple) mapping of sighting events from the virtual to the real environment.

The following is an example of a purely virtual user interacting with the environment. At the user's location is another virtual user, John, and a real person, Jane. Jane herself is physically present at the corresponding location in the real environment whereas the two virtual users are only present at the virtual location. User commands issued by the virtual user from whom the transcript is taken are preceded by a prompt (>) character.

```
You are on the 3rd floor of the Research Laboratory.  A sign on
the wall reads, 'Area 8.'  A sensor in the ceiling is marked, '11.'
John (virtual) is here.
>look at john
John is transparent and has no badge identifier.
>
Jane (real) arrives.
>look at jane
```

```
Jane's badge identifier is 0-0-0-0-10-14.
>
```

This example is very simple primarily for two reasons. First, the text-based interface is not a very realistic presentation of the virtual environment but relies heavily on human imagination. Second, it only uses one type of event: the sighting event. Though this event enables (real and virtual) users to move in the virtual world, it offers no means of social interaction.

One possible application domain for closely interfaced real and virtual environments could be monitoring and control of active/intelligent buildings. It is much easier (especially for software) to *monitor* and *change* the state of a virtual than a real building. Given that the coupling between the two worlds is close enough, the real→virtual mapping of events facilitates *monitoring* and the virtual→real mapping *change.* Another possible application domain could be advanced teleconferencing. It would be relatively straightforward to map *several* (rather than just one) real environments into one virtual environment. A company with branches in different geographical locations could, given suitable layouts of rooms, provide a virtual meeting space by overlaying events in all the physical locations. If the mapping of events back into the physical environments is good, such an environment could let participants in different branches interact in a much more seamless manner than current teleconferencing applications.

One important factor for such environments is the choice of events mapped between environments. We have described only one type of event but other types of events would be required for any rich virtual environment and may require special hardware in the real environment.

Our work has shown how a generic event model, the ECO model, can be used to interface real and virtual environments by relaying events occurring in either world to the other. Even though our virtual world is minimal in almost every respect (especially with respect to presentation) we claim that the idea of mapping events between worlds is general and will be useful with more advanced technology.

5. DVECOM: An Auto-adaptive Model for Collaboration within Distributed Virtual Reality Applications (Zièd Choukair)

Today's computing environments must be distributed to allob collaboration for common purposes [43]. Especially, virtual environments must meet this requirement while ensuring a high level of Quality of Service (QoS) to the user. In Distributed Virtual Environments (DVE), there are still many challenging open problems needing to be addressed [42]. One of the more interesting and difficult problems to be addressed is how to guarantee a sufficient QoS as application-level expectation, as opposed to low-level resource reservation and scheduling. We have developed an application-driven collaboration model to address this issue.

The *Distributed Virtual Environment Collaboration Model* (DVECOM) under development aims to provide an end-user QoS support for distributed virtual reality applications. It aims to reconcile openness and real-time requirements for collaborative relationships using virtual environments. Openness, in opposition to closure, is used here to translate the unknown a priori occurrence of events on behalf of the participants [4, 32]. Real-time requirements mean guaranteeing a periodical synchronization [25, 33], between the displayed scenes, on a set of distributed machines of the same virtual world. The DVECOM model is based partially upon COREMO (Corba Real-Time Extension Model) [3] concepts and further work done in the context of the "Amusement" project [5], an Intelligent Information Interface Esprit Project.

DVECOM integrates QoS provision and management ensuring mandatory display synchronization and then improving the rendering via *best effort* and *least suffering* for virtual world. To improve rendering, the idea is to provide the client-side (receiver updates) the choice between various strategies that will manage resource allocation and display adaptation of the presentation in accordance with the retained rendering strategy. This *presentation polymorphism* on the receiver side will be supported on the sender side by meta-data associated with the update to help the receiver take the appropriate decisions. The receiver-side protocol is based upon the end-user preferences, physical level capability information, as well as the criticality and pertinence of notification to each client (contextual end-user information). The model must be able to guarantee periodical synchronization between the scenes displayed to remote users with as little rendering degradation as possible. To provide mandatory synchronization, we extended our *VirtualArch* [12] platform with a transfer protocol based upon mobile agents moving through a dynamically set ring of local sub-servers coupled with an update algorithm using logical time and stamps.

When available, such guarantees would make it possible to use DVE outside a closed restricted context of industrial collaborative applications with an expected QoS not only from the rendering but especially from the synchronization point of view. Applications could range from distributed collaborative CAM/CAD with virtual prototypes to distributed collaborative simulations where the multiple users can collaborate in a shared virtual environment.

DVECOM objectives through the combination of client-side and server-side protocols are to provide a logical synchronization and, less critically, to optimize the management and the pertinence of the display of the applications and to improve the *rendering* of the virtual environment according to user preferences given by his/her hardware and software capabilities and compliance with real-time constraints.

6. From DASCo to MOOSCo: MOO with Separation of Concerns (António Rito Silva and Miguel Antunes)

MOOs are distributed and concurrent applications. Distributed and concurrent applications development is complex. Besides the current difficulties associated with software development, distributed and concurrent application development is harder due to the diverse domains involved and to the implementation environment. To cope with these problems we developed the DASCo (Development of Distributed Applications with Separation of Concerns) [9] approach based on a "divide and conquer" strategy. This strategy helps to identify minimal domain-specific solutions and how to combine them in different contexts. Moreover, DASCo enforces an incremental development process which incorporates the domain-specific solutions in a stepwise manner and delays implementation in the final target environment.

A minimal domain-specific problem is addressed in isolation as a concern. Each concern identifies a concurrent and distributed aspect for which it is possible to define a construct. Constructs for each concern must be orthogonal to each other. Each concern's constructs are defined as design patterns [18] describing the solution's collaborations and structure.

When applying DASCo approach to MOOs we identify three aspects of the problem: *Domain abstractions*, *Flexibility*, and *Distributed architecture*.

Concepts as scope, object, user, transportation and navigation are examples of *MOO domain abstractions*. These domain abstractions have a set of properties that are perceived by MOO-users. For instance, users perceive objects as persistent since they still there when users return to the MOO. Object ownership is also perceived by MOO-users since since they get some of their operations rejected when accessing another user object.

Flexibility is a key functionality of MOOs. Flexibility allows online object definition and creation. Online actions is supported by a virtual machine that execute a set of built-in functions. Moreover, flexibility allows the dynamic change of players features.

MOO are concurrent and distributed applications. Most of current *MOO distributed architectures* are based on a centralized server with several remote clients that are connected using a protocol as telnet or http.

Separation of concerns techniques can be applied to each one of mentioned aspects. Each MOO *domain abstraction* can be represented as a design pattern and provided as a reusable design artifact integrated in an object-oriented framework. In order to support *flexibility*, the design patterns described in the GoF book [18] may be useful since they describe object-oriented techniques. Note that these patterns are MOO-independent and their intent is to provide a flexible class structure. For instance, the *Chain of Responsibility* [18] design pattern can be applied to decide which verb executes in consequence of a request and, a player can enrich the set of his features in run-time by applying the *Decorator* [18] design pattern. MOO *distributed architecture* benefits from separation of concerns if distribution can be separately introduced and according to the number and location of users. For instance, if a virtual class is going to occur and most of the participants are located in the same place, performance would be improved if the class room is located in a nearby server.

We envision applying DASCo approach to the first and third aspects. In a first step we intend to apply and adapt DASCo design patterns [19, 37, 39, 35, 40, 38] to deal with the MOO domain concerns of replication, recovery, distributed communication, configuration, naming, and synchronization. Moreover, we intend to apply the three-layered architecture [41] to study and experiment the problems associated with composition of MOO concerns.

7. Mining a Pattern Language for MOO Design (Alexandro Fernandez, Alicia Diaz, and Ronald Melster)

Designing virtual environments is not trivial. Functionality and spatial distributions has to be well thought in order to make the virtual environment usable. As they become larger and more complex the need for formalized design techniques arise. Modeling and design techniques must deal with architecture, spatial navigation, the objects inhabiting the VE and the users and groups working or cooperating in the VE [22, 8, 10, 11, 13].

Our approach, to shed light on the design process of object oriented virtual environments, and in particular in MOO environments, consists of recording in a pattern language the expertise of VE designer, in order to help novice ones. Design patterns are abstract design for an application domain, an they are good proven solution [18]. A design pattern has to be instanced according to the current application.

In particular, there are two situations where design becomes difficult: building complex objects and complex behavior. To overcome complexity we can design objects by using two well-known mechanisms: *decomposition* and *abstraction* and combining them we find a powerful mechanism that allows us to derive the object essence from its parts.

In this workshop, we introduce three design patterns that deal with building complex objects: *Cooperation Network.*, *Composite Object*, and *Decentralized System*; and two design patterns that deal with complex behavior: *Collector Object*, and *Subjective Behavior.*

Complex tasks are achieved by a group of cooperating objects instead of a single one. *Cooperation Network* design pattern is useful to model complex objects when they can be obtained by combining simpler ones. In particular, there will be no clues suggesting that the object parts form a whole, it is abstract. For instance, many connected rooms describe the architecture of the building.

The *Composite Object* encapsulates and hides parts within the composite. This can be achieved by making the composite contain its parts. The *Composite Object* defines initialization constructors) verbs to ensure that each composite is created with its own set of parts. MOO editors, characters and robots are examples of this design pattern.

Decentralized behavior is suitable to model natural phenomena. For instance, no one coordinates a herd of elephants. Its behavior results from the autonomous behavior of members. *Decentralized System* design pattern is difficult to design and implement, no one coordinates the herd and context plays a fundamental role. More details and examples of Decentralized Behavior appear in [34], which ones can easily be ported to MOO environments, such as LambaMoo.

There are cases where changes in aspects of an object must be propagated to a group of surrogate objects. The *Collector Object* design pattern is used to tie an aspect of objects in a group to a collector object. The collector is built based on one or more aspects. Collector and collectables can have other aspects independent of the collector object. When an object belongs to a collector, it can not belong to another collector object in the same aspect. Collector activation, state change or movement affecting any of the collector's aspect has to be broadcasted to all collectables.

Objects behave depending on the current context. Context is an abstract concept that describes a particular situation in the virtual environment. The *Subjective Behavior* design pattern is used when it is needed to express the object behavior in relation to its class, its internal state, the class/type or identity of the requestor and the context where the request or action takes place. There are several approximations to implement *Subjective behavior* as is shown in [31].

The above design patterns are part of a catalog that comprises most of the problems/design aspects about complex objects and complex behavior, but there are more patterns for dealing with structural design of virtual worlds, for considering navigational aspects and for managing complex and autonomous behavior.

8. Scalability Issues in MOOs: The Role of Object Migration and Replication (Luís Rodrigues)

A MOO architecture that is based on a single central server to manage all the MOO state is inherently non-scalable. When many simultaneous sessions are maintained, the processing power and the limited network bandwidth of the central server may become a bottleneck. Additionally, MOO users may be geographically dispersed and may experience quite different connectivity when connecting to a single server. A more scalable approach would be to implement the MOO as a set of cooperating servers, and to use migration and replication techniques to place the relevant data near to its users. Having several servers can also be the basis to increase the availability of the environment.

There are several approaches to distribute the load among cooperating servers. The easiest way is to perform a form of static partitioning, by distributing, at configuration time, the objects among the servers. However, in run-time, the distribution of users among servers is not even. It is thus interesting to perform a dynamic partitioning of the MOO state. This requires the ability to migrate clusters of objects (cluster can be defined using application level concepts such as "rooms"). When defining a room location policy, it is also desirable to take into consideration the issue of network latency. This requires the system to collect the delays experienced by its users and to estimate the delays that would result from system reconfiguration.

If fault-tolerance is not considered, the crash of a server may leave the MOO unavailable for a long period. This may discourage users or even defeat the purpose of the MOO. Data replication techniques can be used to provide fault-tolerance, but also to increase the MOO performance by locating data near to its users. Since immutable objects represent no challenge in term of replica consistency with discuss the issue of managing mutable objects. If network-partitions are not considered, a primary-secondary scheme [1] can be used: the servers keep the primary copy of the objects and secondary copies are placed in the clients. If network partitions need to be tolerated, one needs to deal with the conflicting goals of preserving availability and consistency. A typical approach to prevent divergence in partitionable environments is to allow updates on a single partition (usually called the primary partition). In this case, users in the non-primary partitions would be aware of network conditions [7]. Much higher availability can be achieved if the semantics of the object are taken into consideration [14]. For instance, a bag of items could be filled concurrently in different partitions. When the partition disappears, consistency is re-established by merging both bags. MOOs are an excellent environment to apply object-specific replication policies and much of the work in the area of disconnected operation [24] can certainly by applied in this context.

A step further in design of distributed MOOs would be delegate the management of objects in the client themselves, that would synchronize with each other directly, without overloading the server. In such architecture, server would act merely as repository of the MOO state. Unfortunately, this architecture would allows an unreliable or malicious client machine to jeopardize the system operation, simply by disconnecting the client, taking with it important system state. A good compromise between performance and consistency in future large-scale MOOs might be letting servers to "lease" [20] parts of the system state to clients. The server would ensure that either a consistent state is "returned" by the client in due time, or that a backward recovery procedure is triggered to reestablish the availability of the leased state.

In summary, the design of large-scale MOOs raises interesting challenges in term of the management and configuration of distribution, migration and replication, encouraging the use of domain-specific policies.

9. Applying the Distributed Programming Paradigm to Improve Scalability in Multi-user Environments (Erich R. Schmidt, Cristian Ţăpuş, and Daniel M. Zimmerman)

The rapid growth of the Internet played an important role in the growth of the gaming community which caused serious problems for Multi-user Dungeon (MUD) designers; larger numbers of users have crowded game servers and made scalability a critical issue.[30]

The first obvious "solution" to the scalability problem is to dedicate powerful computers to be used solely as game servers. However, hardware performance does not increase over time fast enough to keep up with the popularity of the games and, consequently, with the number of users.

Our approach is fundamentally different. The system we have designed replaces the single server with a pool of servers, addressing the scalability problem by distributing server load across the pool.

Our system is built upon a hierarchical map structure: at the highest level, the *map* is divided into *territories*; each territory is a directed graph of *rooms*, and each room is a directed graph of *cells*.

This hierarchy allowed us to easily design our distributed server system. Each territory is managed by a different *game-server*, and a *meta-server* plays the role of "name-server" for the territories . Of course, this division of the map is completely transparent to the user. Moving on the map and interacting with the environment and the other players are done without the user being aware of the location of the current room and cell on the game-servers; the user sees the entire system as a single server, and only needs the address of the meta-server to connect to the game. The problem of server overload is solved by delegating responsibilities to new game-servers.

We allow rooms to change servers, through a mechanism called *territory division*. This requires us to keep track of the position of each room; this is done by the meta-server, which manages a database of room locations. The database is essentially a hashtable which maps room IDs to hostnames.

We wish to ensure that the load on the system is divided among our multiple game-servers in such a way that each server will experience approximately the same levels of communication and computation. In order to do this, we use *territory division*. When the load on a server increases above a given threshold, the territory managed by the server is split into two new territories; a new server process then starts on a new computer, and one of the new territories is moved to the new host.

Our primary focus in this work has been on distributing the computation in such a way that the user experience is seamless; however, we have identified some possible directions in which the system can be extended, and plan to integrate new features into the system in the future. These include additional structural flexibility, performance maximization, complete decentralization, security, and enhanced game logistics.

Territory overlapping could increase system performance: the rooms on the "edges" of the territories could be managed both by the local game-server and the game-server of the neighboring territory. This would bring up consistency and persistence issues, but it would also provide more transparency to the client.

The meta-server has a key role in the system's functionality. While it does not limit the extensibility and the scalability of the system, the use of the meta-server is not exactly in the spirit of pure distributed systems. We could eliminate the meta-server by storing more data on the game-servers and using IP multicast for queries across the system. Unfortunately, this brings consistency and persistence issues to the forefront, and also increases the communication load in the system.

10. Agora - The Multi-user Environment for Co-authoring Documents (Waldemar Wieczerzycki)

The development of MOO applications require a multi-user database with further evolution of the database technology. The required extensions should be applied simultaneously to both: data modeling techniques and transaction management algorithms. Former techniques have to facilitate modeling data structures that are specific to cooperation processes, while the latter techniques have to support human interaction and exchange of non-committed data.

In such situation we propose a new model of a database that could become a kernel of MOO applications. First, we propose a new data model CDM (Collaborative Data Model) that is oriented for the specificity of multi-user environments, in particular: cooperation scenarios, cooperation techniques and cooperation management. Second, we propose to apply to databases supporting collaboration so called multiuser transactions. multi-user transactions are flat transactions in which, in comparison to classical ACID transactions, the isolation property is relaxed.

In the CDM model a database is viewed as a set of domains. The domain is a set of database objects operated by a group of collaborating users. The users create (modify) domain objects using cooperative database applications associated with the domain.

Every domain is composed of two disjoint subsets of objects: local objects and global objects. First subset contains objects that are available only in the encompassing database domain. These objects are created and modified by multi-user applications corresponding to the domain. Second subset is composed of objects simultaneously available in all database domains.

The multi-user transaction model is inspired by the natural perception, that a team of intensively cooperating users can be considered as a single virtual user, who has more than one brain trying to achieve the assumed goal, and more than two hands operating on keyboards.

Depending on whether database users collaborate or do not, and how tight is their collaboration, we distinguish two levels of users grouping: conferences and teams. A conference groups users who aim at achieving the common goal. Users belonging to the same conference can communicate with each other and be informed about progress of common work by the use of typical conferencing tools.

Tightly collaborating users of the same conference are grouped into the same team. Thus, a team is a subset of users of a corresponding conference.

A multi-user transaction is a set of database operations performed by users of the same team. Thus, is the only unit of communication between a virtual user representing members of a single team, and the database management system.

Two multi-user transactions from two different conferences behave in the classical way, which means that they work in mutual isolation, and they are serialized by database management system.

Two multi-user transactions from the same conference behave in a non-classical way, which means that the isolation property is partially relaxed for them. In case of access conflicts, so called negotiation mechanism is triggered by DBMS, that can resolve the problem.

Finally we combine multi-user transactions with the CDM model. It can be achieved in a very easy way. Every conference from the transaction model is bound to a different domain of the CDM model. Teams working in the scope of the same conference, i.e. multi-user transactions, are addressed to the same domain. There are two possible approaches. First, the domain is monoversion and teams operate on the same database objects. Second, the domain is multiversion and teams operate on different domain versions.

To summarize, the proposed database model is very straightforward and natural, on one hand, and allows practically unrestricted collaboration among members of the same team, on the other hand. Two basic assumptions of this model are: (1) collaborating users can communicate vie non-committed data and (2) collaborating users try to solve their access conflicts at a higher level than the level of a database management system, as it happens classically.[2]

11. Conclusion

The summaries of workshop contributions presented above illustrate the fact that researchers with a variety of interests can use the concept of a MOO as a useful practical test bed for research of a number of issues in Object-Oriented analysis, design, and programming. In view of this, the participants of the workshop have agreed to explore the possibility of collaborating on the design and implementation of a new MOO. The workshop position papers can be downloaded from the workshop web page at www-lifia.info.unlp.edu.ar/MOOEworkshop/.

References

[1] N. Budhiraja, K. Marzullo, F. Schneider, and S. Toueg. The primary-backup approach. In S.J. Mullender, editor, *Distributed Systems, 2nd Edition*, ACM-Press, chapter 8. Addison-Wesley, 1993.

[2] W. Cellary, W. Picard, and W. Wieczerzycki. Web-based business-to-business negotiation support. In *Proceedings of ¡the International Conference on Trends in Electronic Comerce*, Hamburg, Germany, 1998.

[3] Z. Choukair. *COREMO : A CORBA Real-Time Extension Model.* PhD thesis, Orsay U./ENST Bretagne, 1997.

[4] Z. Choukair and al. Contraintes temps-réel des applications multimédia en environnement distribué. Technical report, ENST Bretagne, 1994.

[5] Z. Choukair and al. Distribution architecture overview and representation mechanisms for the amusement project. Technical report, ENST Bretagne, 1998.

[6] E. Churchill and S. Bly. Virtual envirnments at work: Ongoing use of mud's in the workplace. In *Proceedings of WACC'99, ACM Press*, 1999.

[7] F. Cosquer, P. Antunes, and P. Veríssimo. Enhancing dependability of cooperative application in partitionable environments. In *Proceedings of the 2nd European Dependable Computing Conference*, Taormina, Italy, October 1996.

[8] B. Damers. *Avatars!* Peachpit Press, 1998.

[9] DASCo. Development of Distributed Applications with Separation of Concerns Project. DASCo Home Page URL: http://www.esw.inesc.pt/~ars/dasco.

[10] A. Diaz, B. Groth, and R. Melster. 'score' - the virtual museum, development of a distributed, object oriented system for 3d real-time visualization. In *Proceedings of the International Workshop on Communication-Based Systems*, pages 137–146, Berlin, Germany, October 1995. IEEE Computer Society Press. Technical Report 1998-15.

[11] A. Díaz and R. Melster. Designing virtual WWW environments: Flexible design for supporting dynamic bahavior. In *First ICSE Workshop on Web Engineering*, May 1999.

[12] J.L. Diez and al. Virtualarch : A distributed virtual reality platform. Master's thesis, ENST Bretagne, 1998.

[13] P. Dourish and M. Chalmers. Running out of space: Models of information. *HCI'94*, 1994.

[14] A. Downing, I. Greenberg, and J. Peha. Oscar: A system for weak-consistency replication. In *Proceedings of the Workshop on the Management of Replicate Data*, pages 26–30, Houston - USA, November 1990. IEEE.

[15] P. Spellman et al. Collaborative virtual workspace. In *Proceedings of Group'97 ACM SIGGROUP*, pages 197–203, 1997.

[16] V. O'Day et al. Moving practice: From classrooms to moo rooms. *Journal of Collaborative Computing*, 7(1-2), 1998.

[17] S. Evans. Building blocks of text-based virtual environments. Technical report, Computer Science University, University of Virginia, April 1993.

[18] E. Gamma, R. Helm, R. Johnson, and J. Vlissides. *Design Patterns: Elements of Reusable Object-Oriented Software.* Addison Wesley, 1994.

[19] T. Goncalves and A. R. Silva. Passive Replicator: A Design Pattern for Object Replication. In *The* 2nd *European Conference on Pattern Languages of Programming, EuroPLoP '97*, pages 165–178, Kloster Irsee, Germany. Siemens Technical Report 120/SW1/FB, 1997, July 1997.

[20] G. Gray and D. Cheriton. Leases: An efficient fault-tolerant mechanism for distributed file cache consistency. In *Proc. 12th ACM Symposium on Operating Systems Principles*, pages 202–210, Litchfield Park, Arizona, December 1989.

[21] M. Haahr. *Implementation and Evaluation of Scalability Techniques in the ECO Model.* Master's thesis, Department of Computer Science, University of Copenhagen, Denmark, August 1998.

[22] C. Haynes and J. R. Holmevik. *High wired: On the design, use, and theory of educational MOOs.* University of Michigan Press, 1998.

[23] R. Hayton, J. Bacon, J. Bates, and K. Moody. Using Events to Build Large Scale Distributed Applications. In *Proceedings of the Seventh ACM SIGOPS European Workshop*, pages 9–16. Association for Computing Machinery, September 1996.

[24] J. Heidemen, T. Page, R. Guy, and G. Popek. Primarily disconnected operation: Experiences with ficus. In *Proceedings of the Second Workshop on the Management of Replicated Data*, pages 2–5, Monterey, California, November 1992. IEEE.

[25] L. Lamport and al. Time, clocks and the ordering of events in a distributed system. *ACM*, 21(7), 1978.

[26] M. Mateas and S. Lewis. A moo-based virtual training environment. *Journal of Computer-Mediated Communication*, 2(3), 1996.

[27] K. O'Connell. *System Support for Multi-User Distributed Virtual Worlds.* PhD thesis, Trinity College, Department of Computer Science, Dublin, Ireland, October 1997.

[28] A. Ohnishi. Card: an environment for software requirements definition. In *Proc. 2nd Asia Pacific Software Engineering Conference (APSEC'95)*, pages 420–429, December 1995.

[29] A. Ohnishi. Visual software requirements definition environment. In *Proc. IEEE 21st Compsac*, pages 624–629, August 1997.

[30] S. J. Powers, M. R. Hinds, and J. Morphett. Distributed entertainment environment. In *BT Technology Journal Vol 15 No 4*. British Telecommunications, October 1997.

[31] M. Prieto and P. Victory. Subjective object behavior. *Object Expert*, 2(3), 1997.

[32] K. Ramamritham and al. Efficient scheduling algorithms for real-time multiprocessor systems. *IEEE Transactions on Parallel and Distributed Systems*, 1990.

[33] M. Raynal. *Distributed Algorithms and Protocols*. John Wiley, 1988.

[34] M. Resnik, editor. *Turtles, termites and Trafic jamps. Exploration in Massively Parallel Microworlds*. MIT Press, 1994.

[35] F. A. Rosa and A. R. Silva. Functionality and Partitioning Configuration: Design Patterns and Framework. In *IEEE Fourth International Conference on Configurable Distributed Systems*, pages 79–89, Annapolis, Maryland, USA, May 1998.

[36] Roseman, M. Greenberg, and S. TeamRooms. Network places for collaboration. In *Proceedings of CSCW'96*, pages 325–333, 1996.

[37] A. R. Silva, J. Pereira, and J. A. Marques. Object Recovery. In R. Martin, D. Riehle, and F. Buschman, editors, *Pattern Languages of Program Design 3*, chapter 15, pages 261–276. Addison-Wesley, 1997.

[38] A. R. Silva, J. Pereira, and J. A. Marques. Object Synchronizer. In Neil Harrison, Brian Foote, and Hans Rohnert, editors, *Pattern Languages of Program Design 4*, chapter 8. Addison-Wesley, 1999.

[39] A. R. Silva, F. A. Rosa, and T. Goncalves. Distributed Proxy: A Design Pattern for Distributed Object Communication. In *The 4th Conference on Pattern Languages of Programming, PLoP '97(Washington University technical report #WUCS-97-34)*, Allerton Park, Illinois, September 1997.

[40] A. R. Silva, P. Sousa, and M. Antunes. Naming: Design Pattern and Framework. In *IEEE 22nd Annual International Computer Software and Applications Conference*, pages 316–323, Vienna, Austria, August 1998.

[41] António Rito Silva. Development and Extension of a Three-Layered Framework. In Saba Zamir, editor, *Handbook of Object Technology*, chapter 27. New York, CRC Press, 1998.

[42] S Singhal and al. Networked virtual environments. *ACM press*, January 98.

[43] D. Snowdon and al. A review of distributed architectures for networked virtual reality. *Virtual Reality Press*, 2(1):155–175, 1996.

[44] G. Starovic, V. Cahill, and B. Tangney. An Event Based Object Model for Distributed Programming. In J. Murphy and B. Stone, editors, *Proceedings of the 1995 International Conference on Object Oriented Information Systems*, pages 72–86, London, December 1995. Dublin City University, Ireland, Springer-Verlag.

[45] I. Tomek and R. Giles. Virtual environments for work, study, and leisure. *To be published*, 1999.

Formal Techniques for Java Programs

Bart Jacobs, Gary T. Leavens, Peter Müller, and Arnd Poetzsch-Heffter

Bart.Jacobs@cs.kun.nl, Leavens@cs.iastate.edu,
Peter.Mueller@Fernuni-Hagen.de, Arnd.Poetzsch-Heffter@Fernuni-Hagen.de

Abstract. This report explains the motivation for a workshop on formal techniques for Java programs. It gives an overview of the presentations and summarizes the results of the working groups. Furthermore, it contains abstracts of the contributed papers.

Introduction

Motivation: Why Formal Techniques for Java Programs. Formal techniques can help to analyze programs, to precisely describe programming languages, to specify program behavior, to formalize requirements or designs, and to verify program properties. Applying such techniques to object-oriented technology is especially interesting because: (a) The OO-paradigm forms the basis for the software component industry with their need for certification techniques. (b) It is widely used for distributed and network programming. (c) The potential for reuse in OO-programming carries over to reusing specifications and proofs.

Java is a programming language that is more and more used as a platform for OO-research and advanced software-technology projects. It plays an important role in the areas listed above and provides integrated, standardized programming interfaces for a wide range of important computation systems and ressources. Because of the great interest in Java, its high-level programming model, and its integrating role in practical program development, Java is a prominent target for programming related formal techniques.

The aim of the workshop was to bring together people developing formal techniques and tool support for Java. The scope of the workshop included in particular the following topics:

- Interface specification languages
- Automated checking of program properties
- Verification technology and logics
- Specification of library packages
- Specification techniques, in particular for distributed applications
- Modularity and reuse of specifications and proofs

Applying formal techniques to a special programming language and its programs raises two questions: Are the formal techniques mature enough to deal with the language? Is the language an appropriate candidate to be used as a target for formal techniques? The workshop emphasized the first question.

A. Moreira and S. Demeyer (Eds.): ECOOP'99 Workshops, LNCS 1743, pp. 97–115, 1999.

Structure of Workshop and Reader. The one-day workshop was structured into presentation sessions in the morning, working group sessions in the afternoon, and a wrap-up session at the end. In the presentation sessions, short talks about each of the ten accepted papers were given. There were three working groups with the topics "Semantics of Java and Byte Code", "Specification of Programs and Designs", and "Verification and Static Checking of Java Programs". The working groups discussed the integration of the presented ideas and tried to isolate possible directions for further developments. The results of the groups were presented in the wrap-up session. The workshop had 27 participants.

The rest of this reader is structured as follows: Section 2 provides a short overview of the ten presentations, relating them to the topic of the workshop. Section 3 summaries the results of the working groups. Section 4 contains the abstracts of the accepted papers[1]. The proceedings of the workshop are contained in [39].

Overview of Presentations

Semantics. A formal semantics specification of a programming language can be used for several purposes: (a) for language analysis to find inconsistencies; (b) for correctness proofs of tools such as compilers, interpreters, and optimizers; (c) for precise language documentation and standardization; (d) as a foundation for program verification and logics.

In the workshop, we had one contribution addressing goal (a), one contribution addressing goal (b), and two that were mainly concerned with goal (d). V. Kotrajaras and S. Eisenbach presented an analysis of the *threads and main memory semantics* of Java. Based on a formalization of the relevant semantical aspects, they shoby, conditions that allow data inconsistency in a multi-threaded environment and investigated related issues. L. Casset and J. L. Lanet demonstrated *how to formally specify the Java byte code semantics* to prove that certain dynamic checks can be done statically. The goal of this work is to optimize Java code for smart cards. Of course, such optimizations must not affect the security mechanism. P. Cenciarelli explained his approach *towards a modular denotational sematics of Java.* Using so-called monad constructors, he described a modular technique to define a denotational semantics for a concurrent Java subset. B. Reus shoby, how to embed a calculus for sequential, recursive objects into a higher-order logic, yielding the kernel of a *logic for recursive objects.*

Specification and Refinement. Interface specifications play two important roles for software development and usage. (a) They allow the specification of implemented software components without revealing implementation details. Thus, they provide the interface between providers and users of software components. (b) They enable the formal, abstract description of program behavior during the refinement and design phase. This way, they provide an interface between

[1] For one of the contributions, we did not receive an abstract.

requirement and design specifications on one side and implementations on the other side.

In their contribution, S. Cimato and P. Ciancarini sketched *a formal approach to the specification of Java Components.* They combined ideas from the Larch project for the specification of Java components and from architectural description languages for the specification of connectors. Connectors are used to build systems from components. C. Fischer investigated *software development with Object-Z, CSP, and Java.* He used CSP-OZ (a combination of Object-Z and CSP) as a specification language and demonstrated how annotated Java program fragments can be generated from such specifications. The annotations express executable pre- and postconditions as well as class invariants. They provide *a pragmatic link from formal specifications to programs*, because they help to test the manually completed Java fragments. T. Clark presented a techniques for the *formal refinement and proof of a small Java program.* His underlying framework takes the form of a categorical semantics of object-oriented systems behavior and a design language based on λ-notation.

Verification and Analysis Techniques. Verification and analysis techniques for programs should help to find errors and to improve programs w.r.t. clarity and efficiency. Formal verification is typically used to show that programs satisfy certain behavioral properties. Such properties are usually formulated in a specification language, i.e. not in the programming language itself. In general, verification needs interactive theorem proving. However, for many interesting properties fully automatic checkers based on verification technology can produce very valuable analysis reports pointing out program errors or warnings. In addition to this, analysis techniques (similar to compiler optimization techniques) can improve programs by only investigating the program text.

In this area, the workshop had three contributions. M. Huisman, B. Jacob, and J. van den Berg presented *a case study in class library verification.* They demonstrated a formal proof for an invariant property of *Java's vector class* based on a translation from Java code to PVS theories. K. R. M. Leino, J. B. Saxe, and R. Stata explained a technique for *checking Java programs via guarded commands.* Guarded commands are used as a flexible intermediate language to simplify the generation of verification conditions in their Extended Static Checker for Java. K. Yi and B. Chang described a technique for *exception analysis for Java.* The goal of this research is to refine exception types in method signatures in order to provide programmers and compilers with more precise information about possibly raised exceptions.

Results from the Working Groups and Discussions

Semantics of Java and Its Byte Code

This working group had 8 members, namely Ludovic Casset, Pietro Cenciarelli, Alessandro Coglio, Bart Jacobs, Vishnu Kotrajaras, Krimo Nimour, Bernhard

Reus and David Wragg, with Bart acting as moderator and Bernhard taking notes. The background of the members turned out to be rather diverse, and so after some initial discussion we agreed that it would be best to focus on explaining typical issues and problems to each other, in the following three categories.

1. Java byte code specification and verification, especially in the context of JavaCard;
2. Concurrency in Java, with emphasis on modelling memory management for threads;
3. Denotational (or mathematical) semantics.

The first point started with an explanation of Java based smartcards. They contain a small processor, with typically 32K ROM and 8-16K RAM, running a stripped-down version of the JVM. Especially, byte code verification is not part of this JVM, but must be done off-card. Thus, class files must be verified before they are loaded (in compressed form) onto the card. This requires a formalisation of both the JVM, and of the translation from Java source code to the byte code, so that correctness can be established. This is a lot of work, which is currently ongoing in various places. One problem is that there are no clear specifications, and often only reference implementations. Still, this is considered a good area for applications of formal methods, because (1) there is considerable interest from the smart card industry, since errors in smartcard programs can do a lot of damage (both because of their rôle, and because of the numbers in which they will be used); (2) JavaCard programs are relatively small and use a stripped down version of Java (no threads, multidimensional arrays etc.) and only a small library. Formalisation and verification therefore seems feasible with current technology.

The second point continued the discussion after the earlier presentation of the workshop paper "Threads and Main Memory Semantics". The main problem here is the lack of clarity in the specification of the Java memory protocol, especially regarding the interaction between the main memory and the working memories of running threads. The discussion focussed on whether or not it is useful to postulate an intermediate entity.

The third point led to a presentation of, and discussion on, the use of coalgebras as semantical models of classes. Coalgebras involve a set of states, which suitably typed operations that can serve as fields and methods. Some issues in the modelling of class-valued fields were discussed: the use of type theoretic encodings via existential quantification or recursion over types does not work when one uses proof tools like PVS and Isabelle lacking such features.

This workshop did not produce any bold concluding statements. Several issues were clarified among the participants, in a friendly atmosphere. It was generally agreed that Java is a good target for formal methods, because the language is relatively simple and heavily used. The lack of formality and completeness in the language description is felt as a problem (but also as a challenge).

Specification and Refinement

The section summarizes the discussion of the working group on specification and refinement. The members of this group were as follows: Arnd Poetzsch-Heffter, Tony Clark, Stevio Cimato, Osvaldo Doelerlin, Clemens Fischer, Arend Rensick, and Gary Leavens.

Overall, the group's main theme was how to make specifications more useful in practice. The group started with a discussion of where specifications might be most useful, discussed techniques for making specifications more useful, and then discussed other practical issues.

Where Are Specifications Needed? The group discussed several situations where specifications might be particularly needed.

One situation where specifications are needed is in Java programs that use threads. Such programs are very difficult to debug, and thus the incremental payoff from using formal techniques to reason about such programs is greater than it would be for sequential programs.

Component-based software constructed using JavaBeans is another area where specifications are needed. Such components typically have concurrent elements in them. Component-based systems also place a premium on abstraction boundaries. The components of such a system must have well-defined interfaces and behaviors, and thus need behavioral specifications. If one is to use JavaBeans built by other people, then one must have some trust that they do what their specifications say, in which case certification or verification becomes more important.

Another area where specifications are needed is legacy code. We speculated that perhaps using formal specifications would be helpful in maintenance as a tool for documenting the behavior of legacy code.

What Could Make Specifications More Useful? Much of the discussion in this working group centered around techniques for making specifications more useful. An ideal situation would be if specifications were as useful as type checking. That is, if the return from writing formal specifications were as great as the return from writing types in programs. The presentation on ESC/Java at the workshop showed a good direction for research towards this goal.

One notion mentioned along these lines were ways to connect specification languages to development methods such as the Unified Modeling Language (UML). Such connections might help bridge the gap between requirements and specifications. They would also prove very useful in practice, because use of the UML seems to be growing in industry.

Another idea mentioned was the ability to specify Java programs on several levels of abstraction. For example, one should be able to specify at the level of methods, classes, components, and systems. One should have a way to specify the systems at all these levels so that the reader find information about the appropriate level. Interesting areas for research are specification languages that are appropriate for each level, and how to combine such levels formally.

The converse problem is using specifications to help document the decomposition of existing Java programs. It is important to be able to document components at the level of abstraction given by the underlying software architecture. If the specification language is not able to specify components at the appropriate level of abstraction, then this would be more difficult.

Another idea connected with this is the idea of specification facets. A *facet* is some aspect of behavior other than functional behavior; examples are the time or space that a method uses. In general, facets are connected with the use of some resource. For example another facet might be the number of pixels placed on a display by an applet, or the number of colors the uses. Current specification languages are not good at either describing facets or at specifying how different parts of programs relate to them. Even time and space are not usually treated in most specification languages. However such facets are important in many software development projects and are difficult to deal with using ad hoc or informal techniques. There is great potential for the use of specifications in such settings, if there were some formal techniques that could actually aid programmers in budgeting resources.

Perhaps one way to deal with different facets is with special-purpose specification languages. One could imagine a special-purpose language for each facet. In the field of programming languages, special-purpose, or domain-specific, languages have been quite useful. But to date there seems to be little work on special-purpose or domain-specific specification languages. Perhaps this would be a useful direction for future research.

Another idea that would make specifications of Java programs much more useful would be if there were some way to connect them to testing. Testing of course is used in the real world much more often than formal verification.

Practical Issues. As noted above, one practical issue, discussed by the working group on specification, is linking up with current requirement and design notations, such as the UML. For example, the UML features an assertion language called the Object Constraint Language, which could be tied into various formal methods.

There was some discussion about how to design a specification language for Java. Two approaches were discussed. In in the top-down approach, one starts with some existing specification language, such as VDM or Z, and adapts it to Java. An interface definition language defined in this way, would be similar in spirit to a language in the Larch family. In the bottom-up approach, one adds annotations incrementally to Java to accomplish various tasks. The ESC/Java project has essentially followed this approach.

Aliasing is a problem, both for the theory and in the practice of careful software development in Java. Techniques for dealing with aliasing problems must be explicit in the specification or as annotations in Java programs. Leverage for dealing with aliasing related problems may come from some of the following type systems: linear types, universes, balloon types, or ownership types.However, there are many different uses of aliasing in programs, some of which are prohibited by such type systems.

Specification languages must also be able to support invariants and properties of several classes within the same (and possibly different?) packages. Alias control seems essential here, but may not be enough to solve this entire problem.

Composition of program components, such as JavaBeans, can cause problems due to abstraction. When components are combined or when specifications of different facets are combined, the details that are ignored by various abstractions may interact badly. For example, if one component is a specification that has a facet for space, and it is combined with other components that have not had a space facet specified, then there may be no way to reason about the space efficiency of the result .

Needs and Open Problems. The group identified the main needs of specification languages as a better semantics of components and better composition techniques.

The group also identified as open problems the specification of the component and system levels, the specification of object-oriented frameworks, and the specification of facets. However, to be useful, they must have adequate tool support. A reasonable approach would be to use different techniques for the specification of different system levels and facets. However, there must also be some work on combining the specification of different facets.

Verification and Static Checking of Java Programs

This section contains a summary of the discussion of the working group on formal verification and static analysis of Java programs. The participants in this group were: Maria Isabel Gama Nunes, Görel Hedin, Patrik Persson, Raymie Stata, Kwangkeun Yi, and Peter Müller.

The working group discussed two questions which are relevant for everybody who wants to apply formal techniques to Java or deals with verification or static checking: (1) Is Java a good target language to apply formal techniques? (2) What is missing to bring formal verification/static analysis to practice?

Language Issues. Language designers face a trade-off between expressiveness and simple semantics. Whereas expressiveness is desirable for many programmers, a simple semantics is crucial for verification. Although Java initially struck a good balance, there is some concern that (a) some language features do not provide enough support for easy specification and verification, and (b) new language features add more and more complexity to Java.

Among the first group, the following aspects were mentioned: (1) The type system should provide support for null-pointer checking and parameterized types. (2) The concepts for encapsulation, visibility, and packages are insufficient to provide reliable access control to objects and object structures. (3) Abrupt termination, in particular in combination with labeled statements, is difficult to handle for most verification techniques. (4) Verification of concurrent programs would benefit from a stronger specification of the scheduler.

New language features such as inner classes or reflection added a lot of complexity to Java and significantly moved the balance mentioned above from simple semantics towards expressiveness. From a verifier's point of view, it is important that future language extensions (e.g., parameterized or virtual types) do not sacrifice Java's simplicity for expressiveness and downward-compatibility.

In a nutshell, although Java is not an ideal language to apply formal techniques, the working group members agreed that it is the best starting point we have had for years.

Bringing Verification to Practice. The working group identified the immense effort of writing formal specifications as the main obstacle for practical application of formal verification. There are several reasons why programmers don't want to write formal specifications, e.g., (1) it is difficult to write correct specifications (e.g., it is much more likely to correctly guess the type of a variable before the code is written than its exact range), and (2) most specification techniques require a rather complete specification describing the genuine task of a program and several other things such as side-effects and invariants.

To avoid these problems, specification and verification techniques should meet the following requirements: (1) There should be an immediate return on investment for the programmer. Therefore, it would be helpful if specification techniques would support both dynamic checking and formal verification. (2) There should be a way to incrementally increase the effort of writing specifications and the benefit one gets in return. This would allob for a step-by-step introduction of formal techniques into traditional software development practice. (3) Companies should benefit from applying formal techniques. This could be achieved by introducing quality certification for software or software components.

Abstracts of Presentations

How to Formally Specify the Java Bytecode Semantics Using the B Method *(Ludovic Casset and Jean Louis Lanet)*

The new smart card platforms (i.e., Java Card) allow dynamic storage and the execution of downloaded executable content. They are based on a virtual machine for portability across multiple smart card microcontrollers and for security reasons. Due to the reduced amount of resources, a subset of the Java language has been proposed for the Java card industry. The JavaCard 2.1 standard describes the smart card specific features of this virtual machine defining the JCRE (Java Card Runtime Environment). The correctness of the JCRE is important because it is the means to avoid an applet to reference illegally another applet objects. In order to prove such correctness we used formal methods to insure that our implantation respect this property. In our approach, we propose a model based on the refinement technique that guarantees the coherence between the static and the dynamic semantics. Related Work There has been much work on a formal treatment of Java and especially at the Java language level by [52, 25, 61]. They define a formal semantics for a subset of Java in order to prove the soundness of their type system. A work closer to our approach has been done by [58]. The author considers a subset of the byte code and its work aims to prove the run-time type correctness from their static typing. He proposes the proof of the verifier that can be deducted from its virtual machine specification. An interesting work has been partially done by [19] by formally describing a defensive virtual machine. Our approach We propose here to model at an abstract level a Defensive Java Virtual Machine. By successive refinements, we extract the run-time checks in order to de-synchronize verification and execution process. Then, we obtain invariants representing the formal specification of the static checks. It is then possible to correctly implement the interpreter part with respect to the static constraints. Our model has been entirely proved on a subset of the bytecode and we are extending to the complete instruction set. Moreover we are taking into account the firewall dynamic checks by modifying our operational semantics.

Towards a Modular Denotational Semantics of Java *(Pietro Cenciarelli)*

The present paper sketches a denotational semantics of a Java-like programming language featuring concurrent objects. Models are obtained by applying the modular technique introduced in [49] based on the categorical notion of monad, which provides, as advocated in [50], a semantic abstraction of computational features such as non-termination, side-effects, exceptions and so forth. The building blocks of this technique, called *semantic constructors* [12, 10, 11], are functions $\mathcal{F}$ (satisfying certain naturality conditions) mapping monads to monads and equipped with machinery to lift operations defined for a monad T to operations for $\mathcal{F}T$. Models $\mathcal{M}$ rich in computational structure are engineered by composing semantic constructors $\mathcal{F}_1$, $\mathcal{F}_2, \ldots$, $\mathcal{F}_n$, each adding structure for one computational feature, and applying them to a simple model of computation M, that is: $\mathcal{M} = \mathcal{F}_n(\ldots \mathcal{F}_2(\mathcal{F}_1(M))\ldots)$.

In [12] examples are provided of interleaving semantics based on *resumptions* for toy concurrent programs with shared memory. Here we shob that resumptions are not enough to capture multi-threaded object-oriented languages such as Java, and we use the corresponding constructor in conjunction with that for *continuations* to give an account of dynamic creation of threads.

Denotational models of various object calculi can be obtained indirectly by encoding them into type theories or process calculi (see [1, 54, 41]). By using computational types [50], our approach avoids complicated encodings thus making denotational semantics more usable.

Thread and Main Memory Semantics
(Vishnu Kotrajaras and Susan Eisenbach)

The Java Language Specification [33] defines how a thread's working memory should interact with the main memory. It is crucial that programmers understand those rules in order both to predict correctly the behaviour of concurrent programs and to implement correct concurrent programs. Moreover, it is crucial for implementors to follow those definitions in order to implement a correctly behaved runtime system.

In this study, we examine descriptions given in chapter 17 of The Java Language Specification [33]. We formalize these descriptions and prove properties regarding low level working-main memory behaviour. Our main objective is to use the formalization to investigate data consistency amongst threads and the main memory. In single-threaded Java, we show that data consistency holds. In multi-threaded Java, we illustrate conditions that lead to data inconsistency. We then investigate the differences between volatile declarations and synchronized statements. Volatile variables do not maintain data consistency while synchronization provides it. We also propose formal rules that guarantee data consistency of a concurrent program and make the program easier for debugging and reasoning.

Closely related works: Pugh [57] discovered that the use of *prescient store* could introduce behaviour that is not normally possible. He also demonstrated that compiler optimization could destroy data consistency amongst threads. He proposed a memory model which does not interfere with compiler optimization. Pugh also investigated data consistency during object initialization. He proposed some plausible solutions, but did not go into more depth. Gontmakker and Schuster [32] compared Java to existing memory consistency models. They presented a non-operational memory model equivalent to the operational model in [33], in both programmer and implementor's viewpoints. The non-operational model is relatively easier to understand and implement. However, since it is proven to be equivalent to the operational model, it inherits all the faults of the original. The original faults are well worth analyzing before the new model can be really useful.

Other Related works: Drossopoulou and Eisenbach [25, 24, 26] formulated an operational semantics of Java. However, their work did not include concurrent Java. Börger and Schulte [9] used the Abstract State Machine to describe the behaviour of Java threads in a pseudocode-like notation. Their thread-memory description is a good implementation that corresponds to the thread-memory rules. However, they did not formalize the thread-memory rules or study the rules' properties. Coscia and Reggio [20] developed their own version of the operational semantics for concurrent Java. Their work, like [9], focused mainly on execution that synchronizes on every variable access, therefore ignoring the working-main memory rules. [13, 14] transformed the thread-memory rules into logic sentences and went on to use the transformed rules to present the operational semantics for multi-threaded Java. However, the behaviour of Java due to thread-main memory definitions was not studied.

A Logic of Recursive Objects *(Bernhard Reus)*

Following the pioneering work of [46, 42], an axiomatic semantics for an imperative typed object calculus [1] with global state is suggested in [2]. In [44] a version for typed recursive objects is given and [43, 55, 56] present even more axiomatic calculi with global store. On the other hand, [21] suggests a wp-calculus with local state which is also at the heart of the coalgebraic approach [37]. Most of the above work deal with axiomatic semantics in terms of quite complex calculi, sometimes overloaded with huge "background predicates", and exclusively referring to *operational* semantics.

We propagate a *denotational view on objects* and their properties. Just like the *Logic of Computational Functions* [47] (also referred to as "Logic of Domains") allows one to reason about the denotations of functional programs instead of their syntactic representation, we suggest to take the same view on objects and object calculi (see also [36]).

Once having embedded a denotational semantics of an object calculus or OO-programming language in a higher-order logic, one can reason about denotations of objects and prove their properties also using recursive specifications. For the untyped functional and imperative ς-calculus e.g. this can be done quite easily by using greatest fixpoints of functionals on interface specifications (cf. [2, 43, 55, 56]) and coinduction as reasoning principle. Such a logic on denotations might be useful to develop axiomatic calculi, which are more involved and syntactic in nature, and to prove correctness/(relative) completeness w.r.t. to them. By translating the class-based approach to the object-based one and switching from the untyped to the typed world one might obtain a semantics and a logic for a kernel-sublanguage of Java (cf. [14, 51]) in the propagated style.

A Formal Approach to the Specification of Java Components *(S. Cimato and P. Ciancarini)*

The motivation and the starting point of our research was the recognition that while Java is becoming one of the most used programming languages, software designers have few specific tools and techniques at their own disposal to formally reason on the resulting system. Generic specification languages (Z or UML) or architectural description languages (Wright or Darwin) can be effectively exploited, but the generality of the model does not catch all the features of the underlying programming language (Java) and the abstractions needed to make formal descriptions practical and effective. On the other hand, practical approaches for component-based software development (JavaBeans) suffer from the lack of a well-understood formal foundation.

Our research on Java has been conducted towards the development of a methodology for the formal specification and verification of Java components and architectures. At this aim, we have been developing a formal framework for the design and the analysis of Java component based applications which is based on an interface specification language [34, 62] for the component descriptions and an architectural language to combine such components. Furthermore we provide a formal semantics for Java programs, such that the resulting model allows the dynamic analysis of Java applications [15]. In our approach, each component specification integrates both the description of its interface and its functional behavior supported by an algebraic model in which a more abstract description can be given. Those descriptions may be used as the basis for the analysis and as a guide for the designers which have to produce the implementations of the components and to integrate the different parts of the system to work together. Differently from other approaches based on very abstract notations [4, 45], we aim to provide a notation achieving an acceptable compromise between formality and practice, offering both a formal framework where it is possible to reason on the system properties, and an easy way to refine a specification into an implementation.

Formal Refinement and Proof of a Small Java Program *(Tony Clark)*

The aim of this work is to provide a rigorous framework for step-wise object-oriented software development which supports specification, refinement, proof and implementation. The framework takes the form of a categorical semantics of object-oriented system behaviour and a design language based on λ-notation. This work is described in more detail in [16], [17] and [18]; see [60] for a review of formal methods for object-oriented development and [8] for a related approach. The reader is directed to [30], [31], a description of the use of category theory in systems development.

Object-oriented system computation occurs in terms of state transitions resulting from message passing: $\ldots \longrightarrow \Sigma_1 \stackrel{(I,O)}{\longrightarrow} \Sigma_2 \longrightarrow \ldots$ in which a set of object states Σ_1 receives a set of input messages I producing a transition to states Σ_2 and output messages O. The behaviour of a system design is a category of graphs **Obj** whose nodes are labelled with sets of object states and whose edges are labelled with pairs of sets of messages.

System construction is described by standard categorical constructions in **Obj**. Given two behaviours O_1 and O_2 in **Obj** the product $O_1 \times O_2$ exhibits both O_1 and O_2 behaviour subject to structural consistency constraints. The coproduct $O_1 + O_2$ exhibits either O_1 or O_2 behaviour. Equalizers, pull-backs and push-outs can be used to express constraints such that two or more behaviours are consistent. Computational category theory provides an algorithm for computing the behaviour of a system of inter-related components using limits. Object-oriented designs are expressed using a λ-notation whose semantics is given by **Obj**. Refinement can be defined as a program transformation that preserves the meaning in **Obj**.

Software Development with Object-Z, CSP, and Java: A Pragmatic Link from Formal Specifications to Programs *(Clemens Fischer)*

Java is well suited for designing distributed systems which must meet high correctness requirements. But applicable methods for building distributed high quality systems are not widely accepted nor available.

A pragmatic approach for better software quality is Meyer's 'design-by-contract' [46]. The idea is to write predicates that specify properties of systems into the code and to check these predicates during run time.

Missing design-by-contract support in Java is discussed in SUN's list as bug number 4071460. The Jass (Java with assertions) compiler [40, 7] overcomes this problem. Jass programs are normal Java programs augmented with assertions placed in specific comments. The compiler translates these assertions to Java statements that check the predicate during run time.

Design-by-contract, however, is limited to specifying functional, sequential aspects of systems. It is not possible to capture dynamic aspects of communicating distributed systems and it cannot be used to provide high-level interface specifications that not only hide functional implementation details but also conceal architectural design decisions or underlying network technology.

Therefore we suggest a new link from the high level formal specification language CSP-OZ [29] to Jass.

CSP-OZ is a combination of Object-Z [27] and CSP [59]. Object-Z is strong at specifying the state space and methods of a class in a predicative way. This matches nicely the predicates used in a design-by-contract approach. But Object-Z has a powerful type system, schema calculus and a toolkit framework that go far beyond the predicate language used in Jass or Eiffel. It is, however, weak at describing dynamic aspects of distributed communicating systems. This loophole can be filled with the process algebra CSP, which comes with many operators and a mature theory of communicating, distributed systems. CSP, on the other hand, has no high level concepts for the specification of data.

The combination CSP-OZ [29] takes the best of these two worlds. It is a wide range specification language for complex distributed systems like telecommunication, satellite, or rail-road systems.

The key idea presented in the paper, is to generate Jass assertions from CSP-OZ specifications. This task can be automated given a CSP-OZ specification with implementable data types. This step does not guarantee correctness in a mathematical sense. But it combines the advantages of a fully formal specification of a distributed system with the simplicity of a design-by-contract approach. Errors can be found earlier during testing and any assertion violation can be linked directly to the part of the formal specification it stems from, making error interpretation much easier.

A Case Study in Class Library Verification: Java's Vector Class

(Marieke Huisman, Bart Jacobs, and Joachim van den Berg)

One of the reasons for the popularity of object-oriented programming is the possibility it offers for reuse of code. Usually, the distribution of an object-oriented programming language comes together with a collection of ready-to-use classes, in a class library. A clear and correct specification (a contract) of the behaviour of such library classes is highly desirable, both for the implementors (providers) and the clients of these classes. One (post hoc) way to construct such a specification, is by verifying whether a given library class satisfies its required properties. Typical examples of properties that can be verified are termination conditions (in which cases will a method terminate normally, in which cases will it throw an exception), pre-post-condition relations and class invariants.

The full paper describes a case study verification of one particular library class, namely `Vector`, which is in the standard distribution of the programming language Java [6, 33]. The `Vector` class basically consists of an array of objects, which is internally replaced by an array of different size, according to needs. Arrays in Java have a fixed size; vectors are thus useful if it is not known in advance how many storage positions are needed. A verification of an invariant property for this `Vector` class is presented. The property says (essentially) that the actual size of a vector (*i.e.* the number of elements that it contains) is less than or equal to its capacity. This property is maintained by all methods of the `Vector` class, and it holds for all objects created by the constructors of the `Vector` class.

This verification project makes use of two tools: the PVS [53] proof tool, developed at SRI, and the LOOP [38] translation tool. The latter is a compiler which translates Java classes into a series of logical theories in the higher-order logic of PVS. Development of this tool is part of the so-called LOOP project, for Logic of Object-Oriented Programming, in which all three the authors are involved. Initially, this project aimed at reasoning about class specifications, but a new branch of this project concentrated on reasoning about Java [38].

The contribution of the work presented in the paper is twofold. First of all, it shows the feasibility of tool-assisted verification of (standard library) classes in Java. The verification results could be used to improve the class documentation and make it exact, in contrast to informal explanations in ordinary language. Secondly, it is an illustration of the use (and capabilities) of the LOOP translation tool. Although the translation does not cover all of Java yet—threads are not incorporated at the moment—it already allows reasoning about non-trivial, real-life Java programs.

Checking Java Programs via Guarded Commands *(K. Rustan M. Leino, James B. Saxe, and Raymie Stata)*

The Extended Static Checker for Java (ESC/Java) is a tool for finding, by static analysis, common programming errors normally not detected until run-time, if ever [28]. ESC/Java takes as input a Java program, possibly including user annotations, and produces as output a list of warnings of potential errors. It does so by deriving a *verification condition* for each routine (method or constructor), passing these verification conditions to an automatic theorem-prover, and post-processing the prover's output to produce warnings from failed proofs.

Deriving verification conditions for a practical language, rather than for a toy language, can be complex. Furthermore, in designing a tool for automatic checking, one faces trade-offs involving the frequency of spurious warnings, the frequency of missed errors, the efficiency of the tool, and the effort required to annotate programs. To explore and exploit these trade-offs flexibly, it must be easy to change the verification conditions generated by the tool.

To manage complexity and achieve flexibility, our translation from Java to verification conditions is broken into three stages. First, we translate from Java to a sugared high-level, guarded-command-like language (inspired by [23]). Second, we desugar the sugared guarded commands into primitive guarded commands. Finally, we compute verification conditions from these primitive guarded commands. This paper describes guarded-command language, gives its semantics, and discusses how it is used in ESC/Java.

In the translation from Java into sugared guarded commands, we eliminate many of the complexities found in Java, such as `switch` statements and expressions with side effects. This part of the translation is bulky and tedious. We have designed the sugared guarded-command language to make the translation easy to understand and to implement. At the same time, this part of the translation is relatively stable. We find it nice to separate this bulky but stable part of the translation process from other parts that change during experimentation.

The desugaring into primitive guarded commands is where we need a lot of flexibility. The paper gives examples of how different desugarings, possibly chosen under user control, result in different kinds of checking.

The semantics of the primitive guarded-command language is quite simple. The paper gives, in less than half a page, a set of equations for deriving verification conditions from primitive guarded commands.

Exception Analysis for Java *(Kwangkeun Yi and Byeong-Mo Chang)*

Current JDK Java compiler relies too much on programmer's specification for checking against uncaught exceptions of the input program. It is not elaborate enough to remove programmer's unnecessary handlers (when programmer's specifications are too many) nor suggest to programmers for specialized handlings (when programmer's specifications are too general).

We propose a static analysis of Java programs that estimates their exception flows independently of the programmer's specifications. This analysis is an extension of a class analysis to Java's exception mechanism. Its cost-effectiveness balance is suggested by sparsely analyzing the program at method-level (hence reducing the number of unknowns in the flow equations).

We present our exception analysis in the set-constraint framework[35, 3]. Set variable $\mathcal{X}_e$ is for the object classes that program phrase e's normal object belongs to. Variable $\mathcal{P}_e$ is for the exception classes that the phrase e's uncaught exception belongs to. A set constrainst $\mathcal{X} \supseteq se$ describes that set $\mathcal{X}$ contains the set represented by set expression se. Multiple constraints are conjunctions.

Because exception-related expressions are sparse in programs, generating constraints for every expression is wasteful. Hence we have designed a *sparse constraint system* that use small number of unknowns during the analysis. (Similar technique of enlarging constraint granularity has already been successfuly used in ML [48]'s exception analysis [63, 64].) In our sparse constraint system, the number of constraint variables is proportional only to the number of methods, field variables, and the `try` expressions, not to the total number of expressions. For each method f, set variable $\mathcal{X}_f$ is for classes (including exception classes) that are "available" at f, and $\mathcal{P}_f$ is for classes of uncaught exceptions during the call to f. Similarly $\mathcal{X}_x$ for each field variable x. Every catch-variable x of `try` expressions: "`try` e_g `catch` $(c\ x\ e)$" has a separate set variable $\mathcal{X}_x$ which will has the classes of uncaught exceptions from e_g. (The `try` expression's semantics: it catches uncaught exceptions from e_g if their classes are covered by c. The catched exceptions are bound to x and handled in e.) The try-expression e_g has separate set variables $\mathcal{X}_g$ and $\mathcal{P}_g$, which are respectively for available and uncaught exception classes in e_g.

Example rules $f \triangleright e : \mathcal{C}$ to collect constraints $\mathcal{C}$ for Java expression e are as follows. The left-hand-side f indicates that the expression e is a sub-expression of method f.

- For `throw` expression:

$$\frac{f \triangleright e_1 : \mathcal{C}_1}{f \triangleright \texttt{throw}\ e_1 : \{\mathcal{P}_f \supseteq \mathcal{X}_f \cap \mathit{ExnClasses}\} \cup \mathcal{C}_1}$$

  The classes $\mathcal{P}_f$ of uncaught exceptions from method f are the exception classes $(\mathcal{X}_f \cap \mathit{ExnClasses})$ among the classes $\mathcal{X}_f$ available at f.
- For `try` expression:

$$\frac{g \triangleright e_g : \mathcal{C}_g \quad f \triangleright e_1 : \mathcal{C}_1}{f \triangleright \texttt{try}\ e_g\ \texttt{catch}\ (c_1 x_1 e_1) : \{\mathcal{X}_{x_1} \supseteq \mathcal{P}_g \dot{\cap} \{c_1\}\} \cup \mathcal{C}_g \cup \mathcal{C}_1}$$

  The exceptions bound to the handler variable x_1 are the uncaught exceptions $\mathcal{P}_g$ from e_g if the exception's classes are covered by c, hence $\mathcal{X}_{x_1} \supseteq \mathcal{P}_g \dot{\cap} \{c_1\}$. (The operator $\dot{\cap}$ is equivalent to the set intersection with the class inheritance as the subset order.) Note that the constraints $\mathcal{C}_1$ from the try-expression e_g are derived under g.

The least model of the sparse constraints $\mathcal{C}$, which are derived ($\triangleright$ *pgm* : $\mathcal{C}$) from an input program *pgm* is our analysis result. The solutions for $\mathcal{P}_m$ has the exception classes whose exceptions might be thrown and uncaught during m's execution.

References

[1] M. Abadi and L. Cardelli. *A Theory of Objects.* Monographs in Computer Science. Springer-Verlag, New York, 1996. ISBN 0-387-94775-2.

[2] M. Abadi and K.R.M. Leino. A logic of object-oriented programs. In M. Bidoit and M. Dauchet, (eds.): Proc. TAPSOFT '97, 7th Int. Joint Conference CAAP/FASE, vol. 1214, LNCS, pp. 682–696. Springer, 1997.

[3] A. Aiken and N. Heintze, Constraint-based program analysis. *Tutorial of 22th ACM SIGPLAN-SIGACT Symposium on Principles of Programming Languages,* Januaray 1995.

[4] R. Allen and D. Garlan. A Formal Basis for Architectural Connection. *ACM Transactions on Software Engineering and Methodology,* 6(3):213–249, June 1997.

[5] J. Alves-Foss, (ed.): *Formal Syntax and Semantics of Java.* LNCS, vol. 1523, Springer, 1999.
[6] K. Arnold and J. Gosling. *The Java Programming Language.* Addison-Wesley, 2nd edition, 1997.
[7] D. Bartetzko. Parallelität und Vererbung beim 'Programmieren mit Vertrag'. Master's thesis, University of Oldenburg, May 1999. in German.
[8] J. Bicarregui, K. Lano, and T. Maibaum: Towards a Compositional Interpretation of Object Diagrams. Technical Report, Department of Computing, Imperial College, 1997.
[9] E. Börger and W. Schulte. A programmer friendly modular definition of the semantics of Java.
http://www.informatik.uni-ulm.de/pm/mitarbeiter/wolfram.html.
[10] P. Cenciarelli. *Computational applications of calculi based on monads.* PhD thesis, Department of Computer Science, University of Edinburgh, 1995. CST-127-96. Also available as ECS-LFCS-96-346.
[11] P. Cenciarelli. An Algebraic View of Program Composition. In Armando Haeberer, editor, *Proceedings of 7th International Conference on Algebraic Methodology and Software Technology (AMAST'98)*, 1998. LNCS 1548.
[12] P. Cenciarelli and E. Moggi. A syntactic approach to modularity in denotational semantics. In *Proceedings of 5th Biennial Meeting on Category Theory and Computer Science.* CTCS-5, 1993. CWI Tech. Report.
[13] P. Cenciarelli, A. Knapp, B. Reus, and M. Wirsing. From sequential to multi-threaded Java: an event-based operational semantics. In *6 th Conf. Algebraic Methodology and Software Technology, AMAST*, 1997.
[14] P. Cenciarelli, A. Knapp, B. Reus, and M. Wirsing. An Event-Based Structural Operational Semantics of Multi-Threaded Java. In [5].
[15] S. Cimato. *A Methodology for the Specification and Verification of Java Components and Architectures.* PhD thesis, Dept. of Computer Science, University of Bologna, Italy, February 1999.
[16] A. N. Clark and A. S. Evans: Semantic Foundations of the Unified Modelling Language. In the proceedings of the First Workshop on Rigorous Object-Oriented Methods: ROOM 1, Imperial College, June, 1997.
[17] A. N. Clark: A Semantics for Object-Oriented Systems. Presented at the Third Northern Formal Methods Workshop. September 1998. In BCS FACS Electronic Workshops in Computing, 1999.
[18] A. N. Clark: A Semantics for Object-Oriented Design Notations. Technical report, submitted to the BCS FACS Journal, 1999.
[19] R. Cohen. Defensive Java Virtual Machine Specification.
http://www.cli.com/software/djvm.
[20] E. Coscia and G. Reggio. An operational semantics for java. Dipartimento di Informatica e Scienze dell' Informazione, Universita di Genova, http://www.disi.unige.it.
[21] F.S. de Boer. A wp-calculus for OO. In W. Thomas, (ed.), *Foundations of Software Sci. and Comp. Struct.*, vol. 1578 of LNCS. Springer, 1999.
[22] G. DeFouw, D. Grove, and C. Chambers, Fast interprocedural class analysis, *Proceedings of 25th ACM SIGPLAN-SIGACT Symposium on Principles of Programming Languages* pages 222-236, Januaray 1998.
[23] E. W. Dijkstra. *A Discipline of Programming.* Prentice Hall, Englewood Cliffs, NJ, 1976.

[24] S. Drossopoulou and S. Eisenbach. Is the Java type system sound? In Fourth International Workshop on Foundations of Object-Oriented Languages, October 1997. http://outoften.doc.ic.ac.uk/projects/slurp/papers.html.

[25] S. Drossopoulou and S. Eisenbach. Java is type safe — probably. In *11 th European Conference on Object-Oriented Programming*, February 1997. http://outoften.doc.ic.ac.uk/projects/slurp/papers.html.

[26] S. Drossopoulou and S. Eisenbach. Towards an operational semantics and proof of type soundness for java, April 1998. http://outoften.doc.ic.ac.uk/projects/slurp/papers.html.

[27] R. Duke, G. Rose, and G. Smith. Object-Z: A specification language advocated for the description of standards. *Computer Standards and Interfaces*, 17:511–533, 1995.

[28] Extended Static Checking home page, Compaq Systems Research Center. On the Web at www.research.digital.com/SRC/esc/Esc.html.

[29] C. Fischer. CSP-OZ: A combination of Object-Z and CSP. In H. Bowman and J. Derrick, editors, *Formal Methods for Open Object-Based Distributed Systems (FMOODS '97)*, volume 2, pages 423–438. Chapman & Hall, 1997.

[30] J. Goguen: Objects. Int. Journal of General Systems, 1(4):237–243, 1975.

[31] J. Goguen: Sheaf Semantics for Concurrent Interacting Objects. Mathematical Structures in Computer Science, 1990.

[32] A. Gontmakher and A. Schuster. Java consistency: Non-operational characterizations for java memory behaviour. Technical Report CS0922, Computer Science Department, Technion, November 1997.

[33] J. Gosling, B. Joy, and G. Steele. *The Java Language Specification*. Addison-Wesley, 1996.

[34] J. Guttag and J. Horning. *Larch: Languages and Tools for Formal Specification*. Springer-Verlag, Berlin, 1993.

[35] N. Heintze, Set-based program analysis. Ph.D thesis, Carnegie Mellon University, October 1992.

[36] M. Hofmann and B. Pierce. Positive subtyping. *Information and Computation*, 126(1):186–197, 1996.

[37] B. Jacobs. Coalgebraic reasoning about classes in object-oriented languages. In CMCS 1998, number 11 in Electr. Notes in Comp. Sci. Elsevier, 1998.

[38] B. Jacobs, J. van den Berg, M. Huisman, M. van Berkum, U. Hensel, and H. Tews. Reasoning about classes in Java (preliminary report). In *Object-Oriented Programming, Systems, Languages and Applications (OOPSLA)*, pages 329–340. ACM Press, 1998.

[39] B. Jacobs, G. T. Leavens, P. Müller, and A. Poetzsch-Heffter, editors. *Formal Techniques for Java Programs*. Technical Report 251, Fernuniversität Hagen, 1999. URL: `www.informatik.fernuni-hagen.de/pi5/publications.html`.

[40] Jass: Java with assertions, May 1999. http://semantik.informatik.uni-oldenburg.de/˜jass—.

[41] C. Jones. A pi-calculus semantics for an object-based design notation. In *Proc. of CONCUR'93*, 1993. LNCS 715.

[42] G.T. Leavens. Modular specification and verification of object-oriented programs. *IEEE Software*, 8(4):72–80, 1991.

[43] K.R.M. Leino. Ecstatic: An object-oriented programming language with an axiomatic semantics. Tech. Report KRML 65-0, SRC, 1996.

[44] K.R.M. Leino. Recursive object types in a logic of object-oriented programs. *Nordic Journal of Computing*, 5(4):330-360, 1998.

[45] J. Magee, N. Dulay, S. Eisenbach, and J. Kramer. Specifying Distributed Software Architectures. In *Proc. 5th European Software Engineering Conf. (ESEC 95)*, v. 989 of *LNCS*, pp. 137–153, Sitges, Spain, September 1995.
[46] B. Meyer. *Object-Oriented Software Construction*. Prentice Hall, 1988.
[47] R. Milner. Implementation and application of Scott's logic of continuous functions. In *Conf. on Proving Assertions About Programs*, pp. 1–6. SIGPLAN 1, 1972.
[48] R. Milner, M. Tofte, R. Harper, and D. MacQueen. *The Definition of Standard ML (Revised)*. MIT Press, 1997.
[49] E. Moggi. An abstract view of programming languages. Technical Report ECS-LFCS-90-113, University of Edinburgh, Comp. Sci. Dept., 1990.
[50] E. Moggi. Notions of computation and monads. *Information and Computation*, 93(1), 1991.
[51] T. Nipkow and D. von Oheimb. Machine-checking the Java Specification: Proving Type-Saftey. In [5].
[52] T. Nipkow and D. von Oheimb. Javalight is Type-Safe — Definitely. 25th ACM symposium on Principles of Programming Languages, 1998.
[53] S. Owre, S. Rajan, J.M. Rushby, N. Shankar, and M.K. Srivas. PVS: Combining specification, proof checking, and model checking. In R. Alur and T.A. Henzinger, editors, *Computer-Aided Verification (CAV '96)*, volume 1102 of *LNCS*, pages 411–414, New Brunswick, NJ, July/August 1996. Springer-Verlag.
[54] B. Pierce and D. Turner. Concurrent objects in a process calculus. In *Proceedings of TPPP'94*. Springer LNCS 907, 1995.
[55] A. Poetzsch-Heffter. Specification and verification of object-oriented programs. Technical report, Technical University of Munich, 1997. Habilitation Thesis.
[56] A. Poetzsch-Heffter and P. Müller. A programming logic for sequential Java. In S. D. Swierstra, editor, *Programming Languages and Systems (ESOP '99)*, volume 1576, pages 162–176. Springer-Verlag, 1999.
[57] W. Pugh. Fixing the java memory model. In *Java Grande*, June 1999.
[58] Z. Qian. Least Types for Memory Locations in Java Bytecode. Kestrel Institute, Tech Report, 1998.
[59] A. W. Roscoe. *The Theory and Practice of Concurrency*. Prentice-Hall, 1997.
[60] A. Ruiz-Delgado, D. Pitt, and C. Smythe: A Review of Object-Oriented Approaches in Formal Specification. The Computer Journal, 38(10), 1995.
[61] D. Syme. Proving Java Type Soundness. Technical report, University of Cambridge Computer Laboratory, 1997.
[62] J. Wing. Writing Larch Interface Language Specifications. *ACM Transactions on Programming Languages and Systems*, 9(1):1–24, January 1987.
[63] K. Yi and S. Ryu. Towards a cost-effective estimation of uncaught exceptions in SML programs. In *Lecture Notes in Computer Science*, volume 1302, pages 98–113. Springer-Verlag, proceedings of the 4th international static analysis symposium edition, 1997.
[64] K. Yi and S. Ryu. SML/NJ Exception Analysis version 0.98. http://compiler.kaist.ac.kr/pub/exna/, December 1998.

9th Workshop for PhD Students in Object Oriented Systems

Awais Rashid[1], David Parsons[2], and Alexandru Telea[3]

[1] Computing Department, Lancaster University, UK
marash@comp.lancs.ac.uk
[2] The Object People, Epsilon House, Chilworth Science Park, Southampton, UK
davidp@objectpeople.com
[3] Department of Mathematics and Computer Science, Eindhoven University of Technology, The Netherlands
alext@win.tue.nl

Abstract. The PhDOOS workshop covered a wide scope, as its over 20 participants were PhD students in all areas of object orientation. The presentations covered topics such as databases, languages, software engineering and artificial intelligence, components and generative programming, analysis and design, frameworks and patterns, aspected oriented programming, distribution, and middleware. Several topics of shared interest were identified and targeted in separate discussion groups on meta-information, the success or failure of OODBMS, and a general theme on the future of object orientation. As the participants had various research interests covering practically all the OO spectrum, we can confidently state that these topics reflect actually the concerns and needs of the OO community, and emerge from its concrete needs. This document is to be complemented by a workshop proceedings document which will publish the full versions of the presented papers.

1. Introduction

The 9th workshop for PhD Students in Object Oriented Systems (PhDOOS '99) was held on June 14-15, 1999 in Lisbon, Portugal in association with the 13th European Conference on Object Oriented Programming (ECOOP). The workshop was part of the series of PhDOOS workshops held in conjunction with ECOOP each year. The PhDOOS workshops differ from usual workshops. The scope of the presentations is wide. This is because the participants are PhD students and topics are derived from the areas of interest of the participants. The workshops serve as a forum for lively discussion between PhD students doing research in similar areas. For each participant, this is an opportunity to present his/her research to a knowledgeable audience who are working in a similar context. In particular, the presenter may learn about new points of view on this research or about related work, and future research collaboration may be initiated. The workshops also feature invited speakers talking about interesting future research topics in object orientation. This provides the participants an

A. Moreira and S. Demeyer (Eds.): ECOOP'99 Workshops, LNCS 1743, pp. 116–135, 1999.

opportunity to have an "unplugged" discussion with well-known personalities in the field. The workshops also aim at strengthening the international Network of PhD Students in Object-Oriented Systems (PhDOOS[1]), which was initiated at the 1st workshop during ECOOP '91 in Geneva, Switzerland. PhDOOS '99 was organised by Awais Rashid, David Parsons and Alexandru Telea and followed the patterns of its predecessors. The participants were divided into three different categories. First, it was possible to submit a (3-8 page) position paper for review, and to give a 30 minutes presentation at the workshop. Second, it was possible to submit a one-page abstract for review and to give a 15 minutes presentation. Finally, anticipating some last-minute participants a "guest" status was defined for them, including a very short presentation if they wanted to give one. The workshop featured three keynote speakers: Ian Sommerville [2], Gregor Kiczales[3] and Ulrich Eisenecker[4]. The workshop received a total of 30 submissions from 14 countries in 3 continents. Of these 19 were position papers while 11 were abstracts. For the first time in the series of PhDOOS workshops a review process was introduced. Submissions were reviewed by PhD students almost two-thirds into their PhD. The review process was not designed to select the few very best papers, but to ensure that every participant was able to present some relevant material, and was sincere and well prepared. As a result, 17 position papers and 6 abstracts were selected for presentation at the workshop. Accepted papers and abstracts are available on the workshop web site at: http://www.comp.lancs.ac.uk/computing/users/marash/PhDOOS99. They will also be included in the workshop proceedings to be published by University of Eindhoven, The Netherlands.

2. Workshop Structure

The workshop was divided into sessions based on the presenters' areas of interest. These were as follows:

- Databases
- Languages, Software Engineering and Artificial Intelligence
- Components and Generative Programming
- Analysis and Design
- Frameworks and Patterns
- Aspect Oriented Programming
- Distribution and Middleware

The following sections summarise the discussion that took place in the various sessions.

[1] http://www.ecoop.org/phdoos/
[2] Computing Department, Lancaster University, Lancaster, UK
[3] Xerox PARC, USA
[4] University of Applied Sciences, Heidelberg, Germany

2.1. Databases

Juan Trujillo, Awais Rashid, Isabella Merlo, Marlon Dumas and Radovan Chytracek presented their work in this session. Juan Trujillo discussed the recent increased interest in multidimensional databases (MDB) and On-line Analytical Processing (OLAP) scenarios. He pointed out that OLAP systems impose different requirements than On-line Transactional Processing (OLTP) systems, and therefore, different data models and implementation methods are required for each type of system. There have been several different multidimensional data models proposed recently. However, there are certain key issues in multidimensional modelling, such as derived measures, derived dimension attributes and the additivity on fact attributes along dimensions, that are not considered by these proposals. He presented the GOLD model, an Object Oriented (OO) multidimensional model in which all the above-mentioned issues are taken into consideration. Since the GOLD model is based on the OO paradigm, data functionality and behaviour are easily considered, which allows one to encapsulate data and its operations (especially useful when referring to OLAP operations). The GOLD model, therefore, takes advantage of some OO issues such as inheritance and polymorphism and allobs one to build complex multidimensional models. Finally, another main advantage of the GOLD model is that it is supported by an OO formal specification language (GOLD Definition Language, GDL) that allows one to define multidimensional conceptual schemes. More concretely, this GDL is an extension of the OASIS formal specification language (developed in the Technical University of Valencia, Spain) to capture more precisely the features linked to multidimensional databases. In this way, the requirements of the multidimensional conceptual schema can be validated, which allows one to check whether the system properties captured in the specification are correctly defined or not. Awais Rashid proposed a novel hybrid technique for impact analysis in complex object database schemata. He argued that like most database applications, object databases are subject to evolution. Evolution, however, is critical in OO databases since it is the very characteristic of complex applications for which they provide inherent support. These applications not only require dynamic modifications to the data residing within the database but also dynamic modifications to the way the data has been modelled (i.e. both the objects residing within the database and the schema of the database are subject to change). Furthermore, there is a requirement to keep track of the change in case it needs to be reverted. Object database schemata designed to fulfil the above set of requirements can become very large and complex. The large amount of information and complex relationships between the various entities in these schemata combine to make the process of assessing the effect of change expensive, time consuming and error-prone. However, without proper assessment, it is impossible for developers and maintainers to fully appreciate the extent and complexity of proposed changes. For maintainers this makes cost estimation, resource allocation and change feasibility study impractical. For developers, a lack of adequate impact analysis can lead to difficulties in ensuring that all affected entities are updated for each change to the conceptual structure of the database. Impact analysis has been employed to determine the extent and complexity of proposed changes during the various stages of the software life cycle. Although many of these techniques have been suggested for analysing the impact of changes to OO design and code level artefacts, inherent deficiencies in such methods render them unsuitable for performing change impact analysis in an object database schema. The hybrid technique Awais presented combined traditional impact analysis approaches with experience based capabilities in order to support change impact analysis in complex object database schemata. Isabella Merlo was of the view that object database systems (both the pure object oriented systems and the object-relational ones) are the systems that in the next few years will replace conventional relational databases systems, or even older generations systems (such as the hierarchical and the network ones). She pointed out that although many approaches have been proposed in the past to extend object database systems with innovative features and interesting results have been achieved, there is a lack of uniformity and standardization across those approaches. In her opinion one of the reasons is that, the standard for object-oriented databases, ODMG, is recent and not well-established. However, ODMG provides the basis for extending object-oriented databases with new capabilities. Among them, the introduction of temporal and active capabilities in ODMG is an important issue that research in the database area has to address. Her research has introduced temporal and active features in the ODMG standard. The introduction of time and active rules was addressed separately. In future she intends to investigate problems related to their integration in the same model. Marlon Dumas also discussed data models and languages for temporal OO database management systems. He indicated that research in this area has been prolific regarding temporal extension proposals to data models and languages. Whereas in the relational framework these works have led to the consensus language TSQL2, and two proposals to the SQL3 standardization committee, equivalent results are missing in the object-oriented framework. Early attempts to define temporal object data models failed to become widely accepted due to the absence of a standard underlying data model. As the ODMG proposal was released and adopted by the major object database vendors, several temporal extensions of it were defined. Marlon pointed out that these neglect at least some of the following important aspects:

1. migration support, as to ensure a smooth transition of applications running on top of a non-temporal system to a temporal extension of it
2. representation-independent operators for manipulating temporal data, as to exploit the abstraction principle of object-orientation
3. formal semantics

One of the main goals of his work is to propose a general framework for designing DBMS temporal extensions integrating the above features, and to apply it to the ODMG. The design and formalization of the main components of this framework are almost finished, leading to a temporal database model named TEMPOS. In addition to providing temporal extensions of ODMG's object model, schema definition and query languages, TEMPOS includes a language for describing patterns of histories. The feasibility of the proposal was validated through a prototype implementation on top of the O2 DBMS, which has been used to experiment on applications from various contexts. Radovan Chytracek discussed the great importance of database systems in any HEP (High Energy Physics) experiment. HEP community in LHC (Large Hadron Collider) era is in transition from FORTRAN to C++ and from data streams to persistent objects. Together with that a new data management will be necessary, which would allow transition from "files and tapes" approach towards the access to data in the form of objects by selection of their required physics contents. Data volumes of the LHC experiments are expected in the PB (1015 bytes) order of magnitude and this fact makes the job much harder to do. In order to conform to the object-oriented paradigm, LHCb (Large Hadron Collider Beauty; precision measurements of CP-Violation and rare decays) had to heavily investigate the design and development of object databases for both the on-line (data acquisition and real-time processing) and off-line (simulation, reconstruction and analysis) computing environments, e.g. the Event Store, Detector Description Database (DDDB), Calibration and Alignment Database etc. For that purpose the Gaudi framework at LHCb experiment is being developed to cover all stages of physics data processing. The design choices taken at the time of creating the Gaudi architecture take into account specifics of physicists work in order to provide access to object persistency technologies in a transparent way and proper data abstractions to make the physics data handling natural to physicists. Very important part of the framework is DDDB, which holds data describing detector apparatus structure and environment.

2.2. Languages, Software Engineering, and Artificial Intelligence

The languages, software engineering and artificial intelligence stream included contributions from Stefan Chiettini, Moritz Schnizler, John Flackett and Cristian Sminchisescu. Stefan Chiettini opened the session by proposing a technique for the documentation of object interaction. He described how the documentation of object-oriented systems usually consists of two parts: First there is the static part with the description of classes and methods. This part usually contains information about interfaces, inheritance relations and aggregations. The second part, which was the topic of his presentation, describes the dynamic behaviour of the system in a certain situation at run time. Common design and documentation techniques like OMT or UML introduce event trace diagrams (OMT) and sequence diagrams (UML) to visualize run time behaviour of interacting objects. These diagrams show the message sequence in a certain situation at run time. Their major weakness is that they are themselves static and therefore capable of illustrating only one special case, typically called a 'scenario', not the general behaviour of objects. Stefan proposed behaviour diagrams as an extension of existing diagrams to meet the requirements of modern documentation: structured documents with hypertext and multimedia capabilities extended with the possibility to interactively explore the documentation. Behaviour diagrams enable the user to describe general situations in object-oriented systems like conditional message sequences or dynamically bound method calls. Moritz Schnizler followed with his work on a testing approach for program families. Today a popular (because cost efficient) software development approach is the deployment of program families, sometimes called product lines. A program family evolves over time from a successful program. Its main characteristic is that its members have many properties in common, especially their functionality, so object-oriented framework technology is well suited for their implementation. In practice, efficient testing of a program family member remains a problem, often meaning that new tests have to be developed for every single program. The aim of Moritz's work is to develop a more efficient process for testing them. The model for his approach is test benches from other engineering disciplines, e.g. when a car engine is developed. The principle idea is to transfer this approach to the area of software development with object-oriented frameworks. The main problem of this approach is the lack of approved testing methods for object-oriented software. Most testing techniques have their roots in imperative programming and are of little help in testing the interaction of collaborating classes which are a characteristic of object-oriented software. Moritz is investigating the possibility of testing the correct collaboration of classes in the context of frameworks, so that test cases for collaborating classes are developed from the originally intended behaviour for their collaboration. An example for such a testable collaboration is the MVC pattern where, for example, a test case is a state change to the model object requiring appropriate updates from its observing view objects. Based on this, built-in tests are included in the framework that automatically test the correct implementation and use of such pre-implemented collaborations. The final goal is to have built-in tests for all characteristic collaborations that comprise the functionality of a framework. So, using this built-in testing infrastructure, a developer can easily retest the framework's core functionality, when he adapts or extends it, in the context of a new program. For the classes under test that means they need to be more testable, implementing a special test interface that contains, for example, additional inspection methods. John Flackett continued this session with a description of his ConnECT (Connectionist/Symbolic Engine for High-Level Cognitive Tasks) system. ConnECT is concerned with the development of an object-oriented software tool which brings about a synergy of existing knowledge representation techniques, the focus of which is to model an aspect of Natural Language Processing (NLP) by automating text indexing and retrieval. ConnECT exploits object-oriented programming techniques in order to provide a flexible and robust architecture within which to model encapsulated matrices and their operations. Fundamentally, the system is controlled through the use of an envelope class, which in turn utilises object parameter passing as the means for synergising the distinct modular processes. An underlying data class forms the knowledge base upon which extraction operations operate to provide the built in intelligence required for the high level cognitive task proposed. The implementation differs from that of normal object parameter passing, as part of a variable aggregation, in as much as the data object being passed does not simply provide an extension to the receiving objects attributes, rather, it encapsulates all of the required attributes. Concluding this session with a language related presentation, Cristian Sminchisescu described his object-oriented approach to C++ compiler technology. Compilers of language translators front-ends comprise traditionally well-delimited stages like lexical, syntactical, and semantic analysis. Traditional compiler architecture is based on the separate design and implementation of these stages, using tools such as LEX and YACC. Although many text books for compiler design, formal languages, and parsing exist, there are few detailed descriptions regarding the design and implementation of a complete language processor for a complex language like C++. In particular, the C++ language has an inherently ambiguous grammar. This implies that no direct grammar transformation can transform its grammar into a nonambiguous one. Consequently, the traditional lexical-syntactic analysis pipeline will not be effective if one desires to implement the two stages in a modular, decoupled fashion. Most existing C++ compilers (such as the GNU g++ compiler for example) couple the two stages intimately by letting them share and modify complex data structures. The resulting product is monolithic and hard to understand and to maintain from a developer's perspective. Cristian has addressed the above problem by introducing a new, separate stage between the usual lexical and syntactical stages. The stage, called LALEX (lookahead LEX) takes over the C++ context dependency by special processing and introduction of disambiguation tokens. The resulting program pipeline can be built using tools such as LEX and YACC, is modular, and is simple to understand and maintain. Furthermore, the usage of OO techniques in the semantic analysis stage design is made possible by the simplification of its structure due to the LALEX stage. Inside this stage, a C++ program is represented as an (OO) abstract syntax graph whose nodes are classes that model the C++ language semantic constructs. The leaf subclasses of this hierarchy map to the C++ language terminals. The other nodes map to C++ syntactic, C++ semantic, or intermediate 'door' constructs. Modelling the parsed language's constructs as an OO type hierarchy has several advantages. First, semantic rules for constructs can be written as specific class methods. Second, the semantic stage's control mechanism can be written independently of the actual language being parsed, as a generic control algorithm that uses the Visitor design pattern on the syntax graph. Finally, the OO approach to C++ compiler construction has proven efficient in the implementation of the ambiguity resolution mechanisms needed for C++. The interface between the special LALEX stage and the usual parser is kept as simple as possible. LALEX is actually called back by the YACC-style parser to provide tokens. These are provided in a nonambiguous manner by calling back on the classic LEX stage and by using the disambiguation information provided by a specially maintained symbol table. In contrast to other compiler implementations, this symbol table is encapsulated in the LALEX stage and thus differs from the full-scale symbol table used by the parser stage. The above distinction helps for a clear design and implementation of the C++ compiler.

2.3. Components and Generative Programming

The components session was begun by Anthony Lauder, who introduced 'event ports'. Explicit invocation across collaborating components in component-based systems leads to tight component coupling. This diminishes component maintainability, flexibility, and reusability. The implicit invocation model, wherein components register their message interests with a broker, de-couples components and hence reduces inter-component dependencies. This, however, may ignore the historically determined nature of the flow of component message interests. This leads to implementations of message receipt functions polluted with guard code that rejects out-of-sequence messages in order to enforce components' time-ordered protocols. Statecharts, however, are ideally suited to expressing such protocols. By combining statecharts with implicit invocation, direct realization of time-ordered component protocols is achieved without code pollution, offering the potential for a cleaner, more adaptable component collaboration strategy. Anthony presented the development of 'event ports', which reflect this combination and encapsulate a promising new component model. Andreas Speck presented his OO real time (component based) control system. He explained how the rapid evolution of standard hardware such as workstations and PCs has made it possible to develop standard hardware-based universal control systems. Currently the traditional proprietary device-specific controller systems (e.g. robot controls, numeric controls) are ported to this new standard hardware. However, such control systems are still proprietary and device dependent. Andreas posed the question, how can we now build universal and flexible control systems? He has evaluated three approaches that are based on each other: an object-oriented architecture that may be used as an architectural pattern, a conventional object-oriented framework and a component-based framework. In contrast to the today's available control systems all these approaches are much more flexible and can be used to implement different control functionalities. The pattern provides no semi-finished code. However it is very useful when the universal control system should be realized on non standard platforms (e.g. industrial PCs with special real-time operating systems). Both framework approaches (conventional and component-based) already contain reusable base-code which may by adjusted to the user's needs (e.g. to the required control functionality and desired standard platform). Compared with the conventional framework the component framework is more flexible since it is not restricted to predefined flexible hot spots. The free exchange of components leads to a highly flexible system. Moreover the development of a component-based framework needs no specific existing architecture - generic architectural guidance is enough. Ian Oliver argued that animation has been shown to be a useful tool for the validation of the behavioural properties of a model. Animation can be thought of as the 'halfway' house between the specification and the final executable code, relying on some form of execution of the specification. He then discussed how the Object Constraint Language (part of the Unified Modelling Language) may be executed in some sense to provide the basis of an animation environment for OO modelling. Ian's work is based around formulating a mapping between OCL statements and a sequence of atomic operations that perform some form of basic modification to the UML object-diagram. The concepts he is interested in are the class, link and attribute value and so he has defined five operations: modify (value), create/delete (object) and link/unlink (links) that can be employed to modify these components on the diagram. The various presentations were folloby, by a keynote speech from Professor Ulrich Eisenecker who presented a detailed view of components and generative programming. He discussed how most software-engineering methods focus on singlesystem engineering. This also applies to object-oriented methods. In particular, developing for and with reuse are neither explicit activities nor are they adequately supported. Furthermore, there is no explicit domain scoping, which would delineate the domain based on the set of existing and possible systems. Current methods also fail to differentiate between intra-application and inter-application variability. In particular, inter-application variability is often implemented using dynamic variability mechanisms, even if static ones would be more efficient. Analysis and design patterns, frameworks, and components struggle for improving reuse and adaptability, but do not provide a complete solution. For example, despite the fact that frameworks are created in several iterations, there is still a high chance that they contain unnecessary variation points, while important ones are missing. He argued that Domain Engineering overcomes the deficiencies of single-system engineering. It includes a domain scoping activity based on market studies and stakeholder analysis. Analysing commonalities, variabilities, and dependencies lies at the heart of domain engineering. The results of domain engineering (i.e. engineering for reuse) are reusable assets in the form of models, languages, documents, generators, and implementation components. These results represent the input to application engineering (i.e. engineering with reuse). An extremely useful means for capturing features and variation points are feature diagrams, which were originally introduced by the FODA method (Feature-Oriented Domain Analysis). They are augmented by additional information including short descriptions of features, dependencies, rationales for features, default values, etc. Two kinds of languages are then derived from feature models, namely domain specific configuration languages and implementation components configuration languages. The former is used to describe the requirements for a specific system from an application-oriented point of view. The latter is used to describe the implementations of systems in terms of composing components. Configuration knowledge is used to map from requirements specifications to configurations of implementation components. Manual coding of implementation configurations for a large number of variants is a tedious and error prone process. Therefore, generative programming introduces configuration generators translating requirements specifications into optimised configurations of implementation components. An adequate support for implementing such generators requires the ability to define domain-specific languages and representations (e.g. graphical representations), domain-specific optimisations, type systems, and error detection. Furthermore, it is important to be able to implement domain-specific debugging and editing facilities for entering, manipulating, and rendering program representations, as well as domain-specific testing and profiling facilities. A library of domain abstractions, which also contains code extending a programming environment in the above-mentioned areas, is referred to as an active library.

2.4. Analysis and Design

The analysis and design session covered a wide range of subjects and included contributions from Akos Frohner, Glenn Lewis, Christoph Steindl and Fabio Kon. A keynote speech was also delivered by Professor Ian Sommerville. Akos Frohner began by describing layered design visualisation. Designing an object-oriented system is a process that is well supported by a great number of notations and design techniques such as UML. Although UML provides notation for almost all aspects of object-oriented software design, it lacks features for describing aspects that are outside of the design domain or require information from different diagrams. For example, there are no good notations for the visualisation of frameworks, friendship relationships, components, meta-level aspects or security considerations. As a possible solution Akos proposes to use dynamic multi-layer diagrams, in addition to passive, paper oriented diagrams. Such diagrams allob the user of an object-oriented CASE tool to concentrate on the specific feature that she or he is interested in, and filter out the remaining parts. The basic idea is to place related elements of a diagram on to one layer and stack these layers up. If all the layers are used, the final diagram will contain all details, but one may hide any unnecessary layers to focus on a small and comprehensible subset of the components. In an active CASE tool layers can be locked to disable the modification of some elements. Akos also explained the task of framework documentation, showing only the skeleton of a hot-spot, and letting the user add more details by uncovering hidden layers. One may also extend the hot-spot in place on a new layer without modifying the original diagram. Akos gave further examples using the layered structure to support the design of complex systems and their three-dimensional visualisation. The layering technique adds some new notational features to the existing possibilities of UML, but the main impact is on the design work itself. Using layers to associate elements allows users to express their own way of thinking above the logical structure of the model (i.e. package boundaries). Akos' work is part of an ongoing research to use non object-oriented features in the design of large programs, including the storage and visualisation of such information. This presentation was followed by Glenn Lewis, describing a practical approach to behavioural inheritance in the context of coloured Petri Nets. Inheritance means one can begin with an abstract representation of an object that is easy to understand and clutter-free, and incrementally change that to a more concrete representation. In other words, inheritance provides support for abstraction, which is the most common and effective technique for dealing with complexity. The principle of substitutability has been proposed in various forms to give the expectations that an incrementally changed component should comply with if it is to be substituted for a component. One possibility, which is known as weak substitutability, relates to the compatibility of method parameter and result types - it does not require behavioural compatibility. Many consider that weak substitutability is not enough: substitution may still lead to incorrect behaviour even if the weak substitutability principle is satisfied. Another version of the substitutability principle, referred to as strong substitutability, requires behavioural compatibility between the type and subtype. There are a number of proposals for substitutability in the context of concurrent object-oriented systems, but it is unclear whether these proposals are overly constrained for practical application. Glenn presented a discussion of substitutability, and in the context of coloured petri nets he presented a set of three incremental modifications which lie somewhere between weak and strong substitutability. The constraints that he imposes can be checked statically and they have the property that if the refinement is at least as live as the abstraction, then strong substitutability holds (this property cannot be checked statically.) The incremental changes are presented informally. Formal definitions of the proposed increment changes can be found elsewhere, as can an examination of case studies in the literature that suggests the above forms of incremental change are applicable in practice. Christoph Steindl followed with a presentation of static analysis of object-oriented programs, specifically describing his work on program slicing in Oberon. Static analysis derives information by inspection of the source code, and this information must be valid for all possible executions of the program. Conservative assumptions must be taken if the program uses conditional branches and iteration since it is not known at compile time which branches will be taken at run time and how many iterations there will be. Static information is necessarily less precise than dynamic information (obtained by monitoring one specific execution of a program) but it can be computed once for all possible executions, whereas dynamic information must be computed again and again. Two main concepts of object-oriented programming are polymorphism and dynamic binding. These dynamic aspects are difficult to integrate into static analysis, e.g. in most cases the exact destination of polymorphic call sites cannot be determined by static analysis. Additionally, data flow analysis for heap allocated objects is difficult. Since the number of objects is unbounded, they cannot be handled individually. If they are classified into groups, then all objects of a group are aliases for the data flow analysis. Christoph has developed a program slicer that models dynamic aspects of object-oriented programs correctly . Starting from conservative assumptions about dynamic binding and aliases, new user guidance techniques are used to reduce these assumptions. In this way, static analysis can be enriched with user-supplied knowledge to yield information with a precision similar to dynamic information. Fabio Kon presented a framework for dynamically configurable multimedia distribution. Multimedia applications and interfaces will radically change how computer systems will look in the future. Radio and TV broadcasting will assume a digital format and their distribution networks will be integrated with the Internet. Existing hardware and software infrastructures, however, are unable to provide all the scalability and quality of service that these applications require. In previous work, Fabio has developed a framework for building scalable and flexible multimedia distribution systems that greatly improves the possibilities for the provision of quality of service in large-scale, wide-area networks. This framework was successfully deployed in different situations including the live broadcast of a long-term, live audiovisual stream to more than one million clients in dozens of countries across the globe. In his presentation, he identified some significant problems that limited the usability of the previous framework. He proposed mechanisms for attacking these problems and described how he was using mobile configuration agents and a CORBA-based framework for providing efficient code distribution , dynamic reconfiguration, and fault-tolerance to the multimedia distribution framework. The work is based on the infrastructure for dynamic configuration and management of inter-component dependence provided by the 2K Distributed Operating System. 2K is a component-based system that uses a dynamically configurable CORBA communication layer to support on-the-fly adaptation of component-based applications. In his keynote speech Professor Ian Sommerville discussed integration of social and OO analysis. Most methods of analysis focus on technical aspects of the system to be developed and provide little or no support for understanding human, social and organisational factors that may influence the design of a system. While techniques such as use-cases represent an important recognition of the importance of people, there is still the key issue of determining where use-cases come from , what are critical use-cases, etc. His talk presented an overview of a method called Coherence that has been specifically designed to support social analysis of a work setting and to represent this analysis in UML. The motivation for this work was a conviction of the importance of social analysis and the need to take this to the software engineering community in terms that they could understand. The outcome of the social analysis is a set of use-cases that can then be the starting point for more detailed object-oriented analysis.

2.5. Frameworks and Patterns

Nathalie Gaertner, Alexandru Telea, Markus Hof and Aimar Marie led the discussion in this session. Nathalie Gaertner presented her experiences with working with business patterns and frameworks. She defined frameworks as generic applications, described by a set of abstract classes and the way instances of their subclasses collaborate. She pointed out that although frameworks allow a rapid development of new applications through customisation there are two main problems. First, designing a framework is a highly complex , time-consuming work and secondly, understanding the overall architecture and how to use it is difficult. She argued that one way to improve this situation is to include business and design patterns in the framework's architecture since each pattern provides a concise and useful architectural guidance to a related problem. Moreover, the reuse of patterns in software development allobs the integration of flexible modular adaptable well-engineered solutions at a higher level than classes . Business patterns are domain-specific patterns. Integrating these patterns into frameworks - both related to the same business - makes it possible to exploit the generic architecture of frameworks along with the high level abstractions , business knowledge and documentation of the patterns. Nathalie presented a fuzzy logic control framework as an example to demonstrate the synergetic approaches of business patterns and frameworks. Alexandru Telea described the VISSION Simulation System which combines OO and dataflow modelling. He discussed that scientific visualisation and simulation (SimVis) is mostly addressed by frameworks using data and event flow mechanisms for simulation specification, control, and interactivity. Even though OO powerfully and elegantly models many application domains, integration of existing SimVis OO libraries in such systems remains a difficult task. The elegance and simplicity of the OO design usually gets lost in the integration phase, as most systems do not support the combination of OO and dataflow concepts. Practically no SimVis system addresses the needs of its component developers, application designers, and end users in a uniform manner. His proposed solution, VISSION, is a general-purpose visualisation and simulation OO system which merges OO and dataflow modelling in a single abstraction. This abstraction, called a metaclass, extends non- intrusively a C++ class with dataflow notions such as data inputs, outputs, and update operation, to promote it to a higher, more reusable level . VISSION uses a C++ interpreter to execute glue code that connects the metaclasses representing the system's components. Components can be loaded, instantiated and connected dynamically without recompiling or relinking VISSION. The needs of the three user groups mentioned above are addressed extensively and uniformly. Component designers get the full power of C++ to design new components or reuse existing C++ class libraries without having to change them. Application designers get a graphics user interface (GUI) in which component iconic representations can be assembled to build the desired SimVis application as a dataflow network. End users can easily steer a running simulation by the GUIs that VISSION automatically constructs for each component, or by typing C or C++ code that is interpreted dynamically . Alex also presented screenshots of several simulations and visualisations successfully constructed in VISSION.

Markus Hof presented a framework for arbitrary invocation semantics. He first discussed how most object-oriented languages for distributed programming offer either one fixed invocation semantic (synchronous procedure call), or a limited number of invocation semantics. At best, they support a default mode of synchronous remote invocation, plus some keywords to express asynchronous messaging. The very few approaches that offer rich libraries of invocation abstractions usually introduce significant overhead and do not handle the composition of those abstractions. He then described an approach for abstracting remote invocations. Invocation semantics, such as synchronous, asynchronous, transactional, or replicated are all considered first class abstractions. Using a combination of the Strategy and Decorator design patterns, he suggested an effective way to compose various invocation semantics. This technique allobs different semantics on different objects of the same class. It is even possible to have several different views of one and the same object simultaneously. To reduce the overhead induced by the flexibility of the approach, just-in-time stub generation techniques are used. With the help of the semantic information supplied by the programmer, the necessary stub and skeleton code pieces are generated only on demand. This allows for late optimisations and adaptations. The work distinguished between two kinds of invocation abstractions . First, actual abstractions responsible for the execution of the method (synchronous, asynchronous, delayed, etc), and second, invocation filters that decorate an abstraction or other filters (at-most-once, transactional, logging, etc). Aimar Marie 's discussion focused on problems linked to the design of medical diagnostic systems. She pointed out that nowadays, computer-aided systems cannot be black boxes which contain a monolithic process. Systems must contain all components useful to store information, to search for a specific disease, to consult validated clinical tables and to compare the results for several diseases. This suggests the production of strongly inter-connected process modules, sharing a common database of information. Sharing information is possible when the knowledge base is structured regardless of the treatment used. She has adopted an object-oriented architecture to design the knowledge base and a generic model of collaboration between several treatment modules. In this context, she has tested how the use of patterns can help develop such a model and to improve the design of the system. In her opinion the different problems to solve are: to model in the same way pathologies which have heterogeneous signs, to identify generic behaviour into the various procedures of treatment and to design an interface for these procedures to guarantee the communication through the system. She has added to the object model, four patterns which give a solution to these problems. The pattern Composite keeps hidden the complexity of signs and allows treating all of them as simple sign. The pattern Iterator is used to define the generic task common to all diagnostic procedures to access the description elements and give them to a specific diagnostic engine. The pattern State saves the information of "presence" or "absence" of signs without taking into account which treatment is done, numerical calculus, symbolic evaluation and so on. Finally, the pattern Strategy defines a class of reasoning method, all diagnostic procedures are design to respect this interface. The four patterns define four strategic points of the diagnostic system architecture which are not given by the semantic analysis of the domain.

2.6. Aspect Oriented Programming

Gregor Kiczales gave a talk on aspect-oriented programming and the AspectJ tool, an aspect-oriented extension to Java. Using the SpaceWar Game as an example, he explained how 'cross cutting concerns' can appear across other modularised components of a system. For example, issues of game 'look and feel' can be spread amongst many otherwise loosely coupled classes. Given that such cross cutting concerns are inevitable, and that they cause tangled code and difficulties in maintenance, we can usefully modularise them into 'aspects '. An aspect encapsulates a cross cutting concern, 'introducing' fields and methods to classes and 'advising' (extending) existing processes . Gregor went on to describe how aspect orientation is at a stage where empirical testing is required along with theoretical and practical developments analysis to prove its validity and usefulness. Building a user community is essential to researching this approach and showing what results it can produce. Specific issues for research include software engineering (finding aspects, process, program modularity), language design (support for both static and dynamic cross-cuts), tools (programming environments, aspect discovery, refactoring) and theory (language and program semantics, cross-cutting). Gregor concluded his talk with a question and answer session, describing various characteristics of syntax and comparing his work with other approaches such as subject oriented programming.

2.7. Distribution and Middleware

In this session presentations were made by Fabio Costa and Christoph Peter. Fabio Costa talked about middleware platforms, an effective answer to the requirements of open distributed processing. However, in his opinion existing middleware standards do not fulfil important requirements of new application areas like multimedia and mobile computing, which require dynamic adaptability of the underlying platform. He was of the view that such requirements can be met by the adoption of an open engineering approach, based on computational reflection. Reflection offers a principled way to open up both the structure and the behaviour of a system by providing a causally connected self-representation of its implementation, and allobing its inspection and manipulation. He presented his ongoing research on the design and implementation of a reflective architecture for multimedia middleware, which allows the run-time reconfiguration of the components and services of the platform . The design is based on a multi-model reflection framework, whereby the different aspects in the engineering of the platform are identified and each one is represented by a distinct and orthogonal meta-model. There are currently four such meta-models:

- encapsulation (exposes the constitution of interfaces)
- composition (represents the configuration of compound components)
- environment (exposes the mechanisms for message handling at interfaces boundaries)
- resource management (represents the reservation and allocation of resources)

At run-time, meta-objects of any of these meta-models can be created and assigned to individual components of the platform. This makes explicit the corresponding aspect and allows the programmer or some controlling mechanism to dynamically reconfigure the internals of the platform. Christoph Peter argued that languages like C++ and Java have shown that strong, static typing is a good basis for programming. In distributed environments, there are well known calculi like the ss-calculus or Vasconcelos' TyCO. Static type systems for these calculi also exist. But their expressiveness is limited, as none of them can express the sequencing of messages which is an important part of the behaviour of objects. He suggested use of (Static) Process Types, based on a concept which allows to express the sequencing of messages in the type information. This is done by providing changeable state information in the types. When a message is sent, information about the state change of the message's receiver is provided by the type. The sender of the message can update its information about the state of the receiver. His presentation concentrated on applications of the process type concept:

- Examine a matching relationship for process types: Process types provide the subtyping relationship and genericity for re-use. But binary methods can be re-used only with a higher-order subtyping mechanism like matching.
- Using process types for deadlock detection: With asynchronous message passing, an object is blocked while waiting for an answer (message) from another object. If there are cycles of blocking objects, a deadlock occurs. An extension of process types allows to express that a request shall imply an answer. This property can be guaranteed statically and therefore, an important reason for deadlocks can be detected.
- Integrate process types into CORBA: The IDL of CORBA provides little information about the behaviour of an object. A goal of Christoph's research is to examine what possibilities of process types may be used to enhance the interface information but still provide static type checking.

3. Workshop Discussions

Three questions of key interest to the workshop participants were identified during the various sessions. These were as follobs:

- OODBMS: Industrial failure or next generation technology?
- Using meta-information
- New approaches in object orientation - Where will we be tomorrow?

The above questions were discussed by the interested participants who arrived at the follobing conclusions.

3.1. OODBMS: Industrial Failure or Next Generation Technology?

Discussion Participants: Radovan Chytracek, Marlon Dumas, Anthony Lauder, Awais Rashid, Juan Trujillo

Object-oriented programming languages, systems, and methodologies have experienced tremendous industrial success. Object-Oriented Database Management Systems (OODBMS), however, are lagging far behind relational DBMSs in at least three dimensions: market penetration, sales revenue, and consumer awareness. The purpose of the discussion was to elucidate some of the reasons behind this apparent "industrial failure" and to draw some possible conclusions on the subject . In the discussion, participants considered OODBMS to be those which provide classical DBMS services (persistence, transactions , concurrency, etc), under a data model supporting the basic concepts of currently used object-oriented languages (e .g. Java, C++). In particular, Versant, ObjectStore, O2 and Jasmine are considered to be OODBMS while Oracle v8 is not, since it supports neither inheritance nor encapsulation. Some of the OODBMS suppliers (e.g. ObjectStore and Jasmine) are not actually experiencing any commercial or industrial failure (in a financial sense). Nevertheless their visibility and market penetration remain limited. As a result, their long-term prospects are not very clear. Other OODBMS suppliers are currently experiencing severe financial and/or commercial problems. OODBMS suppliers emphasize object-orientedness, and its benefits over the relational paradigm. Typical claimed benefits include reduction of the impedance mismatch between the programming languages and the DBMS, performance advantages (due to navigation from roots and sophisticated caching and swizzling technologies), and transparent support for complex user-defined types. This latter feature has actually enabled OODBMSs to make major in-roads in some niche markets around specialized fields needing complex data such as computer-aided design and computer-aided software engineering. On the other hand, RDBMS suppliers emphasize scalability, reliability, security, and other hard-won DBMS features that are currently (arguably) missing in OODBMS. As a result, RDBMSs have gained (and continue to gain) massive penetration into almost all markets. Furthermore, RDBMS are currently trying to integrate some OO features into their products. Although this will not transform them into fully-fledged OODBMS, it will reduce to some extent their limits regarding complex data management. From these observations we may say that OODBMSs, in contrast to RDBMSs, are a relative failure (compared to early promises in terms of market penetration). There are two viewpoints with respect to what the future may bring. The "optimistic" one states that OODBMS are simply "hibernating", and that their time will come. The contrasting view is that, in the future, a major shakeout will occur, eliminating all but a few OODBMS suppliers addressing small niche markets , with no major penetration ever occurring. Below we enumerate some of reasons underlying the current industrial failure of ODBMSs, and it is, we believe, the way in which these issues are addressed by ODBMS vendor that will determine their future prospects:

- There are many OODBMS suppliers, whereas the RBDMS marketplace has undergone waves of mergers, buyouts, and bankruptcies, leaving a small number of players. This leaves potential buyers of ODBMSs with the uneasy feeling that a similar future shakeout could eliminate any supplier they committed to now.
- Despite the existence of an OMG-sanctioned supposed standard, detailed studies have revealed many inconsistencies within it, and each of the OODBMS companies has followed their own charter leading to portability problems across products.
- Strong OODBMS research in academic labs has had limited commercial pickup, so that OODBMS vendors are having to resolve fundamentally difficult issues on very tight budgets with limited resources.
- OODBMSs lack important features required by industry: e.g. performance with large amounts of data (this is a contentious issue), security, and scalability.

- RDBMSs have proven their reliability though hard-won debugging in the field over many years. OODBMSs have not yet gone through this, leading to uncertainty over their reliability.
- Users are already committed to an RDBMS, with their own layers to resolve impedance mismatches, with mountains of application code, and with staff highly trained and experienced in RDBMS technology.
- It is not clear to what extent the touted advantages of OODBMSs are needed for mainstream applications.

3.2. Using Meta-information

Discussion Participants: Stefan Chiettini, Akos Frohner, Markus Hof, Christoph Steindl, Alexandru Telea.

In the past, systems have been monolithic and static. In the future, systems will be modular and dynamic. The use of meta-information helps to perform this evolutionary step or is an enabling technology for it. When we look at the historical development of programming languages, we see a continuing rise of the level of abstraction of machine details: from machine instructions, via assembly languages and higher programming languages to structured and object-oriented languages. The next step in this development is platform independence. Combined with network transparency, it allobs writing programs that can run on any computer in a networked environment. The composition of new software out of existing components is another promising application area: The programmer composes programs in a visual programming environment by sticking components together or glues them together using scripting languages. The components shall then cooperate, which they only can do if they have some knowledge about each other: their interfaces, properties, facilities and so on. Meta-information seems to be the bridge between abstraction on one hand and knowledge about each other on the other hand. Meta-information makes some knowledge explicit that was previously only implicit. It is also a means to make information available at run time that was usually only available at compile time. Meta-information is also the key to systems that are really extensible where only the required components are active at a time and where additional functionality can be added on demand. Meta-programming can exploit meta-information to several degrees. It can use metainformation to:

- observe and manipulate itself and other running programs (introspection).
- explicitly call functionality that is normally hidden in the run-time system, e.g. creation of new objects, dynamic loading, linking, and unloading of components (interception).
- change the behaviour of language primitives at run time, e.g. object creation and destruction, method dispatch, and access to simple attributes (invocation) The participants agreed that it will be crucial for every computing system and especially programming language to offer a standardized access to meta-information. Many do so already (Lisp, Smalltalk, CLOS, Beta,

Oberon-2, Java), and the implications and principles are apparently well understood. However, in the participants' view it is vital that this access is efficient in memory usage as well as in its run-time behaviour. They saw a wide field for further research and projects in this area: retrieving meta-information from legacy systems in an automatic or semiautomatic way; extending popular languages to handle meta-information; creating visual environments to support various aspects of this field.

3.3. New Approaches in Object Orientation - Where Will We Be Tomorrow?

Discussion Participants: Andreas Speck, Fabio Kon, Ian Oliver, Aimar Marie, Moritz Schnizler, John Flackett, Martin Geier (Guest Participant)

Currently new trends in object-orientation are rising such as aspect-oriented programming (introduced by G. Kiczales' and C. Lopes' group at Xerox PARC), the component generators (U. Eisenecker, K. Czarnecki and D. Batory's work), component-based approaches (C. Szyperski), intentional programming (C. Simonyi) and adaptive programming (K. Lieberherr). The states of these approaches are quite different. While components are already in use and supported by many commercial systems (e.g. CORBA implementations, COM or Java Beans) others are still in evaluation. This great variety of approaches leads to many questions: What is their impact in the future? Do they bear interesting research challenges? Which of them will supersede in the future? Within the PhDOOS community many PhD candidates are doing research in this area. Special crucial points are aspect-oriented programming (especially in connection with object distribution), reflective architectures, component generators, component-based software development including the development of generic architectures for component-based frameworks, and dependence management in component-based distributed systems, dynamically configurable middleware systems as well as secure ports for inter-component communication.

Acknowledgements

We gratefully acknowledge the financial support of AITO and Object Technology International Inc. This support made possible the presentce of many participations at the workshop, as well as the initiative to produce separate workshop proceedings containing the full versions of the presented papers.

Participants List

1. Stefan Chiettini, Institut für Praktische Informatik, Johannes Kepler University Linz, A-4040 Linz, Austria, email: `stefan.chiettini@ssw.uni-linz.ac.at`
2. Radovan Chytracek, CERN, Geneva, Switzerland,
email: `Radovan.Chytracek@cern.ch`
3. Fabio Costa, Computing Department, Lancaster University, Lancaster LA1 4YR,

UK, email: fmc@comp.lancs.ac.uk
4. Marlon Dumas, LSR-IMAG Lab, University of Grenoble, France, email: Marlon.Dumas@imag.fr
5. John C. Flackett, Systems Engineering Faculty, Southampton Institute, East Park Terrace, Southampton, SO14 0YN, UK, email: John.Flackett@solent.ac.uk
6.Akos Frohner, Eotvos Lorand University, Institute of Informatics, Budapest, email: Akos.Frohner@elte.hu
7.Nathalie Gaertner, Laboratoire EEA, Groupe LSI, Universite de Haute-Alsace, 12 rue des freres Lumiere, 68093 Mulhouse Cedex, France, email: n.gaertner@ evhr.net
8.Markus Hof, Institut für Praktische Informatik, Johannes Kepler University Linz, A-4040 Linz, Austria, email: hof@ssw.uni-linz.ac.at
9.Fabio Kon, Department of Computer Science, University of Illinois at Urbana Champaign, USA, email: f-kon@uiuc.edu
10. Anthony Lauder, Computing Laboratory, University of Kent at Canterbury, Canterbury, Kent, CT2 7NF, UK, email: Anthony@Lauder.u-net.com
11. Glenn Lewis, Electrical Engineering and Computer Science, University of Tasmania, email: Glenn.Lewis@utas.edu.au
12. Marie Beurton-Aimar, University of Bordeaux, France, email: Marie.Aimar@dim.ubordeaux2.fr
13. Isabella Merlo, Dipartimento di Informatica e Scienze dell'Informazione, University of Genova, Italy, email: merloisa@disi.unige.it
14. Ian Oliver, University of Kent at Canterbury, England, UK, email: ian.oliver@bcs.org.uk
15. David Parsons, The Object People, Epsilon House, Chilworth Science Park, Southampton SO16 7NS, UK, email: davidp@objectpeople.com
16. Christof Peter, Technische Universität Wien, Institut für Computersprachen, Argentinierstrasse 8, A-1040 Vienna, Austria, email: fchristofg@complang.tuwien.ac.at
17. Awais Rashid, Computing Department, Lancaster University, Lancaster LA1 4YR, UK, email: marash@comp.lancs.ac.uk
18. Moritz Schnizler, Aachen University of Technology, Department of Computer Science III, Software Construction Group, Ahornstr. 55, 52074 Aachen, Germany , email: moritz@informatik.rwth-aachen.de
19. Cristian Sminchisescu, Department of Computer Science, Rutgers University, USA, email: crismin@paul.rugers.edu
20. Andreas Speck, Wilhelm-Schickard-Institut für Informatik, Universität Tübingen, 72076 Tuebingen, Germany, email: speck@informatik.uni-tuebingen.de
21. Christoph Steindl, Institut für Praktische Informatik, Johannes Kepler University Linz, A-4040 Linz, Austria, email: steindl@ssw.uni-linz.ac.at
22. Alexandru Telea, Department of Mathematics and Computing Science, Eindhoven University of Technology, Den Dolech 2, 5600 MB Eindhoven, The Netherlands , email: alext@win.tue.nl
23. Juan Trujillo, Research Group of Logic Programming and Information Systems, Dept. of Financial Economics, University of Alicante, E-03071, Alicante, Spain , email: juan.trujillo@ua.es
24. Martin Geier, University of Erlangen/Nuremberg, Germany (guest participant)

Aliasing in Object Oriented Systems

James Noble[1], Jan Vitek[2], Doug Lea[3], and Paulo Sergio Almeida[4]

[1] Microsoft Research Institute, Australia
kjx@mri.mq.edu.au
[2] Université de Genève
Jan.Vitek@cui.unige.ch
[3] State University of New York at Oswego
dl@cs.oswego.edu
[4] Universidade do Minho
psa@homer.di.uminho.pt

Abstract. This chapter contains summaries of the presentations given at the Intercontinental Workshop on Aliasing in Object-Oriented Systems (IWAOOS'99) at the European Conference on Object-Oriented Programming (ECOOP'99) which was held in Lisbon, Portugal on June 15, 1999.

1. Introduction

Aliasing is endemic in object oriented programming. Because an object can be modified via any alias, object oriented programs are hard to understand, maintain, and analyse. For example, aliasing can cause representation exposure, when an internal implementation object of an aggregate object is accessible outside the aggregate, and argument dependence, when an object's integrity depends upon the state of an aliased object outside its control. These aliasing problems make objects depend on their environment in unpredictable ways, breaking the encapsulation necessary for reliable software components.

On the other hand, understanding aliasing, or more generally, understanding the implicit structure of inter-object references in object-oriented programs, offers many opportunities for improving the implementation of object-oriented systems. The performance of garbage collection, cpu caches, virtual memory, distributed object systems, and object-oriented data bases all depend on the object-oriented program's aliasing structure.

Aliasing has been extensively studied in areas outside object-oriented programs, but features peculiar to object-oriented programs raise many new issues that have not yet been adequately addressed. At ECOOP'91 in Geneva, the workshop on Object-Oriented Formal Methods produced a report called the "Geneva Convention On the Treatment of Object Aliasing" [20] that has continued to define the state of the art during the 1990s, although work on aliasing has begun to appear again at ECOOP and OOPSLA.

In this workshop, we aimed to examine the state of the art in aliasing in object-oriented systems, discuss progress since the Geneva Convention, and identify open questions. We hoped to focus once again on the objects in the "object-

A. Moreira and S. Demeyer (Eds.): ECOOP'99 Workshops, LNCS 1743, pp. 136–163, 1999.

oriented" systems that we build, rather than the classes and types that exist merely to support these objects.

More specifically, the workshop announcement expressed interest in the following issues:

- Models of object ownership, aliasing, and uniqueness.
- Techniques for alias prevention, detection, protection, and advertisement.
- Analysis and Design techniques and notations for describing aliasing.
- Programming language mechanisms for managing aliasing.
- Design guidelines, idioms, and patterns for programming with aliasing.
- Optimisation techniques based on alias analysis.
- Empirical studies of alias structures in programs or alias-based techniques
- Experience programming with alias-aware systems.

Thirteen papers, both short position papers and full length articles were submitted to the workshop. All were reviewed by an international programme committee, and, after some discussion, all were invited to be presented at the workshop.

2. Performance and Analysis

The first session, chaired by John Tang Boyland, considered post-hoc compile-time analysis of programs to detect their aliasing behaviour, and the applicability of such analyses to increasing programs' performance. Each speaker was given approximately five minutes to present an outline their work, and there was also time for questions. Keeping the presentations to five minutes ensured that each presenter had an equal amount of time throughout the day, and the question time allowed them to give more expansive answers where necessary and encouraged discussion between the other workshop participants.

2.1. Using Aliasing Information to Predict Real-Time Garbage Collection (Patrik Persson)

Recent advances in garbage collection scheduling allow languages with garbage collection, like Java, to be used for applications with hard real-time constraints [18]. To determine the required amount of garbage collection work, and thus ensure that processes can execute without running out of memory, a worst-case estimation of the amount of live (i.e., referenced) memory (at any point in time) is required. Other real-time garbage collectors use similar metrics [32].

We have designed an algorithm to estimate the maximum amount of live memory in a program [36]. For simple programs without recursively defined classes, a conservative (albeit pessimistic) estimate can be obtained by assuming all references to denote unique objects. To handle recursive classes, we require every such class to be annotated with a path bound, indicating the maximal number of instances that may be linked together in sequence. Such a path bound corresponds to the length of a linked list or the depth of a binary tree.

The algorithm is based on a classification of references, where references are classified as **links** (introducing cycles into class declarations, such as the 'next' reference in a list element), **entries** (other references to recursive classes, such as the 'first' reference in a list head), **redundant** (references which are always aliased by some other non-redundant reference), and **simple** (non-redundant references to non-recursive classes).

To prevent an overly pessimistic analysis, we require redundant references to be explicitly annotated as such. Such annotations distinguish e.g. a doubly linked list from a binary tree (they both have two recursive pointers, but one is redundant in the doubly linked list). Interesting related questions include:

- How should these annotations be expressed?
- How can we verify (statically and/or dynamically) that the annotations are correct (or at least consistent with the program)?

2.2. Partial Redundancy Elimination for Access Path Expressions (Antony Hosking, Nathaniel Nystrom, David Whitlock, Quintin Cutts, and Amer Diwan)

Pointer traversals pose significant overhead to the execution of object-oriented programs, since every access to an object's state requires a pointer dereference. Objects can refer to other objects, forming graph structures, and they can be modified, with such modifications visible in future accesses. Just as common arithmetic subexpressions often appear in numerical code, common access expressions are often encountered in object-oriented code. Where two such expressions redundantly compute the same value it is desirable to avoid repeated computation of that value by caching the result of the first computation in a temporary variable, and reusing it from the temporary at the later occurrence of the expression. Eliminating redundant computations in this way certainly eliminates redundant CPU overhead. Perhaps just as important for modern machine architectures, eliminating redundant access expressions also has the effect of eliminating redundant memory references, which are often the source of large performance penalties incurred in the memory subsystem.

To evaluate the impact of elimination of redundant access expressions in Java we have built an analysis and optimization tool for Java class files called BLOAT (Bytecode-Level Optimization and Analysis Tool) [34]. BLOAT incorporates several standard optimizations such as dead-code elimination and copy/constant propagation, and SSA-based value numbering [41], as well as *type-based alias analysis* [14] and SSA-based *partial redundancy elimination* (PRE) [8]. BLOAT operates as a bytecode-to-bytecode translator, sourcing and targeting Java class files.

PRE [30] is a powerful global optimization technique that subsumes standard common subexpression elimination (CSE). PRE eliminates computations that are only partially redundant; that is, redundant only on some, but not all, paths to some later re-computation. By inserting evaluations on those paths where the computation does not occur, the later re-evaluation can be eliminated and

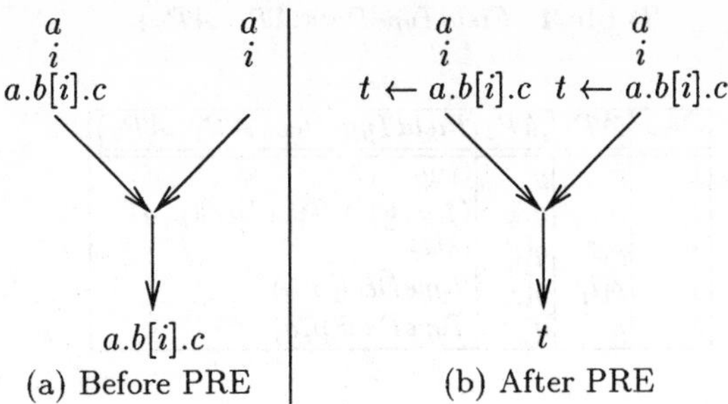

Fig. 1. PRE for access expressions

replaced instead with a use of the precomputed value. Consider the Java access expression $a.b[i].c$, which translates to Java bytecode of the form:

```
aload a     ; load local variable a
getfield b  ; load field b of a
iload i     ; load local variable i
aaload      ; index array b
getfield c  ; load field c of b[i]
```

Traversing the access path requires successively loading the pointer at each memory location along the path and traversing it to the next location in the sequence. Before applying PRE to access path expressions, one must first disambiguate memory references sufficiently to be able safely to assume that no memory location along the access path can be aliased (and so modified) by some lexically distinct access path in the program. Consider the example in Figure 1. The expression $a.b[i].c$ will be redundant at some subsequent reevaluation so long as no store occurs to any one of a, $a.b$, i, $a.b[i]$ or $a.b[i].c$ on the code path between the first evaluation of the expression and the second. In other words, if there are explicit stores to a or i (local variables cannot be aliased in Java) or potential aliases to any one of $a.b$, $a.b[i]$ or $a.b[i].c$ through which those locations *may* be modified between the first and second evaluation of the expression, then that second evaluation cannot be treated as redundant.

Alias analysis refines the set of possible variables to which an access path may refer. Two distinct access paths are said to be possible *aliases* if they may refer to the same variable. Without alias analysis the optimizer must conservatively assume that all access paths are possible aliases of each other. In general, alias analysis in the presence of references is slow and requires the code for the entire program to work. TBAA overcomes these limitations by using type declarations refine the type of variables to which an access path may refer, since only type-compatible access paths can alias the same variable in a type-safe language such as Java. The compile-time type of an access path provides a simple way to do this: two access paths p and q may be aliases only if the relation $\mathit{TypeDecl}(p, q)$

Table 1. $FieldTypeDecl(\mathcal{AP}_1, \mathcal{AP}_2)$

Case	$\mathcal{AP}_1$	$\mathcal{AP}_2$	$FieldTypeDecl(\mathcal{AP}_1, \mathcal{AP}_2)$
1	p	p	true
2	p.f	q.g	$(\texttt{f} = \texttt{g}) \wedge TypeDecl(p, q)$
3	p.f	$q[i]$	false
4	$p[i]$	$q[j]$	$TypeDecl(p, q)$
5	p	q	$TypeDecl(p, q)$

holds, as defined by

$TypeDecl(\mathcal{AP}_1, \mathcal{AP}_2)$
$Subtypes(Type(\mathcal{AP}_1)) \cap Subtypes(Type(\mathcal{AP}_2)) \neq \emptyset$

We write $Subtypes(T)$ to denote all types assignable to T, according to the assignability rules of the Java specification [17]; Thus, an access expression p can legally access variables only of type $Subtypes(Type(p))$.

A more precise alias analysis will distinguish accesses to fields that are the same type yet distinct. This more precise relation, $FieldTypeDecl(p, q)$, is defined by induction on the structure of p and q in Table 1. Again, two access paths p and q may be aliases only if the relation $FieldTypeDecl(p, q)$ holds. It distinguishes accesses such as t.f and t.g that $TypeDecl$ misses. The cases in Table 1 determine that:

1. Identical access paths are always aliases
2. Two field accesses may be aliases if they access the same field of potentially the same object
3. Array accesses cannot alias field accesses and vice versa
4. Two array accesses may be aliases if they may access the same array (the subscript is ignored)
5. All other pairs of access expressions (when none of the above apply) are possible aliases if they have common subtypes

Java's thread and exception models impose several constraints on optimization. Exceptions in Java are *precise*: when an exception is thrown all effects of statements prior to the throw-point must appear to have taken place, while the effects of statements after the throw-point must not. Second, the thread model prevents movement of access expressions across (possible) synchronization points. Explicit synchronization points occur at monitorenter/monitorexit bytecodes. Also, without inter-procedural control-flow analysis every method invocation represents a possible synchronization point. Common access expressions cannot be considered redundant across these synchronization points. Java's memory model also enforces a strict memory coherence semantics for all accesses to the same location. It has been observed that reordering of potentially aliased load instructions can be an illegal transformation under this memory model [39]. Fortunately, for loads that are definitely aliased, PRE-style optimizations as described here *are* legal.

Our experiments measure the impact of BLOAT's optimizations across 9 diverse Java benchmarks, using both static and dynamic metrics, executing in several execution environments: the interpreted JDK reference virtual machine, the Solaris production virtual machine with "just-in-time" (JIT) compilation, and native binaries compiled off-line ("way-ahead-of-time") to C and thence to native code using an optimizing C compiler. The results, reported in full in our position paper, reveal the promise of optimization of Java classes independently of the source-code compiler and the runtime execution engine. They demonstrate significant improvements using TBAA-based PRE over access expressions, with dramatic reductions in memory access operations, and a general trend towards improvement on all metrics for all execution environments.

2.3. MayEqual: A New Alias Question (John Boyland and Aaron Greenhouse)

Introduction. Alias analysis can be defined as determining whether at a particular program point, two pointers refer to the same storage location. One of the two standard aliasing questions can be phrased following Landi [22] (the other question is *MustAlias*):

> $MayAlias_{P[.]}(p_1, p_2)$: In some execution of P, do we have $p_1 = p_2$ at the indicated point $P[.]$?

Algorithmic analyses will return "true" if they cannot rule out equality. Interesting alias analyses for object-oriented languages can be obtained, for example, using Steensgaard's "points-to analysis" [42] (which is flow insensitive) or Sagiv, Reps and Wilhelm's "shape analysis" [40] (which is flow sensitive).

In the course of investigating reordering of statements in the ACT/Fluid project at CMU and UWM, we have found that it is desirable to determine whether a reference computed at one point could equal a reference computed at another point. For instance, if we want to reorder the first two statements in the following loop

```
while (...) { { ...; x.f = ...; ... }
              { ...; ... = y.f; ... }
              ... }
```

we must ensure that the expression `x` could never refer to the same object that is referred to by `y` (assuming both expressions evaluate), or risk changing the results of the program as a consequence of reordering the two statements.

MayAlias appears to be applicable to this problem, but is the wrong question to ask. Because there is no single program point to ask it, the results are not immediately useful; knowing that `x` and `y` might be aliased when `x.f` or `y.f` are

[0] This material is based upon work supported by the Defense Advanced Research Projects Agency and Rome Laboratory, Air Force Materiel Command, USAF, under agreement number F30602-97-2-0241.

dereferenced does not tell us anything about the relationship between **x** *at the point where* ***x.f*** *is dereferenced* and **y** *at the point where* ***y.f*** *is dereferenced.*

The question to ask must also allow for useful flow sensitivity. Consider the following scheme:

```
{ if (x != y) { x.f = ...; } }
{ ...; ... = y.f; ...; }
```

Assume that there are no writes to **y** in the elided code. In this case, the condition around the first expression ensures there cannot be a data dependency (even though the second access is not similarly guarded).

Although we are asserting that *MayAlias* is the wrong question to ask to solve this problem, we do not mean to imply that particular analyses capable of answering the *MayAlias* question cannot be used to solve the problem. We wish only to present the fact that a new question is being asked—one that we believe allows the use of analyses that yield less conservative results.

A New Question. The question we wish analyses to answer is

$$MayEqual_{P[C[.,.]]}(e, e')$$

where P is a program context with a hole for C, which is an execution context with two holes for expressions e and e'. The question has the following meaning:

> Within some execution of C in the program P, do the set of all values to which e evaluates and the set of all values to which e' evaluates have a nonempty intersection?

The inner context, C, focuses the analysis on the part of the program that includes the computations for which we are checking interference. As we shall demonstrate, when checking whether two computations interfere, C should be chosen to be the smallest context that includes both computations. Because of the problems described above, we believe that it is more useful for an analysis to use *MayEqual* as an interface than *MayAlias*. O'Callahan's Ajax analysis system uses a similar construct to expose the results of static analyses to client tools [35].

Let us return to the **while** loop presented above to investigate how choices of C affect the operation on whose behalf *MayEqual* is being asked; in this case the operation is statement reordering. As before, suppose we want to swap the order of the first two compound statements in the loop body. The best choices for the parameters to *MayEqual* are:

$$\begin{aligned} P &= \ldots\texttt{while (...) \{ } \bullet \texttt{ ...\}}\ldots \\ C &= \{\ldots;\bullet\texttt{.f} = \ldots;\ldots\}\{\ldots;\ldots = \bullet\texttt{.f};\ldots\} \\ e &= \texttt{x} \\ e' &= \texttt{y} \end{aligned}$$

With these choices of P and C, the order of the two blocks can safely be swapped if there does not exist an execution of C such that an object referred to by **x** at the first program point is the same as an object referred to by `y` at the second program point (assuming there are no other potential data dependencies). If instead we used the contexts

$P' = \ldots \bullet \ldots$

```
C' = while (...) { { ...; •.f = ...; ... }
                   { ...; ... = •.f; ... }
                   ... }
```

then loop-carried dependencies could be mistakenly viewed as preventing the swapping of statements. Choosing a larger-than-necessary context yields conservative results. However, if we were interested in moving the second compound statement out of the loop, then our choice for C must include the entire `while` statement.

Any analysis that answers the "points-to" question can be used to obtain a conservative answer to the *MayEqual* question with $P = \bullet$ and C being the entire program with holes for the two expressions of interest. An example of a common situation for which a larger-than-necessary C (such as provided by a "points-to" analysis) prevents reordering is if we wanted to ask questions about `x` and `y` in

```
while (...) {
   x = new Node(...);
   x.next = null;                    -- (1)
   y.next = x;                       -- (2)
   y = x;
}
```

No matter how accurate a "points-to" analysis is, it must determine that `x` and `y` could point to the same location, and thus statements labeled (1) and (2) cannot be reordered.

2.4. PAOLA — Program Analysis of Object-Oriented Languages (Wolfram Amme, Markus Schordan Laszlo Böszörmenyi, and Wilhelm Rossak)

PAOLA is a collaboration between University of Klagenfurt (Austria) and University of Jena (Germany). The main focus of the PAOLA project is the development of new techniques for program analysis of object-oriented languages.

In object-oriented languages, objects are accessed via references. An object reference is in principle the same as a pointer to a storage cell. As in imperative languages a correct program analysis of object-oriented languages must be based on the results of a safe alias analysis. One of the main issues is overriding of methods which depends on type information and references to objects established at run-time.

Program analysis often uses a well-known technique of static analysis — monotone data flow analysis. By doing so, a program has to be transformed into a control flow graph in a first step. Thereafter, for each program statement the desired information can be derived by traversing the control graph iteratively.

To be able to determine the methods invoked at run-time we first construct an approximate but safe control flow graph, and give some additional type information to entry nodes of methods. We use the class hierarchy information to restrict this graph.

For a non-virtual function call, we model the control flow in the called method by an interprocedural edge from a *call* node to the corresponding *entry* node. Virtual methods make it impossible to determine the correspondence between a *call* node and an *entry* node before analysis, since the method invoked depends on the type of the receiver at the call site. Therefore we establish multiple edges from the call node to the entry nodes of all methods, that may be called at run-time. Each type corresponds to one edge of the call of a virtual function. Later, by typed alias analysis we are able to restrict the number of edges that carry information. By this we identify overridden methods that are not invoked at run-time. If it is not possible to reduce the number of possibly invoked methods to one the information is combined at the join node of the *exit* nodes.

It is imperative to our analysis that types are computed in the same way as reaching definitions. Additionally the subtype relation and set of types computed for a particular node is used at call nodes to reduce the set of methods that may be invoked at run-time. Since our analysis is a conservative analysis we may not identify all methods that are not invoked but we are able to reduce the number of invoked methods significantly because our method is well suited for computing reaching definitions.

Let us illustrate the basic mechanisms by example. Fig. 2 (b) shows parts of an interprocedural control flow graph, which we derived from the simple Java program listed in Fig. 2 (a). The program consists of three classes. One class *Demo* holds the main method whereas class A is the base class of class B. Further, the method *modifyby* that is defined in A is overridden in class B. We store information about the receiver object, the formal parameters and the actual paramters in the call node. The type information is stored in the entry node of the respective method.

We use typed alias graphs (*TA graphs*) as data flow information sets. Each *TA graph* denotes possible structures of the store and some aspects of its state at a certain point in program execution. In *TA graphs*, alias information is expressed by the set of paths with which we can access an object at one program point. Nodes of a *TA graph* represent the objects present in the store. We mark the nodes of a *TA graph* with the class name of the corresponding object. Additionally, to express the structure of an object we annotate each node with names of variables of the corresponding object. Eventually, a reference of one object to another object is expressed by a labeled edge in the *TA graph*. Figure 2 (c) contains the TA graph, which describes the storage after analyzing the given program, that is before execution of statement 5. As we can see, besides compiler constructed storage cells there could be an object instance of type B in storage which is reachable by the set of variables $\{a, b\}$.

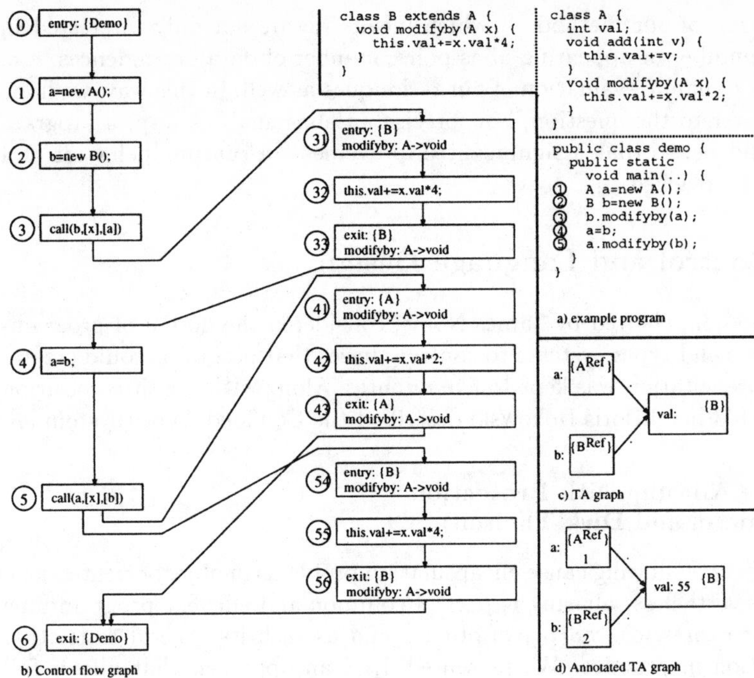

Fig. 2. Source, control flow graph, TA graph, and annotated TA graph.

The availability of object types, which we assign to the nodes of an TA graph, leads to a more precise control flow analysis. With this technique we can choose the target of a calling method during data flow analysis, i.e. with the TA graphs in Fig. 2 (c) we can determine that the calling method in statement 5 must be the modifyby routine of class *B* and not that of class *A*.

To solve our intrinsic task — performing a program analysis of object-oriented languages — we additionally can assign information, which we need for optimization of programs, like value, last definition, last use of an object resp. available expressions, etc., to the nodes of a TA graph. Fig. 2 (d) contains an annotated TA graph for statement 6 in which we hold the program statements that define the contents of a storage object last, i.e., the reaching definitions. Integrating such kind of annotations into the data flow analysis leads to an elegant form of program analysis. With the additional type information at program point 5 we are able to determine which method is invoked and we compute that it must be program point 55 where a value is assigned to the variable `val` of the dynamically allocated object that is referenced by variable `a`.

A very significant point of research work in the PAOLA project will be the evaluation of our methods by means of real applications. By doing so, we hope to answer the question, how far an optimization of object oriented programs, which is based on our program analysis, can improve the runtime behavior of a program. In contrast to other works we are not only interested in performing a static evaluation of our method — which means we are not only interested in measures as number of appearing alias pairs, number of data dependences, etc. We perform a dynamic evaluation of our techniques as well. In this way, we hope to get an answer to the question, how precise an alias analysis resp. a program analysis should be, so that a significant improvement in runtime behavior of a program can be reached.

3. Alias Control and Language Design

The second session, chaired by James Noble, considered the design of programming languages and types systems to control aliases that programs could create. Again, each presentation was kept to five minutes. Along with the three position papers presented here, Boris Bokowski described the Confined Types system [4].

3.1. Flexible Aliasing with Protection (Günter Kniesel and Dirk Theisen)

Unwanted effects of aliasing cause encapsulation problems in object oriented programming. Nevertheless, aliasing is part of common and efficient programming techniques for expressing *sharing* of objects and as such its general restriction is not an option in practice. We presented JAC an approach that allows full referential object sharing but adds access control to object references to limit the *effects* of aliasing.

JAC – Java with Access Control. Our goal was to offer sufficient protection from unwanted aliasing effects and still provide a simple and *practical* solution that has no run-time overhead and can be implemented in Java without changes to the Java Virtual Machine ([25]) and the Java type system ([17]). Therefore JAC limits itself to the simplest possible set of access rights: full access and read-only access. One main characteristic of JAC is the scope of access rights, which apply to the *full* (local and transitive) state of an object.

So, in a nutshell, JAC is an extension of Java with transitive readonly access control.

Readonly Types. In JAC, for every programmer-defined type (class or interface) T there exists one *implicit* readonly type, T_{ro}. It contains the signatures of the methods from T that do not modify the state of `this` (we call them *readonly methods*). This is a common technique, often proposed as a design pattern for write-protecting objects [13, 23].

The peculiarity of JAC is that in a readonly type each original return type T_i is replaced by its readonly counterpart $T_{i ro}$.

The modification of return types in readonly types is the key to achieve *transitive protection*: when a method is called on a reciever of readonly type it will only return a result of readonly type, although it might return a result of writable type when called on a writable reciever.

Expressions can be declared to be of a readonly type by prepending the **readonly** type modifier to a type declaration. Only readonly methods may be called on expressions of readonly type.

Because each readonly type is a supertype of the programmer-supplied type definition, writable objects may be passed to readonly expressions (where they will be write-protected) but readonly values will never be passed into writable contexts.

A declarative definition of readonly types is:

> For an expression of a readonly type that evaluates to an object reference *o* the *full* state of the referenced object is protected against changes performed via *o*.

The `mutable` Type Modifier. The constructive definition of readonly types given first is slightly more restricitve than the declarative one given above. For instance, it would also write-protect results that do *not* refer to the state of `this` e.g. references passed in as parameters and references to objects newly created within the method body.

Intuitively, such references should not be affected by the access protection applicable to `this`.

This may be expressed in JAC by explicitly annotating a return type with the keyword `mutable` meaning "writeable, even in a readonly context"[1].

The primary effect of the `mutable` annotation is that the annotated result type will also be contained in the readonly signature of the corresponding method[2].

GJAC – Generic JAC. The ability to model containers with arbitrarily shareable elements that are guaranteed not to modify the objects stored in them has repeatedly been described as a desirable property of alias management techniques ([21, 33]). This property is trivially fulfilled by JAC.

However, JAC would sometimes be too protective. A writable element added to a readonly container will be returned as a readonly element. This is no real limitation because JAC's notion of readonly types smoothly extends to systems that support genericity, like GJ ([7]), pmg ([6]), and, presumably, future versions of Java.

Combining genericity and readonly types makes it easy to model containers that return exactly the type of elements that had previously been inserted.

A full range of protection schemes that can be achieved using (G)JAC is discussed in [43] together with further aspects that cannot be mentioned here for obvious lack of space.

---

[1] We adopted this keyword from C++ and extended its use as a return type modifier. C++ uses `mutable` just as an annotation of instance variables.

[2] Now the complete definition of readonly types reads: "... with each *non-mutable* return type T_i, replaced by its readonly counterpart $T_{i\,ro}$".

State of the Project. Our proof-of-concept implementation of JAC as an extension to Java introduces is fully *backward compatible* with standard Java. JAC is also *efficient* in that it imposes no run-time costs, all access control checking being purely static. The mapping of JAC's protection scheme to the standard Java type system and emerging extensions thereof make our approach *simple* and *generally applicable*.

3.2. Alias Killing: Unique Variables without Destructive Reads (John Boyland)

Several researchers (including Wadler [44], Hogg [21], Baker [3] and Minsky [29]) have proposed extending programming languages to express the concept of a unique or linear variable. Such a variable is either empty or else its value is the sole reference to an object. The object is then known as an *unshared* object. An unshared object can be destructively updated without affecting any other variable. Destructive updates on unshared objects can thus be permitted even in a language without side-effects. In an imperative language, the holder of an unshared object knows that no other part of the system can mutate the object. For instance, if a module has sole access to a file stream object, then its implementation can be changed to buffer input from the file, with the client of the module observing no change of behavior. Being able to declare which variables are expected to be unique and to have these declarations checked can make code more understandable and maintainable.

Reasoning about programs with unique variables can ensure that the objects referred to by unique variables are indeed unshared. An object is unshared when first created and it will remain unshared as long as the reference is stored in only one variable. Similarly, if a unique variable is read at most once, any resulting object will be unshared. If this "variable" is a field of a dynamically allocated objects, it is difficult to ensure it will be read at most once. Instead, a system with unique variables may require them to read *destructively*, that is, after reading the value of a unique variable, the variable is *nullified* (made empty).[3] Emptiness is marked using a special "null" or "void" pointer. This latter restriction is the one used by Hogg and Minsky in their respective proposals [21, 29]. Baker also briefly mentions destructive reads when discussing how unshared objects can be stored in possibly shared objects.

Requiring reads of unique variables to be destructive is sufficient to prevent them from being *compromised*, that is aliased with another variable. But destructive reads of unique fields, by their very nature, modify the object containing the field. This fact has several unfortunate consequences. First, programs are more complex when they have to continually re-establish field values. Second, destructive reads may make a method or procedure appear to have more side-effects than it conceptually performs. Third, it would seem that adding unique variables to a programming language necessitates the further addition of destructive reads.

[3] Instead of a destructive read, an atomic swap can be used to solve the same problem in much the same way. A rather different approach is to "deep copy" the value.

Alias Killing is an alternate check for uniqueness: when a field annotated as 'unique' is read, any existing aliases are required to be dead. This condition can be checked statically, and in conjunction with annotations on procedures, the checking can proceed modularly. (The procedure annotations are checked at the same time that the uniqueness annotations are checked.) If a program passes the check, then it has the same behavior with or without the uniqueness annotations; no implicit nullification takes place.

The annotations can be stripped out and ignored whenever the program is implemented and executed. As a result, existing compilers and run-time systems can be used unchanged. Thus one achieves the benefits of uniqueness annotations without having to extend the base language implementation.

3.3. Overcoming Representation Exposure (David Clarke, James Noble, and John Potter)

Through their reliance on reference semantics, what objects gain in flexibility they lose in their ability to control access to their internal implementation details — this is the problem of *representation exposure*. Our earlier work dealing with ownership types achieved a limited form of representation containment, whereby each object's representation was contained within that object, its owner. Inter-object accessibility was constrained so that owners were dominators of the objects they owned. Unfortunately, this approach lacked flexibility, so that common programming techniques became overly cumbersome to implement.

Representation Exposure Tension. Aliasing is problematic because it breaks the encapsulation necessary for building reliable software components [26]. In earlier work we presented *ownership types* [10], which is based on labelling each object with its owner and recording this information in the object's type. Ownership is fixed for an object's lifetime and there is a distinction between being an *owner of* and having a *reference to* an object. This allows, for example, an object to be stored in a container even though they are not owned by the container. The evolving object graph of a well-typed program has the property, called *representation containment*, that all access paths from the root of the system to an object pass through that object's owner, making an object's owner a dominator for such paths [38]. To our knowledge, ownership types constitute the first type system which enforced representation containment — related work is surveyed in our previous papers [10, 33, 38].

Representation Containment. In our previous work [10], we presented a type system for a class-based programming language (without inheritance) which prevented representation exposure. The types, called *ownership types*, express the owner of an object in the object's type. Every object has an owner which is another object or the ambient root object of the system.

We use *contexts* to denote owners. Contexts and the rules which govern them describe and limit the extent of object access. They are represented by paths π

and path variable α specified as follows:

$$p, q ::= \pi \mid \alpha$$
$$\pi ::= \epsilon \mid \pi.\kappa$$

where κ is a denumerable collection of names. The empty path, ϵ, represents the root, and a path $\pi.\kappa$ is a context inside context π. The relation $\subset$ between contexts, called *inside*, is defined as follows:

$$p \subseteq q \text{ if and only if } q \text{ is a prefix of } p$$

All contexts are inside the context ϵ, that is, for all p, we have $p \subseteq \epsilon$.

Each object has two associated contexts: the object's owner, and its representation context, the owner of its representation. The owner is used to determine which other objects can keep a reference to this object. The representation context is used to determine which objects this can keep a reference to. We specify the owner when creating a new object. The representation context, however, is a distinct new context.

In our earlier work, if an object had owner π, the the representation context was $\pi.\kappa$, where κ was a fresh atom [10][4]. By identifying objects with their representation contexts, we see that objects are inside their owners.

We proved that if the following constraint is maintained for all objects α and β

$$\alpha \to \beta \Rightarrow rep(\alpha) \subseteq owner(\beta) \qquad (*)$$

where $\alpha \to \beta$ means α has a reference to β, $rep(\alpha)$ is α's representation context, and $owner(\beta)$ is β's owner, *then* every object's owner was a dominator for paths from the root of the system to that object, and that the tree of contexts was the dominator tree for the object graph [38]. This means that external access to an object's representation must be through an object's owner. We also proved that programs well-typed in the ownership type system satisfied the constraint (*) [10].

Unfortunately this basic model is not expressive enough. To be practical, the we must allow coding styles such as iterators and public inner objects, even when they potentially expose represention.

We have developed an extended model (using Abadi and Cardelli's object calculus [1] to allow multiple objects to access an object's representation. This is achieved by relaxing constraints on where the representation context is created. Previously an object's representation is created directly inside the object's owner. We now allow the representation context to be created anywhere inside the owner of the object. In particular this allows us to create an object with the same owner as a given object, but with its representation context inside the first object's representation context. Because these two objects have the same owner, they are accessible by the same objects. But since the second object's

[4] The presentation differs in [10], but the underlying semantics are the same as described here.

representation context is inside the first object's, the second object has access to the first object's representation. We maintain the same invariant (*) with appropriately modified definitions of *rep*() and *owner*().

Using this extended model, we are able to express a number of programming idioms that are inadmissible in the basic model, including:

- Objects that present multiple interfaces such as COM components or JavaBeans.
- Objects that share structure within complex aggregates such as iterators over linked lists.
- Writing methods that are *owner-indifferent*, such as a binary method to compare two linked lists.
- Initializing objects with externally created parameters which become part of the new object's representation with no external aliases, such as initializing a parser with a lexer subcomponent.
- Providing direct but safe access to an object's representation, for efficiency reasons.

Unfortunately, this position paper is too narrow to describe them.

Of course, many issues remain unresolved, including the incorporation of the ideas into programming languages in a manner acceptable to programmers. Details of the formal underpinnings of the ideas in this presentation, including an accompanying type system, are in preparation.

Acknowledgements. The members of the Object Technology Group were invaluable with their comments and support. The referees provided helpful suggestions including the term *owner indifferent*.

3.4. Implementing "Object Ownership to Order" (Boris Bokowski)

So far, no practical way of controlling aliasing in object-oriented programming has been found. On the one hand, approaches like Eiffel's **expanded** [27], Hogg's Islands [21], Almeida's Balloons [2], and Confined Types [4] are too restrictive because they rule out common programming idioms and patterns. On the other hand, Flexible Alias Protection [33, 10] claims to be a more flexible way of controlling aliasing that still allows common programming styles. However, the proposed scheme is rather complex, so that it is difficult to make such a claim without having experience with larger alias-protected example programs. Moreover, it is not yet clear whether the scheme can be integrated into a non-toy programming language.

Using CoffeeStrainer [5], a framework for checking programmer-defined constraints on Java programs, we have implemented "Object Ownership to Order" [9], a refinement of the original Flexible Alias Protection proposal. The implementation serves two purposes: First, it shows that the CoffeeStrainer framework is useful for implementing language extensions that can be expressed as static constraints. Second, it helps validating the theoretical results for a real-world programming language, it allows experimenting with variations of the alias protection scheme, and it enables automated checking of larger examples.

Usually, implementing language extensions is difficult. Either a new compiler has to be written, or an existing compiler has to be modified. Unfortunately, the latter approach does not work well because most compilers are monolithic programs that are not open to modifications and extensions. With the implementation of "Object Ownership to Order", we have shown that CoffeeStrainer is useful for implementing language extensions that can be expressed as static constraints. Originally, CoffeeStrainer has been written for framework programmers who want to express constraints how to use their framework correctly. The constraints, which are embedded within special comments in classes or interfaces, may apply to the *definition* of the classes and interfaces in which they appear, and to all places in a program where these classes or interfaces are *used*.

The experiences while implementing "Object Ownership to Order" are threefold: experiences with automated alias-checking of larger example programs, Java-specific issues, and repercussions on the original proposal.

Experiences with alias-checking: Using the implementation, we have alias-checked a number of example programs. As expected, programs that are designed with the program's aliasing properties in mind can be annotated as is. However, adding ownership tags in a way that tries to control aliasing as much as possible leads to a large number of ownership parameters for each class. Other programs that have been designed with less care (or more design patterns) seem to prevent alias protection to a certain degree. For example, annotating and checking the original implementation of `java.lang.Vector` showed that it is not yet possible to define binary methods such as `equals()` when using Flexible Alias Protection. Another problem is the implementation of the corresponding `Enumeration` class which directly accesses internals of the vector object.

Java-specific issues: While it was easy to handle some features not present in the original proposal, such as `null`, arrays, and primitive types, others were problematic. Unlike instance fields and methods, which have a context in which the most important rule - no role confusion - can be checked, there is no such context for static methods and fields. Consequently, no objects may be manipulated by static methods or stored in static fields. Of course, this is not satisfactory; a solution seems to be to parameterize static methods with ownership tags similar to the parameterization of classes. Inner classes are not supported, because this would require an extension of the proposal as inner objects have access to their enclosing instances.

Repercussions on the original proposal: In addition to the extensions of the original proposal that have been hinted at in the previous paragraph, we found that the flat parameterization with ownership tags is not sufficient: Simple objects can be stored in alias-protected containers, but if alias-protected containers themselves are to be stored in other alias-protected containers, nested parameterization is needed. Additionally, it could be useful to allow parameterization not only of static methods, but of methods in general.

4. Designing, Programming, and Verifying with Aliasing

The third session, chaired by Doug Lea, considered more practical uses of aliasing in programming and program analysis.

4.1. Towards Safer Aliasing with the Eiffel Language (Olivier Zendra and Dominique Colnet)

We believe aliasing offers some significant advantages in terms of performance and thus may be worth relying on. Our Eiffel [27] compiler — SmallEiffel, The GNU Eiffel Compiler [5] — makes intensive but carefully designed use of aliasing, trying to reconcile both performance and safety through use of design by contract technics.

Aliasing is of course not specific to compiler implementations. However, compilers appear to be prone to using aliasing, for example when encountering an identifier. The basic idea of aliasing here is to use exactly the same string when several symbols have the same name. This way, it is possible to compare two symbol names with a mere pointer comparison, instead of having to look at the (potentially complete) contents of the name. This avoids having duplicates of the same string, which saves a lot of memory. There also seems to be a possible gain in terms of speed.

Of course, strings are not the only "aliasable" objects in a compiler, but since they are very common and well understood objects, we use them as a basic example in our presentation. Indeed, although local aliased object management is quite easy and intuitive in a routine or small algorithm, this is not the case anymore when aliasing has to be managed on a system-wide basis. To achieve its purpose, it is above all very important that the STRING_ ALIASER object be unique in the whole system. A singleton pattern [15] perfectly suits this purpose.

It is of course also very important that in the whole system all objects use the alias provider, and that none keeps its own duplicate versions of aliased strings. This way only one single, unique version of the string is ever created and is managed by the alias provider. So all classes of the system have to respect the rules of the game, and use the alias provider. They also have to take part in the whole system security by checking that their providers themselves do use the alias provider. This can be easily done in Eiffel by using the preconditions and postconditions of routines.

Of course, enforcing the use of the aliaser is not enough to safely cope with aliasing. One also has to strictly control who modifies the aliased object and where. More generally, aliasing mutable (and actually *mutated*) objects causes less problems when dealing with objects which have been *designed to be aliased.*

An example of such objects are instances of type BASE_CLASS which represent classes after they have been parsed. These objects are much more complex than strings since they include all the information about the class they represent: name, ancestors, attributes, routines, etc. If a class FOO is present in the system

[5] http://SmallEiffel.loria.fr

only one instance of the corresponding BASE_CLASS is ever created, whatever the number of occurrences of FOO in client code. Obviously, aliasing this kind of objects is mandatory. Doing otherwise would only result in a tremendous amount of instances of BASE_CLASS and would be utterly inefficient.

The mechanism used is very similar to the one for strings. The alias provider for BASE_CLASS objects is the EIFFEL_PARSER singleton. Its role is to ensure that each class source file is only (lazily) parsed once, for obvious performance reasons, and to provide aliases for BASE_CLASS objects. Indeed, the EIFFEL_PARSER is the only object allowed to create instances of BASE_CLASS. Thanks to the selective export mechanism of Eiffel, this property can be *statically guaranteed.*

In order to precisely quantify the impact of aliasing, two versions of our compiler should be run: one with (full) aliasing and another without any. The latter would have meant major and lengthy rewriting. Furthermore, as mentioned above, it even seems impossible to write a compiler without some kind of aliasing, e.g. for BASE_CLASS. Consequently, we decided to restrict our benchmarking to string aliasing only. It is worth noting this was made easier by the fact that the whole aliasing process was in the STRING_ALIASER. All reference equality tests between two STRINGs were also replaced by the `is_equal` structure comparison.

The benefit *from the sole string aliasing* represents a more than 14% decrease and is thus quite significant. This footprint reduction is also a good thing in terms of execution speed, since decreasing memory use also eases the burden on the garbage collector [12] and lowers swapping.

The downside of string aliasing is that the management of the STRING_ALIASER has a cost. Indeed, each time a new string is found, it is necessary to check whether it is already in the aliaser and in case it is not the new object has to be created and then inserted in the aliaser. It was thus reasonable to wonder whether the cost of interning strings would outweigh the benefits of mere pointer comparisons.

The experiments we made show that *string aliasing alone* actually leads to an improvement of more than 10% on the whole compilation time. It is important to note that these significant performance improvements come from the sole string aliasing. It is not unreasonable to think that the other kinds of aliasing (on BASE_CLASSes, LOCAL_NAMEs, etc.) also cause footprint and speed improvements which are quite significant. Aliasing under various forms thus seems to play a major part in the very good performance [11] of the SmallEiffel compiler.

4.2. Alias Control Is Crucial for Modular Verification of Object-Oriented Programs (Peter Müller and Arnd Poetzsch-Heffter)

One of the most important motivations for alias control is to support program verification. In object-oriented settings, *modular* verification techniques are required to prove that an OO-module behaves according to its specification in all contexts it is (re-)used. We argue that alias protection is crucial for modular verification of OO-programs. If objects can be shared in an arbitrary way, the absence of certain kinds of side-effects cannot be guaranteed by state-of-the-art verification techniques.

Overview. Based on the formal specification and verification technique presented in [31], we describe situations in which unwanted sharing of objects leads to side-effects that cannot be detected by modular verification. We sketch a type system that allows one to prevent such situations by alias control.

Specification Technique. To handle data abstraction and encapsulation, we use so-called abstract attributes to formalize the abstract values of object structures. In implementations, an abstract attribute A is represented by a set of concrete attributes C_i. We say that A *depends on* C_i. Following [24], we require these dependencies to be declared explicitly.

Frame properties of a method m are specified by a modifies-clause describing the set of attributes that might be modified by m. To handle encapsulation and subtyping, the permission to modify an abstract attribute A includes the right to modify all attributes A depends on.

Modular Verification of Frame Properties. The context of a module M consists of M and all modules imported by M. Modular verification means to guarantee that properties of a module M that have been proven in the context of M carry over to all contexts in which M is used.

Modular verification is particularly difficult for frame properties since one has to ensure that a method m does not affect attributes that are not covered by its modifies-clause, even if these attributes are declared outside m's context. The following example illustrates the most prominent problem: Two classes C_1 and C_2 declared in different contexts contain attributes A_1 and A_2 which depend on an attribute A of an imported class. If two instances of A_1 and A_2 depend on the same instance of A, a method m of C_1 with the permission to modify A_1 might also modify A_2 via the shared instance of A. This side-effect cannot be detected during the verification of m since A_2 does not belong to the context of C_1.

Alias Control with Universes. To prevent undetectable side-effects, objects of imported types must not be shared among objects of types declared in different contexts. To achieve that, we equip each module with a so-called *universe*. Universes are partitions of the object store that belong exclusively to the objects of the types declared in the corresponding module (so-called owner objects). Objects inside a universe U can only be directly referenced by other objects of U or by U's owner objects.

This behavior is enforced by an extended type system: Objects in different universes are regarded to be of different types. I.e., types consist of a type identifier and a universe. A type T of universe U is only accessible in U and U's owner module. I.e., outside U, it cannot occur as parameter or return type of public methods which guarantees that references are never passed beyond U's owner objects. Therefore, universes control both static and dynamic aliases. Data can be exchanged between different universes by a clone operation which performs a deep copy of an object structure.

Alias control on the level of modules is sufficient for modular verification, since more fine-grained sharing properties can be guaranteed by verification (cf. [31] for a discussion). The effort of proving such properties can be significantly reduced by refining universes to allow for alias control on the object level (cf. [10] and [2] for such type systems).

4.3. Intercontinental Workshop on Aliasing in Object-Oriented Systems (Phillip M. Yelland)

In this submission, I'd like to take the opportunity presented by the workshop to reprise some of the material that originated in my Ph.D. work [45]. Though almost eight years old, the results of this research are still fairly obscure—an upshot of my own indolence (the thesis itself was never published) and of a general indifference that (with a few honorable exceptions) prevailed at the time of original writing.

I began the research with the intention of devising models for object-oriented languages based on the algebraic semantics popularized by the "ADJ group" in the late '70s and early '80s [16]. Since algebraic semantics were devised with the intent of supporting specification languages and formal verification, my hope was that constructing such models for object-oriented languages would legitimate the application of Hoare-style datatype verification methods to OOL's. (You might recall that a number of researchers in OOL's—particularly those associated with Eiffel—advocated the use of such methods [28].)

Unfortunately, in attempting to come up with such models, I had terrible problems dealing with the subject of this workshop—the chains of reference intrinsic to conventional object-oriented programming languages. Many of my early essays collapsed into complex jumbles, with a profusion of low-level details needed to cope with references. These models only sanctioned proof methods so complicated and turgid as to be almost useless.

Eventually, I realized I needed "abstract" denotational models of OOL's. Such models would ascribe a representation to a collection of objects (or equivalently, classes) bereft of all internal details that were inaccessible to objects outside of that collection. (As you'd no doubt suspect, this notion of abstractness is a weakening of Plotkin's definition of "full abstraction" [37].) Abstract algebraic models yield proof methods that are "the best one can do", in as far as they address only the complexities that arise from the characteristics of the subject language itself, without introducing extraneous complications.

I began by devising an abstract model for the language that Hoare used in presenting his seminal work on data type verification [19]. Though it's apparently not widely appreciated, Hoare very wisely excluded any possibility of aliasing involving objects in his language (all assignment and parameter-passing is accomplished by copying). Naturally enough, the abstract model gives rise to a proof method that coincides precisely with that Hoare proposed.

I found that once aliasing is introduced, however, abstract models (and their associated proof methods) become considerably more convoluted. Problems arise not only from the updating of shared objects described in the workshop rubric, but from the cycles of reference all to easy to contrive in conventional object-oriented languages. Cycles, for example, allow an object to be observed in an inconsistent state, if an operation invokes another operation on a subsidiary object that has a reference back to the original. Even worse, a cycle can lead to the non-termination of a program in an OOL in a way that's not at all evident from an inspection of the code.

The results of my thesis work serve to motivate the construction of mechanisms for controlling aliasing in object-oriented languages. For they establish that without such mechanisms, formal (or indeed informal but rigorous) verification must deal with significant complexity that originates not in the formal notation or proof methods used but in the programming languages themselves. Hoare's elegant (if somewhat idealized) presentation shows that by reigning in the effects of aliasing, we can produce object-oriented programming systems which are significantly easier to reason about and which therefore comprise much more propitious bases for the construction of reliable software.

5. Unifying Views of Aliasing

The final section of the workshop, chaired by Paulo Almeida, aimed to find common ground among the workshop participants and other related work, and to establish a basis for continued work in the field. There was only on position paper presentation in this session. After the position paper, the workshop broke into three focus groups and finally reconvened for a closing plenary.

5.1. The Objects of Aliasing (James Noble)

In recent years, there have been a number of valiant attempts to address the problems caused by aliasing in object-oriented languages. In some sense, the problems caused by aliasing are endemic to object-orientation, in that aliasing problems stem directly from two of the foundations of object-orientation: object identity and mutable object state [33]. In this position paper we outline (extremely briefly) a number of the issues involved in managing aliases in object-oriented systems, and attempt to illustrate how the various approaches fit together. The aim of this position paper was to initiate discussion during the workshop, rather than to present a comprehensive survey of finished work.

The Aim of Alias Management. The *Geneva Convention on the Treatment of Object Aliasing* [20] outlined four main strategies for managing aliasing: detection, prevention, control, and advertisement. Alias prevention prevents aliasing from ever occurring in programs, detection determines when aliasing is present in programs, advertisement allows the programmer to declare when aliasing may occur, and control ensures aliasing is restricted to only certain parts of the program.

We use the term "alias management" to cover any and all of these strategies. This is because many alias management techniques combine several of these strategies — perhaps preventing aliases in some regions of the program, requiring the programmer to advertise when aliases may occur in other regions, and then controlling any aliases which do occur so they do not grant access to those parts of the program where aliases are forbidden.

The aim of most alias management schemes is to prevent the problems caused by aliasing — and it is important to note that preventing the problems caused by aliasing is a different matter to preventing aliasing *per se*. Generally, problems arise when an object is examined or modified via an alias, while the existence of an alias merely creates the potential for such a problem to occur.

The classic problem caused by aliasing is *representation exposure* [26] when details of the representation of an abstraction are leaked out across the abstraction's encapsulation boundary. Many alias management schemes aim to prevent representation exposure, by ensuring an abstraction's representation can never leak across its boundary. A related problem is *argument dependence* [33], when the implementation of an abstraction depends upon an aliased object which is imported across the boundary from outside. Again, many alias management schemes also address argument dependence, often by tightly restricting the import operation (as in Islands [21]), or by limiting the visibility out across the boundary (as in Flexible Alias Protection [33]).

Alias management schemes vary along a number of axes:

- Name vs. Object Aliasing — object aliasing means that one object can be reached by more than one path though other objects in memory, while name aliasing means that one object can be referenced by more than one name in the program's text.
- Drawing Abstraction Boundaries — Islands and Balloons provide an encapsulation boundary around an object and all objects reachable from that object. Flexible alias protection schemes relax this restriction, making a distinction between an object's *representation* which is within the boundary and its *arguments* to which it can refer but which lie outside its boundary [33, 10]. COM-style components have yet another style of encapsulation, where several objects provide interfaces to a component, and share many other components as their representation.
- Static vs. Dynamic Aliases — static aliases originate from the heap while dynamic aliases orignate from the stack Static aliases are generally worse than dynamic aliases, because dynamic aliases cease to exist when their stack frame is released, while static aliases may persist arbitrarily in the heap.
- Mutability — Aliasing problems arise when state is modified, so some aliasing management schemes address the mutability of state.

  Several alias protection schemes employ "functional sublanguages" which enforce restrictions on the mutability or access to mutable state, often as a transitive "readonly" or "const" mode which permits objects to read state but not to change it.

- Uniqueness — A unique object is only every accessible through precisely one "unique" pointer from another object, or perhaps on the stack. A unique object can be created, modified, and passed quite freely around the program — its ownership or access paths can change dynamically — and, provided its uniqueness conditions are maintained, no aliases are introduced. A number of different programming language mechanisms can be used to support uniqueness, including destructive reads, copy assignment, swapping, alias killing, and linearity.
- Ownership — several alias management schemes do not depend on full uniqueness, but rather limit those objects which may refer to the protected object.
- Phase and Granulatiry — alias management schemes may be implemented using compile time or run-time checking, and may be require anything from a single method to an entire program to be checked as a unit.
- Implementation — to be useful, alias management must be integrated into programming languages. There seem to be three major approaches: supplementing the language via extratextual comments, extending programming languages, and using external assertion languages.

Conclusion. Aliasing is endemic in object-oriented programming [20, 33] and quite a large number number of programming language mechanisms have been proposed to manage, control, serve, and protect objects against the pernicious effects of aliasing. A successful alias management scheme has to balance flexibility and expressibility against protection and paranoia, while somehow integrating within existing programming languages and supporting common programming styles. This is not a easy task, and many open questions remain unanswered.

Acknowlegements. Thanks to David Clarke for his comments on this position paper, to John Potter for his email, and to the anonymous reviewers. This work was supported by Microsoft Australia Pty Ltd

5.2. Focus Groups and Closing Plenary

The focus groups and especially the closing plenary sessions were curtailed by the time remaining after the workshop presentations. It is difficult to know how this could have been avoided, given that the pleanry discussions drew heavily on the earlier presentations. As a result, several of the focus group participants expressed interest in continuing to work together after the end of the confereence.

The discussion in the plenary was quite wide-ranging, however, some of the main points included the following. Workshop attendees are working actively on many of these and other issues.

Canonical Problems Caused by Aliasing. The workshop recognised the following categories of problems caused by aliasing:

Problem	Solution	
Representation Exposure	Representation Containment	incoming aliases
Argument Dependence	Argument Independence	outgoing aliases
Role Confusion	Role Separation	aliasing type parameters
Reentrancy	Non-Reentrancy	cycles in objects or calls

Extent of Language Mechanisms. A mechanism's extent describes what objects it affects — the topology of the boundary it draws around objects. Extent is orthogonal to the kind of protection provided. For example, C++ provides a shallow read-only annotation, JAC provides a transitive annotation, and GJAC a flexible annotation. Islands and Balloons [21, 2] provide transitive uniqueness annotations, while *u*-pointers [29] provide shallow uniquness.

Single or Shallow	a single object, like C++ const
Transitive or Deep	the transitive closure of an object
Flexible	separates containers and contents [33]
Post-Flexible or Fractal	supports iterators, inner objects etc.

Semantics of Qualifiers. The various qualifiers used in alias management schemes can be described by a common lattice of basic capabilities — Read, Write, Store, Identity, each of which may be unique to the reference or also usable by "other" references. A standard reference has all capabilities, a unique refernce only the unique capabilities, a readonly reference lacks the unique-write capability, and an immutable reference lacks the unique-write and other-write capabilities.

6. Conclusion

Overall, the workshop was considered to have been a worthwhile exercise by most of the participants. As well as producing this report, some of the organisers and attendees are continuing to work together to produce a second report on aliasing in object-oriented systems, following the style of the Geneva convention, to attempt to bring the problems and issues of aliasing to the attention of the wider object-oriented research community.

Workshop Attendees

Paulo Sergio Almeida `psa@di.uminho.pt`
Wolfram Amme `amme@informatik.uni-jena.de`
Boris Bokowski `bokowski@acm.org`
John Tang Boyland `boyland@cs.uwm.edu`
Aaron Greenhouse `aarong@cs.cmu.edu`
Guenter Kniesel `gk@cs.uni-bonn.de`
Tony Hosking `hosking@cs.purdue.edu`
Doug Lea `dl@altair.cs.oswego.edu`

Tony Hoare	`Tony.Hoare@comlab.ox.ac.uk`
Peter Mueller	`Peter.Mueller@FernUni-Hagen.de`
James Noble	`kjx@mri.mq.edu.au`
Patrik Persson	`Patrik.Persson@cs.lth.se`
Arnd Poetzsch-Heffter	`poetzsch@informatik.tu-muenchen.de`
Markus Schordan	`markuss@ifi.uni-klu.ac.at`
Dirk Theisen	`theisen@akaMail.com`
Jan Vitek	`jv@cs.purdue.edu`
Phillip Yelland	`phillip.yelland@sun.com`
Olivier Zendra	`Olivier.Zendra@loria.fr`

Programme Committee

Ole Agesen, (Sun Microsystems Laboratories)
Paulo Sergio Almeida, (Universidade do Minho)
John Tang Boyland, (U. Wisconsin-Milwaukee)
Laurie Hendren, (McGill University)
John Hogg, (ObjecTime)
Doug Lea, (State University of New York at Oswego)
Rustan Leino, (COMPAQ Systems Research Center)
James Noble, (Microsoft Research, Macquarie)
Jens Palsberg, (Purdue University)
Bill Pugh, (University of Maryland)
Jan Vitek, (Université de Genève)

References

[1] Martín Abadi and Luca Cardelli. *A Theory of Objects.* Springer-Verlag, New York, 1996.

[2] Paulo Sergio Almeida. Balloon types: Controlling sharing of state in data types. In Mehmet Akşit and Satoshi Matsuoka, editors, *ECOOP'97 — Object-Oriented Programming, 11th European Conference*, volume 1241 of *Lecture Notes in Computer Science*, pages 32–59, Berlin, Heidelberg, New York, 1997. Springer.

[3] Henry G. Baker. 'Use-once' variables and linear objects—storage management, reflection and multi-threading. *ACM SIGPLAN Notices*, 30(1):45–52, January 1995.

[4] B. Bokowski and J. Vitek. Confined types. In *OOPSLA '99 Conference Proceedings*. ACM, 1999.

[5] Boris Bokowski. Coffeestrainer: Statically-checked constraints on the definition and use of types in java. In *Proceedings of ESEC/FSE'99*, Toulouse, France, September 1999.

[6] Boris Bokowski and Markus Dahm. Poor man's genericity for Java. *Presentation at ECOOP'98, http://www.inf.fu-berlin.de/ bokowski/pmgjava/*, 1998.

[7] G. Braha, Martin Odersky, D. Stoutamire, and P. Wadler. Making the future safe for the past: Adding genericity to the Java programming language. *Proceedings of OOPSLA'98, ACM SIGPLAN Notices*, 33, 1998.

[8] Fred Chow, Sun Chan, Robert Kennedy, Shin-Ming Liu, Raymond Lo, and Peng Tu. A new algorithm for partial redundancy elimination based on SSA form. In *Proceedings of the ACM Conference on Programming Language Design and Implementation*, pages 273–286, 1997.

[9] D. G. Clarke, R. Shelswell, J. M. Potter, and J. Noble. Object ownership to order. manuscript, 1998.

[10] David G. Clarke, John M. Potter, and James Noble. Ownership types for flexible alias protection. In *OOPSLA '98 Conference Proceedings*, volume 33(10) of *ACM SIGPLAN Notices*, pages 48–64. ACM, October 1998.

[11] Suzanne Collin, Dominique Colnet, and Olivier Zendra. Type Inference for Late Binding. The SmallEiffel Compiler. In *Joint Modular Languages Conference*, volume 1204 of *Lecture Notes in Computer Sciences*, pages 67–81. Springer-Verlag, 1997.

[12] Dominique Colnet, Philippe Coucaud, and Olivier Zendra. Compiler Support to Customize the Mark and Sweep Algorithm. In *ACM SIGPLAN International Symposium on Memory Management (ISMM'98)*, pages 154–165, October 1998.

[13] Mark Davis. Immutables. *Java-Report*, 4(4):70–77, April 1999.

[14] Amer Diwan, Kathryn S. McKinley, and J. Eliot B. Moss. Type-based alias analysis. In *Proceedings of the ACM Conference on Programming Language Design and Implementation*, pages 106–117, 1998.

[15] Erich Gamma, Richard Helm, Ralph Johnson, and John Vlissides. *Design Patterns: Elements of Reusable Object-Oriented Software*. Addison-Wesley, 1994.

[16] J. Goguen, J. Thatcher, and E. Wagner. An initial algebra approach to the specification, correctness and implementation of abstract datatypes. In R. Yeh, editor, *Current Trends in Programming Methodology (Vol. IV: Data Structuring)*. Prentice-Hall, 1978.

[17] James Gosling, Bill Joy, and Guy Steele. *The Java Language Specification*. Addison-Wesley, 1996.

[18] Roger Henriksson. *Scheduling Garbage Collection in Embedded Systems*. PhD thesis, Department of Computer Science, Lund University, Sweden, 1998.

[19] C. A. R. Hoare. Proof of correctness of data representations. *Acta Informatica*, (1), 1972.

[20] J. Hogg, D. Lea, A. Wills, D. de Champeaux, and Richard Holt. Report on ECOOP'91 workshop W3: The Geneva convention on the treatment of object aliasing. *OOPS Messenger*, 3(2):11–16, 1992.

[21] John Hogg. Islands: Aliasing Protection in Object-Oriented Languages. In *Proceedings of the OOPSLA '91 Conference on Object-oriented Programming Systems, Languages and Applications*, pages 271–285, November 1991. Published as ACM SIGPLAN Notices, volume 26, number 11.

[22] William Landi. Undecidability of static analysis. *ACM Letters on Programming Languages and Systems*, 1(4), December 1992.

[23] Doug Lea. *Concurrent Programming in Java – Design Principles and Patterns*. Addison Wesley, 1996.

[24] K. R. M. Leino. *Toward Reliable Modular Programs*. PhD thesis, California Institute of Technology, 1995.

[25] Tim Lindholm and Frank Yellin. *The Java Virtual Machine Specification*. Addison-Wesley, 1997.

[26] Barbara Liskov and John V. Guttag. *Abstraction and Specification in Program Development*. MIT Press/McGraw-Hill, 1986.

[27] B. Meyer. *Eiffel: The Language*. Object-Oriented Series. Prentice Hall, New York, N.Y., 1992.

[28] Bertrand Meyer. *Object-Oriented Software Construction*. Prentice-Hall, 1988.

[29] Naftaly Minsky. Towards alias-free pointers. In Pierre Cointe, editor, *ECOOP'96 — Object-Oriented Programming, 10th European Conference*, volume 1098 of *Lecture Notes in Computer Science*, pages 189–209, Berlin, Heidelberg, New York, July 1996. Springer.

[30] E. Morel and C. Renvoise. Global optimization by suppression of partial redundancies. *Communications of the ACM*, 22(2):96–103, February 1979.

[31] P. Müller and A. Poetzsch-Heffter. Modular specification and verification techniques for object-oriented software components. In G. Leavens and M. Sitaraman, editors, *Foundations of Component-Based Systems.* Cambridge University Press, 1999. (to appear).

[32] Kelvin Nilsen. Reliable Real-Time Garbage Collection of C++. *Computing Systems*, 7(4):467–504, 1994.

[33] James Noble, Jan Vitek, and John Potter. Flexible alias protection. In *Proceedings of ECOOP'98*, number 1445 in LNCS, pages 158–185. Springer Verlag, 1998.

[34] Nathaniel John Nystrom. Bytecode level analysis and optimization of Java classes. Master's thesis, Purdue University, August 1998.

[35] Robert O'Callahan. The design of program analysis services. Technical Report CMU-CS-99-135, Carnegie Mellon University, Pittsburgh, PA 15213, June 1999.

[36] Patrik Persson. Live Memory Analysis for Garbage Collection in Embedded Systems. In *Proceedings of the ACM SIGPLAN 1999 Workshop on Languages, Compil ers, and Tools for Embedded Systems (LCTES'99), SIGPLAN Notices 34(7)*, pages 45–54. ACM Press, 1999.

[37] G. Plotkin. LCF considered as a programming language. *Theoretical Computer Science*, 5(3), 1977.

[38] John Potter, James Noble, and David Clarke. The ins and outs of objects. In *Australian Software Engineering Conference (ASWEC)*, 1998.

[39] William Pugh. Fixing the Java memory model. In *ACM Java Grande Conference*, 1999.

[40] Mooly Sagiv, Thomas Reps, and Reinhard Wilhelm. Solving shape-analysis problems in languages with destructive updating. *ACM Transactions on Programming Languages and Systems*, 20(1):1–50, January 1998.

[41] Loren Taylor Simpson. *Value-Driven Redundancy Elimination.* PhD thesis, Rice University, Houston, Texas, April 1996.

[42] Bjarne Steensgaard. Points-to analysis in almost linear time. In *Conference Record of the Twenty-third Annual ACM SIGACT/SIGPLAN Symposium on Principles of Programming Languages*, pages 32–41, New York, 1996. ACM Press.

[43] Dirk Theisen. Enhancing Encapsulation in OOP – A Practical Approach. Masters thesis, CS Dept. III, University of Bonn, Germany, 1999.

[44] Philip Wadler. Linear types can change the world! In M. Broy and C. B. Jones, editors, *Programming Concepts and Methods.* Elsevier, North-Holland, 1990.

[45] Phillip Yelland. *Models of Modularity: A Study of Object-Oriented Programming.* PhD thesis, Cambridge University, Cambridge, U.K., 1991.

Experiences in Object-Oriented Re-engineering

Stéphane Ducasse[1] and Oliver Ciupke[2]

[1] University of Bern, IAM-SCG
ducasse@iam.unibe.ch, http://www.iam.unibe.ch/ ducasse/
[2] Forschungszentrum Informatik of Karlsruhe (FZI)
ciupke@fzi.de, http://www.fzi.de/ciupke.html

1. Workshop Summary

This paper reports the activities that took place during the third edition of the workshop on Experiences in Object-Oriented Reengineering (Previous editions were held during ECOOP'97 and ECOOP'98 [3] [2]). This year seventeen participants attended the workshop. The overall organization stayed the same. Prior to the workshop each participant was asked to read the full version of the submitted papers that have been edited as internal proceedings. Then each participant presented his paper in 10 minutes followed by 10 minutes discussion. Then during the afternoon the two focus groups were formed to discuss the following topics: (1) Metrics, Visualisation and Problem Detection, and (2) Program Understanding, (Re)-documentation and Refactoring Composition.

Suggested further reading are the previous edition of the proceedings [2], the proceedings of this workshop containing the full versions of the papers[1], and look at the FAMOOS Esprit project whose main goal is reengineering object-oriented applications (`http://www.iam.unibe.be/~famoos`, `http://www.sema.es/projects/FAMOOS/`).

The report is organized as follow: first we summarize the presented work then second we report on the group discussions. Every participant sent a summary of her/his work with up to five references on their own work. The submitted papers are categorized in the following groups: Problem Detection, Program Understanding based on Metrics, Program Visualization, Framework Documentation, Dynamic Analysis, and Behavior based Architecture Extraction, and Support for Evolution.

2. Problem Detection

Metrics-Based Problem Detection in Object-Oriented Legacy Systems Using Audit-Reengineer

Authors: Anne-Marie Sassen and Radu Marinescu
Emails: `anne-marie.sassen@sema.es, radum@cs.utt.ro`

Object oriented programming has often been promoted as the most effective approach to build inherently flexible software, and was quickly adopted by industry in the recent years. There are already applications consisting of millions of

A. Moreira and S. Demeyer (Eds.): ECOOP'99 Workshops, LNCS 1743, pp. 164–183, 1999.

lines of code developed in several hundred man-years. While the benefits of object oriented technology are widely recognized, its utilization does not necessarily result in general, adaptable families of systems. These large applications are often suffering from improper use of object oriented techniques (like inheritance) and the lack of object oriented methods being geared towards the construction of families of systems instead of building single applications. The result is a new generation of inflexible legacy systems, which need to be reengineered. Because of the large numbers of lines of a legacy system, tool support is indispensable.

In this article we present Audit-Reengineer, a product based on Concerto2/Audit, SEMA's tool for quality assessment, and on the results of ESPRIT project 21975 FAMOOS. We have assessed the suitability of the metrics included in the tool from the perspective of re-engineering. We validated the tool on two medium sized case studies. The tested metrics were: Tight Class Cohesion (TCC): Measures the cohesion of a class as the relative number of directly connected methods. (Methods are considered to be connected when they use common instance variables.) Change Dependency Between Classes (CDBC): Determines the potential amount of follow-up work to be done in a client class when the server class is being modified, by counting the number of methods in the client class that might need to be changed because of a change in the server class. Data Abstraction Coupling (DAC): Measures coupling between classes as given by the declaration of complex attributes, i.e. attributes that have another class of the system as a type. Weighted Method Count (WMC): Measures the complexity of a class by adding up the complexities of the methods defined in the class. The complexity measurement of a method is the McCabe cyclomatic complexity. Reuse of Ancestors (RA): Measures how much of a class is reused from one of its superclasses.

The general conclusion is that the metrics included in the tool work very well for model capture. For problem detection however, we found less evidence of their suitability. A likely reason for this is that the case studies were well designed and that they are no legacy systems. In fact they are maintained until now without any specific difficulty. Therefore, our next step in the evaluation of Audit-Reengineer will be to apply it to real legacy systems.

References

[Audit 98] User Manual Concerto2/Audit-CC++, Sema Group, 56 rue Roger Salengro, 94126 Fontenay-Sous-Bois Cedex - France , 1998

[CDDN 99] O. Ciupke, S. Demeyer, S. Ducasse, R. Nebbe, T. Richner, M. Rieger, B. Schulz, S. Tichelaar, J. Weisbrod. The Famoos Handbook of Reengineering, Deliverable 5.6.1 of FAMOOS, 1999.

[Mar 97] R. Marinescu. The use of Software Metrics in the Design of Object Oriented Systems. Diploma thesis at the "Politechnica" University in Timisoara, 1997.

[Mar 98] R. Marinescu. Refined Metrics and Heuristics. Internal FAMOOS achievement, RMETH A2.5.1, 1998.

Detecting Design Defects in Object-Oriented Software

Authors: Marcelo Machado Feres
Emails: mferes@emn.fr, mferes@cefetcampos.br

Although object-oriented techniques allow software systems to be more flexible, reusable and maintainable, there are many practices in the software development process that compromise the software quality and make it difficult to evolve, therefore generating defects. It is desirable to avoid those practices and and as much as possible to detect them automatically. We have been investigating design heuristics and antipatterns to identify what are the main practices that represent design defects often present in object-oriented software and which tools and techniques could be useful to their detection.

In order to detect some design defects we have developed a practical approach to detect design defects in Java legacy systems. This approach consists of specifying design defects as queries to be applied in the UML design information generated by a reverse engineering tool.

The process consists of take a Java source code and apply a reverse engineering tool that generates as a result the design information following the UML metamodel and some relevant code information such as instantiation, message sending, etc. After that, the information generated is converted to an appropriate format to be understood by an expert system (we have used JESS - Java Expert System Shell), as a fact list. The design defects or guideline violations we want to detect are specified as rules in JESS.

The final results are the representation of parts of the source code that contain potential design defects. Our approach follows the technique proposed by Oliver Ciupke to automatic problem detection, but we have chosen to represent the source code through the UML metamodel, therefore it was possible to detect some design defects and guideline violations stated as not automatically detectable, for example method overridden with no operation that represents a violation of a design heuristic proposed by Arthur Riel.

References

[Fere99] M. M. Feres. Detecting Design Defects in Object-Oriented Software Master Thesis. Ecole des Mines de Nantes - France. August/1999. (http://www.emn.fr)

[Riel96] A. J. Riel. Object-Oriented Design Heuristics. Addison-Wesley, 1996.

[BM98] W. J. Brown, R. C. Malveau, H. W. "Skip" McCormick III, T. J. Mowbary. AntiPatterns. Refactoring software, architectures, and projects in crisis. Wiley computer publishing, 1998.

[BC98] H. Bär and O. Ciupke. Exploiting design heuristics for automatic problem detection. In Proceedings of the ECOOP Workshop on Experiences in Object-Oriented Re-Engineering, number 6/7/98 in FZI Report, June 1998.

A Guideline to Detect Reusable Components

Authors: Lucia Torres Gastal
Emails: luli@atlas.ucpel.tche.br

The work described here addresses the field of software reuse. Software reuse is widely considered as a way to increase the productivity in software development. Moreover it can bring more quality and reliability to the resultant software systems. Identifying, extracting and reengineering software components from legacy code is a promising cost-effective way to support reuse. Considering this assumption, this sense in Object-Oriented (OO) legacy system. In order to compose this Guideline some existing techniques to detect reusable components were evaluated. From them the main aspects concerning object-oriented concepts are taken into account. In addition, the basic concerns of object-oriented paradigm are considered since they hold in themselves the goal to tackle reuse. After showing the Guideline composition process and the principles covered in its context, some of the directives stated are applied in a case study to demonstrate their use in practice.

3. Metrics for Program Understanding

Understanding Object Oriented Software Systems without Source Code Inspection

Authors: Gerd Köhler, Heinrich Rust and Frank Simon
Emails: {hgk,rust,simon}@informatik.tu-cottbus.de

An approach for metrics-based tool support for the task of understanding object oriented software systems is presented. Understandability of software is one of the most important quality factors, which is sometimes directly demanded and sometimes a refined criterion. It is a precondition for assessing a software system [KöRuSi98]. The task of understanding large software systems is made easier if more structural properties can be made explicit to the software engineer. Object oriented programming languages allow to express more of the software structure in an explicit, syntactically fixed way than do other programming paradigms. This additionally structure can also be used to define software measures which typically concentrate many structural features into statistics.

In our work, we propose the combined presentation of structural information and of different types of metrics in hyperdocument form for the identification of large and small system components and usage and inheritance relations of the system components with each other. We distinguish program components on several granularity levels of the software system: The whole system (represented by a directory tree with all its content) consists of subsystems (represented by the directories of the tree). Each subsystem consists of files, which in turn contain classes, which finally consist of methods and attributes. This is the lowest granularity level we consider. The is-direct-component-of relation turns the system components of the different levels into a tree. We developed a tool which, for each component, generates a hyperdocument. These hyperdocuments are linked by hyperlinks representing different relations between components. These include the transitive part-of relation, the is-direct-component relation, for each component the uses relation and the is-used-by relation to components of the same or of a bigger granularity. Additionally, we collected two types of metrics for each of the components, which are presented in the hyperdocument: Different size metrics were used which measure the number of sub-components or smaller elements (like number of characters of a method definition), while different coupling metrics were used which represent different intensities of mutual uses of system components. The measures and links between the hyperdocuments which our tool has to generate are configurable. They have the form of parameterised SQL-statements in an HTML-skeleton file. The SQL statements are used to extract the relevant information from a database which represents the symbol-table information of a CASE-Tool (cf. [LeSi98]).

We developed the thesis that the understandability of a large software system can be improved by adding this type of explicit documentation to the system. A small exploratory student experiment with ten participants was performed which was used to validate our approach; in this experiment, both our tool and other approaches were used to restructure given software systems into subsystems, i.e. the systems were given as flat sets of files which were to be grouped into several subsystems (cf. [AbPeSo98]). To be able to compare the results with respect to the effort spent, we restricted the time for each restructuring to 120 minutes. This was our way to operationalise understandability. Each student restructured two systems (each with about 60 classes), one with the information presented by our tool and one without, in which source-code analysis was performed in any other way the students chose to. We collected information about which kind of information the students used in the projects, and we compared the different results, e.g. with respect to forgotten classes. Our basic assumptions were confirmed, e.g. when our tool was used, the students used more different types of information in the same time than when it was not used. Students reported that the extra data presented by our tool was helpful for their understanding.

References

[AbPeSo98] F. B. e Abreu, C. Pereira, P. Sousa. "Reengineering the Modularity of Object Oriented Systems", in Workshop "Techniques, Tools and Formalisms for Capturing and Assessing the Architectural Quality in Object Oriented Software", ECOOP'98.

[LeSi98] C. Lewerentz, F. Simon. "A Product Metrics Tool Integrated into a Software Development Environment", in Proceedings of Workshop on Object-Oriented Product Metrics for Software Quality Assessment, ECOOP'98, CRIM Montréal 1998.

[KöRuSi98] G. Köhler, H. Rust, F. Simon. "An Assessment of Large Object Oriented Software Systems", in Proceedings of Workshop on Object-Oriented Product Metrics for Software Quality Assessment, ECOOP'98, CRIM Montréal 1998.

Reverse Engineering Based on Metrics and Program Visualization

Authors: Michele Lanza, Stéphane Ducasse and Serge Demeyer
Emails: `{lanza,ducasse,demeyer}@iam.unibe.ch`
URLs: `http://www.iam.unibe.ch/ lanza,ducasse,demeyer/`

The reverse engineering of large scale object-oriented legacy systems is a challenging task with a definite need for approaches providing a fast overview and focussing on the problematic parts. We investigate a hybrid approach, combining the immediate appeal of visualizations with the scalability of metrics. Moreover, we impose ourselves the extra constraint of simplicity: i.e. (a) that the graph layout should be *quite trivial* and (b) that the extracted metrics should be *simple* to compute. Indeed, our goal is to identify useful combinations of graphs and metrics that can be easily reproduceable by reverse engineers using some scriptable reengineering toolset. We validate such a hybrid approach by showing how CodeCrawler —the experimental platform we built— allowed us to reverse engineer a small to medium software system.

Principle. We enrich a simple graph with metric information of the object-oriented entities it represents. In a two-dimensional graph we render up to five metrics on a single node at the same time.

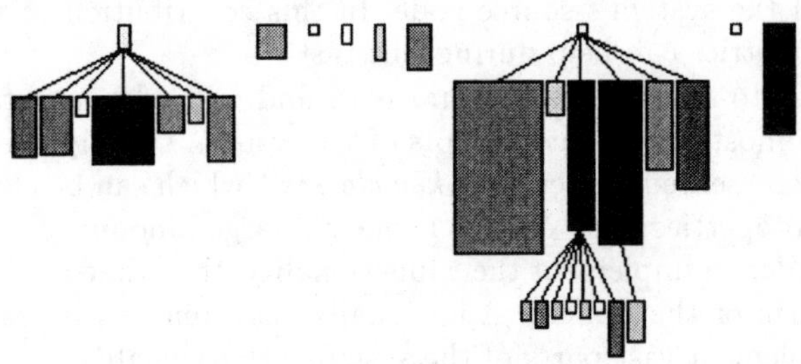

Fig. 1. Inheritance Tree; node width = NIV, node height = NOM and color = NCV.

As an example 1 shows an inheritance tree graph of CodeCrawler. The nodes represent the classes, the edges represent the inheritance relationships. The size of the nodes reflects the number of instance variables (width) and the number of methods (height) of the class, while the color tone represent the number of class variables. The position of a node does not reveal a metric as it is used to show the location in the inheritance tree.

CodeCrawler. CodeCrawler is developed within the VisualWorks 2.0 Smalltalk environment, relying on the HotDraw framework [John92] for its visualization. Moreover, it uses the facilities provided by the VisualWorks 2.0 environment for the Smalltalk code parsing, whereas for other languages like C++ and Java it relies on Sniff+ to generate code representation coded using the FAMIX Model [Tich98]. For more information see
`http://www.iam.unibe.ch/~lanza/codecrawler/`

References

[Duca99] S. Ducasse, S. Demeyer and M. Lanza, A Hybrid Reverse Engineering Approach Combining Metrics and Program Visualization, Accepted to WCRE'99.

[Lanz99] M. Lanza, Master thesis, Combining Metrics and Graphs to Reverse Engineer OO Applications, University of Berne, 1999.

Analysing Software Systems by Using Combinations of Metrics
Authors: Markus Bauer
Emails: `bauer@fzi.de`
URLs: `http://www.fzi.de/bauer.html`

Usually, one of the first steps when reengineering a legacy system is to get some basic understanding on how the system works and on how it is structured. This task is called *model capture* and usually requires some rather time consuming analysis of the system's source code. In this contribution to the workshop, we show how metrics can help during this task.

A good way to start model capture is to find out, which parts (i.e. classes) implement the most important concepts of the system. Usually, these concepts of a system are represented by very few *key classes*[1], which can be characterised by the following properties: Key classes *manage* a large amount of other classes or *use* them in order to implement their functionality, thus they are tightly *coupled* with other parts of the system. Additionally they tend to be rather *complex*, since they implement vast parts of the system's functionality.

After having made that observation, it is easy to identify these key classes by using both, a complexity metric like WMC [CK94] and a coupling metric like DAC [LH93] and combine the measurement results. Figure 2 shows a diagram that can be used for such an analysis – the classes of the legacy system are placed into a coordinate system according to their complexity and coupling measurements. Classes that are complex and tightly coupled with the rest of the system fall into the upper right corner and are good candidates for these key classes. To understand, how the legacy system works, we should thus concentrate on understanding these classes and their interactions by studying their source code. This focuses our effort during model capture to very few parts of the system and thus saves a lot of time and costs.

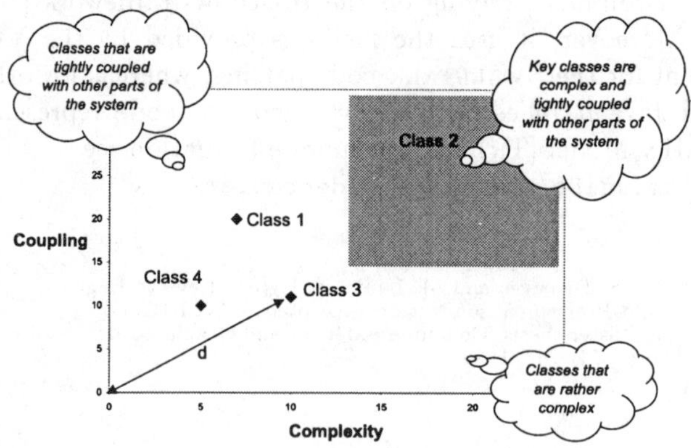

Fig. 2. Finding the key classes in a legacy system.

[1] Case studies indicate that about 10 % of the classes of a system can be considered as key classes

We believe, that two principles made our approach work rather well: using a combination of metrics with *a well defined meaning* (we clearly knew what coupling and complexity properties key classes have) and relying on a *graphical evaluation* technique that is easy to understand. Therefore, we should apply these principles in other reengineering tasks as well.

References

[CDT99] Ciupke O., Ducasse S., Tichelaar S. et al.: The FAMOOS Handbook of Reengineering. Software Composition Group, University of Berne, Switzerland, 1999.

[CK94] Chidamber S.R., Kemerer C.F.: A Metric Suite for Object-Oriented Design. In: IEEE Transactions on Software Engineering, June 1994.

[LH93] Li W., Henry S.: Maintenance Metrics for the Object-Oriented Paradigm. In: IEEE Proc. First International Software Metrics, May 1993.

4. Program Visualization, Software Documentation, and UML

Simplification of Class Diagrams Using Graph Compression Techniques

Authors: Ferenc Dósa Rácz and Kai Koskimies
Emails: `ferenc.dosa@nokia.com`, `kk@cs.tut.fi`

Understanding a class diagram of a legacy software system is definittely a non-scalable task: human eyes and brain is capable surveying a diagram containing some tens of classes but in case of hundreds or thousands of classes - which is most probable in case of reverse engineering - it becomes impossible to grasp the overall architecture of the system. The usual learning process of brain propose a way for us: by classifying individual experiences by their features we can get from the individuals to abstract knowledge represented by groups. Applying this to class diagrams: using a specific information [see later] we group class symbols, and we can simply hide the classes belonging to the same groups, and represent them by the group they belong to. The user should be able to look at the hidden class symbols thus we will need an uncompression operation defined on compressed diagrams to show the formerly invisible classes.

Principle. Our aim is to create a compressed graph which is semantically valid, or at least close to valid. In order to perform a hiding [called compression] operation we need a set of features to classify by: the associations between classes has been chosen. During compression we set up a containment hierarchy, and we register the association the compression was performed by for being able to perform further compressions or uncompressions in a consistent way. For automatic compression [in case of reverse engineering] we can use inheritance, aggregation, and implementation of interface associations to compress by. Other compressions can be performed only by user interaction.

Comments.

- The exact method of automatic compressions and the validness of compressed diagrams are still in question and research as well as user interactive version of the compression technique.
- A compressed diagram is just another kind of view to the same model therefore it should not affect the graphical layout of the diagram. During compression we hide and during uncompression we show class symbols - this definittely affects the layout, though. Meaningful presentation options for compressed class diagrams are under investigaton as well. [Different graph layout methods, inner views i.e. being able to explore containment hierarchies.]

References

[RJB99] Rumbaugh J., Jacobson I., Booch G.: The Unified Modeling Language Reference Manual. Addison-Wesley 1999.

[Kos98] Koskimies K.: Extracting high-level views of UML class diagrams. In: Proc. of NOSA '98 (First Nordic Workshop on Software Architecture), Research Report 14/98, Department of Computer Science, University of Karlskrona/Ronneby, August 1998.

Minimalist Documentation of Frameworks

Authors: Kasper Østerbye
Emails: `kasper@daimi.au.dk`

Programmers are like most other humans - they prefer to act rather than read. In the context of application frameworks, this means that a programmer is more inclined to "try it out" than to read its manual. Rather than trying to force programmers to stop this all too human habit, this paper examine ways in which documentation can be organized so that a programmer is supported in learning through doing rather than learning through reading. The programmer is most open to study documentation during a breakdown of his understanding of the framework, and must in that case be led to the appropriate pieces of documentation.

Minimalist documentation is a documentation style developed by John Carroll [Carr90] for end user documentation for software systems. It tries to come up with a new documentation paradigm, in which the documentation does not strive to be complete, but sufficient, and where the documentation is intended to be studied along with using the system, rather than read as a standalone piece of writing. The rationale is that the new user will create a model of the software more efficiently while using the system, and by encouraging use, the user will also easier bring his or her background experiences to bear in the new system.

The approach presented in the workshop paper examines how framework documentation can benefit from Carroll's ideas on minimalist documentation. The documentation is organised in a manner that will allow the programmer to be active within minutes of starting with the framework and its documentation. The main points in our approach are:

- Example based tutorial based on full running examples.
- A fairly traditional reference manual.
- Extensive run-time checks in the framework, as a designer you must assume all rules will be broken.
- Hypertext linking between reference manual and examples, and from runtime errors to manual and examples.

The paper examines framework documentation in the context for a discrete event simulation framework BetaSIM for the programming language BETA.

The BetaSIM tutorial starts out with an example that can be compiled and run, and indicates what can be changed without the program breaking down. Only then does the tutorial spend some time explaining what the program does. To keep the tutorial terse, it does not give the exact meaning of all aspects of the framework, but focuses on overall effects. This is deliberate - to support a more detailed understanding, all usage of framework classes and methods are linked to the reference manual. This makes it easy to seek more information, or not to do so if one understands the program as it is.

A reference manual must satisfy several important criteria. It must be complete, correct, up to date, and not the least, it must be well indexed. The reference manual for BetaSIM is organized in the same way as JavaDoc [Frie95], with a page per class. However, most classes have hypertext references which links back to the relevant locations in the tutorial.

In his minimalist instruction, John Carroll operates with the notion of training wheels, which are special support from the system to support beginners, so that their errors need not be fatal. The BetaSIM framework performs extensive error checking, and tries to explain the possible courses. The main thesis behind this work is that breakdowns are an opportunity where the programmer is prepared to switch from doing to learning. An example, not from BetaSIM, but from a container library, could be to have an indexed insert operation on a stack, which reported an error that briefly explains the difference between a stack and an indexed collection. The idea being that the user might not have used a wrong operation on a stack, but a wrong data structure. The error messages will often refer back to the tutorial to illustrate correct usage.

The paper also contains a discussion of tool support for writing such documentation, and it discusses related work.

References

[Carr90] J. M. Carroll. The Nurnberg Funnel: Designing Minimalist Instruction for Practical Computer Skill. The MIT Press, 1990.

[Frie95] L. Friendly. The design of distributed hyperlinked programming documentation. In International Workshop on Hypermedia Design, 1995, page 159, June 1995. Proceedings to be republished summer 95 by Springer Verlag.

Formalization of UML Using Algebraic Specifications
Authors: Rachel Pires Vieira de Vasconcelos
Emails: rachelpires@censa.com.br@emn.fr

We describe an algebraic semantic framework covering the formalization of the main static model elements of UML. As UML is the unification of Object-Oriented (OO) analysis and design modeling languages, the formalization process presented here can be easily extended to other similar OO notation sets. Moreover it can contribute towards a standardization of OO modeling concepts. In the semantic framework presented in this work model elements are formal described through algebraic specifications defining abstract data types. Abstract data types allow the specification of the semantics in an abstract way being really suitable to the description of OO models. The formal specifications are written in Larch Prover (LP). LP is a theorem prover that allows verifications and validations to be applied to the formal specifications. From these validations, properties and inconsistencies about the models can be proved what leads to early detection of errors in the software development process. These formal specifications to be interpreted by LP are generated from a UML CASE tool built in Graphtalk metatool. The integration between the CASE tool and the formal specifications is provided through a set of mapping rules established in this work.

5. Dynamic Analysis

Dynamic Reverse Engineering of Java Software
Authors: Tarja Systä
Emails: cstasy@cs.uta.fi
URLs: http://www.cs.uta.fi/~cstasy

Software maintenance, re-engineering, and reuse are complex and expensive because of program comprehension difficulties. Thus, the need for software engineering methods and tools that facilitate program understanding is compelling. A variety of reverse engineering tools provide means to help program understanding. Reverse engineering aims producing design models from the software. The application of reverse engineering techniques is not limited to understanding old legacy systems. They can and should be applied for forward engineering as well, e.g., to document the implementation steps.

To fully understand existing software both static and dynamic information need to be extracted. Static information describes the structure of the software the way it is written in the source code, while dynamic information describes its run-time behavior. Extracting information about the dynamic behavior of the software is especially important when examining object-oriented software. This is due to the dynamic nature of object-oriented programs: object creation, object deletion/garbage collection, and dynamic binding make it very difficult, and in many cases impossible, to understand the behavior by just examining the source code.

A prototype environment that has been built to reverse engineer Java software. The static information is extracted from the byte code and analyzed with Rigi reverse engineering environment [MWT94]. The dynamic event trace information is generated automatically as a result of running the target system under a debugger. SCED [KMST98] is used to view the event trace as scenario diagrams. In SCED state diagrams can be synthesized automatically from scenario diagrams. This facility is used to examine the total behavior of a class, an object, or a single method, disconnected from the rest of the system.

For testing the usability of the prototype reverse engineering environment a target Java software, FUJABA [RoH98] has been examined. Based on the feedback received from FUJABA group the resulting dynamic models were self-explanatory and they correspond to their understanding of the behavior. In addition, a source of one known bug was identified by examining the generated scenarios.

References

[KMST98] Koskimies K., Männistö T., Systä T., and Tuomi J.: Automated Support for Modeling OO Software, IEEE Software, 15, 1, Janyary/February 1998, pp. 87-94.

[MWT94] Muller H., Wong K., and Tilley S.: Understanding software systems using reverse engineering technology, In the Proceedings of the 62nd Congress of L'Association Canadienne Française pour l'Avancement des Sciences (ACFAS), 1994.

[RoH98] Rockel I. and Heimes F.: FUJABA - Homepage, `http://www.uni-paderborn.de/fachbereich/AG/schaefer/ag_dt/PG/Fujaba/fujaba.html`, February, 1999.

6. Refactoring and Evolution

Tool-Supported Component Evolution

Authors: Thomas Genßler and Benedikt Schulz
Emails: {`genssler,bschulz`}`@fzi.de`

In this paper we present an approach to the tool-based evolution of legacy components. Our technique is rooted in the concepts of aspect-oriented programming. The main idea behind our approach is to identify fragments of so-called aspect code within existing components and to provide a means to adapt this code to new requirements. Static meta-programming provides the implementation basis for our approach We have implemented a number of meta-programming adaptation and configuration operators. Those operators are meta-programs written in a standard programming language and perform complex reorganization operations on legacy components such as replacing communication links, increasing flexibility, and wrapping. We present some examples of how to apply our technique, ranging from flexibility-improving reorganizations to the adaptation of components to new middle-ware platforms.

Automated Application of Design Patterns to Legacy Code

Authors: Mel Ó Cinnéide and Paddy Nixon
Emails: `Mel.OCinneide@ucd.ie`, `Paddy.Nixon@cs.tcd.ie`

Legacy systems frequently suffer from a lack of flexibility that hampers the further development of the system. A common approach to this problem is to apply design patterns [Gam95] to the places in the system where extra flexibility is required. This task is usually performed by hand, without the benefit of tool support. While in general the application of a design pattern requires designer judgement, many aspects of the process are automatable and this is the focus of our work.

In developing a design pattern transformation we commence by considering the starting point for the transformation. We assume that the intent of the pattern exists in the code in some simple but inflexible way, and this structure is termed a precursor. The transformation must therefore bridge the gap between the precursor and the design pattern structure itself. We attempt to decompose this gap into a number of minipatterns. Minipatterns are the design motifs that occur frequently in the design pattern descriptions. For each minipattern a minitransformation is developed that can apply this minipattern. Minitransformations serve as the unit of reuse for our transformations.

Design pattern transformations are to be applied to an existing system so it is important that they do not affect the observable behaviour of the program. For each design pattern transformation we develop a structured behaviour preservation argument in a similar way to earlier work on C++ refactorings [Opd92]. We define a set of primitive refactorings and, using these as a basis, argue that the minitransformations, and consequently the design pattern transformations themselves, are behaviour preserving.

Our methodology has been applied successfully to structure-rich creational patterns such as Abstract Factory, Factory Method, Singleton and Builder. We also applied an earlier version of this methodology to a structural pattern, Decorator [OCi97]. The applicability of this approach to strongly behavioural patterns, where the structure of the pattern is less important than its dynamic aspects, has yet to be established. Our current work involves applying this methodology to a broad variety of design patterns and evaluating our software tool further in a practical context. For more detail please see [OCi99].

References

[Gam95] Gamma, E. et al, Design Patterns: Elements of Reusable Object-Oriented Software, Addison-Wesley, 1995.

[OCi97] Ó Cinnéide, M., Towards Automating the Introduction of the Decorator Pattern to Avoid Subclass Explosion, Technical Report TR-97-7, Department of Computer Science, University College Dublin, Ireland.

[OCi99] Ó Cinnéide, M. and Nixon, P., A Methodology for the Automated Introduction of Design Patterns, Proceedings of the International Conference on Software Maintenance, Oxford, August 1999 (to appear).

[Opd92] Opdyke, W. F., Refactoring Object-Oriented Frameworks, PhD thesis, University of Illinois, 1992.

Tool Support for Refactoring Duplicated OO Code

Authors: Matthias Rieger, Stéphane Ducasse and Georges Golomingi
Emails: {ducasse, rieger, goloming}@iam.unibe.ch
URLs: http://www.iam.unibe.ch/~scg/

Code duplication is a well-known problem in software maintenance, bloating up source code and complicating the extermination of errors. Refactorings are a way to transform an application in a behaviour preserving manner [OJ92] . Duplication is one important aspect of code where refactorings can be used to improve the source code. We propose to use a duplication detection tool, Duploc [DRD99], to guide the refactoring process.

Combining Duplication Information and a Static OO Model. The approach is based on availability of information about duplication as well as the ability to represent a program in terms of object-oriented entities, like for example classes, methods and attributes.

The Approach Step-by-Step. To refactor applications based on duplication information we combine the tools presented above in the following process: (1) We represent the object-oriented application we want to analyse using the FAMIX meta model [DTS98]. The entities of the meta-model contain source anchors. (2) According to an object-oriented refactoring scenarios (see below) entities from the application model are selected and their source code is fetched. (3) The duplication information is generated by running the source code through Duploc. (4) Analysis of the duplication in the context of the refactoring scenario selected in step 2: can the duplication be refactored? Note that this step requires the interaction with a human operator.

General Refactoring Operations to Counter Code Duplication. In our analysis of duplication we see two cases where refactoring operations can be applied: (a) A complete function is duplicated exactly. The solution is to remove all but one copy of the function and adjust the calls to the function accordingly. (b) A piece of code is found as part of a number of functions. The solution is to extract the piece and create a new function F from it, replacing the duplicated code with calls to F.

Before applying the refactoring operation, additional analysis is needed to determine the context in which the duplicated code is found. The context consists in local variables and parameters that are accessed by the duplicated code. This analysis is complicated even more in object-oriented code. Analysis of this kind can be supported by tools as is shown in [RBJ97].

Refactoring Duplication in an Object-Oriented Context. We have identified three situations of relationships between object-oriented software entities and discuss the refactorings that can be applied in each of the cases: (a) Duplication inside of a Single Class. To execute the refactorings, no special care has to be taken about class borders, the whole class can be seen as a procedural program. (b) Duplication between Sibling Classes. To simplify the analysis, we only consider situations where *all* the subclasses of a common superclass contain the duplication. The solution in this case is to move the the one method that has been left over after the refactoring has been executed to the common superclass. (c) Duplication between Unrelated Classes. If the same functionality is found in different classes, this might indicate a new responsibility which could be factored out into its own class.

References

[DRD99] S. Ducasse, M. Rieger, and S. Demeyer. A Language Independent Approach for Detecting Duplicated Code, to appear in ICSM'99.

[DTS98] S. Demeyer, S. Tichelaar, and P. Steyaert. Definition of a common exchange model. Technical report, University of Berne, July 1998.

[OJ92] W.F. Opdyke and R.E. Johnson. Creating abstract superclasses by refactoring.1992.

[RBJ97] D. Roberts, J. Brant, and R. E. Johnson. A refactoring tool for smalltalk. *Journal of Theory and Practice of Object Systems (TAPOS)*, 3(4):253–263, 1997.

7. Architecture Extraction

Extracting Architecture: The Behavioural Point of View

Authors: Xavier Alvarez and Isabelle Borne
Emails: {`Xavier.Alvarez,Isabelle.Borne`}`@emn.fr`

The reengineering of architectures in Object-Oriented systems hasn't been achieved in a systematic way. Usually, the recovery of architecture is highly dependent on the previous knowledge of the system, ad-hoc techniques and the use of tools with a wide spectrum of complexity and effectiveness. The quality of the results varies too much and the applicability is not always as expected. Current approaches provide a helpful insight on the systems but fail to transmit the full picture of the collaborations between objects due to the underlying idea that 'structure determines behaviour', whereas we believe that it's the other way around.

The Problem. In the process of reverse engineering architecture the static information that is retrieved from the source code is too rudimentary. Or more likely the emphasis under which such information is examined is off-target. Objects enforce the encapsulation of their internal structure, leaving only the interaction through messages. This obviously conflicts with the idea of rebuilding the model based on the internal structure of the classes - which is the most common approach. Things like instance variables and inheritance are things that denote a structure - but of the internals. This kind of 'structural' analysis can be performed by humans simply because there's lot of semantic information in the names of classes, methods, variables, etc. This semantic information guides the analysis towards things that are semantically important for the application. Automatic recovery can't use this kind of information.

The Proposed Approach. From the paradigm's perspective, objects can only send messages between them, and the objects have a method on how to respond to a given message. From this perspective instance variables and inheritance doesn't matter too much, because they only reflect one of the possible implementations. We must note that we are dealing with a concrete application, therefore with a very concrete implementation so we'll have to address at some point the real structure (inheritance and like). The issue is 'when'. If we address this too early, we'll get tangled by the possible errors (perceived, real or otherwise) that are present in the application. For example: misuse of inheritance or other problems with the concrete structure, and the reason why we're trying to examine the architecture in the first place. Methods provide a powerful approach to determine the real collaborations between different elements and objects of the architecture. Not only because they 'send messages' but also because they incarnate the concept that expresses how a given responsibility is carried out. That is, the delegations, collaborations and services that are done by an object. For example, there's a bias in considering messages to instance variables 'more important' than arguments or temporals, but the truth is that the method needs all of them to carry out effectively. When building a 'traditional' architectural view of a system we must decide where does a given class fit into. This is particularly stressful when the class has been reused/adapted from one application to another (thus having 'mixed' behaviour and responsibilities). Deciding for any of the possible architectural elements can produce several violations to the intended architecture. So using the methods to build the architecture (instead of the classes) we introduce a finer grain of detail that allows to preserve architectures that otherwise would be considered invalid (or deteriorated).

Conclusions. It's our belief that over using the internal structure information retrieved from models is a limited (and possibly) erroneous way of reconstructing the architectures. More emphasis should be placed in the elements that actually carry out the behaviour of the objects to really understand how they behave instead on how they were built.

8. Report of Working Group on Metrics, Visualisation, and Problem Detection (Oliver Ciupke)

This discussion group was formed around the topics *software metrics*, *visualisation*, and *problem detection*. Whereas problem detection is a task in a reengineering process, metrics and visualisation are techniques which can potentially be used in several reengineering tasks. Consequently, a big issue during the discussion was the actual applicability of these techniques in problem detection. *Guidelines*, especially those dealing with the design of a system were also discussed in this context.

Guidelines. Informal knowledge about how to develop good systems is often expressed in the form of guidelines or heuristics. For example, many heuristics are published on how to design a software system. On the other hand, when examining a legacy system, searching for violations of such guidelines can also serve as a starting point for detecting problems in such a system.

It was discussed, to what degree guidelines can be useful in the context of reengineering, and if mandatory guidelines exist, i.e., guidelines which should be obeyed in any case. Everybody agreed, that there are no guidelines, for which you cannot think of reasonable exceptions. (E.g., even the well accepted rule to avoid goto statements may have its exception in the implementation of state machines.) Some participants reported however, that there were some guidelines for which at least in their experience so far, all violations found in existing systems had actually pointed to a real problem.

To give some examples, P. Steyaert uses the following guidelines in the development of multi-media and scheduling related software in Smalltalk: (1) No navigation code (Law of Demeter). In praxi: avoid path expressions, such as a.b.c.d(). (2) No code duplication. (3) No polymorphism simulated by case or if–then–else statements. and (4) Localise and encapsulate problematic parts of your system. (Intentionally build abstractions.)

Furthermore O. Ciupke reported, every cycle in the static structure of C++ programs he has examined so far, pointed to a design fragment he personally considered as an actual design flaw (i.e., its removal would considerably increase flexibility or simplicity).

For some guidelines it is not sure though, if a violation is due to a bad design or just due to a bad implementation. This can make it hard to come to a strategy for actually solving a corresponding problem.

Metrics. Software metrics are one of the most discussed topics in software reengineering. However, many questions even regarding their general applicability and usefulness still remain open: What do metrics really measure? Can they really be used to detect problems? In case they detect problems – they do not show what the problem really is.

Metric authors often do not make it clear, what they really want to measure with a metric they define. But to apply metrics, it is necessary for the user to first define the goal of the whole analysis, to select a suite of metrics measuring properties according to that goal, and to evaluate and interpret the results.

Many participants had experience in using metrics for the purpose of reengineering. They were still unsure, whether metrics are actually suitable to be applied in problem detection. If so, identifying the kind of the problem found as well as providing a solution to it are both not supported.

Maybe very "simple" metrics, such as lines of code or number of methods or attributes per class could be very useful. For example, the largest classes or methods in a existing systems mostly comprise potential for improvements with respect to flexibility. However, these kind of metrics are mostly neglected by research and tools in favour for more "sophisticated" ones.

Many metrics try to measure different notions of complexity. But what is seen as system complexity from a programmer point of view is difficult to map to a metric. Frank cited N. Fenton who sees this as even intrinsically impossible.

Combinations of metrics turned out to be useful in a case study done by M.Bauer E.g., classes which have a high value in WMC (a complexity metric), but low value in TCC (a coupling metric) are often more procedural oriented collections of functions and variables, instead of a single abstraction or an object of the application domain.

Visualisation. Visualisation of software structures can be done on different levels of abstraction. Typical for object-oriented systems are on the lower level the visualisation of the interaction and dependencies between methods and attributes. At higher level there are those between classes or then between subsystems (aka. packages, modules, etc.) Important for the user is that he can choose the level of abstraction he needs for his purposes and depending on the size of the system.

A common issue discussed together with all of the mentioned techniques was, to what degree certain tasks can actually be automated and what remains to be done in an interactive manner in the different cases. When detecting problems for example, every suspicious code fragment detected by tools needs further judgement by a human expert. The ability to support this kind of semi-automatic tasks could be one of the strongest points of visualisation.

9. Report of Working Group on Refactorings, and Frameworks (Re)-documentation (Stéphane Ducasse)

Refactorings Composition. The discussion focused on the combining of elementary refactorings into more complex ones. One of the questions was how to derive the preconditions of a complex refactoring from its constituent refactorings. A refactoring is a behaviour preserving operation that possesses a precondition that must hold before its application and a postcondition that is valid after its application. In the composition of elementary refactorings, checking all the preconditions of the elementary refactorings before applying the complex refactoring is not sufficient because even though the precondition of R_n might be true before the application of the composite refactoring, the refactoring R_{n-1} might invalidate this precondition. The inverse is also true: a valid composition could be thought to be invalid. For example, the precondition of R_n might fail before the application of the complex refactoring when in fact the refactoring R_{n-1} would have made it true.

Thomas Genssler and Mel O'Cinneide proposed two ways of achieving this composition of refactorings. One approach was to compose the refactorings *dynamically* from a library of elementary ones. The second approach was to provide the user with a useful set of complex refactorings, such as those that apply common design patterns.

With the first approach, the difficulty is to derive automatically the precondition of the complex refactoring from the elementary ones that compose it. The possible use of temporal logic was raised but without a really positive answer due to the intrinsic complexity of its introduction into the object paradigm and to the implied paradigm change. It was also argued that temporal logic was not needed in this case and that a simple right-to-left processing of the refactorings preconditions was sufficient.

As a pragmatic approach, it was suggested that since the elementary refactorings involve nearly orthogonal code transformations and therefore few composition problems, it could be interesting to see if the composability of a refactoring could be made explicit. Then the composition could be checked dynamically. Another discussion was the possibility of undoing a refactoring in case of a precondition failing during the execution of a complex one.

UML Extraction and Design Pattern Identification. The extraction of UML from the source code was discussed. In particular the issue that in Java as in Smalltalk the aggregation and composition is hard to extract directly from the source code without extra computation. In Smalltalk this situation is due to the fact that the language is dynamically typed and in Java to the absence of templates or generic types.

Several possibilities were discussed like searching for the explicit cast on collection elements in the abstract syntax tree, performing a dataflow analysis or using the dynamic behavior of the program to collect and synthetize the type.

Then the question of the correctness of the extraction was raised. Different points of view on the need for such a synchronization between the source code and the extracted design were discussed. It was said that from a reengineering point of view, keeping UML class diagrams in synchronization with the source code is far from ideal because the reengineer does not need to present code with boxes and arrows but to extract the design i.e. the principal elements of the code, their responsibilities, their relationships and collaborations. This view implies an interpretation of the code entities so clearly desynchronizing the code and the extracted design. However note that the mapping between the code entities and the extracted design entities can be kept to support the evolution of the code while preserving the design extraction heuristics.

The importance of the *behavior* of the entities was stressed in the context of object oriented entities that exchange message and hide their internal structure and representation. We foresee the following possible future research tracks: how role information or behavior information can serve as a base to reverse engineer and reengineer object-oriented applications following the ideas promoted by Reenskaug in his OORAM methodology.

The discussion derives to the topic of the identification of design patterns the code and the representation of design pattern as language constructs. Different views were enonced from the fact that design patterns should not be introduced as language constructs to the opposite, the reasonable view being that patterns could be introduced as language constructs if they would let the programmer enough flexibility and freedom. For the identification of design patterns into the code the variability of a possible implementation was raised and works using fuzzy logic and prolog rules were cited. However none of the participants had a real experience with these techniques.

Frameworks (Re)-Documentation. The documentation of frameworks and the redocumentation of applications was a long discuted topics.

Framework documentation difficulties were discussed how to document what is possible to achieve for a given framework, how to extend a framework so that it supports new functionalities, what is not possible to do with a framework, what is the level of granularity that we want to document, how a literate approach can be applied?

We summarize here the results of the discussion as a list of advices that somebody assigned to document a framework may follow. It was reported that the following practice was followed in industry: the documentation is often the task of a newcomer. The reason being that he will have to learn the framework anyway so the gain is double. However issue on the quality of the resulting documentation is still an open question.

Use automatic to semi-automatic solutions. Javadoc like approaches are interesting because they are scalable. They emphasize literate programming approach minimazing the distance between the code and its comments.

The examples should be really carefully chosen because they represent the intent of the frameworks. So the user will be somehow conditioned by these examples. Use growing examples to drive your explanations.

Try to link the errors and the problems an user can face to his own code and avoid abstract descriptions. Introduce hyperlinks from within the environment itself to the documentation.

Among the various sources of information that were examined, the FAQ (Frequently Asked Questions) is a definitive appealing one especially because of its ''How to " structure. Possible research tracks could be how to support simple and integrated user extension of the frameworks documentation. This could take into account multi users and central or distributed documentation.

Experiences on Framework Redocumentation. After discussing the frameworks documentation we discussed the frameworks redocumentation. One of the participants explained a technique that a company followed to redocument one of their framework. This company used a Javadoc approach for the complete framework. It also applied the same technique to the frameworks applications. Then the company grouped all the methods with the same name together presenting the method of the frameworks and its possible extensions

References

[1] O. Ciupke and S. Ducasse, editors. *Proceedings of the ECOOP'99 Workshop on Experiences in Object-Oriented Re-Engineering,* number FZI 2-6-6/99, Forschungszentrum Informatik, Haid-und-Neu-Straße 10-14, 76131 Karlsruhe, Germany, June 1999.

[2] S. Ducasse and J. Weisbrod, editors. *Proceedings of the ECOOP'98 Workshop on Experiences in Object-Oriented Re-Engineering*, number FZI 6/7/98, Forschungszentrum Informatik, Haid-und-Neu-Straße 10-14, 76131 Karlsruhe, Germany, June 1998.

[3] S. Ducasse and J. Weisbrod. *Report of the ECOOP'98 Workshop on Experiences in Object-Oriented Re-Engineering,* pages 72–96. LNCS 1543. Springer-Verlag, 1998.

Component-Oriented Programming

Clemens Szyperski[1], Jan Bosch[2], and Wolfgang Weck[3]

[1] Microsoft Research, Redmond, Washington
cszypers@microsoft.com - www.research.microsoft.com/users/cszypers/
[2] University of Karlskrona, Ronneby, Sweden
jan.bosch@ide.hk-r.se - www.ipd.hk-r.se/bosch/
[3] Oberon microsystems, Zurich, Switzerland
weck@oberon.ch - www.oberon.ch/

Abstract. This report summarizes the presentations, discussions, and thoughts expressed during the workshop sessions. *Full proceedings are available as a technical report* of the Department of Software Engineering and Computer Science at the University of Karlskrona/Ronneby, Sweden (http://www.ipd.hk-r.se/).

1. Introduction

WCOP'99, held together with ECOOP'99 in Lisboa, Portugal, was the fourth workshop in the successful series of workshops on component-oriented programming. The previous workshops were held in conjunction with the respective ECOOP conferences in Linz, Austria, Jyväskylä, Finland, and Brussels, Belgium. WCOP'96 had focussed on the principal idea of software components and worked towards definitions of terms. In particular, a high-level definition of what a software component is was formed. WCOP'97 concentrated on compositional aspects, architecture and gluing, substitutability, interface evolution, and non-functional requirements. WCOP'98 had a closer look at issues arising in industrial practice and developed a major focus on the issues of adaptation. WCOP'99 moved on to address issues of component frameworks, structured architecture, and some bigger systems built using components frameworks.

This report summarizes the presentations, discussions, and thoughts expressed during the workshop sessions. *Full proceedings are available as a technical report* of the Department of Software Engineering and Computer Science at the University of Karlskrona/Ronneby, Sweden (http://www.ipd.hk-r.se/).

WCOP'98 had been announced as follows:

> WCOP'99 is the fourth event in a series of highly successful workshops, which took place in conjunction with every ECOOP since 1996, focusing on the important field of component-oriented programming (COP).
>
> COP has been described as the natural extension of object-oriented programming to the realm of independently extensible systems. Several important approaches have emerged over the recent years, including

A. Moreira and S. Demeyer (Eds.): ECOOP'99 Workshops, LNCS 1743, pp. 184–192, 1999.

CORBA, COM (COM+, DCOM, ActiveX, DirectX, ...), JavaBeans. A component is not an object, but provides the resources to instantiate objects. Often, a single component will provide interfaces to several closely related classes. Hence, COP is about architecture and packaging, besides interoperation between objects.

After WCOP'96 focused on the fundamental terminology of COP, the subsequent workshops expanded into the many related facets of component software. WCOP'99 shall emphasis architectural design and construction of component-based systems beyond ad-hoc reuse of unrelated components. To enable lively and productive discussions, the workshop will be limited to 25 participants. Depending on the actually submitted positions papers, the workshop will be organized into three or four subsequent mini-sessions, each initiated by a presentation of two or three selected positions and followed by discussions. Instead of splitting the workshop into task forces, it is intended to provoke lively discussion by preparing lists of critical questions and some, perhaps provocative, statements (to be used on demand).

Position papers will be formally reviewed, each by at least two independent reviewers. As an incentive for submission of high quality statements, the best position statements will be combined with transcripts of workshop results and published.

Last year's WCOP'98 report observed: "The call for contributions in the area of systems rather than individual components and their pairwise coupling was addressed in only a minority of the submissions. It can be speculated that this is symptomatic for the relative youth of the component software discipline." Interestingly, this has changed and WCOP'99 did attract a large number of submissions in the area of component frameworks.

21 papers from nine countries were submitted to the workshop and formally reviewed. Eleven papers were accepted for presentation at the workshop and publication in the proceedings. About 40 participants from around the world participated in the workshop.

Based on the range of submissions and the relatively weak response from attendees when asked to submit ahead of time topics for discussion, the organizers decided to deviate from the announced workshop format. The workshop was organized into two morning sessions with presentations, one afternoon breakout session with four focus groups, and one final afternoon session gathering reports form the breakout session and discussing future direction.

2. Presentations

This section summarizes briefly the contributions of the eleven presenters.

Colin Atkinson (joint work with Thomas Kühne and Christian Bunse) pointed to what they call the "interface vicissitude problem." The observation is that the same logical operation requires different levels of detail at different architectural levels, *all* of which are 'real' in that they are actually realized in an implementation. An example is a *write* operation that accepts some datum and writes it to a file. At a high level this might be architected as a method on a file object: `f.write(d)`. Within the file system implementation, the operation likely turns into `fm.write(f,d)`, i.e., a method on a file manager object that takes both the datum and the file as arguments. Finally, on the level of an ORB the operation might be coded: `orb.request("write",f,d)`. Obviously, none of these levels is the only "right" one—and, equally, none of the corresponding architectural views is "better" than any of the others. Instead, it is useful to view such architecture as *stratified*, where each strata corresponds to a particular refinement level. Colin and Thomas observed that reflective architectures are a special case of stratified architectures.

Günter Graw introduced an approach to the formalization of Catalysis, aiming at the specification of behaviour in component frameworks. His approach, called cTLA (compositional TLA) is based on Lamport's Temporal Logic of Actions and supports constraints on processes, processes interacting via joint actions, added flexibility over TLA, structured verification as is required to support components, and a basis to build theorems. Relating Günter's work to the idea of architectural strata above, it was observed that cTLA might be applied usefully to capture the mapping between strata as a set of local refinements with established properties.

Sotirios Terzis (in joint work with Paddy Nixon) observed that current concepts of trading in distributed systems are largely based on syntactic notions, which they perceive as insufficient for locating useful components. Therefore, they propose a Component Description Language (CDL) that, in conjunction with semantic trading, would allow to broaden the offering a trader comes up with when requested to locate a matching component. Attendants raised some concern whether such semantic trading was feasible.

Constantinos Constantinides (joint work with Atef Bader and Tzilla Elrad) presented an aspect-oriented design framework for concurrent systems. They view aspects and components as two orthogonal dimensions: aspects cut across a system and cannot be encapsulated. Examples include synchronization, persistence, error handling, and security. They propose a new kind of "module" that itself cuts across traditional modules (or components). Deviating from the standard "weaver" approach, which requires access to source code and which tends to explode in complexity with the introduction of new aspects, they propose to follow a moderator pattern. A moderator is an object that moderates between components and aspects by coordinating semantic interaction of components and aspects. Moderators aim to mingle binary code instead of source code–some kind of "just in time" weaving. To get moderators into the picture, all components have to be written to include fully abstract calls to moderators at critical points.

James Noble aimed to characterize the nature of component frameworks. Wondering about the difference between Brad Cox's "evolutionary programming" and component frameworks (with their provision for controlled evolution), James claims that the following three technical features are characteristic of component frameworks:

1. Component containment—the representation and implementation of a component is not exposed by its interfaces.
2. Multiple instances of interfaces—a single object (single identity) can implement multiple interfaces.
3. Interface dispatch—each interface potentially needs its own state and behaviour (the folding of interfaces with like-named methods, as in Java, is not generally acceptable).

During the following discussion it became clear that James refered to component models (such as COM) as component frameworks; his three characteristic properties therefore really characterize components, not component frameworks. Attendants wondered whether interface accessibility should be linked to levels of refinement (like architectural strata).

Alex Telea presented his Vission System, a component framework supporting the construction of rich and diverse visualization and simulation systems. As a mechanism, Alex enhanced C++ with a dataflow mechanism and provided his Vission environment as a frontend. The approach combines the advantages from object orientation (persistance, subtyping/polymorphism) with advantages from dataflow approaches (modularity, visual programming). His components use inheritance to incorporate aspects. Using meta-class wrapping, Vission can reuse the massive existing base of scientific and visualization code—his presentation included a number of impressive examples.

Ole Madsen reported that he had been intrigued by a suggestion by Clemens Szyperski at last year's WCOP, where Clemens suggested that first-class COM support in Beta would be a good way to help Beta off its "island". Ole had followed through since then and reported about the lessons learned from supporting COM in Beta. They used nested classes to implement multiple interfaces, which worked well and which naturally allows Beta to implement COM classes. While COM was found nice conceptually, there are a number of messy details such as the parameter space. The rather weak available "specification" of COM IDL was seen as a major obstacle.

Ulrik Schultz discussed his idea of "blackbox program specialization." Program specialization aims to configure a generic component to perform well in a set of specific situations. Specialization operations require access to the implementation, while the selection of a specialization operation depends on the intended usage. Thus, in a component world, it is the component implementer that understands how specialization can be applied and what benefits can be gained, but it is the client using a component that knows which particular specialization would be applied best. Ulrik therefore proposes that components should implement extra interfaces that provide access to specialization operations. These can then be called by the client in its particular context.

Henrik Nielsen (joint work with Rene Elmstrom) pointed out that there is a huge practical problem arising from the combination of blackbox abstraction and versioning. Fundamentally, with components one cannot trust what cannot be *locally* verified. Therefore, detailed (formal) documents and guarding run-time checks (perhaps using wrappers) are all required. Further, since component management is quite cumbersome, he suggests that better tool support for dependency management among generations of groups of components is needed. Henrik pointed out that there is a Danish national initiative that addresses some of these issues: the Centre for Object Technology (http://www.cit.dk/cot).

Jing Dong (joint work with Paulo Alencar and Donald Cowan) focused on design components and the question on how to compose these properly. By "correct composition" he means that components don't gaine or lose properties under composition. He illustrated his point by showing how the iterator and the composite design pattern can be composed. To reason about composition of design patterns, patterns need to be enriched by theories. Composition then is theory composition and correctness of a composition can then be proved by showing that all involved component theories still hold. Jing claimed that this approach could be generalized to other (non-design) components. When asked, Jing explained that his specifications deal with aliasing explicitly and that state changes are restricted by specified constraints.

David Helton proposed the view that coarse-grained components actually work in practice and could be seen as an alternative to finer-grained ones embedded in component frameworks. He pointed to Gio Wiederholt's CHMIS project at Standord: a research system that uses coarse-grained components. David emphasized that such coarse-grained components are reality today, mentioning systems by SAP, Baan, and PeopleSoft as examples. Aiming for a synthesis, he suggests that several concepts from the small-grained component world should be questioned when considering coarse-grained ones instead. For example, are classes, polymorphism, and other OO concepts needed at this level? (He thought: probably not!) He proposed to eliminate at the highest level all of implementation and interface inheritance, polymorphism, and possibly even instantiation, and claimed that this was similar to what was done in the CHMIS project.

Jan Bosch closed the morning presentations with a brief statement of his own, entitled "Software Architecture / Product Line Architectures and the real world." His presentation started with the identification that components can be reused at three levels, i.e., across versions of a product—which is mostly understood, across product versions and a product family—the current state of practice is learning this, and, finally, across product versions and product families and organizational boundaries—except for narrow, well established domains, we are nowhere near learning this trick. His main advice to organizations interested in converting to component-based software engineering was to first establish a culture in which intra-organizational component reuse was appreciated, before proceeding with full-scale third party component reuse. The main argument for this was that, in his experience with a number or industrial software development organizations, establishing a software product-line, which is based on intra-organizational component reuse, already results in so many problems that adding the additional dimension of complexity caused by third party components may exceed the ability of the organization. In addition, the benefits of a software product line over traditional product-oriented development are already quite substantial.

3. Breakout Session

The following five breakout groups were formed:

1. Architectural strata and refinements.
2. Adaptation, aspect moderation, and trading.
3. Component frameworks.
4. Implementation problems with "real COM".
5. Practice versus theory/academia.

Most of the groups had between five and twelve members (one had only three), all with a designated scribe and a designated moderator. The following subsections summarize each groups findings.

3.1 Architectural Strata and Refinements

This group did not agree on interaction refinement as *the* mechanism for architectural refinement, but did agree that interaction refinement is an important concept. The group observed that strata refinement is sometimes automatic (as is the case with remoting infrastructure) and that in such cases the stratification itself is abstracted into separate components. The group wasn't clear whether there was a difference between interaction refinement and normal decomposition (and if there was a difference, which these differences would be). They perceived a spectrum of solutions between "inlining" and abstraction into separate components.

3.2 Adaptation, Aspect Moderation, and Trading

This group came up with a taxonomy of adaptation levels:

- adaptation
  - system (adaptation from inside)
    - collection of components (replace component)
    - composition of components (rewire components) [1]
      - topology
      - semantics of connectors
  - component (adaptation from outside)
    - appearance (interfaces)

[1] Two remarks: (a) Colin Atkinson observed that this distinction might be equivalent to the system versus component distinction at the top-level, if properly applying interaction refinements; (b) Walt Hill pointed out that it would be useful to separate the specialization of adapters from the rewiring/reconfiguring step.

  * behavior
    - properties (data)
    - implementation/specialization (code)

They also noted further dimensions of adaptation:

- blackbox vs. whitebox
- functional vs. non-functional (perceived as a more difficult, less quantifiable, and therefore unclear front of attack)
- when to adapt? (with a full spectrum between compile-time and fully lazy - for safety and performace: do as early as possible)
- ORB vs. Trader vs. Specialization

3.3 Component Frameworks

This group tried to apply the notion of architecture classification (Atkinson et al.) to the Vission framework (Telea). They observed a tension for architectural classification: levels vs. layers. The traditional approach suggests the following layering picture:

enduser	
data flow manager	GUI manager
meta classes	
C++ classes	

Unfortunately, this layer structure is disturbed by cross-layer relations preventing any linear ordering of the bottom three layers. There are relations between layer 3 and 2, layer 2 and 1, and layer 3 and 1.

The same architecture is described very differently when using architectural strata. One stratum is assigned to each class of user of the system: one for endusers, one for application designers, and one for component designers.

stratum	structure
enduser	GUI Mgr dataflow components
application designer	GUI Mgr DF Mgr meta classes
component designer	GUI Mgr DF Mgr meta classes C++ classes

It is possible to understand strata top-down (similar to proper layers).

The group concluded that mapping user layers to architectural strata worked well in this example. Also, layer and strata views are complementary. An open research question is whether component relations can be constrained to reside within strata rather than crossing strata.

An interesting further observation is that, at least in this example, components are found in successive strata. It was speculated whether indeed those things that—once revealed by a stratum—stay, can be captured by separate components. That is, strata-based diagrams seem to expose the notion of components (objects?) explicitly, as these are the entities that appear in successive strata.

A number of issues are considered open:

- Is traditional "strict" layering too rigid?
- Does it conflict with object segregation?
- Would the stratum model improve on this?
- What's the relation between strata and aspects? (Some relation seems plausible.)
- Is it a problem of layering that it tries to segregate interfaces *and* implementations?

3.4 Implementation Problems with "Real COM"

This group started discussing the Beta implementation of COM but then progressed to more general issues. A summary of the topics discussed let to the following laundry list:

- Components should have strong specifications (including pre/post- conditions and invariants).
- Making robust components on top of non-robust/not-well-defined platforms is *hard*.
- Technology-independent components are an important research goal; but this is *very* difficult. (Clarification: the independence looked for is independence from platform-specific services and implementations.)
- Component technology vendors need to provide examples and explanations which make it easier for implementers who are building components.

A question from the audience as to how to teach people to get all these things right was answered by one of the group members: "You don't. This will remain largely the expertise of a few." (A pesimistic view indeed—although backed by the industrial experience with other non-IT component technologies: after initial shakeouts only a few champions remain in the race, usually with a rich repertoir of proprietary expertise and technology.)

The suggestion that linguistic support for specification aspects was required (such as pre/post-conditions) was seen as a good idea.

3.5 Practice versus Theory/Academia

This group considered the success factors for using theory in practice:

- Mature domains: creation of stable domain models is possible.
- Degree of criticality/complexity: there is a compelling reason to reason.
- Organizational maturity level (in the CMM sense) required to get this right.

- Scoped usage of theory: don't try to throw the biggest hammer at everything. (This last point in particular requires great care. It is not obvious how to contain the "spread" of a theory.)

In the context of components the group observed:

- Theory/formal methods can be naturally confined to specific components, leading to a natural scoping approach.
- Components can bridge the gap between theory and practice: the results of applying a particular theory in to a specific problem can be reused in component form, helping to ammortize the initial investment.

There are two further issues:

- Politics/culture: component approach establishes new dependencies inside and between organizations.
- Cost/benefit: component approach requires an ammortization model.

4. Concluding Remarks

Concluding, we are able to state that, on the one hand, also the fourth workshop on component-oriented programming was a highly successful event that was appreciated by the participants, but, on the other hand, that the issues surrounding component-oriented programming have not been solved and that future events remain necessary to further the state of the art.

One interesting trend that we have identified over the years is a change in focus. Whereas the first workshops aimed at the individual components, especially during the last event there was a clear consensus that the focus should be on the component architecture, i.e., the cooperation between components. In particular, not the component-'wiring' standards, such as CORBA, COM and JavaBeans, but rather the system design level issues, such as software architectures and component frameworks.

Object Technology for Product-Line Architectures

Philippe Lalanda[1], Jan Bosch[2], Ramon Lerchundi[3], and Sophie Cherki[4]

[1] Schneider Electric, France,
philippe_lalanda@mail.schneider.fr
[2] University of Karlskrona, Sweden,
Jan.Bosch@ide.hk-r.se
[3] ESI, Spain,
Ramon.Lerchundi@esi.es
[4] Thomson-CSF/LCR, France,
cherki@lcr.thomson-csf.com

1. Introduction

1.1 Product-Line Architectures

The industry of software-intensive systems is facing today both economical and technical challenges. On one hand, shrinking budgets and sharp competition require to reduce significantly development and maintenance costs, shorten lead time, and improve predictability. On the other hand, the size and complexity of systems have dramatically increased in the past few years and have brought considerable technological problems. In order to face these issues, major changes are required regarding the way software products are developed.

A promising approach, which is gaining wide acceptance, is to replace traditional development models by product-line development. Traditional life cycle models have originally been conceived under the assumption that they apply to the development of individual software products, inhibiting the sharing of common assets between projects. Product-line development is based on a different approach, which naturally promotes and supports software reuse. In a product-line approach, products addressing a same domain are regarded as a whole and developed as members of a product family.

More precisely, a software product-line is a collection of products sharing a common set of features that address the specific needs of a given business area [4]. In a product-line context, products are built from reusable software artifacts, called reusable assets, which are managed at the product-line level. Core assets concern every software artifact that can be reused, including requirements, software components, software architecture, test cases, budget estimation, development structures, etc. These reusable assets have to be generic enough to be appropriate for several products in the product-line, and specific enough to be reusable in a straightforward manner and then provide a real added value.

A. Moreira and S. Demeyer (Eds.): ECOOP'99 Workshops, LNCS 1743, pp. 193–206, 1999.

The development of core assets is generally termed as domain engineering. The development of new products from the set of reusable assets is generally called application engineering. The whole process is allowed by an adequate organization and a coordinated management.

There is a number of specific practices that are needed to develop and exploit the core assets in a product-line. These practices are not always mature and most of the time only emerging in the context of one-shot developments, that is the developments of single products with no reuse in mind. The levels of reusability and adaptability required by the product-line approach bring additional complexity and formidable challenges with regard to the current technology. Such complexity is today almost not dealt with, and requires significant improvements for the current state-of-the-art in software engineering.

The SEI (Software Engineering Institute) has listed the essential practices required to produce core assets and products in a product-line and to manage the process at multiple level [1]. In this product-line framework, practice areas have been divided into three categories: software engineering practices (including domain analysis, assets mining, architecture exploration and definition), technical management practices (including data collection, metrics, and tracking and product-line scoping) and organizational management practices. On the other hand, the PRAISE project (Product-line Realisation and Assessment in Industrial Settings) sponsored by the European Community is providing integrated and validated methodological support to the development of large software product families in industrial settings. A Process model and a Benefit assessment model have been built [2].

One of the major core assets is the software architecture, called product-line architecture, which is shared by all the products in a product-line. The architecture brings the minimal level of similarity between products that is mandatory to build shareable assets like software components, test cases, requirements, cost and time analysis, etc. For example, software architecture defines the software components that can be reused in the product-line: The architecture provides the specification for the components and ensures their integrability and, to some extent, their interoperability in future products. The design, development and exploitation of product-line architectures raise important issues and require excellence in many specific areas. It requires to handle essential practice areas related to the usual development of software architectures, but also practice areas necessary to deal with the additional complexity due to the specific nature of product-line architectures.

Practice areas which are essential to the development of single product architecture include:

- Software architectures design,
- Software architectures representation,
- Software architectures evaluation,
- Software architectures implementation in conformance with specifications,

- Traceability with requirements (functional and non functional).

The specificity of product-line based development brings additional areas where excellence is required:

- Generic, adaptable software architectures,
- Reusable components design and development,
- Component and software architecture mining,
- Traceability with common and variable requirements in a family of products.

1.2 The Workshop

The first international workshop on Object Technology and Product Line Architecture was organized in conjunction with ECOOP'99 (European Conference on Object Oriented Programming). It was held in Lisbon on June 15, 1999.

Its purpose was to build upon the work done in the PRAISE project and to bring together practitioners and researchers in order to:

- Share their experience in the application of object technologies to the development of adaptable software architectures,
- Explore innovative object techniques to deal with the various aspects of a product-line architecture.

More precisely the topics covered during the workshop, either through papers, talks or working groups, included:

- Modeling common and variable requirements in a product family,
- Tracing requirements onto an adaptable architecture,
- Adaptable architectures,
- Patterns for the design of adaptable architectures,
- Object-oriented techniques for the representation of adaptable architectures,
- Object-oriented frameworks.

The workshop participants included:

- Mathias Braux, University of Nantes (France)
- Sholom Cohen, Software Engineering Institute (USA)
- Denis Conan, Alcatel (France)
- Krzysztof Czarnecki, Daimler Chrisler AG (Germany)
- Mikko Hamalainen, University of Helsinki (Finland)
- Juha Hautamaki, University of Tampere (Finland)
- Andreas Hein, Robert Bosch (Germany)
- Tuomas Ihme, VTT Electronics (Finland)
- Bo Jorgensen, University of Odense (Denmark)
- Tomoji Kishi, NEC Corporation (Japan)
- Natsuko Noda, NEC Corporation (Japan)
- Linda Northrop, Software Engineering Institute (USA)

- Ramkumar Ramaswamy, Infosys Technologies Limited (India)
- Juha Savolainen, University of Helsinki (Finland)
- Yannis Smaragdakis, University of Texas (USA)
- Perdita Stevens, University of Edinburgh (Scotland)
- Jukka Viljamaa, University of Helsinki (Finland)
- Renato Vinga-Martins, Robert Bosch (Germany)

It was organized by:

- Philippe Lalanda, Schneider Electric Research Center (France)
- Jan Bosch, University of Karlskrona (Sweden)
- Sophie Cherki, Thomson-CSF Research Center (France)
- Ramon Lerchundi, European Software Institute (Spain)

Participants with an accepted paper presented their work in the domain of product-line architectures. All of them participated in working groups dedicated to special interest discussions. Papers and working groups results are presented hereafter.

Proceedings of the workshop are published by the European Software Institute (see http://www.esi.es/Projects/Reuse/Praise/).

2. Presentations

Twelve papers have been accepted for the workshop: authors were actually asked to make a short presentation of their work. Presentations were grouped into three major themes in order to get maximum coherency and allow well focused questions and discussions. The three themes, which emerged naturally from the issues treated by the papers accepted to the workshop, were the following: the design of product-line architectures, the representation and documentation of such architectures, and product-line experiment reports.

2.1 Designing Product-Line Architectures

A product line architecture has to capture architectural features that are common to many products and encapsulate variable features in a way that it can be adapted to specific requirements. Hence, techniques allowing to capture variability in an architecture are most relevant.

The workshop included five papers on this subject. More precisely, papers dealt with the following issues:

- The definition and use of software components classification to drive the design of product line architectures,
- The definition and use of a refinement methodology to design extensible software applications,
- The use of interaction patterns to design product line architectures,

- The use of partial evaluation to overcome performance default due to framework genericity,
- The effect of domain standards on product line architecture.

Ramkumar Ramaswamy, from Infosys Technologies Limited, presented a paper entitled “Creating Malleable Architectures for Application Software Product Families”, written with Uttara Nerurkar. His aim is to deal with the issue of designing software architectures in such a way that variability could be handled incrementally, as it is discovered. In the paper, a brief presentation of the case study, a commercial banking product named Bancs2000, and of some issues requiring a variability oriented architecting is first given. Then, a definition of software components classification (vertical vs. horizontal, logical vs. physical, mandatory vs. optional) aimed to drive the design of product line architectures is proposed and its applicability to characterization of software components is discussed. With regards to this classification, variability is characterized in terms of occurrence and type. Coarse-grained solutions are given to design software architecture with regards to it.

Yannis Smaragdakis, from the University of Texas, presented a paper entitled “Building Product-Lines with Mixin-Layers”, written with Don Batory. His aim is to provide a methodology for designing software extensible via the addition and removal of components. Their methodology, called GenVoca, lies on the definition of stepwise refinements adapted to component granularity. Encapsulation of refinement classes defines a layer (or collaboration) and every composition of layers defines an application of a product line. Implementation of the methodology is finally presented: the paper then focuses on inheritance as mechanism for composition.

Bo Nørregaard Jorgensen, from Odense University, presented a paper entitled “Standardizing Component Interaction Patterns in Product-Lines Architectures”, written with Wouter Joosen. In this paper, the authors describe five interactions patterns extending existing Java Beans framework from reactive applications to industrial control applications which include periodic activities. The first pattern, named “property”, applies to components configuration at both composition-time and run-time. The second pattern, named “event”, applies to communication of events without temporal constraints of event processing imposed by event source. The third pattern, named “publisher”, applies to periodic communication of data in applications where regular amounts of data are processed at fixed time intervals. The fourth pattern, named “synchronous service provider”, applies to synchronous invocation of a service which is provided by external component and which is performed in the same thread as actions performed by invocation source component. Finally, the fifth pattern, named “asynchronous service provider”, applies to invocation of a service which is provided by external component and which is performed in a different thread allowing the invocation source component to perform other actions concurrently. Then, the authors show when and how the previously described patterns could be used on a robot control system.

Mathias Braux, from the Ecole des Mines de Nantes, presented a paper entitled "Speeding up the Java Serialization Framework through Partial Evaluation". The purpose of his work is to improve the performance of framework-based applications using reflection as a way to achieve flexibility. To address this goal, the author proposes a technique for removing run-time reflection using partial evaluation during compilation phase. This technique was applied to the Java Serialization framework.

The fifth paper by Mikko Hämäläinen and Juha Savolainen, entitled "The Effect of Standardization on Product Development", focuses on the way standards emerging in a domain affect product development within the domain by reducing variability at the design level. First, standardization is discussed versus variability. Then, Wireless Application Protocol standard in telecommunications market is presented with regards to its rationale, its architecture, its market, and product line it infers.

2.2 Representing and Documenting Product-Line Architectures

An architecture is an abstraction of important structures of a software system. It is essentially manipulated through its representation (if we except some emerging code analysis techniques). The way an architecture is represented, or specified, is therefore of major importance. This, of course, also applies to product-line architectures. In addition, a product-line architecture has to integrate information on how it should be used in order to derive single-application architectures.

The workshop included four complementary papers on this subject. More precisely, papers dealt with the following issues:

- The use of a production plan to bridge the conceptual gap between architecture and new systems,
- The use of specialization templates to document object-oriented frameworks,
- The use of UML to describe product-line architectures,
- The traceability between requirements and architecture.

Sholom Cohen, from the Software Engineering Institute, presented a paper entitled "From Product-Line Architectures to Products". This paper acknowledges the importance of product-line architectures but shows that, in practice, there is rarely sufficient support for the process of adapting product-line architectures to specific requirements. First, the author reviews important factors that influence the extent of the gap between requirements and architecture (including the degree of abstraction of the architecture, bounds of variability, variability mechanisms employed, availability of automatic support, etc.). Then, he argues that production plans should be carefully prepared in order to control the transition. A production plan must detail the steps necessary to bridge the conceptual gap between assets and systems. Production plans can take various forms with regard to the actual assets that are part of the product-line, and particularly the architecture. The author provides four examples, going from manual to automated composition of systems, and shows the nature of production plans that are needed in each case.

The second paper by Markku Hakala, Juha Hautamaki, Jyrki Tuomi, Antti Viljamaa, Jukka Viljamma, Kai Koskimies and Jukka Paakki, entitled "Managing Object-Oriented Frameworks with Specialization Templates", focuses on object-oriented frameworks. The authors also acknowledge the necessity to provide guidance to the users of a framework, and propose to integrate such knowledge in the framework description. They introduce the concepts of design contract and specialization template as basic design artifacts and documentation means. Design contracts, which are application-independent descriptions of certain OO design aspects, are described formally with a language called Cola (Contract Language). A specialization template is a framework-specific design solution to a particular flexibility requirement. A specialization template is based on a design contract: essentially it binds a design contract to a particular framework and its flexibility requirements. A prototype tool for Java frameworks, called FRED, is implemented based on a formalization of specialization templates. The authors' vision is that a Java framework can be specialized under the guidance of FRED.

The third paper "UML for Describing Product-Line Architectures?", by Perdita Stevens from the University of Edinburgh, reports some work in progress on the use of UML as a notation for describing product-line architectures. The author argues that the users of product-line architectures are most likely to know UML and that such familiarity with the notation is an essential ingredient in using correctly and efficiently an architecture. The author then reviews UML notations that can be used for describing software architectures and rapidly focuses on the special issues of product-line architectures. The main point is to assess how UML can allow the representation of the variability which is and which is not permitted in a product-line architecture. The author discusses the different views of an architecture than can be described by UML (externally visible behavior, static structure, dynamic structure, state diagrams, and deployment) and shows how variability can be dealt with for each of them.

Finally, the paper "Requirements Traceability for Product-Lines", by Renato Vinga-Martins from Robert Bosch, deals with the traceability links that should be maintained between domain analysis models and product-line architectures in order to facilitate the delivery of new applications. The author argues that a requirement model and a feature model are indispensable in a product-line context because each of them conveys information needed during reuse. The feature model, as know from FODA, captures common and variable user-visible features. It is extended with an architectural part to provide support for traces from quality requirements onto the product-line architecture. On the other hand, use-case models, information model and operational model are seen as optional in a product-line context. They can be added in the domain analysis if needed. The author then presents in more details the different models previously mentioned and shows how they can be traced to the product-line architecture. In particular, traceability to architectural patterns within the architecture is developed.

2.3 Experiment Reports

The product-line approach has received wide attention in companies specialized in software-intensive systems and several initiatives have been launched recently in industrial settings. Such experiments are full of lessons that are rarely communicated to a large audience.

The workshop included three papers relating real-scale product-line projects and focusing on the product-line architectures developed during these projects. The papers addressed three significant domains:

- Real-time embedded control software,
- Embedded software for information terminals,
- Command and control software.

The first paper entitled "A ROOM Framework for the Spectrometer Controller Product-Line" by Tuomas Ihme from VTT Electronics, presents a framework for the design of scientific on-board X-ray spectrometer control software. The author first argues that embedded systems are rarely developed from scratch: they are often re-engineered from existing systems. In such situation, product-line and reusable software components are suitable approaches. The paper presents snapshots of the domain analysis outputs and of the architecture of the framework. UML, including use cases to describe typical interactions, has been used to support domain analysis. The framework is designed using the ROOM (Real-time Object-Oriented Modeling) language and the ObjecTime Developer tool, by ObjecTime Limited, that proved suitable for the development of product-line architectures based on object technology. The author emphasizes the role played by design patterns in the framework design. In particular, he argues that the strategy pattern appeared to be useful in the documentation of the reuse strategies of the framework. Special means are still needed however for the configuration rules of components. Since the size and quality of the target code generated by ObjecTime Developer from the framework does not fulfil the requirements for on-board software, some parts of the target code have to be implemented manually.

A second paper entitled "Analysing Hot/Frozen Spot from Performance Aspect" by Tomoji Kishi and Natsuko Noda from NEC corporation, deals with performance requirements in a product-line architecture. It presents a product-line architecture for a family of embedded software for information terminals that retrieve information stored in CD-ROM databases. The main variability in this product-line is the CD-ROM format which is different in the Japanese market and in the U.S. market. The authors argue that such a variability at the level of the supporting technology has to be considered very early in the product-line and drives architectural design. In particular, in order to meet performance requirements, CD-ROM formats have to considered in many architectural spots. The authors present an approach based on performance aspects to identify hot and frozen (stable) spots in a product-line architecture. The overall approach is exemplified on a well defined product-line and expected to be refined during other systems development.

The third paper entitled "CCT: A Component-Based Product Line Architecture for Satellite-Based Command and Control Systems" by Clifford Hollander and John Ohlinger from Hollander Group, Inc. and National Reconnaissance Office, presents results and lessons learned from their experiment in the project Control Channel Toolkit, which aim was to develop a component-based reference architecture. More precisely, assets base is first described followed by variability identification. Then, the reference architecture that has been designed is presented and discussed with regards to modeling notation used, variability handling, documentation associated, architectural evaluation, and process.

3. Working Groups

Working groups dedicated to special interest discussions were held during the afternoon. Discussions lasted about two hours and were summarized afterwards in plenary session. Themes tackled in the working groups were the following:

- The design of product-line architectures
- The representation of product-line architectures
- The launching of a product-line

3.1 WG1: The Design of Product-Line Architectures

The purpose of the first working group was to investigate issues related to the design of product-line architectures. Several members of the workshop had actually proposed techniques to build evolving software architectures and were ideally positioned to contribute to the discussions.

Participants of the group decided to focus on the important notion of variability within a product-line architecture and how it should be dealt with.

First, three kinds of variability were identified:

- Component variability stands at the component level. It is concerned with different ways to perform a given function within a component. Such variability is generally treated with variation points or dedicated patterns.
- Protocol variability stands at the connection level. It is concerned with the various ways to design and implement the communication between two or several components. Such variability can be tackled with changeable protocols or with the implementation of a special purpose components taking care of the variability (a broker for example).

- Transverse variability stands at the level of a group of components. Such variability generally concerns quality attribute and is often hard to handle.

Design and architectural patterns were then identified during the discussion as a major technique to express these kinds of variability. The use of patterns leads to the creation of architectural elements (components, tasks, ...) to encapsulate variabilities and to prepare for their adaptations. With this approach, variation points take the form of micro-architectures describing the way a few components are structured and interact with each other along with quality attributes.

Most patterns for adaptability are based on the creation of specific-purpose components and on indirection techniques. In order to meet product-specific requirements, appropriate components are integrated in the architecture. Adding product-specific features can be made alternatively by:

- Plugging a new, more adapted component in the architecture,
- Instantiating a component to meet the expected requirements,
- Generating a component in order to meet the expected requirements.

3.2 WG2: The Representation of Product-Line Architectures

The purpose of the second working group was to discuss important issues related to the representation of product-line architectures. Several papers of the workshop dealt with this concerns and served as a basis to the discussion.

The first question of course was to determine what needs to be represented in a product-line architecture. Several participants reminded that the following views are generally used to describe software architectures:

- The logical view describes the components of a system and their connections from a static point of view. In this view, all the potential components and connections are displayed. This view provides information on how the system is structured, how the control is shared, and how data are exchanged. There is however no indication on whether a connection is effectively used, or when it is used: the logical view does not contain any temporal information.
- The behavioral view describes the dynamics of the system. It contains the same components and connections defined in the logical view, but focuses on the exchanged data and on the temporal aspects of the communication. It describes the sequences of communication between components, the points of synchronisation, the nature of transmitted data, etc. In most cases, this view has to take into account the run-time context since the communication flow can be quite different depending on the state of the system.
- The execution view describes the different processes and tasks that are executed in the system. This represents a higher level than the behavioural view: the processes and tasks are the computational structures where threads of communication take place.

- The physical view describes the mapping of the architecture onto an execution platform (which can be a middleware, an operating system, etc). This view shows how dynamic (cpu, memory, bandwidth) and static (code size) resources of hardware and middleware platforms are used by the system.

Participants agreed that such views were adequate to represent product-line architectures. They however constitute a minimal set that may be extended to deal with specific needs. Also, it was agreed that variability could be incorporated in each of these views. Two major ways to express variability in a view were then identified. The first one is by adding specific notations in order to highlight a variation point in a view (this is discussed later in more details). The second approach consists in omitting information in a view. In particular, the level of abstraction of a view is very important. Abstraction is definitely a way to express variability in an architectural view (everything that is not shown is variable).

The group then focused on the languages that can be used to represent architectural views in a product-line context. UML was at the center of the discussion. Industrial members of the group were attracted by the "universality" of this language. As stated by a participant, users of product-line architectures are most likely to know UML and such familiarity is an important asset for a successful use of the architecture. UML was seen as very useful to represent static views and associated variability. More concerns were emitted regarding the behavioral views and even more regarding the physical view. Further work is clearly needed to cope with variability in these views.

Finally, the group discussed rapidly about traceability between product-line requirements and product-line architecture. Industrial participants insisted that such traceability was of major importance in a product-line context. In order to be used efficiently and correctly, architectural decisions need to be linked to domain requirements (which may be variable). The issue of a federating fifth view came in the discussion. As stated by one participant, this view could be a commonality and variability view that is tied to a configuration view in design.

3.3 WG3: The Launching of a Product-Line

The third working group was concerned with organizational aspects of a product-line. This group took benefits from the experience of industrial participants to launch successful product-lines (at VTT Electronics and NEC Corporation).

The first issue raised during the discussion was related to the starting of a product-line. Basically, many industrial companies are very interested in setting product-line practices but do not know how and where to start. The working group identified three different situations that required different approaches:

- The Greenfield approach: In this case, there is no product available to start from and the product-line has to be built from scratch. This is a complex situation where risks have to be carefully evaluated and managed. Such situation, which may seem extreme, occur when many similar applications have

to be developed simultaneously (and sometimes when there is a shortage of human resources).
- The evolutionary approach. Different software artifacts are managed in a coordinated way in a company. It can be for example a set of requirements documents of a software component which is reused in several applications. In this situation, the intended scope of the product-line has to be carefully determined (some shared artifacts may fall out of the scope). The sharing of assets can then be made progressively.
- The revolutionary approach. Different similar products exist but are managed separately in a company. In this situation, reverse engineering activities can be done in order to identify the main artifacts of the product-line.

It is to be noted that the so called Greenfield approach raised discussions. Some believe that such approach does not exist: product-lines differ from general purpose developments in that they focus on existing and related future products, capitalized experience, business goals, etc. If no product is available in a product-line, some prototyped are needed to clarify the situation. Then, are we still in a Greenfield approach ?

The working group then decided to discuss two major concerns that need to be addressed when launching a product-line: the organization structure and tool support. Several open questions were raised during the discussion.

First, are Domain Engineering units (or groups, or departments) necessary? In some industries, Domain Engineering Groups have been built with senior Systems/Software Engineers, trying to get one member from each important product.

Then, how is a product-line architecture team built ? Is it a stable and permanent team, or a group of part-time product architects? Experience shows that the time-line for these groups is quite short (some months) because interest of the business units decreases very rapidly with time. Then the product-line people go back to their "product groups" and try to apply directly the product-line approach in their products.

The management of product-line assets also raises important questions. Is it necessary to create a new structure to manage the shared assets ? Who pays for the shared assets in product oriented accounting companies: each product pays a part, or a common account? Some organizations have done that. But in organizations where each product presents its own balance sheet, it is not so easy to decide. Another typical question that appears when re-using: Who is responsible for the shared assets? For these questions, there is not a rule. Each company has to decide how to fit the product-line.

Also, are life cycles for building products good enough for the product-line approach where application derivation is the key issue? Traditionally, life cycles (both software and systems) have been conceived for the development of unique products. In the product-line approach, it seems the "typical" processes are not longer valid. For instance, the management of requirements for product-line is different from the single product approach.

Furthermore, people were very concerned about the lacks of existing tooling to address properly product-line. The traceability of requirements during the life cycle, down to the common assets, is very poorly treated in existing tools. Even tools that come from the same vendor but treat different assets, are very poorly integrated.

4. Conclusion

This first workshop on product-line architectures was very successful. It brought together practitioners and researchers in the product-line field, tackled important issues of the field and initiated lively discussions. Three major research areas naturally emerged during the workshop.

The first theme concerns the design of product-line architectures. Current papers are very much driven by object-oriented patterns [3] and frameworks. This approach is obviously pertinent. However, we feel that more work is needed at the architectural level. This includes the definition of new architectural patterns, the standardization of interfaces and interaction mechanisms, and architecture-based tools to derive specific architectures. Works in the Aspect Oriented Programming field, providing a transverse handle on architectures, are also of high interest for the design of product-line architectures.

The second theme is the representation and documentation of product-line architectures. The importance of guidance for derivation within the architecture has been stressed by many participants. Early works presented during the workshop, going from production plans to template-based documentation, are very promising. Representing a product-line architecture is also a challenge in itself. The workshop confirmed the dominant situation of UML but also showed that a lot of work is still needed to completely model product-line architectures with UML. In particular, variability cannot be expressed satisfactorily today in the different UML views. Finally, the need for traceability links, from requirements to reusable components, has also been emphasized during the workshop.

The third theme deals with the launching of product-line experiments in industrial settings. Three papers from the industry show that product-line practices raise high expectations in the industry. They also reveal however that more guidance on organizational matters is needed. In particular, industrial companies need to know how to launch a product-line given their initial situation. It is clear, though, that progressive actions are needed in order to change the way products are developed and to adapt people organization.

References

[1] P. Clements and L. Northrop. A framework for software product-line practice - version 1.0. Technical report, Software Engineering Institute, September 1998.

[2] Thomson-CSF (France), Robert Bosch Gmbh (Germany), Ericsson (Sweden), and the European Software Institute (Spain). Praise project (product-line realisation and assessment in industrial settings). ESPRIT Project 28651, 1999. (http://www.esi.es/Projects/Reuse/Praise).

[3] E. Gamma, R. Johnson, R. Helm, and J. Vlissides. *Design patterns: Elements of reusable object-oriented software.* Addison Wesley, 1995.

[4] European Software Institute. Product-line architectures and technologies to manage them. Technical report, European Software Institute, 1998.

Object-Oriented Databases

Giovanna Guerrini[1], Isabella Merlo[1], Elena Ferrari[2],
Gerti Kappel[3], and Adoracion de Miguel[4]

[1] DISI - Università di Genova, Italy
{guerrini,merloisa}@disi.unige.it
[2] DSI - Università di Milano, Italy
ferrarie@dsi.unimi.it
[3] Johannes Kepler University of Linz, Austria
gerti@ifs.uni-linz.ac.at
[4] Universidad Carlos III de Madrid, Spain
admiguel@inf.uc3m.es

Abstract. The goal of the *First ECOOP Workshop on Object-Oriented Databases* was to bring together researchers working in the field of object-oriented databases, to discuss the work which is going on. The aim of the workshop was twofold: to discuss the current status of research in the field and to critically evaluate object-oriented database systems in terms of their current usage, of their successes and limitations, and their potential for new applications. The workshop thus consisted of a number of presentations of reviewed papers and of discussions on the topics mentioned above.

1. Introduction

Three different directions can be devised aiming at integrating object-orientation and databases: the attempt of adding object-oriented features to the relational database standard SQL, which has lead to object-relational database systems [15, 16]; the extension of object-oriented programming languages to support persistent objects (e.g. PJama) [11]; the attempt of definig a standard for "pure" object-oriented databases, namely, ODMG [3]. At the same time, some efforts have been made to extend the core object data model with richer modeling constructs, to better supporting integrity constraints, reactive capabilities, temporal data, schema evolution capabilities and to design efficient storage structures and implementation techniques for object databases. Object-oriented database systems have claimed of being more adequate than relational ones for handling non-traditional data, such as multimedia and semi-structured data, and for non-traditional applications, such as CADE/CASE, medical information systems, and for integrating heterogeneous database systems.

If you look at the programs of the last object-oriented and database conferences, however, there are very few papers on object-oriented databases. Thus, a first aim of the *First ECOOP Workshop on Object-Oriented Databases* has been to test whether there is still someone researching in that field. Fortunately,

A. Moreira and S. Demeyer (Eds.): ECOOP'99 Workshops, LNCS 1743, pp. 207–221, 1999.

the answer has been positive. Together with these researchers, at the workshop, we aimed at discussing whether there is still anything to research and at critically evaluating the current state of the field. Are we satisfied about the reached results? Have all the problems of object-oriented databases been solved, or simply isn't there anyone interested in solving them, since relational DBMSs would never be overcome? Is the future in object-relational DBMSs and in persistent object-oriented languages? Does the web and web-related data open new perspective for object-oriented databases?

Thus, the aim of the workshop was to discuss the research going on in the object-oriented database field, critically evaluating object-oriented database systems in terms of their current usage, of their successes and limitations, and their potential for new applications. The discussion have covered all the aspects of object-oriented databases, ranging from data modeling issues, to implementation issues and practical evaluations of OODBMSs.

Submission of papers describing mature results or on-going work were invited for all aspects of object-oriented databases, including, but non limited to:

- data modeling concepts,
- performance, storage structures, query processing and optimization,
- experiences in using OODBMSs,
- object-oriented database standards,
- object-relational DBMSs,
- persistent object-oriented languages,
- interoperability and heterogeneity,
- active object-oriented databases,
- spatial and temporal aspects,
- applications in handling multimedia and semi-structured data.

A program committee of 14 people active in the field of object-oriented databases was assembled during the workshop preparation. The program committee members are experts in several aspects concerning object-oriented databases, ranging from theoretical foundations of object-oriented databases to object-oriented system implementations. The program committee members and their affiliations are listed below.

Suad Alagiċ	Wichita State University, USA
Elisa Bertino	University of Milano, Italy
Mary Fernandez	AT&T Labs Research, USA
Giorgio Ghelli	University of Pisa, Italy
Guido Moerkotte	University of Mannheim, Germany
Tamer Ozsu	University of Alberta, Canada
Isidro Ramos	Polytechnic University of Valencia, Spain
Awais Rashid	Lancaster University, UK
Elke Rundensteiner	Worcester Polytechnic Institute, USA
Gunter Saake	Magdeburg University, Germany
Markku Sakkinen	University of Jyväskylä, Finland
Marc Scholl	University of Konstanz, Germany
Roel Wieringa	University of Twente, The Netherlands
Roberto Zicari	Johann Wolfgang Goethe University, Germany

The workshop has been advertised inside both the object-oriented and the database communities, and many research groups active in object-oriented databases were directly contacted to encourage them to participate at the forum.

A total of 28 papers were submitted for presentation at the workshop. Submissions were attracted from 15 different countries giving a truly international flavour to the workshop. All the submitted papers were thoroughly reviewed by the programme committee and finally the organizing committee carefully selected the 10 papers to be presented at the workshop. Most of the submitted papers were of very good quality and the number of accepted papers has been limited by time restrictions.

The accepted papers were grouped into five main categories: evaluation of commercial systems, persistent object-oriented programming languages, query languages and heterogenous databases, extension of object-oriented databases with temporal features, and, finally, consistency and verification. Each accepted paper has been presented by one of the authors. Each presentation has been devoted 30 minutes: about 20 minutes for the paper presentation and ten minutes for questions and discussion. We have decided to devote at least ten minutes for questions and discussion to encourage the interaction among who was presenting the paper and other workshop participants, and we believe we have achieved good results: some discussions have been continued during lunch time! Informal proceedings were produced for the workshop and they have been given to the participant at the beginning of the workshop.

23 people participated at the workshop and most of them actively participated at the final discussion, giving a significant contribution to the workshop. Most of the participants came from the academy, though some of them came from the industry. The list of participants can be found at the end of the report.

The report is organized as follows. Section 2 describes the session dealing with the evaluation of commercial object-oriented database systems. Section 3 is devoted to the session on persistent object languages and systems. Section 4 describes the session devoted to query languages and to the management of heterogeneous information. Section 5 reports on the session discussing work aiming at extending object-oriented databases with temporal features. Section 6 is devoted to the session dealing with consistency and verification in object-oriented databases. For all those sessions, we present the abstracts of the works presented in the session, and briefly report on the discussion on all of them. Section 7 reports on the last session of the workshop, which was entirely dedicated to discussion. Finally, Section 8 concludes the workshop report.

2. Evaluation of Object-Oriented Database Systems

In this session two very interesting papers giving an evaluation of object-oriented database systems from a "user" point of view were presented. The first one focuses on the requirements of organizations that have to deal with really very large databases, whereas the second one is centered around the capabilities offered by various systems for data and schema evolution.

2.1. Object Databases and Petabyte Storage - Dreams or Reality? (Dirk Düllmann and Jamie Shiers)

The European Laboratory for Particle Physics (CERN) is located on the border between France and Switzerland, just outside Geneva. Much of the on-going activities of the laboratory are focused on a new accelerator, the Large Hadron Collider (LHC), that is currently under construction. Scheduled to enter operation in 2005, experiments at this facility will generate enormous amounts of data. Over an estimated 20 year running period, some 100PB - 10^{17} bytes - of data will be acquired at rates ranging from 100MB/s to 1.5GB/s. A number of research and development projects have been initiated to find solutions to the many challenges that the LHC will pose. Among these, the RD45 project has focused on the problems of providing persistent storage to these vast quantities of data. Starting in 1995, this project has focused exclusively on object-oriented solutions and object database management systems in particular. In the paper [6], presented by Jamie Shiers, the authors describe the criteria by which the object-oriented technology have been choosen, issues related to product selection, and their experience in using OODBMSs in production. Finally, the risks involved with the current strategy and outline future directions for the project are discussed.

The discussion following the paper presentation was very animated. Both the system selected for the project (Objectivity/DB) and those examined as candidates were discussed, with strong emphasis on the architectural issues arosen in the presentation. The presentation was very interesting since it really evaluated object-oriented database systems in terms of their potential practical usage in a very relevant application. Another important contribution of the presentation was indeed to recall to all the participants from the database community what *very large databases* mean.

2.2. Evaluation for Evolution: How Well Commercial Systems Do (Awais Rashid and Peter Sawyer)

The conceptual structure of an object-oriented database application may not remain constant and may vary to a large extent. The need for these variations (evolution) arises due to a variety of reasons, e.g. to correct mistakes in the database design or to reflect changes in the structure of the real world artefacts modeled in the database. Therefore, like any other database application object database applications are subject to evolution. However, in object-oriented databases, support for evolution is a critical requirement since it is a characteristic of complex applications for which they provide inherent support. These applications require dynamic modifications to both the data residing within the database and the way the data has been modelled i.e. both the objects residing within the database and the schema of the database are subject to change. Furthermore, there is a requirement to keep track of the change in case it needs to be reverted. The paper [13], presented by Awais Rashid, discusses the evolution facilities offered by some of the existing systems. The authors first provide an overview of the ODMG 2.0 standard from an evolution viewpoint. Then, they describe the extension to the database evolution features specified by the ODMG 2.0 standard. Using this extension as a basis, they form evaluation criteria, which are employed to assess the various evolution facilities offered by four commercially available object database management systems: POET, Versant, O2 and Jasmine.

Also in this case the presentation of the paper has been followed by an extensive discussion, and also in this case the choice of the systems considered in the comparison has been debated and motivated. The choice of the evolution primitives considered was also discussed, and the feeling that they should be driven by experiments on real projects rather than from the literature emerged. The other main issues arisen in the discussion concern typing problems caused by schema evolution, that is, whether the notions of schema evolution and of type safety can be conciled, and the potential offered by reflection to achieve type safety in an evolving environment.

3. Persistent Object-Oriented Languages

In this session two papers dealing with persistent object systems were presented. The first one deals with the problem of schema evolution in the context of the PJama persistent object language, whereas the second one describes how persistence has been added to the BETA object-oriented programming language in the Mjølner system.

3.1. Evolutionary Data Conversion in the PJama Persistent Language (Misha Dmitriev and Malcom P. Atkinson)

PJama is an experimental persistent programming system for the Java programming language. It has much in common with modern object-oriented database systems used together with Java. Therefore, the problem of schema and data evolution is really important for PJama and will be even more important if it becomes a product.

The approach to and the implementation of schema (class) evolution in PJama was described in [5]. This paper [4], presented by Misha Dmitriev, deals with persistent object conversion (data evolution) facilities which have been recently developed. These facilities include default (automatic) and custom conversion, the latter meaning that the programmer can explicitly encode in Java the transformations for the objects that make these objects match new declarations of the respective classes. If custom conversion is needed, the programmer has a choice between *bulk* and *fully* controlled conversion. In the first case, a conversion method (function) should be written for each evolved class. The system then scans the persistent store, applying a suitable method for every evolving object that it finds. In case of fully controlled conversion, a complete program should be written, that can transform individual objects, as well as any larger data structures in arbitrary order. During any kind of conversion the "old" object graph remains unchanged, that is, substitute objects are not directly reachable from it, making their own, separate world. The paper shows that this is crucial for comprehensible semantics of evolution code. The author believes that the present set of facilities is complete, i.e. it is enough to convert any persistent store instead of rebuilding it from scratch. However, the question of whether this can be generally proven is raised.

The discussion following the presentation covered three main issues. First, the comparison with lazy and eager data conversion mechanisms offered by some OODBMSs, in particular by Objectivity/DB. Then, the fact that while the inspiring principle of PJama was to extend the Java programming language with persistence without modifying it, schema evolution capabilities lead to the violation of the Java type system rules. Again, the issue of schema evolution versus type safety has raised. Finally, the more appropriateness of lazy data conversion mechanisms to a transactional context where "stopping" the computation is unacceptable was pointed out.

3.2. Transparent, Scalable, Efficient OO-Persistence (Stephan Korsholm)

Doing garbage collection and handling persistent objects have much in common. Especially the marking phase of a mark-sweep garbage collector, during which the transitive closure of some set of garbage collection roots is traversed and marked. This phase of the garbage collector does in many respects perform the same kind of work as when the transitive closure of some set of persistent roots is serialized and exported from memory onto secondary storage. This work [10], developed within the Desartee project (Esprit LTR project no 31870), describes how efficient, scalable persistence has been transparently added to the Mjølner System (MS) by changing the generational garbage collector to identify and remove persistent objects from memory onto persistent storage, while hardware support has been utilized to load persistent objects on demand. Transparency has been achieved both at the user and at the machine level, while scalability is intended both with respect to time and to space. MS supports development of programs written in BETA, which are statically typed, garbage collected and compiled into binary machine code. The changes introduced to support persistence have not affected the size, layout or handling of non-persistent objects.

The discussion following the presentation pointed out that, according to this approach, objects are loaded when they must be used and are saved when garbage collecting, thus the transactional notions of commit and rollback are missing. The possibility of integrating transactional principles in the approach by forcing garbage collection upon commit has been discussed. Moreover, the applicability of the presented techniques to Java without modifications to the Java Virtual Machine was also debated. Finally, the possibility of extending the approach with distribution and concurrency features was discussed.

4. Query Languages and Heterogeneous Databases

This session has been devoted to query languages and interoperability. The first paper describes a multi-database system exploiting the object-oriented technology, whereas the second one describes a visual query language based on OQL.

4.1. Distributed Mediation Using a Light-Weight OODBMS (Vanja Josifovski and Tore Risch)

Tore Risch presented this work [9] in which an overview is given of a light-weight, object-oriented, multi-database system, named Amos II. Object-oriented multi-database queries and views can be defined where external data sources of different kinds are translated through Amos II and integrated through its object-oriented mediation primitives. Through its multi-database facilities many distributed Amos II systems can interoperate. Since most data reside in the data sources, and to achieve good performance, the system is designed as a main-memory DBMS having a storage manager, query optimizer, transactions, client-server interface, etc. The Amos II data manager is optimized for main-memory and is extensible so that new data types and query operators can be added or implemented in some external programming language. Such extensibility is essential for data integration.

The presentation of the paper provided several hints for discussion. A first issue concerned the various levels and granularities of optimization that can be exploited in such a system. Then the applicability of that approach to applications requiring the storage of huge amounts of data was discussed, pointing out that a possible mean to reduce the amount of stored data to a reasonable size is to distribute them into different databases. Finally, problems related to method dispatch and its efficiency in this context were debated.

4.2. VOODOO: A Visual Object-Oriented Database Language for ODMG OQL (Leonidas Fegaras)

Query and data visualization are key components of many commercial database systems, such as Microsoft Access and Paradox. Object-oriented databases offer excellent opportunities for visual data browsing because they provide a direct and natural mapping of real-word objects and relationships into equivalent constructs. Even though there is already a sizable number of graphical user interfaces for object browsing, which include commercial products, such as O2Look and O2Tools of O2, there is a little work on visual query formulation in OODBs. Some researchers believe that, since OODB queries can be arbitrarily complex, this complexity must be reflected in the query formulation tool itself. In this work [8], the author shows that this is not necessarily true. According to the author point of view, if a query language is well-designed and uniform, as it is the case of ODMG OQL [3], it would require very few visual constructs for query formulation, since it would map similar features into similar visual constructs.

This paper presents VOODOO (which stands for a Visual Object-Oriented Database language for ODMG OQL) which is a simple and effective visual language to express ODMG OQL queries. The language is expressive enough to allow most types of query nesting, aggregation, universal and existential quantifications, group-by, and sorting, and at the same time is uniform and very simple to learn and use. The visual language is strongly typed in the sense that the queries constructed are always type-correct. In addition, there is sufficient type information displayed by the system that guides every stage of the query construction. The main difference between this language and other related visual query languages is that only one generic visual construct, called a *template*, is used instead of inventing a new one for each OQL syntactic feature.

The main issue arisen in the discussion on the paper concerned the extensibility of the visual query language to queries containing method invocations.

5. Temporal Object-Oriented Databases

The extension of object-oriented databases with temporal features is addressed in the papers presented in this session. In particular, the first one proposes a flexible versioning mechanism allowing one to keep different portions of the object data over time. The second one, by contrast, deals with the problem of querying temporal document databases.

5.1. Outdating Outdated Objects (Holger Riedel)

Nowadays a lot of information is collected by many applications. Although storing mass data causes no problems, the processing of interesting queries poses many restrictions. Especially collecting temporal data leads to increasing costs for updates and queries, while the worth of such information shrinks quite rapidly. Working with such outdated data is insufficiently supported in current research and products. Within temporal databases, the concept of vacuuming was proposed to destroy a certain amount of historical data of a temporal relation. An even simpler solution is used in data warehouses, where the information which might be useful in the future is selected when transferring data from the operational database to the data warehouse.

In this paper [14] the author proposes a flexible temporal versioning schema for object-oriented databases which supports controlled restructuring of the history of objects. Therefore, arbitrary parts can be marked for deletion according to a temporal condition. These parts are put into different versions organized in a linear order. Thus, each object of such a versioned class walks through these versions in a fixed way. Although this leads to versioning on the object-level, arbitrary OQL queries including additional temporal constructs can be used, either ignoring or explicitly using the versions of a specific class. In order to get type-correct query results, specific null values are provided in a promising way. The author shows how this approach can be implemented by the use of lazy and eager evaluation schemes for version migration, flexible object-oriented storage structures, and enhanced query transformers and optimizers.

The relationships between versioning and the inheritance hierarchy, that is, the impact of versioning a class on its subclasses and superclasses were discussed after the presentation.

5.2. Retrieval of Information from Temporal Document Databases (María José Aramburu Cabo and Rafael Berlanga Llavori)

Current technology allows us to create large databases of documents from where they can be retrieved in several ways. However, the resulting systems do not offer proper tools for retrieving historical information from the stored documents by considering their temporal properties. Starting from the TOODOR object-oriented database model for representing up-to-date documents, the main proposal of this paper [1], presented by María José Aramburu Cabo, is a family of new document retrieval operators called *chronicles*. The temporal object-oriented data model of TOODOR supports two different temporal features of documents: publication and event times. The publication time represents the evolution of document classes and the time instants at which documents are published. The event time of a document is defined as the temporal projection of its contents, purpose or structure. By means of event times, chronicles can be used to group retrieved documents according to several predefined temporal patterns. These object operators are able to find out documents that refer to the same reported event, which is described by the user through an information retrieval condition, some time granularity and a temporal pattern. Among other things, chronicles are useful to determine the evolution of events, to search for certain temporal patterns, and to find out cause-effect relationships among documents.

During the presentation of the paper, a number of interesting issues have arisen and have been discussed. In particular, the differences between the event and publication times supported by the model and the classical notions of valid and transaction times of temporal database systems have been discussed. The motivations for providing an ad-hoc model and language for temporal document databases and the reasons of inadequacy of available models were also debated.

6. Consistency and Verification

This session deals with consistency and verification in the context of object-oriented database schemas. Two papers were presented in this session, the first one dealing with integrity constraint specification and consistency management, and the second one devoted to verification of schema requirements for an advanced transaction model.

6.1. Consistency Management in Object-Oriented Databases (Hussien Oakasha, Stefan Conrad, and Gunter Saake)

The paper [12], presented by Gunter Saake, illustrates concepts and ideas underlying an approach for consistency management in object-oriented databases. In this approach constraints are structured as first class citizens and stored in a meta-database called constraint catalog. The structure of a constraint is an aggregation of two parts. The first part is called the *kernel* which is an object that is sharable among interrelated objects that are subject to the same constraint. The second part is called the *shell* which is an object being sharable among objects of the same class. When an object is created, constraints of this object are retrieved from the constraint catalog and relationships between these constraints and the object are established. The structure of constraints has several features that enhance consistency management in OODBMSs which do not exist in conventional approaches in a satisfactory way. These features are:

- monitoring object consistency at different levels of update granularity,
- integrity independence,
- efficiency of constraint maintenance,
- controlling inconsistent objects,
- enabling and disabling of constraints globally to all objects of database as well as locally to individual objects, and
- the possibility of declaring constraints on individual objects.

All these features are provided by means of basic notions of object-oriented data models.

The presentation of the paper stimulated discussion on several issues. Among the discussed topics, we mention criteria to establish how and when constraints should be checked in a context where data are accessed through programs whose execution may be very long. In addition, the possibility of exploiting reflection techniques to gain the chance of performing type checks over constraints was debated (such checks are impossible if constraints are codified as strings).

6.2. Compensation Methods to Support Generic Graph Editing: A Case Study in Automated Verification of Schema Requirements for an Advanced Transaction Model (Susan Even and David Spelt)

Compensation plays an important role in advanced transaction models, cooperative work, and workflow systems. However, compensation operations are often simply written as a^{-1} in transaction model literature. This notation ignores any operation parameters, results, and side effects. A schema designer intending to use an advanced transaction model is expected (required) to write correct method code. However, in the days of cut-and-paste, this is much easier said than done. The authors demonstrate in this paper [7], presented by Susan Even, the feasibility of using an off-the-shelf theorem prover (also called a proof assistant) to perform *automated* verification of compensation requirements for an OODB schema. In addition, they discuss the results of a case study in verification for a particular advanced transaction model that supports cooperative applications. The case study is based on an OODB schema that provides generic graph editing functionality for the creation, insertion, and manipulation of nodes and links.

Most of the discussion following the presentation focused on performance result of the developed tool, on the applicability of the approach to verify other properties about methods, and to different method definition languages.

7. Panel Discussion

In order not to start from scratch, we started the discussion with some comments on the *Asilomar Report* [2]. The Asilomar Report is a very interesting document published in 1998 on SIGMOD Record. On August 1998, a group of 16 among the most famous and important database system researchers from academy, industry, and government met at Asilomar (California), to assess the database system research agenda for the next decade. The goal of this meeting was to discuss the current database system research agenda and, if appropriate, to report their recommendations. The Asilomar Report summarizes the results of that meeting. Several interesting results are presented in the document which makes one thinking about the status of the research in computer science, not only in databases, nowadays. What is surprising is that object-oriented databases are not even mentioned in [2].

This fact, together with the small number of papers on object-oriented databases presented in international database conferences, makes one thinking that the research in object-oriented databases is “almost” finished. We came up with the conclusion that this is completely false. To testify that there is the success of the workshop, that, at its first edition, received a number of papers comparable to the one of a small conference. On this conclusion there has been a total agreement of the audience, perhaps even because that was the right audience.

It is, however, undoubted that the object-oriented database community is going through a frustration phase, mainly because of market reasons. That is, object-oriented DBMSs represent somehow a mature technology (most systems came into the market at the beginning of the 90s) but they are still not obtaining much commercial success. A proof of that can also be found in the fact that, though the workshop solicited the participation of people from the industry experiencing object-oriented DBMSs in real applications, the industrial representation at the workshop was really low (the only non-academic users reporting experiences of using OODBMSs were the CERN group). Thus, the general impression could be that of no industrial interest in OODBMSs, that is, no market for them.

This is however surprising, since if we take a look of the industrial market in computer science the object-oriented paradigm has proved itself successful in many respects. First, we would like to mention the success of the Java object-oriented programming language, which is the leading programming language on the Web. Moreover, we can mention UML, the new unified modeling language in software engineering, which is object-oriented, the success of the CORBA (Common Object Request Broker Architecture) architecture in distributed systems, and so on. By contrast, if we take a look of the database industrial market we notice that the leading systems are still totally based on the relational model. Recently, some efforts have been made by most successful relational DBMS producers to extend their systems with object-oriented features. The last systems are thus *object-relational*, that is, they support the possibility to define abstract data types as values of attributes and to refer to tuples via object identifiers. The relation, however, still remains the main construct for organizing data. The extent to which the object-oriented paradigm has been incorporated in object-relational (also known as *universal*) database systems is thus not fully satisfactory. The people at the workshop were all in agreement on the fact that there has not been a strong financial support by the industrial world for researching and improving object-oriented database systems. A reason for that can perhaps be that it is very hard to change ones mind when this is used to something for a long time, as relational databases, even though there are several advantages. Another reason can be found in the presence of the huge number of legacy systems based on relational databases which are still in use. We were not claiming, of course, that object-oriented DBMSs would be better than relational ones in an absolute way, rather than they can offer several advantages at least with respect to certain kinds of applications. Thus, there was the consensus of the workshop participants on the fact that the object-relational and the object-oriented database markets could coexist, simply because they fulfill different applicative requirements.

An important negative point of object-oriented DBMSs in their completion with object-relational DBMSs is surely represented by their weakness with respect to traditional database features. ObjectStore, for instance, is one of the most successful object-oriented DBMSs from the market point of view, and it misses many DBMS features: it has no declarative query language, no constraints, no complex transaction support, no security mechanism. Thus, a cause of the problems of object-oriented DBMSs can be to call them database management systems when they are (still) not full-fledged database management systems. ObjectStore itself can perhaps be better characterized as an *object repository* rather than a DBMS. That is the reason why persistent object languages could be more successful, offering some solution to the "static" market of object-oriented databases. If object-oriented programming languages are the programming languages of the future, the database community has to deal with managing data "inside" this languages. It is well known that embedded SQL suffers of several problems that could be avoided extending the used language with some facilities. Thus, the first step in this direction is the addition of persistent capabilities to object-oriented programming language. The model of persistence that they should offer should be orthogonal, that is objects of any type may be persistent or transient. A starting point in the development of the Mjølner System [10], for instance, was that the border between the application and the

DBMS, which was sharp in the relational context, should not be stressed in the object-oriented context. Thus, their aim was to provide some functionalities, not to build a complete DBMS. The issue then arises of whether extending object-oriented programming languages with persistence features is enough. Database systems offer several features that completely lack in object-oriented programming languages, such as efficient set-oriented data manipulation, query languages, constraint specification, active and temporal features, index management, and so on.

In addition to architectural aspects such as indexes, clustering, transaction support, access control, a key DBMS feature missing in persistent object languages is related to declarativity: declarative query languages working on collections of objects, and integrity constraints. For instance, the PJama system, which extends Java, lacks all these features, since Java has not been conceived as a database programming language. Similarly, most OODBMSs, also among those which adhere to the ODMG standard, are actually not providing any declarative query language; only few of them implemented a subset of OQL. Thus, the issue was debated of whether switching to the object-oriented context would necessarily mean to impose procedural programming to database users. The general feeling was against this conclusion.

Finally, taking advantage of the presence of Jamie Shiers, reviewer member of ODMG, and of Suad Alagic, who is also very close to the ODMG group, and who have participated to many ODMG meetings, also the current status of the work of the group and of the standard has been discussed. In spite of the fact that ODMG 3.0 is expected to be released at the end of this year, the work of the group seems somehow frozen, and in particular the C++ group (that is, the group working on the C++ binding) has almost stopped its activity, and this can be seen as a witness of the Java "hegemony". The name of the group is to be changed from Object Database Management Group to Object Data Management Group, and this could be interpreted as a bad signal for OODBMSs. Some participants pointed out that the ODMG standard is de facto not promoted by the companies participating in it, and that it seems to have gained more attention from the academy rather than from the industry.

Thus, the conclusion of the discussion was that there is still much to work for the object-oriented database community in the direction of making the OODBMS technology competitive with the relational one. Anyway, a necessary condition to the success of that is the market financial support.

8. Conclusion

The results of the First ECOOP Workshop on Object-Oriented Databases were, in our opinion, very positive, both in terms of number and quality of submissions, of number of participants, and of discussion at the workshop. We would like to remark that the workshop would not have been possible without the help and support of many people. The program committee and additional reviewers have input their time, skills and knowledge in reviewing the submissions of the workshop. The final program is due to their hard work. We would also like to thank the Workshop Chair of ECOOP'99, Ana Moreira, for the scheduling and the local arrangements.

List of Participants

In the following we list the participants at the workshop, their affiliations and their e-mail addresses.

Name	Affliation	E-mail address
Alagiĉ Suad	Wichita State University, USA	alagic@cs.twsu.edu
Àlvarez-Gutiérrez Darío	University of Oviedo, Spain	darioa@lsi.uniovi.es
Aramburu Cabo María José	Universitat Jaume I, Spain	aramburu@inf.uji.es
Belen Martinez Prieto	University of Oviedo, Spain	belen@lsi.uniovi.es
Dmitriev Misha	University of Glasgow, UK	misha@dcs.gla.ac.uk
Düllmann Dirk	CERN Geneva, Switzerland	Dirk.Duellman@cern.ch
Even Susan	University of Twente, NL	seven@cs.utwente.nl
Fegaras Leonidas	University of Texas, USA	fegaras@lambda.uta.edu
Grouleff Morten	Mjølner Informatics, Denmark	mg@mjolner.dk
Guerrini Giovanna	Università di Genova, Italy	guerrini@disi.unige.it
Heide Damm Christian	University of Aarhus, Denmark	damm@daimi.au.dk
Korsholm Stephan	Mjølner Informatics, Denmark	sek@mjolner.dk
Merlo Isabella	Università di Genova, Italy	merloisa@disi.unige.it
Nylorg Mads	Technical University of Denmark	mn@iac.dtu.dk
Rashid Awais	Lancaster University, UK	marash@comp.lancs.ac.uk
Riedel Holger	University of Konstanz, Germany	Holger.Riedel@uni-konstanz.de
Risch Tore	University of Linköping, Sweden	torri@ida.liu.se
Rodrìguez M. Elena	Universtity of Catalonia, Spain	malena@lsi.upc.es
Saake Gunter	Magdeburg University, Germany	saake@iti.cs.uni-magdeburg.de
Sakkinen Markku	University of Jyväskylä, Finland	sakkinen@cs.jyu.fi
Shiers Jamie	CERN Geneva, Switzerland	Jamie.Shiers@cern.ch
Spelt David	University of Twente, NL	spelt@cs.utwente.nl
Torvill Bjorvand Anders	University of Oslo, Norway	torvill@trolldata.no

References

[1] M. J. Aramburu-Cabo and R. Berlanga-Llavori. Retrieval of Information from Temporal Document Databases. Available at ftp://www.disi.unige.it/person/GuerriniG/ecoopws99/final12.ps.gz.

[2] P.A. Bernstein, M.L. Brodie, S. Ceri, M.J. Franklin D. J. DeWitt, H. Garcia-Molina, J. Gray, G. Held, J. M. Hellerstein, H. V. Jagadish, M. Lesk, D. Maier, J. F. Naughton, H. Pirahesh, M. Stonebraker, and J. D. Ullman. The Asilomar Report on Database Research. *SIGMOD Record*, 27(4):74–80, 1998.

[3] R. Cattel, D. Barry, D. Bartels, M. Berler, J. Eastman, S. Gamerman, D. Jordan, A. Springer, H. Strickland, and D. Wade. *The Object Database Standard: ODMG 2.0.* Morgan Kaufmann, 1997.

[4] M. Dimitriev and M. Atkinson. Evolutionary Data conversion in the PJama Persistent Language. Available at ftp://www.disi.unige.it/person/ GuerriniG/ecoopws99/final14.ps.gz.

[5] M. Dmitriev. The First Experience of Class Evolution Support in PJama. In *Advances in Persistent Object System. Proc. of the 8th International Workshop on Persistent Object Systems (POS-8) and the 3rd International Workshop on Persistence and Java (PJAVA-3)*, pages 279–296, 1999.

[6] D. Dullman and J. Shiers. Object Database and Petabyte Storage - Dreams or Reality? Available at ftp://www.disi.unige.it/person/GuerriniG/ecoopws99/final1.ps.gz.

[7] S. Even and D. Spelt. Compensation Methods to Support Generic Graph Editing: A Case Study in Automated Verification of Schema Requirements for an Advanced Transaction Model. Available at ftp://www.disi.unige.it/person/ GuerriniG/ecoopws99/final16.ps.gz.

[8] L. Fegaras. VOODOO: A Visual Object-Oriented Database Language For ODMG OQL. Available at ftp://www.disi.unige.it/person/GuerriniG/ecoopws99/final13.ps.gz.

[9] V. Josifovski and T. Risch. Distributed Mediation using a Light-Weight OODBMS. Available at ftp://www.disi.unige.it/person/GuerriniG/ecoopws99/final25.ps.gz.

[10] S. Korsholm. Transparent, Scalable, Efficient OO-Persistence. Available at ftp://www.disi.unige.it/person/GuerriniG/ecoopws99/final10.ps.gz.

[11] Ronald Morrison, Mick J. Jordan, and Malcolm P. Atkinson, editors. *Advances in Persistent Object System. Proc. of the 8th International Workshop on Persistent Object Systems (POS-8) and the 3rd International Workshop on Persistence and Java (PJAVA-3)*. Morgan Kaufmann, 1999.

[12] H. Oakasha, S. Conrad, and G. Saake. Consistency Management in Object-Oriented Databases. Available at ftp://www.disi.unige.it/person/GuerriniG/ecoopws99/final20.ps.gz.

[13] A. Rashid and P. Sawyer. Evaluation for Evolution: How Well Commercial Systems Do. Available at ftp://www.disi.unige.it/person/GuerriniG/ecoopws99/final5.ps.gz.

[14] H. Riedel. Outdating Outdated Objects. Available at ftp://www.disi.unige.it/person/GuerriniG/ecoopws99/final11.ps.gz.

[15] C.M. Saracco. *Universal database management*. Morgan Kaufmann, 1998.

[16] M. Stonebraker. *Object-relational DBMSs*. Morgan Kaufmann, 1999.

Parallel/High-Performance Object-Oriented Scientific Computing

Bernd Mohr[1], Federico Bassetti, Kei Davis[2] (Organizers),
Stefan Hüttemann[3], Pascale Launay[4], Dan C. Marinescu[5], David J. Miller,
Ruthe L. Vandewart[6], Matthias Müller[7], and Augustin Prodan[8]

[1] Forschungszentrum Jülich GmbH, ZAM, Germany
b.mohr@fz-juelich.de
[2] Los Alamos National Laboratory, CIC-19, U.S.A.
kei@lanl.gv, fede@lanl.gov
[3] Technische Informatik, Universität Tübingen, Germany
hutteman@informatik.uni-tuebingen.de
[4] IRISA, Campus de Beaulieu, Rennes, France
Pascale.Launay@irisa.fr
[5] Department of Computer Sciences, Purdue University, U.S.A.
dcm@cs.purdue.edu
[6] Sandia National Laboratories, U.S.A
djmille@sandia.gov, rlvande@sandia.gov
[7] High Performance Computing Center (HLRS), Stuttgart, Germany
mueller@hlrs.de
[8] Iuliu Haţieganu University, Romania
aprodan@umfcluj.ro

Abstract. This chapter contains a summary of the presentations given at the Workshop on Parallel/High-Performance Object-Oriented Scientific Computing (POOSC'99) at the European Conference on Object-Oriented Programming (ECOOP'99) which was held in Lisbon, Portugal on June 15, 1999. The workshop was organized jointly by the Special Interest Group on Object-Oriented Technologies of the Esprit Working Group EuroTools and Los Alamos National Laboratory.

1. Introduction

While object-oriented programming is being embraced in industry, particularly in the form of C++ and Java, its acceptance by the parallel/high-performance scientific programming community is tentative at best. In this latter domain, performance is invariably of paramount importance, where even the transition from FORTRAN 77 to C is incomplete, primarily because of performance loss. On the other hand, three factors together practically dictate the use of language features that provide better paradigms for abstraction: increasingly complex numerical algorithms, application requirements, and hardware (e.g., deep memory hierarchies, numbers of processors, communication and I/O).

In spite of considerable skepticism in the community, various small groups are developing significant parallel scientific applications and software frameworks in

A. Moreira and S. Demeyer (Eds.): ECOOP'99 Workshops, LNCS 1743, pp. 222–239, 1999.

C++ and FORTRAN 90; others are investigating the use of Java. This workshop seeks to bring together practitioners and researchers in this emerging field to 'compare notes' on their work – describe existing, developing, or proposed software; tried and proposed programming languages and techniques; performance issues and their realized or proposed resolution; and discuss points of concern for progress and acceptance of object-oriented scientific computing.

The workshop had seven selected presentations organized in four sessions about scientific computing with C++, problem solving environments, scientific computing with Java, and requirements/issues for (performance) tools for C++ and Java. This report contains the summary and discussions of the presentations at the workshop. For a more detailed description of the work presented here, see the proceedings of the workshop which were published as a technical report [1].

2. Scientific Computing with C++

More and more scientific and engineering problems become amenable to numerical treatment and ever more complex and efficient algorithms are being developed to make even better use of the existing computing power. However, in order to enable researchers to make efficient use of both, it is necessary to provide software that hides the complexity of the computing platform and of the algorithm alike.

With the increasing complexity of modern numerical algorithms, the advantage of object-oriented programming techniques is obvious. A language that supports this techniques is preferable to languages that lack this support. However, in the scientific community where performance is one of the major criteria, a language that suffers a performance loss or is not available on supercomputers will not be widely accepted. C++ is available on most supercomputers as well as on the workstations where the code is developed. In addition, the language was designed to have no or only a minimal runtime overhead while still offering the advantages of an object-oriented language. Moreover C++ is a multi-paradigm language that allows one to use the programming style that is best suited for the problem to be solved. However, compared to the lifetime of many scientific software, C++ is still a young language and we need to gain experience with abstraction techniques or paradigms that offer the most advantages but suffer no performance drawback. An advantage that was again visible in this workshop is the similarity between C++ and Java. This frequently allows one to use concepts from either language without a major redesign.

2.1. Object-Oriented Concepts for Parallel Smoothed Particle Hydrodynamics Simulations (Stefan Hüttemann)

In the first presentation, Stefan Hüttemann described object-oriented concepts for parallel smoothed particle hydrodynamics simulations based on a 3 year work experience in a government funded project with computer scientists, physicists and mathematicians.[1] For more details please see [1], [16] and [17].

Motivation. Astrophysical problems of interest include open boundary problems involving viscous compressible fluids. Smoothed Particle Hydrodynamics (SPH) is the method used by astrophysicists to solve a Navier-Stokes equation. SPH became widely popular in recent years. SPH is now also used as an alternative for grid-based CFD simulations (e.g., in automobile industry).

SPH uses particles that move with the fluid instead of grid points as in other CFD simulation methods. This makes SPH much more difficult to parallelize than grid-based CFD methods.

Parallel SPH using DTS. Using a portable parallel programming environment called "Distributed threads system" (DTS), Hüttemann could show that SPH can be parallelized on shared memory machines (NEC SX-4) with parallel efficiencies of up to 90% (see [16]). On machines with distributed memory (Cray T3E) it is possible to achieve speedups with efficiencies of 65% (see figure 1). On the Cray T3E, the native Cray SHMEM library was used to parallelize SPH simulations.

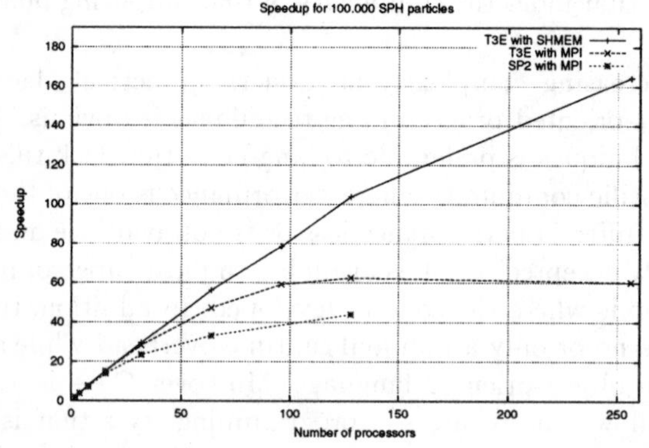

Fig. 1. Speedup SPH on Cray T3E with SHMEM and MPI and on IBM SP with MPI for a mid-size problem with 100 000 SPH particles.

The Need for Object-Oriented Techniques. For these simulation methods, it seems to be most natural to use message objects to communicate between concurrent program units. Also, the growing complexity of the simulation programs

[1] SFB 382: "Verfahren und Algorithmen zur Simulation physikalischer Prozesse auf Höchstleistungsrechnern" (Methods and algorithms to simulate physical processes on supercomputers)

requires structural elements in the programming paradigm not offered by FORTRAN or C. Therefore, project participants started programming in C++, and there is now an increasing demand for object-oriented solutions.

Towards Object-Oriented Parallel SPH. To support object-orientation for parallel programming, the users extended their model of parallel computing with threads on machines with distributed memory using C++ objects. In this model, an object – extended for architectures with distributed memory – is the basic entity of data communication. Objects can be migrated between different address spaces and replicated to improve performance. Also work was done on the integration of the STL, i.e., transferring STL containers as well as using iterators for send and receive calls. On the application level, known design patterns were modified and applied to the problem.

Discussion/Questions.

Q: Which design patterns are useful for parallel scientific computing?

A: We used modifications of standard design patterns. They proved useful especially for domain-decomposition algorithms. The programmer can use high-level constructs like monitors and active objects for parallel programming.

Q: How can you motivate more scientists (physicists) to use object-oriented techniques for scientific computing?

A: From our experience, the only way to get physicists to code their simulations in C++, is to provide a simulation framework that is as fast as a comparable FORTRAN program.

Q: You should compare your results with other similar work.

A: This contribution to the workshop was a presentation of a work in progress. More details of our work can be found in [1], [16] and [17].

2.2. Molecular Dynamics with C++. An Object-Oriented Approach (Matthias Müller)

Principles of Molecular Dynamics. In the second part of this section, Matthias Müller of the High Performance Computing Center in Stuttgart presented his work on Molecular Dynamics (MD).

The principle of an MD program is: find the interaction partners for every particle, calculate the forces between the particles and integrate the equations of motion. A real MD program can be rather complex, e.g., by using optimization techniques such as linked-cell algorithms for short range interaction. Different MD programs need different types of particles with different degrees of freedom and forces.

With this in mind, an MD package for short range interaction was developped. It allows easy modification of particle type, interaction force, and integration scheme, and allows one to switch between serial and parallel implementation without changing the main program. For the implementation, C++ and the Message Passing Interface (MPI) were used.

The parallel paradigm applied here is domain decomposition, and therefore every CPU is responsible for a part of the domain and has to exchange information about the border of its domain with its adjacent neighbors. Instead of exchanging them directly with all 8 or 26 neighbors in two or three dimensions respectively, the Plimpton scheme[2] is applied.

Design of the Particle Container. To free the ordinary programmer from the details of bookkeeping and still provide him with the freedom to implement his own particle types, forces, and integration schemes, a template container for particles is provided, similar to the containers of the standard template library (STL). In addition to the normal members provided by an STL container, a particle container provides a template member `for_each_pair` to allow for iterations over pairs of particles. Here the function object concept of STL is applied, and the force class has to supply an operator() for two particles:

```
template<class PARTICLE>
class Force{
public:
  inline void operator()(PARTICLE & p1 , PARTICLE & p2){
     Vector force;
     // calculation of f goes here
     p1.force += force;
     p2.force -= force;  // actio = reactio
  }
};
```

This example also demonstrates the possibility of formulating the algorithm in a natural, dimension-independent way. To avoid possible performance problems due to the many small vectors used, the template expression technique [3] is used to perform loop unrolling, inlining, and other optimizations at compile time.

The main loop of an MD simulation will look similar to this example:

```
PartContLC<Particle,3> box(ll,ur,bound_cond,cut_off);
double dt=0.1;                                 // time step
MD_int_vv_start<Particle>  int_start(dt);    // integration
MD_int_vv_finish<Particle> int_finish(dt);
while( t<maxT ){
  // velocity verlet integration first part:
  for_each_particle(box.begin(),box.end(),int_start);
  // force calculation:
  box.update();                                // communication
  box.for_each_pair(myForce);
  // velocity verlet integration second part:
  for_each_particle(box.begin(),box.end(),int_finish);
  // advance time:
  t+=dt;
}
```

In the STL, algorithms and containers are separated as much as possible. However, in order to have an efficient search algorithm for interaction pairs, it had to be incorporated into the container, much like the sort algorithm for lists in the STL. The member function `for_each_pair` performs a pair search with the well-known linked-cell algorithm. The function object concept is of course not limited to integration and force calculation, but can be used whenever all particles or pairs of particles have to be "visited", e.g., for general data extraction, calculation of pair correlation functions, or even computational steering.

Performance. While recent benchmarks have shown that C++ can compete with C or Fortran [4], it is not clear whether this holds for a particular application. The performance depends on the abstraction techniques used [5, 6]. Therefore, it is a non-trivial task to find a suitable balance between certain techniques and performance. Since the force calculation is the most time consuming part in an MD simulation, the danger of an abstraction penalty at this point is high. In our experience, the performance of the described MD algorithm is comparable with a similar implementation in C [1]. However, this depends on the compiler used. It is not unusual to get three times slower execution times just by using a different compiler on the same platform.

Conclusion. It has been demonstrated that object-oriented concepts help to design flexible, portable, and easy-to-use tools for molecular dynamics. In particular, judicious application of the template and inlining mechanisms of C++ *can* lead to program performance on par with that of classical procedural languages. In several cases, the container abstractions described above have proved to yield programs which are easily portable to parallel platforms and which can utilize 2 or 3 dimensions. The achieved flexibility also allows an easier integration into frameworks such as PSEs or computational steering.

Discussion/Questions.

Q: What happens if a particle changes the domain in the course of a simulation?
A: The particle container takes care of this. It will be automatically transferred between the CPUs.

3. Problem Solving Environments

Until recently, the focus of Problem Solving Environments for parallel high-performance computing has been the development of better codes and tools to enable higher fidelity, full physics simulations. This has included the ability to create more complex computer models, better meshing techniques, a wider variety of analysis algorithms, and more sophisticated technologies for visualizing results. However, little emphasis has been placed on integrating these tools and providing easy desktop access to them and the information they generate.

With the advent of the internet and a shifting focus toward distance and distributed computing, attention is now being paid to the development of metasystems and frameworks which view computing resources (both hardware and software) as large networked grids. These metasystems are being designed to manage such grids and to provide product designers transparent desktop access to them without requiring detailed knowledge of computing infrastructures. Utilizing technologies such as browsers, Java, agents, and distributed computing middleware, integrated Problem Solving Environments are being created which allow a designer to access high-performance modeling and simulation tools in a way that focuses on designer-oriented issues rather than computing issues. Two papers presented as part of the Problem Solving Environment section of this workshop discuss different approaches to provide such environments.

3.1. An Agent-Based Design for Problem Solving Environments (Dan C. Marinescu)

First, Dan Marinescu of Purdue University presented the Bond system [7], [9], [10], and [11].

Motivation and Introduction. Many problems in science and engineering involve computer modeling of physical phenomena. Often, computer simulation involves large groups of scientists and engineers, large collections of experimental data and theoretical models, as well as multiple programs developed independently and possibly running on systems with different architectures. Problem Solving Environments, PSEs, are software systems, designed to hide the intricacies of computer simulation and guide a researcher or an engineer towards a meaningful solution. Traditionally, the developers of PSEs are computational scientists, the authors of the component programs.

There are at least two directions for further development of Problem Solving Environments. One is to build "intelligent PSEs", the other is to support distributed applications. Both directions require structural changes in the software engineering of Problem Solving Environments.

Complex computer simulations require domain knowledge, thus it seems appropriate to abstract such knowledge into a set of rules. The process of knowledge representation requires "conceptualization", namely identification of the basic objects in the domain-specific area and defining the relations among these objects. The PSE should have the means to gather facts related to the specific application.

Once the rules and the facts are embedded into the working memory of an inference engine, new facts can be generated and actions determined by these new facts can be triggered. Examples of rules are: (condition C) then (A) else (B). For example, condition (C) may be determined by facts such as the size of the data set, the shape of a domain, etc. and the facts (A, B) could be the suitability of one algorithm or another for one processing step. Recent practical results in the area of knowledge representation, e.g., the development of the

Knowledge Interchange Format (KIF) by Geneserth et al. at Stanford [8], will certainly facilitate the development of intelligent PSEs. Though a number of efforts in this area have been reported in the literature, successful use of a PSE embedding an inference engine has not yet been reported.

Another dimension of Problem Solving Environments is their ability to support distributed applications. Some computer modeling applications are naturally distributed over a wide-area network. Such applications require gathering experimental data, processing raw data, plugging the results of this processing into theoretical models, and repeating the process with various sets of model parameters. Other applications require legacy components, distributed over a wide-area network, to collaborate towards a common goal. In both cases the distributed applications have common requirements: (a) the need to start-up and monitor the execution of individual components that often are legacy programs, (b) components developed independently must be coordinated, (c) data files need to migrate from the point where the data is generated to the consumption site, (d) data annotation is necessary in view of large number of data files, (e) heterogeneity of the hardware and the diversity of the software should be accommodated.

Traditional PSEs are monolithic. The main objective of their designers is to provide a solution to a specific problem rather than identify common functions and build a common PSE platform. Monolithic PSEs for distributed applications are very complex. The development of an infrastructure will help the scientific community create the software it needs for complex experiments and sophisticated computer simulation.

Software Composition. The idea of building a program out of ready-made components has been around since the dawn of the computing age, backworldsmen have practiced it very successfully. Most scientific programs use mathematical libraries, parallel programs use communication libraries, graphics programs rely on graphics libraries, and so on.

Modern programming languages like Java, take the composition process one step further. A software component, be it a package or a function, carries with itself a number of properties that can be queried and/or set to specific values to customize the component according to the needs of an application which wishes to embed the component. The mechanism supporting these functions is called introspection. Properties can even be queried at execution time. Reflection mechanisms allow us to determine run time conditions, for example the source of an event generated during the computation. The reader may recognize the reference to Java Beans, but other component architectures exists, including Active X based on Microsoft's COM and LiveConnect from Netscape to name a few.

Can these ideas be extended to other types of computational objects besides software components, for example, to data, services, and hardware components? What can be achieved by creating metaobjects describing network objects like programs, data, or hardware?

Informally, a Problem Solving Environment is the "glue" for a number of components developed independently. Often the components are legacy codes that cannot be modified with ease. In this case, wrapper components around legacy programs can be created called software agents. Each wrapper is tailored to the specific legacy application. Then interoperability between components is ensured by federation of agents.

Conclusions. Bond is a Java-based, agent-based, distributed object system that has been under development for the past few years. Bond provides a framework for interoperability based upon (1) metaobjects that provide information about network objects, and (2) software agents capable of using the information about network objects to carry out complex tasks. Some of its components, e.g., the agent framework, the scheduling agents, the monitoring and security frameworks, are generic and can be expected to be included in other applications like distance learning, or possibly electronic commerce. The design of a Problem Solving Environment based upon a network of PDE solvers is one of the applications of Bond that illustrates the advantages of a component based architecture versus a monolithic design of a PSE. A beta version of the Bond system was released in mid March 1999 under an open source license, LPGL, and can be downloaded from our web site, `http://bond.cs.purdue.edu`.

3.2. An Object-Based Metasystem for Distributed High Performance Simulation and Product Realization (David J. Miller and Ruthe L. Vandewart)

The second paper in the Problem Solving Environment section of the workshop was presented by David J. Miller of Sandia National Laboratories in Albuquerque, NM. It focuses on software being developed at Sandia known as the Simulation Intranet/Product Database Operator, or SI/PDO.

Motivation. The SI/PDO embodies an architecture for satisfying Sandia's long term goal of providing integrated software services for high fidelity full physics simulations in a high-performance, distributed, and distance computing environment. The talk began with a statement of a vision to develop a product-oriented environment for designers which provides desktop access to computer-based tools, processes, and modeling/validation techniques distributed across the Department of Energy laboratory and production complex in support of science-based simulation and virtual prototyping missions. In accomplishing this vision, it would be necessary to integrate distributed computing with high-performance computing, and take advantage of commodity-based computing clusters being constructed at the laboratories.

Requirements. Some of the system requirements presented for SI/PDO include the ability to work in a heterogeneous computing environment, the use of object-oriented development principles and a component-based architecture, the characteristics of machine and tool independence, network transparency, and an iterative, evolutionary implementation path. Because of the magnitude of the mission, three initial thrusts were addressed in the first implementation: provide desktop access to massively parallel machines for running analysis codes, integrate visualization with analysis to provide image snapshots on the desktop of a simulation's progress, and develop the concept of the Product Database Operator, or PDO. The PDO includes the ability to capture large quantities of data generated by analyses in an object repository, classify this data into a taxonomy, and make relevant information easily available to the users to solve new problems.

Architecture. Then, a detailed discussion of the software architecture model was presented. It is designed for a grid-like computing network and consists of desktop clients, distributed business objects, and data persistence. A web browser is used on the desktop to access applications and services that the user requires. It is implemented in Java, using Java Bean components to represent the desktop pieces of the distributed services and a Java applet which serves as the container for the beans. Transparent connections and communication are provided between the Web Top and distributed services through the use of the Common Object Request Broker Architecture (CORBA). The business objects are the legacy codes and new codes provided by scientists and commercial vendors which implement the modeling and simulation services required by the designers. These services are made to look like distributed CORBA-based components which are accessible from anywhere on the network and may execute on workstation nodes or massively parallel machines. Finally, data persistence is implemented by the PDO through the use of a commercial object-oriented database management system and a CORBA service which allows transparent network access to the PDO and hides the details of database programming.

Implementation. A focused problem domain was selected for the first prototype implementation. It consists of providing desktop access to a structural finite element code called Alegra executing on a Linux-based high-performance computing cluster of several hundred DEC Alpha processors. In addition, the first implementation provides a spyglass capability which feeds back JPEG images of data generated by the analysis code at each time step. On the Web Top are components to configure, execute, monitor, and display results of an analysis run. All components are tied to the PDO which maintains dynamic state of each process, communicates asynchronous events of state changes, and manages the information generated.

Future Work. Finally, a discussion of future work included the need for providing access to additional services and high performance clusters, extending the concept of the PDO, addressing security through secure ORB technology, and looking at more advanced capabilities involving drag-and-drop programming environments for building distributed design assistants which target specific modeling and simulation Problem Solving Environments. The majority of questions and comments following the talk focused on the similarities and differences between the two approaches presented in this section of the workshop and potential collaboration in future implementations. Additional information and full papers discussing the SI/PDO can be obtained by contacting the authors through the email addresses provided above.

4. Scientific Computing with Java

The use of Java for scientific computing is providing an eligible alternative, despite the fact that the Java language has not been designed with that aim in mind. Initiatives such as the JavaGrande Forum (http://www.javagrande.org) are focusing on making Java a language suitable for high-performance computing.

Java is an easy to understand and "clean" object-oriented language. Moreover, this language has many nice features for parallelism and distribution, such as threads and RMI integrated into the language. Therefore, many programmers have now switched to this language.

New tools, libraries, and environments are now needed for scientific computing in Java. These environments have to take advantage of Java's characteristics, so tools developed for other languages such as Fortran can not be used efficiently. The projects presented in this session aim at providing environments for scientific computing in Java: the *Do!* environment, designed for parallel and distributed programming in Java, is presented first. This approach is based on the use of collections to structure parallelism and program distribution. The second part presents an experimental work using the Java language for simulation and modelling applications. This approach relies on the generation of random variables in Java.

4.1. Using Collections to Structure Parallelism and Distribution (Pascale Launay)

First, Pascale Launay of IRISA in France introduced the *Do!* project. The aim of the *Do!* project [12, 13, 14, 15] is to ease the task of programming scientific parallel and distributed applications using Java. The use of collections provides a unified way to structure parallelism and distribution. A parallel framework, based on collections, has been defined which allows one to write parallel applications in a centralized fashion (all objects are on a single host). "Distributed" collections are provided for distributed execution of these applications (objects are mapped on distinct hosts). The framework library comprises static collections (arrays) and dynamic collections (lists). It has been targeted to the Java language and runs on any standard Java environment.

Collections and Parallelism. Parallelism is *introduced* through active objects: an active object has its own sequential activity, private attributes, and an argument (that can be used for communications and synchronizations with other objects). Active objects are implemented using Java THREADS.

Parallelism is *structured* through collections: collections are large object aggregates, responsible for the storage and accessing of their elements. Operators express global operations on collections: an *operator* is an object processing an operation on elements of a collection, provided by an *iterator*, independently from the collection shape. Two sorts of operators have been developped for collections of active objects: START for the activation of active objects, and JOIN for their termination and the synchronization. Several parallel models are defined by combining iterators and operators (START and JOIN and their descendants). The parallel framework is represented by a PAR class or a descendant, implementing a parallel model (parallel construct):

- the PAR class (basic) defines independent parallelism between active objects;
- the DATAPAR class defines data parallelism, through multiple copies of an active object operating on a data aggregate;
- the SHAREDPAR class defines dependent active objects accessing a single shared object.

Collections and Distribution. Distribution is *introduced* through the mapping of objects on distinct hosts (JVMs). Runtime classes process remote creations to map objects on hosts, and remote method invocations implement communication between remote objects using the Java RMI. Because using Java RMI requires important modifications in the code of classes, seamless location of objects is provided through code transformations of classes (*accessible* classes).

Distribution is *structured* through distributed collections (collections with elements that are located on distinct hosts). Distributed collections manage access to distributed elements. The distribution of collections is described in a specific class called a *distribution layout manager* (DLM): DLMs encapsulate all computations depending on the type of distribution (owner retrieving and key transformation). For each type of collection, there are several DLMs to describe different kinds of distributions. A specific DLM is associated with each distributed collection. It is used by the collection to process accesses, and it is used to determine where to create an object that will be stored in a distributed collection. The operators process operations on elements of distributed collections. Accesses to distributed elements are managed by the distributed collection and the seamless location of accessible objects, so there is no need to modify iterators, operators, and parallel constructs. DLMs are associated with non-distributed collections as well. In that case, they have no effect; they are included in a program to specify how to distribute it.

Conclusion and Discussions. Performance is one of the main concerns in scientific computing. The *Do!* environment is targeted to the Java language, using

THREADS and RMI. The current implementation of the Sun JVM is not satisfying in terms of performance, but some environments are now available which make it possible to use Java for high performance computing. The overhead of using the *Do!* framework and code transformations for *accessible* classes is negligible.

The main contribution of this work is to provide an integrated framework for parallelism and distribution through the use of collections, allowing the expression of several parallel models. The distribution of collections leads to the distribution of their elements and therefore to the generation of distributed programs. Usually, distributed collections are used to express data parallelism only. Some distributed collection libraries exist, for example Parallel STL (part of the HPC++ project). In that project, distribution is part of the collections. In our environment, distribution is expressed through special objects (DLMs) encapsulating all aspects depending on the type of distribution. This allows one to implement any type of distribution and allows the users to easily extend the library to their specific needs. That way, dynamic collections and dynamic DLMs have been implemented, integrating load balancing strategies through the mapping of objects when they are created.

A first release of the *Do!* environment is currently available online (http://www.irisa.fr/caps/PROJECTS/Do), comprising arrays and static DLMs. It is illustrated by a complete example of a distributed program written using the *Do!* framework. A second release integrating lists and dynamic DLMs has already been implemented and will be available soon. Applications have been implemented using the *Do!* environment and high performance Java environments will be used in a future release. A foreseen extension is to include object migration in order to allow load balancing during active objects execution. This technique will also be ported to a CORBA environment, Java being used only as a coordination language.

4.2. Simulating and Modeling in Java (Augustin Prodan)

Introduction and Previous Research. Augustin Prodan of Iuliu Haţieganu University presented some results of a study concerning the possibilities offered by the Java language for simulation and modeling applications. This study is the result of an experimental work developed in the Department of Mathematics and Informatics, Iuliu Haţieganu University Cluj-Napoca, in collaboration with the University of Medicine and Pharmacy Craiova.

Previous research has shown that stochastic models are advantageous tools for representation of the real world. Based on theoretical work in stochastic modeling [19], an incremental development of an object-oriented Java framework containing the main elements for building and implementing stochastic models has been produced.

The first result of this research is an object-oriented approach to the simulation of random variables by means of classical distributions. The second part of the work is devoted to the applications. Methods for simulating and modeling the flow of patients in the departments of geriatric medicine are presented.

The Fundamentals of Simulation in Java. There are three levels of simulation to be considered. The first level consists in simulating random numbers, as they are the basis of any stochastic simulation study. The so-called pseudo-random numbers, generated via Java's built-in linear congruential generator, can be used to simulate random numbers [18].

Based on the first level, the second level of simulation used for classical distributions is built. The classical random variables are the most simple stochastic models, so called distributional models, which enter into the composition of other complex models. A hierarchy of Java classes which models the classical distributions is proposed. Each distribution is determined by a set of parameters and a distribution function. Based on these elements, a polymorphic method is specified by each distribution class in turn, in order to simulate a specific value. An instance of a particular class can be used to simulate a set of values for the corresponding random variable, by calling this polymorphic method as many times as needed. The particular implementation for each class is based on one or more of the following techniques: the Inverse Transform Technique, the Acceptance-Rejection Technique, and the Composition Technique.

The third level of simulation is devoted to applications and is based on the previous two levels.

A Model for Geriatric Medicine. The population of geriatrics in a given hospital district is relatively stable and therefore it is possible to model the movement of geriatric patients by considering both their entrance into the hospital and their stay in the geriatric unit. Geriatric departments usually practice two different types of care: acute and long-stay, well-known as two-compartment medical care. The in-patient care is modeled as a mixed-exponential phase-type distribution, applying the composition technique with the composed density function $f(t) = \rho\alpha_1 e^{-\alpha_1 t} + (1-\rho)\alpha_2 e^{-\alpha_2 t}$, $t \geq 0$. As far the admission policy is concerned, the best solution is to be modeled as a Poisson process. The Poisson arrival model introduces more variability into the system and hence increases its consistency. Once the model has been shown to accurately represent the movement of geriatric patients, given expert knowledge of feasible changes to the system and the costs associated, the theoretical effects of modifications to the system may be calculated. Furthermore, the costs can be assessed without having to implement the changes in a real setting, which could be costly. Therefore, it is possible to maximize the efficiency of the geriatric department, thus optimizing the use of hospital resources, in order to improve hospital care.

Conclusions and Future Work. A set of base line Java classes for simulation of classical distributions was introduced. Based on their design and implementation, a model was created which accurately represents the movement of geriatric patients. Both geriatricians and hospital administrators agreed that such a model can be used to maximize the efficiency of the geriatric department and to optimize the use of hospital resources in order to improve hospital care. For future work, the continuation of the incremental development with new Java classes for implementing simulation and model techniques is intended. A model for estimating tumor sizes by using the Hit or Miss Monte Carlo integration will be created. Future research effort will also be oriented towards the development of new models, model analysis, statistical data mining, and visualisations.

Discussion/Questions.

Q: The *simulation* of random numbers means in fact the *generation* of random numbers?

A: Yes, in the field of computational probability and stochastic applications, the problems of how to *generate*, or how to *simulate* random numbers are synonyms. We say that a method in our application *simulates* uniform (0, 1) random variables using Java's built-in random number generator.

Q: Have you verified if Java's built-in random number generator works well?

A: No, we haven't yet. I read somewhere that Java's simple linear congruential generator is non-random in certain situations by generating undesirable regularities. To overcome this, we intend to build a class as an improvement over the one supplied by Java.

Q: How did you decide what distributions to use in your application?

A: This is a problem of stochastic modeling research. Our stochastic model is based on some results obtained by Harrison, Millard and McClean [1]. We have used data described by P. H. Millard (1991) on the movement of geriatric patients (over 10,000 admissions) between 1969 and 1984 for hospitals within the district containing St. George's Hospital, London, U.K. By applying the maximum likelihood equations to data, the above distributions were validated and estimations of the distribution parameters were obtained.

Q: Why did you use Java in your work and not one of the languages oriented towards stochastic applications?

A: I like Java.

5. Requirements/Issues for (Performance) Tools for C++ and Java (Bernd Mohr)

In the last session, Bernd Mohr presented a list of requirements and problem areas for performance tools for object-oriented programming. As a member of the Special Interest Group on Object-Oriented Technologies of the Esprit Working Group EuroTools, he was interested in collecting feedback from "real" users with respect to this list in order to improve future performance tools. Current tools were designed and implemented with traditional programming languages like Fortran or C in mind, and their use in object-oriented environments is limited or even impossible. His list was divided into four parts:

Issues Regarding Object-Orientation in General. The first part described problem areas for tools which apply to object-oriented programming in general and are not specific to a particular language.

1. Object-orientation is mostly about abstractions and re-use. Abstractions of a specific application area are typically implemented as a set of classes and put in a library for re-use. Such a set of classes is also called a framework. In the object-oriented field, people are more willing to use/re-use other libraries and frameworks as a "black box". This means that (performance) tools should present their results to them on the level of the abstractions the framework/library provides. However, to do this, a way is needed to describe attributes/features of frameworks to tools.
2. For object-oriented programming, the unit of most interest is a class with its methods (and not procedures/functions like it is for procedural programming). Also, classes are often related to each other through inheritance ("is-a") and composition ("has-a"). This has consequenses for tools: they should be able to calculate and present information on a per class basis. However, simply the summing-up of all performance indices of all methods of a class is not enough, as data collected for inherited methods would get counted for the base and not the derived class. This also means that tools must know about inheritance/composition relationship in addition to the call graph.
3. Typically, procedural programming leads to a set of "longish" procedures while object-oriented programming results in a set of classes with lots of short methods. Inlining is therefore very important for efficient object-oriented programs. But inlining introduces problems for tools. First, inline functions and methods do not "exist" for object code based tools (e.g., debuggers). Second, measurement/instrumentation overhead for small functions is very high. In addition, adding instrumentation code might prohibit inlining. Last, if inlined, optimizers might rearrange (instrumentation) code leading to false results.
4. Object-oriented programming languages support virtual functions, i.e., different functions get called based on the dynamic type of an object. This is a problem for static analysis tools because they can only determine the set of possibly called functions. In addition, virtual functions are often implemented through indirect calls (i.e., function pointers). So, tools must be able to handle these.

C++ Specific Issues. Next, Bernd presented a list for the programming language C++. This list is longer than the others because, firstly, C++ is a very complex language, and secondly, being now over 20 years old, much more experience exists about its usage and problems.

1. The C++ language is very complex (and became even more complex in the recent standardization). This means that no (working, complete) public domain parser is available for research groups. This makes it hard to implement static analysis or source code instrumentation tools.
2. Other than with procedural programming languages, plain function/method names are not unique as C++ allows function overloading and in addition, the same name can be used for methods in different classes and namespaces. But tools often use these names for legends and labeling. Therefore, tools for

C++ must present the "fully qualified" name to the user including class and namespace prefixes and argument types. But this name can get very long easily. The C++ standard suggests a *minimum* length of 1024 characters! In addition, names can contain blanks and special characters. Many current tools cannot handle this. Finally, the "object code" name of a C++ object is different from its "source code" name (*name mangling*), so tools need to know the mapping between these names. Complicating the issue is that different compilers use different mangling schemes.
3. A lot of functions/methods are called implictly by the compiler (not explicitly by the programmer), e.g., constructors, destructors, conversion operators, or operator functions like overloaded assignment or addition. That means that not all function calls are directly "visible" in the source code, complicating static analysis and result display.
4. C++ supports generic programming through template classes and functions. A list of actual template instantiations is very hard to determine (even impossible to know) in advance. This complicates source code instrumentation (e.g., determining a unique identification for instrumenting a function defined as a template). Also, templates require even more inlining to be efficient (see above).
5. In addition to classes, C++ allows grouping of classes and global functions into namespaces. This is a relatively new addition to the language. Therefore, there are basically no tools supporting this yet (e.g., for presentation/organization of performance data).
6. Finally, C++ allows the definition of objects of class type in global scope. This implies that code can possibly executed before/after `main()` through constructors/destructors of these global objects. Tracing/measurement tools which traditionally initialize/wrap-up in `main()` don't work anymore.

Java Specific Issues. Java is a relatively "young" language so there do not exist many tools for it yet. Also, experiences with tool design and implementation for Java environments are still very limited. Therefore, the list presented was relatively short and not very specific.

1. First, Java is traditionally byte-code interpreted. Therefore, tools need to be able to get (performance) information on both the Java program and the interpreter.
2. Second, Java has built-in threading. So, tools must be able to handle multithreading.

Distributed Object-Oriented Programming. Finally, Bernd asked whether issues for distributed object-oriented programming are basically the combination of the issues for object-orientation (see above) plus the issues for distributed programs (e.g., heterogenity and global time) or whether there are other specific problems unique to this programming style. The audience favored the first but it might be possible that the usage of middleware like CORBA or DCOM might require further tool adaptation/extensions.

References

[1] F. Bassetti, K. Davis, B. Mohr (Eds.). Proceedings of the Workshop on Parallel/High-Performance Object-Oriented Scientific Computing (POOSC'99), European Conference on Object-Oriented Programming (ECOOP'99). Technical Report IB-9906, Forschungszentrum Jülich, Germany, June 1999.

[2] S. Plimpton. Fast parallel algorithms for short-range molecular dynamics. *Journal of Computational Physics*, 117:1–19, 1995.

[3] T. Veldhuizen. Expression templates. *C++ Report*, pages 26–31, June 1995.

[4] T. Veldhuizen. Scientific computing: C++ vs. Fortran. *Dr. Dobb's Journal*, November 1997.

[5] S. Haney. Is C++ fast enough for scientific computing? *Computers in Physics*, 8(6):690–694, Nov/Dec 1994.

[6] A. D. Robison. C++ gets faster for scientific computing. *Computers in Physics*, 10:458–462, 1996.

[7] Bölöni, L., and D.C. Marinescu, *An Object-Oriented Framework for Building Collaborative Network Agents.* Kluever Publishers, 1999.

[8] Genesereth, M. R., *An Agent-Based Framework for Interoperability*, in J. M. Bradshaw Ed. *Software Agents*, MIT Press, pp. 317-345, 1997.

[9] Hao, R., L. Bölöni, K.K. Jun, and D.C. Marinescu, *An Aspect-Oriented Approach to Distributed Object Security*, Proc. 4-th IEEE Symp. on Computers and Communications, IEEE Press, (1999).

[10] Marinescu, D.C., and Bölöni L., *A Component-Based Architecture for Problem Solving Environments*, 1999.

[11] Tsompanopoulou, P., L. Bölöni, D.C. Marinescu, and J.R.Rice, *The Design of Software Agents for a Network of PDE Solvers* Proceedings of Workshop on Autonomous Agents, IEEE Press, 1999.

[12] *Do!* Project Web Site. http://www.irisa.fr/caps/PROJECTS/Do

[13] P. Launay and J.-L. Pazat. Generation of Distributed Parallel Java Programs. In *Euro-Par'98*, number 1470 in Lecture Notes in Computer Science, pages 729–732, Southampton, UK, September 1998. Springer Verlag.

[14] P. Launay and J.-L. Pazat. The Do! Project: Distributed Programming Using Java. In *First UK Workshop Java for High Performance Network Computing*, Southampton, UK, September 1998. http://www.cs.cf.ac.uk/hpjworkshop.

[15] P. Launay and J.-L. Pazat. A Framework for Parallel Programming in Java. In *International Conference on High-Performance Computing and Networking (HPCN'98)*, number 1401 in Lecture Notes in Computer Science, pages 628–637, Amsterdam, The Netherlands, April 1998. Springer Verlag.

[16] Bubeck, T., Hipp, M., Hüttemann, S., Kunze, S., Ritt, M., Rosenstiel, W., Ruder, H., Speith, R.: *Parallel SPH on Cray T3E and NEC SX-4 using DTS* High Performance Computing in Science and Engineering '98, Springer (1999) 396–410

[17] Hipp, M., Hüttemann, Konold, M., Klingler, M., Leinen, P., Ritt, M., Rosenstiel, W., Ruder, H., Speith, R., Yserentant, H.: *A Parallel Object-Oriented Framework for Particle Methods* High Performance Computing in Science and Engineering '99, Springer (1999)

[18] A. Prodan, M. Prodan. *Mediul Java pentru Internet.* Ed. ProMedia-plus, ISBN 973-9275-07-9, Cluj-Napoca, 1997.

[19] S.M. Ross. *A Course in Simulation.* Macmillan Publishing Company, New York, 1990.

Integrating Human Factors into Use Cases and Object-Oriented Methods

Ahmed Seffah[1] and Cameron Hayne[2]

[1] Computer Research Centre of Montreal
aseffah@crim.ca
[2] Computer Research Centre of Montreal
hayne@crim.ca

Abstract. This article summarizes the workshop on human factors in use cases and object-oriented development methods. The following questions were the main focus of the workshop: Can use cases be improved by the incorporation or consideration of formal task analysis models and human centered design techniques in general? Are there ways of integrating human factors and user-centered techniques into use cases and object-oriented methods? The workshop brought a multidisciplinary blend of researchers and practitioners involved in user-centered design together with those interested by user requirements and use cases. It highlighted fundamental problems arising from the integration of human factors in use cases and OO methods.

1. Introduction

Industry practices and academic research have led to several object-oriented methods which seem highly adequate for the development of systems with little or no user interaction. However, for interactive systems – those with a significant user interface – these methods have a major gap. Most do not propose mechanisms (models) for:

1. Explicitly and empirically identifying and specifying user needs, its profile and the his or her social and organizational environment
2. Testing and validating requirements with end-users before, during and after development.

As a result of this weakness, interactive systems developed using such methods can meet all technical requirements, and yet be unusable. This problem explains a large part of the frequently observed phenomenon whereby large numbers of change requests to modify the services of an application are made after its deployment.

The solution to this problem consists of adopting a user-centered design approach, which is characterized by [8]:

– The active involvement of users, as well as a clear understanding of the context of use, the tasks and the end-user requirements.

A. Moreira and S. Demeyer (Eds.): ECOOP'99 Workshops, LNCS 1743, pp. 240–254, 1999.

- An appropriate allocation of function between users and technology – specifying which functions should be carried out by the users.
- The iteration of design solutions in which user feedback becomes a critical source of information.
- A multidisciplinary design perspective that requires a variety of skills (usability engineers, software developers, end-users and stakeholders.)

Use cases, a potential technique for user-centered design, provide a mechanism for determining system boundaries, as well as a user-oriented requirement model. They can be considered as a starting point towards a method for specifying end-user needs and in general for integrating human factors in the development process. Task analysis is another potential technique widely used in the human computer interaction (HCI) community. Task analysis aims to achieve a generic and thus abstract model of end-user tasks, typically in a hierarchical form of goals and sub-goals. There appears to be much commonality between task analysis and use cases.

The following are the main issues that have been addressed:

- Ways for extending use cases to support interactive systems design and usability engineering.
- Techniques object-oriented developers can use to communicate with task analysis specialists when developing interactive systems.
- Differences and commonality between task analysis methods and the use case-driven approach.
- Methods for describing end-user requirements and achieving a better understanding between end-users and developers.

2. Summary of Position Papers

In this section, we give summaries of the papers presented by the workshop participants with some discussion of the issues raised. These summaries have been supplied by the presenters and have been lightly edited by the authors of this article. The list of presenters is given in a later section. Full versions of the position papers can be downloaded from the workshop home page:
http://www.crim.ca/~aseffah/ecoop

2.1. Detailing Use-Cases with Activity Diagrams and Object Views (Nuno Jardim Nunes and João Falcão e Cunha)

Our approach, WISDOM (White Water Interactive System Development with Object Models), extends use-cases to support HCI techniques. Three techniques pay a major role in our proposal:

1. Annotating non-functional requirements to use cases enables developers to minimize the number of artifacts to manage and prevents problems in later stages of development.

2. Detailing use cases with activity diagrams reduces the burden of managing multiple success and failure scenarios for one use-case. We also found out this technique simple enough to be used in participatory sessions under the form of sticky notes, fostering user-centered design.
3. Finally we use views (stereotyped analysis and design classes) as the conceptual building block of interaction design. We believe they are essential to model the interaction between the system and it's actors and model the complete user interface architecture. In views we introduced stereotyped attributes for input and output information and distinguished the operations done on an object (actions on views) from operations done by the object (operations in general analysis classes). WISDOM organizes views in several diagrams; in class diagrams representing structural relationships between them; in activity diagrams illustrating the navigational model with behavioral relationships and finally; in state chart diagrams to detail the internal behavior of views.

2.2. Integration of the User Model and Human Factors in an Object Oriented Software Production Environment (María Dolores Lozano and Isidro Ramos)

We use a methodology for specifying user interfaces within an automatic software production environment. This environment is supported by an object-oriented model, called OASIS (Open and Active Specification of Information Systems) [11] and a methodology associated to the model called OO-Method [13], [12]. The methodology and the environment are developed by one of the research groups of the department of information systems and computation from the Technical University of Valencia (Spain) covering the typical phases of Analysis, Design and Implementation within the principles of the Object Oriented Paradigm. Our aim in this work is to enrich this formal and Object-Oriented Specification Language, OASIS, by including aspects of user interface specification. The user interface is an important entity placed between the user and the application that the user needs to interact with the system. Thus, the user interface must be designed to be capable of communicating with both the end user and the application.

We propose a user model, which models the user-system interaction. Besides, we also show a specific example in which this methodology is applied in the phases of Analysis and Design, showing the different steps in which it is developed. The model we propose includes the generation of graphical and object-oriented diagrams to represent user interface issues.

Analysis Phase: The user model is represented by means of what we have called the *user diagrams*. These *user diagrams* consist of three different types of diagrams:

- The Dialog Structure Diagram, which represents the windows and dialogs that the user needs to complete all the tasks he requires from the system, and the user selections to pass from one window to another.

- The Component Specification Diagrams, which models the contents of every one of the windows and dialogs represented in the previous diagram. Every window is composed of components and tools.
- Components Behavior Definition Table in which every one of the components and tools represented in the previous diagram is accurately described so that the user can understand the meaning of the components and tools through which he interacts and retrieves information from the system.

Design Phase: The Graphical Models obtained in the first phase of Analysis are translated into an OASIS specification, which is the design tool within this methodology.

Implementation Phase: This is the last step of the process. Implementation is tackled in a different way depending on the programming environment used. In this phase we can use a Graphic User Interface Builder to get the visualization of the specified interface.

Therefore, we can conclude that this methodology offers a set of operational methods, which allows the design of user interfaces in an object-oriented environment. Above all, we want to point out the importance of designing interaction between the end-user and the application before starting filling windows and windows with arbitrary sets of widgets and other graphical elements. First to this, it is crucial to think about how should be the structure of the user interface of the system, considering first the general lines and then the details and final appearance, but only after having analyzed the tasks, operations and components needed to fulfil the user's needs.

Besides, this object-oriented approach facilitates the possibility of reusing user interface components. This possibility permits the construction of user interfaces using library classes with the advantage of implementing each individual feature only once.

2.3. The Requirements/Service/Interface (RSI) Approach to Use Case Analysis (Mark Collins-Cope)

The RSI approach provides a framework for analyzing and understanding potential use case deliverables and their inter-relationships, with a view to answering the questions detailed above. The RSI approach also aims to assist in maximizing software re-use - by partitioning functionality into those aspects which are concerned with 'managing the interface' to an actor, and those areas which make up the re-usable core of the system.

RSI divides use cases three categories, shown by the UML stereotypes: <<requirement>>, <<service>> and <<interface>>:

- <<Requirement>> use-cases document business processes for which automated support may be required. They detail the requirements driving the development of a system, but do not define the detail of a system's functionality.
- <<Interface>> use cases provide a detailed description of the interfaces presented to the system's actors and association functionality.

- <<Service>> use cases provide a detailed description of the underlying functionality a system offers in a manner independent of the needs of any particular interface.

The separation of <<interface>> and <<service>> use cases can also be viewed as a layering of the functionality of a system, with <<interface>> use cases providing a 'translation' role between the nuances of a particular interface and the essential core of a system.

The benefits of dividing use cases into three categories lie in the answers to the following questions:

- What is the appropriate level of granularity for use cases? The answer to this depends on your objectives in undertaking use case analysis, which may vary over the duration of your analysis. In brief, if you want to broadly scope your system, use the <<requirement>> level; if you want to clearly and rigorously define the system you are going to build, use the <<interface>> level; and finally, if you want to factor out the re-usable core of your system, use the <<service>> level.
- If large grained use cases are used, should they decomposed into 'lower level' use cases? Yes, potentially at least. The relationship between RSI categories of use cases is one of scooping and requirement. <<requirement>> use cases may be scoped, and then refined into <<interface>> use cases, which in turn may be refined into <<service>> use cases. The RSI approach provides a clear structure and purpose to use case decomposition.
- If so, at what point should this decomposition stop, and how should these sub-use cases be used? <<Interface>> use cases are used to clearly define the interface (user or external system) of the system that you are intending to implement. <<Service>> use cases can be used to develop a problem domain object model (a specification or core model) in a formal or semi-formal manner. <<Service>> use cases are not decomposed further.
- Should user or external system interface functionality be described in use case text? The RSI approach provides a clear placeholder for such descriptions if required, at the <<interface>> level. Some projects may choose to defer detailed interface design past the use cases analysis phase, however even then this may be back documented in the RSI use case model.
- How do dialog descriptions fit in? Where do report layouts go? Should user interface dynamics be included? The RSI approach provides the <<interface>> level for dialog descriptions (including detailed descriptions of user interface dynamics) and report layout definitions.
- Should interchange file formats, or interface protocols form part of the documentation? Again, the RSI approach provides the <<interface>> level for such descriptions.

2.4. The Knight Project: Tool Support for Cooperation in Object-Oriented Modelling (Klaus Marius Hansen)

We believe that analysis, design, and implementation of software systems is best done in a way that is object-oriented, incremental, evolutionary, and cooperative

[5]. Since model building is a cardinal point in system development [14], support for modelling in a process with these characteristics becomes important.

Basically, two types of technology exist for doing object-oriented modelling, namely whiteboards and CASE tools. Use of whiteboards are informal, supports synchronous collaboration, and enables extensions of notations. CASE tools, on the other hand, combine a formal notation with the possibility for asynchronous collaboration and tool integration. To facilitate effective user collaboration in modelling activities, these two technologies need to be combined.

To ground development in practice, we have made user studies of different user groups. From our analysis of the user studies a number of lessons on the collaborative, communicative and coordinative aspects of object-oriented modelling can be learned.

Although most of the drawing elements made were in the form of UML diagrams, these elements were combined with non-UML elements in one of two forms. Either as rich "freehand" elements that explained part of the problem domain, or as formal additions to the UML such as notations for inner classes or grouping. This means that a tool supporting collaborative object-oriented modelling should, ideally, facilitate: drawing in a formal modelling notation, drawing of "freehand" additions, and the ability to tailor the notation "on the fly".

Filtering was used for several reasons. First, even whiteboard real estate is limited. Second, not all parts of a diagram are interesting at all times. Third, users may employ a specific semantic filtering to decide the important elements of a diagram. In all user studies, drawing has been transferred to and from CASE tools. This naturally implies that the tool we develop integrate with a CASE tool.

It has been a striking fact in our user studies that modelling has been coordinated as turn taking. We believe it to be general for the kind of work that (object-oriented) modelling is all about. Verbal communication and use of other artefacts was not coordinated via turn taking. The people engaged in the meetings would e.g. discuss among themselves while another person was drawing at the whiteboard, or they would use other artefacts concurrently. This has design implications, especially if distributed collaboration is to be considered.

We are currently developing a tool based on the user studies and further evaluations. It combines a large, shared touch sensitive drawing surface (currently a SMART Board ^{TM}) with ordinary CASE tools. Since interaction on the drawing surface is done via gestures (drawing a box e.g. creates a UML class) the ease of interaction with a whiteboard is combined with the computational power of ordinary CASE tools.
The Knight Project homepage has more information:
http://www.daimi.au.dk/~knight.

2.5. Characterizing Task Formalisms: Towards a Taxonomy (Sandrine Balbo, Cécile Paris, and Nadine Ozkan)

A number of task formalisms have been developed in the Human-Computer Interaction community, often with different goals and thus different strengths. Without an explicit understanding of the different attributes of these formalisms, it is difficult to select a specific one to achieve one's goals. To address this issue, we have tried to organize the various formalisms in a taxonomy consisting of several dimensions, combining and building on our own experience, and also the work of Balbo [2], and Brun and Beaudoin-Lafon [4]. The elements of the taxonomy have been defined according to various criteria we have found useful to consider when having to decide on a specific methodology or task model formalism.

The main drivers for our taxonomy are:

- The phase of the Software Development Life Cycle (SDLC) the formalism intends to support, and more generally the aim of the formalism, and
- The characteristics of the formalism, including readability and usability of the formalism.

Dimension 1: Aim of the Formalism Our first dimension is the aim of the formalism, which refers to the phase of the SDLC for which the methodology is intended. We have chosen a coarse-grained decomposition of the SDLC, for purposes of generality and in order to avoid adherence to a specific methodology. The phases we consider are:

- Requirement analysis,
- User interface design,
- Software design,
- Implementation. We keep Brun and Beaudoin-Lafon's distinction and consider that a formalism could aim to achieve two purposes:
  - the derivation of the generic functions of the system, and
  - Automatic generation of all or parts of the final system;
- Evaluation, and more specifically if the formalism can be used for predictive evaluation of the system. (Prediction is, to our knowledge, the only use of task formalisms at this phase of the SDLC.)

Dimension 2: Characteristics of the Formalism

As general characteristics, we retain from Balbo the driving element, the readability, and the usability; from Brun and Beaudoin-Lafon, the extensibility. With extensibility, we are not concerned with the applicability of the formalism to a range of tasks (as described in Brun and Beaudoin-Lafon) but whether or not the formalism can be extended easily to fit a new situation when necessary. We have found that feature to be an important one as we apply task models in novel and varied situations, to be exploited in innovative ways. We also keep the representation of mandatory *vs* optional tasks, and the representation as to who must perform the action (user, system, both).

For the describing power, we extend the notion to include not only the levels of decomposition and temporal relations, but also whether the formalism allows for the representation of the interface feedback to the end-user, and the management of errors.

For the temporal relations, we look at the synchronization of actions (sequencing, alternatives, composition – i.e., A and/or B –, and iteration), at the amount of parallelism allowed (interleaved or true parallelism), and, finally, we consider delays.

In this summary, we presented the attributes of a taxonomy built to help compare and contrast task models and identify their strengths. This taxonomy provides us with a basis on which to choose a task model for a specific situation. The taxonomy allowed us to determine more explicitly the similarities and differences between these various models. It also enabled us to compare the different task formalisms in order to conduct our choices in cases where we needed to select task formalism.

2.6. Use Cases and Task Analysis (E. Kantorowitz)

Before starting a discussion, it is useful to define the employed terminology. The organizer's definition of task analysis, which I can accept, is:

Task analysis aims to achieve a generic and thus abstract model of end-user tasks, typically in a hierarchical form of goals and sub-goals.

The purpose of task analysis is thus the identification of the tasks that the users are expected to accomplish with the help of the system. Each task identified through task analysis is thus a use case of the system. A use case may be specified in UML notation [3]. The next step in the software development process is to take each one of the identified use cases, and to design the human-computer process that accomplishes the task. Following Jacobson's approach [9] this process is specified by a detailed scenario written in the natural language that the user understands. The idea is that the users should participate in the validation of the scenarios. To enable this validation the scenario must specify all the aspects of the process with all their details. This includes the detailed structures of all the user interfaces together with the systems reactions to all possible kinds of user inputs. Reactions to faulty user actions are included. Fault handling is important for several reasons. The first is that users make mistakes, the second is that many users learn to use a system by trial and error. This is often an efficient learning method as users can immediately observe the consequences of their actions. A further purpose of the scenario is to enable HCI experts validate and improve the process with the help of their expertise.

Considering that neither the users nor the HCI experts may be trained in employing formal notations, the use of a combination of natural language text, diagrams and drawings is often the best way to specify a scenario. Even people trained in employing formal systems can have difficulties in understanding them, and are doing many mistakes [15]. Future formal systems may be designed to be less error prone. Considering the high costs of faults in the design of the human-computer process, it is advisable to employ the notation that enables the designers of this process to be most productive. To make the design and validation more effective, some industries built system prototypes that visualize the scenarios. It is noted that the costs of implementing prototypes are high, and that some important aspects are often omitted. When the difficult task of designing the scenarios is completed they provides a detailed specification of the behavior of the system. The next step is to analyze the scenarios and produce an equivalent formal requirements model, possibly in UML notation.

The described process has been employed successfully in the industry for many years [9]. We have also tried it at my university with student projects. The detailed scenarios are quite bulky, but our students and we feel that the investment is worthwhile. We ask the students to quality check the scenarios. The students document the quality checks, so we can see how much was done. The student also record the number of hours invested in each stage of the process. We observed that student who make a considerable investment in detailed scenarios and their quality checking, complete in general their projects with less work hours than students who invest less effort in the task analysis and scenario construction.

2.7. Comparing Use Cases and Task Analysis: A Concrete Example (Cameron Hayne, Ahmed Seffah, and Daniel Engelberg)

We compare the techniques of use-case analysis (often used by software engineers engaged in object-oriented development) and task analysis (often used by "human-factors people" engaged in user-interface requirements analysis). This comparison is centered around a substantial real-world example (handling of health service requests) where we have attempted to write a set of use cases which would reproduce the content of an existing task analysis document.

Task analysis usually aims to describe the way that people currently do their work. Use cases usually describe the way in which a future system will be used. However, they can also be used in reverse engineering an existing system. Communication in a use case is between the various actors. Usually there are two main actors: the system and the user. Human to human communications do not usually appear in use cases (unless these communications are mediated by the system). Human to human communication are often an important part of task analysis.

The task analysis outlined [in the full version of this paper] describes the ways that requests are handled at the CLSC in the current paper-based system. The tasks of the social workers involves a lot of communication with other people (the requestor, the client, other health professionals) and the task analysis does not specify which parts of the work might be computerized and how this future system will integrate with the remaining (non-computerized) parts of the work. The original task analysis document did state, however, that use of a computer would likely be too obtrusive during the evaluation phase when the social worker is meeting the client. This implies that the social worker would have to take notes on paper and later transcribe them into the computer.

The use cases were derived from the existing task analysis and hence they also describe more the existing way of working than the future computerized version. But this example makes it evident that it is possible to express the results of a task analysis in terms of use cases. Cockburn's formulation of use cases allows the flexibility to incorporate arbitrary information on non-functional requirements. And, although it is common for the communication in use cases to be between two actors (the system and the user), this is not a necessary restriction - use cases can easily describe communication among larger numbers of actors. Perhaps the above use cases should have been more explicit on the nature of the actions and responsibilities of the human actors to make this point clear.

The use cases we outlined do not seem at a level sufficient to determine the requirements for the system. A second phase of analysis needs to be done to decide how computers will be introduced into the work. The results of this second phase of analysis would be a second set of use cases that would specify the communications between the Social Worker and the computer system as well as the communications between humans.

The process of writing the use cases corresponding to the existing task analysis has made us realize that the semi-formal nature of Cockburn's use case formulation is very useful in forcing consideration of error conditions and failure modes. Having to supply pre and post conditions for each use case forced us to think more logically (if ... then ... else) about the users' tasks and goals.

2.8. Use-Case Storyboards in the Rational Unified Process (Philippe Kruchten)

The *Rational Unified Process* (RUP) is a software engineering process developed and commercialized by Rational Software [10], [3]. It captures some of the best practices of the industry for software development. It is use-case driven, and takes an iterative approach to the software development lifecycle. It embeds object-oriented techniques, and many activities focus on the development of *models*, described using the Unified Modeling Language (UML) in particular a *use-case model*.

In the RUP, *User-Interface Design* (UID) is covered by the following process elements: one worker: the *User-interface designer*, involved in two activities: User-interface modeling and User-interface prototyping, where two artifacts are developed: *Use-case storyboards* and *User-interface prototype*.

A *use-case storyboard* is a logical and conceptual description of how a *use case* is provided by the user interface, including the interaction required between the actor(s) and the system. It is represented in UML as a collaboration, stereotyped as <<use-case storyboard>>. Use-case storyboards are used to understand and reason about the requirements of the user interface, including usability requirements. They represent a high-level understanding of the user interface, and are much faster to develop than the actual user interface. The use-case storyboards can thus be used to create and reason about several versions of the user interface before it is prototyped, designed, and implemented.

A use-case storyboard is described in terms of boundary classes and their static and dynamic relationships, such as aggregations, associations, and links. Each boundary class is in turn a high-level representation of a *window* or similar construct in the user interface. The benefits of this approach are the following:

- It provides a high-level view of static window relationships such as window containment hierarchies and other associations between objects in the user interface.
- It provides a high-level view of dynamic window relationships such as window navigation paths and other navigation paths between objects in the user interface.
- It provides a way of capturing the requirements of each window or similar construct in the user interface, by describing a corresponding boundary class. Each one defines responsibilities, attributes, relationships, etc. that have a direct mapping to the corresponding construct in the user interface.
- It provides a trace to a specific use case, thereby providing a seamless integration with a use-case-driven approach for software engineering. As a result, the user interface will be driven by the use cases that the system is required to provide, and by the actors' roles in, and expectations of, these use cases.

A use-case storyboard in the analysis model is traced (one-to-one) to a use case in the use case model. Use-case storyboards are used by:

- User-interface designers, to build a model of the user interface;
- Designers of the boundary objects participating in the use-case storyboard, to understand the objects' roles in the use cases and how the objects interact, and then to design and implement the boundary objects;
- Testers of the system's use cases;
- Managers to plan and follow up the analysis and design work.
- Maintainers of the system to understand how the system carries out the flow of events in terms of boundary objects. For example, a change may affect a limited number of use cases, in which case the designers need to see the realization of their flow of events;

2.9. Relations between Use Cases and Task Analysis (Peter Forbrig and Anke Dittmar)

Use cases and specifications of tasks both describe work in different ways. There are a lot of similarities between them. Beside classes and objects, which have nearly the same meaning in both approaches there, are *roles* and *actors*, which are synonyms. The same is true for *tasks* and *use cases*.

Work is described in a more informal way by use cases. These documents are not yet precise enough to guarantee the implementation of software with the desired functionality. But, they can be a useful starting point for the application of the introduced model-based method.

A task model is a little bit more precise. It describes all possible scenarios of the created use cases by using process equations. There are mappings of the actors of the use cases to the roles in the user model and between tasks and use cases. Task descriptions can be seen as refinements of use cases. They are related to a business-object model, which has to be a refined view of the classes in the use cases.

A model-based approach using task, business-object and user models allows prototyping in a very early project stage. These models can also be used to generate scenarios such as interaction diagrams or collaboration diagrams. This is especially useful in the design phase of a software product in order to illustrate the functionality of a prototype by generated task-oriented scenarios. The described specification of tasks is in some sense more precise and more general than specifications actually used for use cases. Interaction diagrams can be generated from these specifications. The same is true for collaboration diagrams. We want to support Artim [1] opinion "One model but many views" and believe that different notations for the same thing may help to communicate with users. Task hierarchies, process algebras, use cases and scenarios in different notations should be available during software development. Tool support is strongly recommended. It can help to construct one view with the help of others or can check whether different views are contradictory or not. We are working on such tools. Cockburn [6] discusses some problems concerning use cases. He relates use cases to goal structures.

From our point of view hierarchy of use cases is not so important for many people. In our approach we start by ignoring the relations between use cases. At first a collection of tasks (use cases) is sampled. The goal, the actors, the tools, the artifacts and all the other things also mentioned by Cockburn are collected for each task.

Later the task structure is developed. But this structure is described in a more formal way and this specification is the basis for further development. Main success scenarios, scenario extensions and scenario variations are notes only. They should have been specified in a structured way in a natural language. Interaction diagrams are of limited use only. Using this methodology the problem of scenario explosion does not exist. Expressions in an algebra are able to describe an infinite number of scenarios.

During the workshop we have shortly revealed the origins and different applications of specification principles of use cases and tasks. We have argued that a combination use of these methods can improve the software development process.

A framework of task models, object models and user models was introduced. These multiple dimensions require tools enabling the manipulation of all these models along the different phases of software development. These tools should be able to propagate changes from one model to the other models. During this propagation process it has to be decided whether the changes have influence on the model which is the destination of the propagation. In order to achieve this goal algorithms checking consistency and completeness have to be considered in the course of further developments.

We did not discuss within this workshop the problem of models describing existing or envisioned work situations, which has also to be handled by tools. This is discussed in [7].

2.10. Enhancing Use Case Driven Process with Elements of a User-Centered Requirements Framework (Rachida Djouab, Ahmed Seffah, Moncef Bari, and Ghislain Lévesque)

We discuss the main issues for enhancing the use case driven requirements workflow as suggested in RUP [3], [10] using elements of RESPECT, one of the most advanced user-centered requirements framework. The URL (http://www.nectar.org/respect/index.htm) contains further information about the RESPECT project and products.

There are, at least four complementary ways, for enhancing the use case approach:

1. Extending the use case model and notation using artifacts and headings collected in RESPECT.
2. Adding to the use case requirements driven process by activities described in RESPECT and user-centered design processes.
3. Using RESPECT and UCD techniques to capture non-functional requirements in the use case-driven software development lifecycle
4. Improving communication between all the persons involved in the requirements process and more specifically between usability specialists, software engineers and end-users.

Behind this specific example (Use case and RESPECT), our investigations aims to establish the basic foundation for (1) cost-effectively integrating user-centered design techniques into the traditional software development lifecycle, and (2) unifying the software and usability engineering processes.

3. Discussion

Some of the questions discussed at the workshop were the following:

- Is there an *essential* difference between task analysis and use case analysis?
- Can we fit use case techniques into Sandine Balbo's taxonomy?
- How useful are computerized tools in these analyses?
- Who are the use cases aimed at? (i.e. who is the audience for use cases?)
- Should there be separate use cases for the user interface and the rest of the system?
- Does the use case approach lacking essential items to make it "user-centred" or is the problem merely that use cases are often poorly done?
- Should use cases include non-computerized functionality ?
- At what stage should use case analysis be done ? Should it come before or after design of the user interface?

Workshop Presenters

Philippe Kruchten	Rational Software Corporation pbk@rational.com
Nuno Jardim Nunes	University of Madeira, Portugal dnnunes@uma.pt
Peter Forbrig	University of Rostock, Germany pforbrig@informatik.uni-rostock.de
E. Kantorowitz	Technion – Israel Institute of Technology kantor@cs.technion.ac.il
María Dolores Lozano	University of Castilla-La Mancha Albacete, Spain mlozano@info-ab.uclm.es
Sandrine Balbo	CSIRO, Mathematical and Information Sciences, Australia Sandrine.Balbo@cmis.csiro.au
Cameron Hayne	Computer Research Institute of Montreal hayne@crim.ca
Klaus Marius Hansen	University of Aarhus, Denmark marius@daimi.au.dk
Ghislain Lévesque	University of Quebec at Montreal levesque.ghislain@uqam.ca
Mark Collins-Cope	Ratio Group Ltd markcc@ratio.co.uk

References

[1] J. M. Artim, M. Van Harmelen, et al. Incorporating work, process and task analysis into commercial and industrial object-oriented systems development. *ACM SIGCHI Bulletin*, 30(4), oct 1998.

[2] S. Balbo. *Évaluation ergonomique des interfaces utilisateur: un pas vers l'automatisation.* PhD thesis, University of Grenoble, Grenoble, France, sep 1994.

[3] G. Booch, J. Rumbaugh, and I. Jacobson. *The Unified Modeling Language User Guide.* Addison Wesley, Reading, MA, 1999.

[4] P. Brun and M. Baudouin Lafon. A taxonomy and evaluation of formalisms for the specification of interactive systems. In *Proceedings of HCI'95*, 1995.

[5] M. Christensen et al. The M.A.D. experience: Multi-perspective Application Development in evolutionary prototyping. In *Proceedings of the 12th European Conference on Object-Oriented Programming (ECOOP '98)*, 1998.

[6] A. Cockburn. Structuring use cases with goals. *Journal of Object-Oriented Programming*, 10(7), 1997.

[7] P. Forbrig and C. Stary. From task to dialog: How many and what kind of models do developers need? (CHI workshop "from task to dialogue: Task-based user interface design"), 1998.

[8] ISO. ISO/DIS 13407 standard: Human centered design processes for interactive systems. Technical report, ISO, 1998.

[9] I. Jacobson, M. Christerson, et al. *Object-Oriented Software Engineering: A Use Case Driven Approach.* Addison Wesley, Reading, MA, 1992.

[10] P. Kruchten. *The Rational Unified Process—An Introduction.* Addison Wesley, Reading, MA, 1999.

[11] P. Letelier, I. Ramos, P. Sanchez, and O. Pastor. OASIS version 3.0: A formal approach for object oriented conceptual modeling. Technical Report SPUPV-98.4011, Technical University of Valencia, Spain, 1998.

[12] M.D. Lozano, I. Ramos, and P. Cuenca. Application of an object-oriented methodology for automatic software production: OO-Method. In *Proceedings of the IEEE Pacific Rim Conference on Communications, Computers and Signal Processing (PACRIM'97)*, 1997.

[13] O. Pastor, E. Insfran, V. Pelechano, J. Romero, and J. Meseguer. OO-Method: An OO software production environment combining conventional and formal methods. In *Proceedings of the 9th International Conference, CAiSE'97*, 1997.

[14] J. Rumbaugh, I. Jacobson, and G. Booch. *The Unified Modeling Language Reference Manual.* Addison Wesley, Reading, MA, 1999.

[15] R. Vinter, M. Loomes, and D. Diana Kornbrot. Applying software metrics to formal specifications: A cognitive approach. In *Proceedings of the Fifth IEEE International Software Metrics Symposium*, 1998.

Object-Oriented and Constraint Programming for Time Critical Applications

Frank S. de Boer

Utrecht University, The Netherlands
frankb@cs.uu.nl

Abstract. The aim of this workshop was to discuss any aspect of time critical applications which are based on (a combination of) object-oriented and constraint technology: Language design, implementation, hybrid systems, temporal deductive databases, semantic models, specification, verification and analysis methods, constraint domains and solvers for temporal reasoning, temporal aspects of internet and multimedia computing, applications. Papers illustrating products and protoypes were particularly encouraged.

1. Introduction

Many applications in, for example, robotics, worldwide information networks, decision support systems, distributed multimedia computing and deductive temporal databases have time critical aspects. The overall aim of this workshop was to discuss extensions of object-oriented technology for time critical applications. A particular emphasis is on such extensions based on constraint technology. Recently several extensions of constraint programming have been proposed in order to deal with the difficulties of time-critical applications. In fact, some of these difficulties can be better resolved within a framework which facilitates the transition from specifications to programs, supports rapid prototyping, allows simple methodologies for program correctness and admits simple concurrent extensions.

Summarizing, the aim of this workshop was to discuss any aspect of time critical applications based on (a combination of) object-oriented and constraint technology: Language design, implementation, hybrid systems, temporal deductive databases, semantic models, specification, verification and analysis methods, constraint domains and solvers for temporal reasoning, temporal aspects of internet and multimedia computing, applications. Papers illustrating products and prototypes were particularly encouraged.

The workshop was supported by the ESPRIT Working Group 23677 COTIC (concurrent constraint programming for time critical applications [1]) and was held together with the third meeting of the Working Group.

The program of the workshop consisted of presentations of the following position papers:

[1] http://www.cs.ruu.nl/people/frankb/www.dvi

A. Moreira and S. Demeyer (Eds.): ECOOP'99 Workshops, LNCS 1743, pp. 255–266, 1999.

1. S. Tini and A. Maggiolo-Schettini. A truly concurrent semantics for timed default concurrent constraint programming.
2. J.M. Howe and A. King. Specialising finite domain programs using polyhedra.
3. P. Dechering and E. de Jong. Transparent process replication in a shared data space architecture for distributed systems.
4. E. Monfroy. From solver collaboration expressions to communicating and coordinated agents.
5. J. Luebcke and U. Nilsson. On-the-fly model checking of CTL formulas using constraint logic programming.
6. M.C. Meo. On the expressiveness of concurrent constraint languages.
7. J. Dospisil and E. Kendall. Redesigning constraint based applications with aspects.
8. F.S. de Boer, R.M. van Eijk, W. van der Hoek, and J.-J. Meyer. Failure semantics for the exchange of information in multi-agent systems.

2. The Position Papers

In this section we discuss briefly the presented papers.

2.1. A Truly Concurrent Semantics for Timed Default Concurrent Constraint Programming

Timed Default Concurrent Constraint Programming (`tdccp`) has been proposed by Saraswat, Jagadeesan, and Gupta as a *synchronous model* of concurrent computations in *reactive systems.*

We recall that a computation system is reactive if it continuously reacts to stimuli from the external environment by producing responses within temporal bounds fixed by the environment. Synchronous models are based on the *synchronous hypothesis* which has been proposed by Berry to simplify reasoning about reactive systems. This hypothesis states that reactions of a system to external stimuli are instantaneous, so that inputs from the environment and outputs from the system come instantaneously. In practice, this amounts to requiring that the environment is invariant w.r.t. the system during reactions.

`tdccp` extends the Concurrent Constraint Programming (`ccp`) model with combinators to deal with defaults for negative information and with discrete time. `ccp` is obtained by assuming a notion of computation as deduction over systems of partial information. Information accumulates monotonically in a distributed context: a multiset of *agents* cooperate to produce *constraints* on shared variables. A set of primitive constraints (*tokens*) are assumed to specify (possibly partial) information on the values of a finite set of variables. Tokens are equipped with an *entailment relation*: $a_1, \ldots, a_n \vdash a$ holds exactly if the information given by a follows from the information given by $a_1, \ldots, a_n$. A `ccp` program consists of a multiset of agents which cooperate by posting tokens in a *store* and by querying the store about the validity of tokens. So, the agent "`tell` a" posts the token a in the store and the agent "`if` a `then` A" behaves as the agent A when the store entails a.

In `tdccp`, agents can query the store also about the nonvalidity of tokens: the agent "`if` a `else` A" behaves as A if the store does not entail a. Moreover, the combinator "`next` _" permits to sequentialize, w.r.to a discrete time, agent interaction with the store: the agent "`next` A" will behave as A at the next instant of time. Finally, according to the synchronous hypothesis, agents post tokens in the store and query the store without consuming time. In practice, a `tdccp` program has a discrete behavior: at each instant of time it reacts to an input, namely to a set of tokens posted in the store by the external environment. The reaction implies an accumulation of tokens in the store, so that the resulting store is interpreted as the response of the program. The store is refreshed between any instant of time and the subsequent one.

According to the original operational semantics, an observer of a `tdccp` program P can observe sequences of pairs of sets of tokens $(i_1, o_1), \ldots, (i_n, o_n), \ldots$, with i_n the set of tokens supplied by the environment at the nth instant and o_n the set of tokens produced by P at the same instant. The observer cannot associate to each token $a \in o_n$ its *causes*, namely the subset of tokens supplied by the environment up to the nth instant which are sufficient to have the token a as response of P at the nth instant.

Now, the knowledge of causes of tokens produced by `tdccp` programs could be useful for two purposes:

- *Modeling application-level causality.* The `ccp` model has been extensively used to model physical systems. Each system component is modeled as a transducer which accepts input and control signals, operates in a given set of modes and produces output signals. In order to schedule such a system one must determine input and control signals which must be supplied to the system to cause a certain output. To do this one is interested in knowing the minimal cause of the output considered, namely the minimal set of input and control signals causing a certain answer of the system.
- *Observer monitoring verification.* This technique has been proposed by Halbwachs for the verification of safety properties. Note that most interesting properties of reactive systems are safety properties. A safety property ϕ expressing logic relations over inputs and outputs of an agent A is translated into an agent Ω_ϕ which runs in parallel with A and *observes* the behavior of A by reading at each instant of time the input and the output of A, so that it is able to detect when A violates ϕ. If Ω_ϕ detects that A has violated ϕ then it produces an "alarm" token α. Now, finite computations where the alarm α appears are counterexamples showing the A does not satisfy ϕ. If we can observe the causes of α then we are able to isolate the part of A responsible of the violation of ϕ.

So, our aim is to give a *causal semantics* for `tdccp`, namely a semantics from which causes of tokens produced by programs can be recovered.

We recall that a causal semantics for ccp has been given by Saraswat, Jagadeesan, and Gupta to refine the original *interleaving* semantic. According to the interleaving semantics, the observer of a ccp program can observe the final store resulting from its execution, namely the set of tokens produced by the program. In the causal semantics, the observable final store consists of a set of *contexted tokens* of the form $a^{\{a_1,\ldots,a_h\}}$, where the *context* $\{a_1,\ldots,a_h\}$ contains exactly the tokens causing a.

Now, if we consider ccp extended with the combinator "if _ else _", tokens may be caused by the absence of other tokens. So, contexts must carry information about the absence of tokens. We may consider contexted tokens of the form $a^{\{a_1,\ldots,a_h,\overline{a_{h+1}},\ldots,\overline{a_k}\}}$ to represent that a is caused by the presence of $a_1,\ldots,a_h$ and by the absence of $a_{h+1},\ldots,a_k$.

Moreover, if we consider the combinator "next _", tokens produced by a program at the nth instant can be caused by the presence or by the absence of tokens at instants $i \leq n$. For this reason, we consider contexted tokens of the form $a^{\{(a_1,i_1),\ldots,(a_h,i_h),(\overline{a_{h+1}},i_{h+1}),\ldots,(\overline{a_k},i_k)\}}$ to represent that a is caused by the presence of a_j at instant i_j, $1 \leq j \leq h$, and by the absence of a_j at instant i_j, $h+1 \leq j \leq k$.

Technically, we proceed by giving firstly a Structural Operational Semantics (SOS) in terms of a Proved Transition System (PTS), namely a labeled transition system where transition labels encode transition proofs. Then we show the agreement between our SOS semantics and the original semantics of tdccp, namely we prove that the semantics of Saraswat, Jagadeesan, and Gupta can be recovered from our PTS. From the information in the PTS we can derive the causes of tokens produced by programs. By unfolding the PTS we obtain a Proved Tree. By relabeling the Proved Tree so that these causes are highlighted, we obtain a Causal Tree which is interpreted as a causal semantic model for tdccp. Finally, we show that if we view ccp programs as tdccp programs then the causal semantics of ccp agrees with our causal semantics, namely we prove that the causal semantics of ccp can be recovered from our Causal Tree.

2.2. Specialising Finite Domain Programs Using Polyhedra

Abstraction interpretation centres on tracing properties of programs using descriptions. In the context of constraint programming, descriptions often capture numeric properties of the store. For example, LSign is useful for checking the satisfiability of linear constraints [9, 15]; intervals have been proposed for refining domain constraints of finite domain programs [1]; polyhedra have been applied to optimise CLP($\mathcal{R}$) programs [8]. To obtain finiteness, analyses usually trace information in an approximation of the concrete domain. This paper, however, uses a slightly different tactic. Finite domain constraint programs are reinterpreted as constraint programs over linear equations, and polyhedral abstraction is then applied to propagate information in this domain. This enables information to be inferred which cannot be deduced with an approximation of the concrete domain.

Howe and King argue in [5] that constraint propagation performed at compile-time by an analysis should complement the run-time propagation of the solver. Specifically, they demonstrate that a significant speedup (sometimes of several orders of magnitude) can be obtained by using polyhedra to infer deep inter-variable relationships in finite domain programs which cannot be traced by run-time (interval based) bound propagation. The crucial tactic is to combine the constraints deduced by the analysis with a program specialisation based on projection. To be precise, finite domain constraints are interpreted as relations over sets of points. These constraints are over-approximated and represented as a polyhedron. The intersection of polyhedra corresponds to composing constraints. Projection onto an integer grid gives (low valency) domain constraints that can be added to the program without compromising efficiency. The speedup follows from reducing the search. Interestingly, the analysis can be interpreted as a compile-time solution to combining constraint solvers [10].

This paper formalises the analysis of [5] in terms of abstract interpretation. Correctness of the analysis and of the associated program transformation is established. The analysis is constructed in terms of operations on polyhedra, for example, calculating the closure of the convex hulls of polyhedra, and also uses fixed-point acceleration techniques, such as widening, to obtain convergence. Correctness is proved with respect to a ground fixpoint semantics for (positive) constraint logic programs [6]. The analysis does not preserve the set of computed answer constraints (but increases it).

Work that is particularly closely related to this paper is an analysis of deductive database queries [7] that uses polyhedral abstractions to propagate constraints. The current paper applies similar abstraction techniques, though the analysis and the transformation differ significantly in detail. One crucial difference in the work presented here is the way that projection is used to constrain individual program variables of finite domain programs with domain constraints. Without this step, the analysis would have little effect.

2.3. Transparent Process Replication in a Shared Data Space Architecture for Distributed Systems

In mission-critical systems fault-tolerance is often one of the primary requirements in order to ensure a sufficiently high level of reliability, availability, and safety during systems' operation. Replication of software components on commercially off-the-shelf hardware is a generally applicable and cost-effective way of implementing fault-tolerance. However, guaranteeing correct system behaviour in an environment where replicated software components exist and may fail at arbitrary moments is a difficult problem that is often solved using application specific techniques. Failing components may either produce erroneous data, for instance due to faulty communication links, or completely stop producing data, because the component crashed. In this paper, we particularly focus on replication techniques to recover from or mask crash failures.

This paper presents a new software architecture in which replication of components and recovery from crash failures are transparent. The architecture is based on a shared data space through which components interact. The architecture is defined by a denotational semantics in which the possible behaviours of a component are defined by a set of state transition traces. Using the semantics, some fundamental algebraic properties of the architecture are derived, that reflect transparent replication and crash recovery.

More conventional approaches towards replication for fault-tolerance usually assume a message-passing (or client-server) model. Over the past years group communication has been developed as a framework in which replication of services is transparent to client applications. However, maintaining consistency among replicated services, using either active, passive, or semi-active replication, requires the implementation of complicated communication protocols.

In the architecture that is introduced, replication comes for free. Consequently, fault-tolerant services can be implemented fairly easily and with low overhead during run-time, which is particularly important for time-critical applications. Synchronisation either between active copies or between a primary process and its back-ups is not required. Furthermore, the implementation does not depend on a perfect failure detector, because correct system behaviour is still retained if, in the case of passive or semi-active replication, one of the back-up processes is activated while the primary process is still running.

2.4. From Solver Collaboration Expressions to Communicating and Coordinated Agents

The need for constraint solver collaboration, i.e., that is solver combination [13] and cooperation [2], is widely recognized. The general approach consists of making several solvers cooperate in order to process constraints that could not be solved (at least not efficiently) by a single solver.

Bali is a realization of such a system, composed of a language for constraint solver collaboration and a language for constraint programming. Solver collaboration is a glass-box mechanism for linking heterogeneous black-box tools, i.e., the solvers. Bali provides a general framework for integration and re-usability of heterogeneous solvers, together with a language for designing and implementing their collaborations. Solver collaborations are created by composing solvers using collaboration primitives (implementing, e.g., sequential, concurrent, and parallel schemes) and control primitives (such as fixed-points, iterators, and conditionals).

In [11], theoretical basis of Bali are settled. Distinction between cooperation and combination, and analogies between solvers and collaborations are discussed. Some more practical aspects are tackled in [12], such as a simplified operational semantics of the collaboration language, and applications over various domains.

From collaboration expressions of heterogeneous solvers to "running" distributed cooperative architectures actually able to solve constraints there is a big gap. In the paper "From Solver Collaboration Expressions to Communicating and Coordinated Agents", E. Monfroy is concerned with the intermediate steps that are essential for realizing a system that fulfills and respects the requirements of a framework like Bali. Heterogeneous solvers are homogenized in order to be easily integrated and to freely communicate in spite of their differences. This mechanism, called encapsulation, leads to the notion of homogeneous agents. Communication between such agents is then established with respect to the communication protocol of Bali. The behavior of such architectures is formalized in order to verify that the "running" architectures actually implement computations defined by solver collaboration language expressions. A transition system formalizes the behavior of the architecture with respect to message passing. Whereas the operational semantics of Bali describes constraint transformation/solving in terms of application of functions (i.e., solvers), the organizational model describes the same process in terms of data exchange/communication and solver states. These two aspects lead to an implementation that actually respects the formal framework of Bali.

2.5. On-the-Fly Model Checking of CTL Formulas Using Constraint Logic Programming

Model checking is one of the more successful approached for verifying that a *finite state system* satisfies a temporal *specification*, often expressed in some temporal logic. Model checking can be used to verify safety properties as well as deadlock and liveness, and can also been extended to real-time properties. However, model checking is computationally expensive since systems, even in case of finite ones, may contain a large number of states and checking the property in all of those states is not feasible. One way of dealing with the state space explosion is to represent sets of states *symbolically* (symbolic model checking); another complementary approach to reduce the state space is to interleave the checking with a reachability analysis starting from some set of initial states (so-called *local* model checking).

We propose a framework for doing model checking in a *functionally complete* fragment of the temporal specification language CTL (Computation Tree Logic). Our approach combines techniques from *constraint logic programming*, *constructive negation* and *tabled resolution*. The framework is *symbolic* in that it encodes and manipulates sets of states using constraints; it also supports *local* model checking using tabulation techniques from the field of deductive databases. The framework is parameterized by the constraint domain – any constraint domain closed under conjunction, disjunction, projection and complementation can be used in the framework. We show how the semantic equations of CTL can be encoded straightforwardly as a constraint logic program, and describe an abstract execution model that facilitate local checking of properties. A prototype implementation is available.

2.6. On the Expressiveness of Concurrent Constraint Languages

This paper compares the expressive power of three different concurrent constraint languages. The first is a timed concurrent constraint language, called *tccp* and introduced in [3], which is obtained by a natural timed interpretation of the usual concurrent constraint programming constructs: action-prefixing is interpreted as the next-time operator and the parallel execution of agents follows the scheduling policy of maximal parallelism. Additionally, *tccp* includes a simple primitive now then else which allows one to specify timing constraints. The second language considered is concurrent constraint programming itself, that is, the language *ccp* as introduced in [16]. Finally we consider confluent (in the sense of [4]) *ccp*.

In this paper it is shown that *tccp* is strictly more expressive than *ccp* which, in its turn, is strictly more expressive than confluent *ccp*. The separation results show that fair merge [14] can be expressed in *tccp* and not in *ccp*, while angelic merge [14] can be expressed in *ccp* and not in confluent *ccp*.

The basic idea underlying the *ccp* (*tccp*) paradigm is that computation progresses via monotonic accumulation of information in a *global store*. The information is produced (in form of constraints) by the concurrent and asynchronous activity of several agents which can *add* a constraint c to the store by performing the basic action tell(c). Dually, agents can also *check* whether a constraint c is entailed by the store by using an ask(c) action. This allows the synchronization of different agents.

Non-determinism arises by introducing a *guarded choice* operator: The agent $\sum_{i=1}^{n} \mathsf{ask}(c_i) \rightarrow A_i$ nondeterministically selects one $\mathsf{ask}(c_i)$ which is enabled in the current store and then behaves like A_i. If no guard is enabled, then this agent *suspends*, waiting for other (parallel) agents to add information to the store. *Deterministic ccp* is obtained by imposing the restriction $n = 1$ in the above construct. The || operator allows one to express parallel composition of two agents A || B and finally a notion of locality is obtained by introducing the agent ∃xA which behaves like A, with x considered *local* to A.

The language *tccp* includes now construct, which allows one to specify the behavior at the *next* time instant. We interpret the agent now c then A else B in terms of instantaneous reaction as follows: If c is entailed by the store then the above agent behaves as A, otherwise it behaves as B (at the current time instant).

The syntax of *tccp declarations* and *agents* [3] and the operational model of *tccp* is described by a transition system $T = (\mathsf{Conf}, \rightarrow)$ where configurations (in) Conf are pairs consisting of a process and a constraint (representing the common *store*), while the transition relation $\rightarrow \subseteq \mathsf{Conf} \times \mathsf{Conf}$ is described by the (least relation satisfying the) rules **R1-R11** of Table 1.

A *tccp process* P is then an object of the form D.A, where D is a set of procedure declarations of the form p(x) : −A and A is an agent.

A computation ξ for a configuration $\langle A_0, c_0 \rangle$ is a (finite or infinite) sequence $\langle A_0, c_0 \rangle \longrightarrow \langle A_1, c_1 \rangle \longrightarrow \ldots \langle A_i, c_i \rangle \longrightarrow \ldots$ and we denote by $\mathit{Result}(\xi) = \bigwedge_i c_i$. In order to simplify the notation, we will use the infix operator + instead of $\sum$ and we will use tell(c) → A as a shorthand for tell(c) || (ask(true) → A).

The language *ccp* is obtained from *tccp* by dropping the now then else statement and by interpreting the parallel operator in terms of interleaving rather than maximal parallelism.

R1	$\langle \mathsf{tell(c)}, d\rangle \longrightarrow \langle \mathsf{stop}, c \sqcup d\rangle$	
R2	$\langle \sum_{i=1}^{n} \mathsf{ask(c_i)} \rightarrow \mathsf{A_i}, d\rangle \longrightarrow \langle \mathsf{A_j}, d\rangle$	$j \in [1,n]$ *and* $d \vdash c_j$
R3	$\dfrac{\langle \mathsf{A}, d\rangle \longrightarrow \langle \mathsf{A'}, d'\rangle}{\langle \mathsf{now\ c\ then\ A\ else\ B}, d\rangle \longrightarrow \langle \mathsf{A'}, d'\rangle}$	$d \vdash c$
R4	$\dfrac{\langle \mathsf{A}, d\rangle \not\longrightarrow}{\langle \mathsf{now\ c\ then\ A\ else\ B}, d\rangle \longrightarrow \langle \mathsf{A}, d\rangle}$	$d \vdash c$
R5	$\dfrac{\langle \mathsf{B}, d\rangle \longrightarrow \langle \mathsf{B'}, d'\rangle}{\langle \mathsf{now\ c\ then\ A\ else\ B}, d\rangle \longrightarrow \langle \mathsf{B'}, d'\rangle}$	$d \not\vdash c$
R6	$\dfrac{\langle \mathsf{B}, d\rangle \not\longrightarrow}{\langle \mathsf{now\ c\ then\ A\ else\ B}, d\rangle \longrightarrow \langle \mathsf{B}, d\rangle}$	$d \not\vdash c$
R7	$\dfrac{\langle \mathsf{A}, c\rangle \longrightarrow \langle \mathsf{A'}, c'\rangle \quad \langle \mathsf{B}, c\rangle \longrightarrow \langle \mathsf{B'}, d'\rangle}{\langle \mathsf{A} \parallel \mathsf{B}, c\rangle \longrightarrow \langle \mathsf{A'} \parallel \mathsf{B'}, c' \sqcup d'\rangle}$	
R8	$\dfrac{\langle \mathsf{A}, c\rangle \longrightarrow \langle \mathsf{A'}, c'\rangle \quad \langle \mathsf{B}, c\rangle \not\longrightarrow}{\begin{array}{c}\langle \mathsf{A} \parallel \mathsf{B}, c\rangle \longrightarrow \langle \mathsf{A'} \parallel \mathsf{B}, c'\rangle \\ \langle \mathsf{B} \parallel \mathsf{A}, c\rangle \longrightarrow \langle \mathsf{B} \parallel \mathsf{A'}, c'\rangle\end{array}}$	
R9	$\dfrac{\langle \mathsf{A}, d \sqcup \exists_x c\rangle \longrightarrow \langle \mathsf{B}, d'\rangle}{\langle \exists^{\mathsf{d}} \mathsf{xA}, c\rangle \longrightarrow \langle \exists^{\mathsf{d'}} \mathsf{xB}, c \sqcup \exists_x d'\rangle}$	
R10	$\langle \mathsf{p(y)}, c\rangle \longrightarrow \langle \exists^{\mathsf{d_{xy}}} \mathsf{xA}, c\rangle$	$\mathsf{p(x) : -A \in D,\ x \neq y}$
R11	$\langle \mathsf{p(x)}, c\rangle \longrightarrow \langle \mathsf{A, c}\rangle$	$\mathsf{p(x) : -A \in D}$

Table 1. The transition system for *tccp*.

Following [14], the three levels of expressivity that we consider in this paper correspond to the possibility of implementing different versions of the merge process. This is a typically interactive process which merges the data (tokens) arriving on two input streams l_1 and l_2 to produce a single output stream l. The tokens arriving on the input streams are transmitted to the output stream and their relative ordering (on a single input stream) is preserved on the output. Examples of merge processes are arbiters, resource handlers etc. A merge process is called *fair* if it transmits sooner or later all data available in either l_1 or l_2, while it is called *angelic* whenever it satisfies the following requirement: if from a certain moment on no data will be available in l_1 (l_2) then all data in l_2 (l_1) will appear in l. Thus a fair merge is also an angelic merge, while angelic merge behaves like a fair merge in case both the sequences of data in input are finite.

Intuitively fair merge requires sensitivity to the presence or the absence of data to the input streams. For this reason it can be implemented in *tccp*, since the presence of the now then else statement enforce a kind of non-monotonic behavior which allows to check for absence of information, while it cannot be implemented in standard *ccp*.

As for the angelic merge, observe that such a process can avoid to get stuck at input ports with no input, but it does not need no be fair on infinite input streams. Intuitively the presence of an external choice construct (as in *ccp*) allows one to implement angelic merge (since it allows to discard a deadlocked branch) while when only internal choice is available (as in confluent *ccp*) the angelic merge process cannot be implemented.

We provide now a formal justification for these intuitions by showing that *tccp* cannot be embedded into *ccp*. We use a property of *ccp* agents saying that if d is the result of a computation which starts with an input c, then whenever we start with an input greater than c it is always possible to construct a computation whose result is greater than d. Such a property is analogous to Hoare monotonicity given in [14] for distributed systems. The intuition behind the definition of Hoare monotonicity is that, in a monotone network, arrival of new data at input streams cannot disable output of data that were already enabled.

The Hoare monotonicity does not hold for *tccp*. In fact, the presence of the now the else statement enforces a non-monotonic behavior in the sense that adding more information to the store can inhibit some computations, because the corresponding else branches are discarded.

By using this monotonicity property of *ccp* agents, we can prove that no total subset of input-output relation of fair merge can be implemented by a *ccp* program.

On the other hand, we can implement a fair merge $\mathsf{merge}(\mathsf{l}_1, \mathsf{l}_2, \mathsf{l})$ in *tccp* as follows.

$\mathsf{ask}(\mathsf{l}_1 \doteq \mathsf{nil}) \rightarrow \mathsf{tell}(\mathsf{l} = \mathsf{l}_2)$
$+$
$\mathsf{ask}(\exists \mathsf{v}, \mathsf{l}_1'.\ \mathsf{l}_1 = [\mathsf{v}|\mathsf{l}_1']) \rightarrow$
$\mathsf{now}\ \exists \mathsf{w}, \mathsf{l}_2'.\ \mathsf{l}_2 = [\mathsf{w}|\mathsf{l}_2']$
$\mathsf{then}\ \exists \mathsf{v}, \mathsf{w}\, \mathsf{l}_1', \mathsf{l}_2', \mathsf{l}'(\mathsf{tell}(\mathsf{l}_1 = [\mathsf{v}|\mathsf{l}_1']) \parallel \mathsf{tell}(\mathsf{l}_2 = [\mathsf{w}|\mathsf{l}_2']) \parallel \mathsf{tell}(\mathsf{l} = [\mathsf{v}|\mathsf{w}|\mathsf{l}']) \parallel \mathsf{merge}(\mathsf{l}_1', \mathsf{l}_2', \mathsf{l}'))$
$\mathsf{else}\ \exists \mathsf{v}, \mathsf{l}_1', \mathsf{l}'(\mathsf{tell}(\mathsf{l}_1 = [\mathsf{v}|\mathsf{l}_1']) \parallel \mathsf{tell}(\mathsf{l} = [\mathsf{v}|\mathsf{l}']) \parallel \mathsf{merge}(\mathsf{l}_1', \mathsf{l}_2, \mathsf{l}'))$
$+$
% *an analogous group for the list* l_2

It is easy to check that the process merge implements a fair merge.

Analogously, we can prove that angelic merge cannot be implemented in confluent *ccp*. In order to prove this result we need to observe that that for confluent *ccp* a kind of dual of Hoare monotonicity holds: if there exists a computation ξ for an agent A with input constraint c, producing an output constraint d, then given an input constraint c' weaker than c there exists a computation ξ' for A and c' producing an output constraint weaker than d. This property is analogous to Smyth monotonicity as defined in [14]. Note that this property does not hold for full *ccp*, because a smaller input can force the activation of a branch which brings to a greater or incomparable result.

By using the Smyth monotonicity of confluent *ccp* agents, we can prove that no total subset of input-output relation of angelic merge can be implemented by a confluent *ccp* program.

On the other hand, observe that we can implement an angelic merge $\mathsf{merge}(\mathsf{l}_1, \mathsf{l}_2, \mathsf{l})$ in standard *ccp* as follows.

$\mathsf{ask}(\mathsf{l}_1 = \mathsf{nil}) \to \mathsf{tell}(\mathsf{l} = \mathsf{l}_2)$

$+$

$\mathsf{ask}(\exists \mathsf{v}, \mathsf{l}_1'.\ \mathsf{l}_1 = [\mathsf{v}|\mathsf{l}_1']) \to (\exists \mathsf{v}, \mathsf{l}_1', \mathsf{l}'(\mathsf{tell}(\mathsf{l}_1 = [\mathsf{v}|\mathsf{l}_1']) \parallel \mathsf{tell}(\mathsf{l} = [\mathsf{v}|\mathsf{l}']) \parallel \mathsf{merge}(\mathsf{l}_1', \mathsf{l}_2, \mathsf{l}')))$

$+$

% *an analogous group for the list* l_2

2.7. Redesigning Constraint Based Applications with Aspects

Constraint solvers and Constraint Satisfaction Problems (CSP) are powerful but complex; the code features a high degree of redundancy and code tangling. The complexity typically makes it very difficult to debug and maintain such applications. Aspect oriented programming (AOP) is a relatively new approach to alleviating code tangling and redundancy in object-oriented designs and implementations. This paper describes the problems that commonly occur in object-oriented CSP and illustrates how AOP can potentially be used to improve them.

2.8. Failure Semantics for the Exchange of Information in Multi-agent Systems

In this paper, a semantic theory for the exchange of information in multi-agent systems is presented. A concurrent constraint programming language is introduced for the description of the behavior of concurrently executing agents. The basic underlying concept of the programming language is the expression of information by constraints (of a given constraint system). The agents of a system maintain their own private stores of information. Agents interact only by means of a synchronous communication mechanism that allows for the exchange of information as expressed by constraints. Such a communication involves the interaction of two agents, one of which asks the other agent to provide some information. The semantics of the language, which is based on a generalisation of traditional failure semantics, is shown to be fully-abstract with respect to observing of each terminating computation its final global store of information.

References

[1] R. Bagnara. *Data-flow Analysis for Constraint Logic-based Languages.* PhD thesis, 1997.

[2] F. Benhamou and L. Granvilliers. Combining local consistency, symbolic rewriting, and interval methods. In *Proceedings of AISMC3*, 1996.

[3] F.S. de Boer, M. Gabbrielli, and M.C. Meo. A timed concurrent constraint language. Information and Computation (to appear).

[4] M. Falaschi, M. Gabbrielli, K. Marriott, and C. Palamidessi. Confluence and concurrent constraint programming. In *Proceedings of AMAST'95*, number 936 in LNCS, pages 531–545. Springer-Verlag, 1995.

[5] J.M. Howe and A. King. Specialising finite domain programs using polyhedra. In *Logic Program Synthesis and Transformation*, 1999.

[6] J. Jaffar and J.-L. Lassez. Constraint logic programming. In *Proceedings of the Symposium on Principles of Programming Languages*, pages 111–119. ACM Press, 1987.

[7] D.B. Kemp and P.J. Stuckey. Analysis based constraint query optimization. In *Proceedings of the International Conference on Logic Programming*, pages 666–682. MIT Press, 1993. Long version available http://www.cs.mu.oz.au/ kemp/.

[8] K. Marriott and P.J. Stuckey. The 3 r's of optimizing constraint logic programs: Refinement, removal and reordering. In *Proceedings of the Twentieth Annual ACM Symposium on Principles of Programming Languages*, pages 334–344. ACM Press, 1993.

[9] K. Marriott and P.J. Stuckey. Approximating interaction between linear arithmetic constraints. In *Proceedings of the Internation Symposium on Logic Programming*. MIT Press, 1994.

[10] E. Monfroy. An environment for designing/executing constraint solver collaborations. *Electronic Notes in Theoretical Computer Science*, 16(1), 1998.

[11] E. Monfroy. An environment for designing/executing constraint solver collaborations. Number 16(1) in ENTCS (Electronic Notes in Theoretical Computer Science), 1998.

[12] E. Monfroy. The constraint solver collaboration language of bali. In *Proceedings of the International Workshop Frontiers of Combining Systems, FroCoS'98*, Logic and Computation Series. Research Study Press Ltd, 1999.

[13] C. G. Nelson and D. C. Oppen. Simplifications by cooperating decision procedures. Number 1(2) in ACM Trans. Prog. Lang. Syst., 1979.

[14] P. Panangaden and V. Shanbhogue. The expressive power of indeterminate dataflow primitives. Information and Computation, pages 99–131, 1992.

[15] V. Ramachandran and P.Van Hentenryck. Lsign reordered. In *Proceedings of the Second Internation Symposium on Static Analysis*, pages 330–347. Springer-Verlag, 1995. LNCS 983.

[16] S. Saraswat. *Concurrent Constraint Programming Languages*. PhD thesis, 1989.

Interactive System Design and Object Models

Nuno Jardim Nunes[1], Marco Toranzo[2], João Falcão e Cunha[3], Jaelson Castro[4], Srdjan Kovacevic[5], Dave Roberts[6], Jean-Claude Tarby[7], Mark Collins-Cope[9], and Mark van Harmelen[8]

[1] Universidade da Madeira, Portugal
dnnunes@uma.pt
[2] Universidade Federal de Pernanbuco, Brasil
matc@di.ufpe.br
[3] Faculdade de Engenharia da Universidade do Porto, Portugal
jfcunha@fe.up.pt
[4] Universidade Federal de Pernambuco, Brasil
jbc@di.ufpe.br
[5] Aonix, United States of America
srdjan@acm.org
[6] IBM Easy of Use, UK
DaveRoberts@uk.ibm.com
[7] Universite de Lille, France
Jean-claude.Tarby@univ-lille1.fr
[8] Ratio Group, UK
markcc@ratio.co.uk
[9] Cutting Edge Systems, UK
mark@cutsys.com

Abstract. This paper reports the activities of the ECOOP'99 Workshop on Interactive System Design with Object Models (WISDOM'99). The paper presents the workshop rational, format, the discussion framework and its four identified issues: architecture, process, notation and traceability. The results of the workshop are proposals for a meta-architecture to develop interactive systems, an user-centered software development process framework, some comments on notation issues and finally a traceability model of user interface design. Furthermore this paper contains abstracts of all position papers presented at the workshop.

1. Introduction

The Workshop on Interactive System Design and Object Models (WISDOM'99) was held in June 15 under the auspicious of the 13th European Conference on Object-Oriented Programming (ECOOP'99) in Lisbon, Portugal.

Two previous workshops held at the Computer-Human Interaction Conference (CHI'97 and CHI'98) discussed the use of object models in user interface design. The CHI'97 [30] workshop focused particularly on the current practice and theory of object modeling in user interface design. As a result, the participants formulated a general framework for object modeling in user interface. The

A. Moreira and S. Demeyer (Eds.): ECOOP'99 Workshops, LNCS 1743, pp. 267–287, 1999.

CHI'98 workshop [1] took the framework developed in the previous year and tried to bridge the conceptual gulf between current human-computer interaction (HCI) practice and current development practice. The outcome was a set of extensions to the unified modeling language (UML), addressing HCI issues.

The goal of WISDOM'99 was to discuss the role of object-oriented modeling in the design of interactive system, taking as a starting point the characterization of object models developed at the CHI'97 workshop (Fig. 1). The workshop call for papers focused four main issues:

1. The proposed characterization from the object-oriented community perspective;
2. The relation of these object models to other descriptions, in particular, task models, business models and user interface design descriptions;
3. The role and impact of object-oriented architectures and patterns for interactive system design and specification; and finally;
4. New notations to improve object models better supporting interactive systems design.

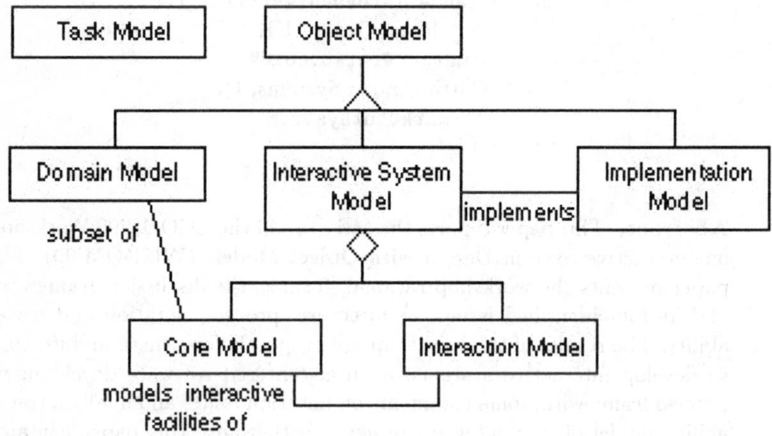

Fig. 1. Model of the Useful Object Models (part of the CHI'97 meta-model [30])

With this approach we hoped to help bridge the gap between human-computer interaction (HCI) modeling and object-oriented software engineering (OOSE), using the object-oriented analysis and design notation and semantics as the common ground.

1.1. Workshop Format

Participation in the workshop was by invitation only, based on the evaluation of the participant's position papers by the WISDOM'99 international program committee. Ten position papers were accepted for presentation at the workshop. Full versions are available at the workshop site `http://math.uma.pt/wisdom99`.

The workshop had a total of 18 participants, including contributors, organizers and observers. In order to maximize time for discussion, participants with accepted position papers were asked to present their ideas in very short 10 minutes sessions. That way we were able to wrap up presentations and initial discussion about each position paper in the morning session. The afternoon session was totally dedicated to discussion of the workshop topics.

The position papers presented at the workshop addressed different issues under the WISDOM'99 topics. There were 4 broad areas covered by the position papers:

- Relationships between high level abstraction models (business, domain and task models) and user interface specification [24] [12] [26] [9]
- Methods to specify interactive systems using OO notations [20] [2]
- Traceability between models in interactive system design [27]
- Architectures and patterns in interactive system development [6] [4] [23]

WISDOM'99 had two focused and very interactive invited talks. In the morning session, Mark van Harmelen presented the CHI'97 framework giving participants an inside perspective on this meta-model [29] and an overview of the goals and findings of the two previous workshops at CHI'97 and 98. Participants with background on object-oriented software engineering (OOSE) expressed some problems with this human-computer interaction (HCI) perspective. Some participants stated that the meta-model was not very clear in expressing the problem of bridging HCI and OOSE. In particular, they argued that current OOSE theory and practice already addressed the problem of producing high quality user interfaces.

In the afternoon session, Srdjan Kovacevic presented a talk about tool issues for user-interface design. During his talk he presented a different interpretation of the CHI'97 meta-model and isolated three dimensions for integrating user-interface design in the software development lifecycle (process, architecture and notation). Participants decided to adopt this modified version of the CHI'97 meta-model as the discussion framework for WISDOM'99. Some participants with background on OOSE stated that this modified version of the meta-model was clearer in expressing the problem of bridging HCI and OOSE. Although equivalent in the essence, this version adopted different definitions for the useful object models and introduced the concept of user interface. This version also denoted relationships between some of the models as dependencies assuming a very clear separation between abstract models (interactive system model, interaction model and domain model) and more concrete models (user interface, functional core and implementation). During this brief discussion it seemed clear that people with background on OOSE were more concerned about the later concepts, while people with background on HCI were concerned with the former ones. This initial discussion was very important to reach consensus over a framework that globally satisfied the majority of the participants with different backgrounds.

1.2. People Involved in the Workshop

- Alberto Silva, Technical University of Lisbon, Portugal (Observer, Program Committee)
- António Silva Filho, State University of Maringa, Brazil (Position Paper)
- Cécile Paris, CSIRO, Australia (Position Paper)
- Dave Roberts, IBM Ease of Use Warwick, UK (Organization, Program Committe)
- Elizier Kantorowitz, Technion, Israel (Position Paper)
- Jaelson Castro, Federal University of Pernambuco, Brazil (Organization, Program Committee, Position Paper)
- Jean-Claude Tarby, University of Lille, France (Position Paper)
- João Falcão e Cunha, University of Oporto, Portugal (Organization, Program Committee, Position Paper)
- Marc Evers, University of Twente, The Netherlands (Position Paper)
- Maria Lozano, University of Castilla-La Mancha, Spain (Observer)
- Mario Rui Gomes, Technical University of Lisbon, Portugal (Observer, Program Committee)
- Mark Collins-Cope, Ratio Group Ltd, UK (Position Paper)
- Mark van Harmelen, Cutting Edge Systems, UK (Organization, Invited Speaker, Program Committee)
- Michael Thomsen, University of Aarhus, Denmark (Position Paper)
- Marco Toranzo, Federal University of Pernambuco, Brazil (Position Paper)
- Nuno Guimarães, University of Lisbon, Portugal (Organization, Program Committee)
- Nuno J. Nunes, University of Madeira, Portugal (Organization, Program Committee, Position Paper)
- Peter Forbrig, University of Rostock, Germay (Observer)
- Philip GRAY, University of Glasgow, UK (Position Paper)
- Richard Cooper, University of Glasgow, UK (Position Paper)
- Shijian Lu, CSIRO, Australia (Position Paper)
- Srdjan Kovacevic, Aonix, USA (Organization, Invited Speaker, Program Committee)

1.3. Initial Discussion Topics

During the Workshop participants revised and selected issues for discussion from the original workshop topics. The selection process took into consideration that:

- Topic (i) would be addressed with the inclusion of several participants from the OO community at the workshop. Therefore we concluded that there was no need to explicitly address this topic;
- Topic (ii) was considered the main topic for discussion at WISDOM'99;
- Topic (iv) was considered closely related to topic (ii) and was also included as the main discussion of WISDOM'99;
- Topic (iii) was commonly considered a very important topic for discussion but due to time limitations we would not address this topic.

Therefore we decided to focus the discussion of WISDOM'99 on the relation of a selection of CHI object models to other descriptions, in particular, business models, domain models and user interface design descriptions. As a result of this discussion we would address notations to improve object models to support interactive systems design.

During the workshop a lot of time was spent trying to expand the selected topics for discussion. Participants were asked, individually, to write their thoughts, ideas and insights over the selected topics for discussion. Afterwards, one of the organizers summarized the notes and we achieved an initial framework for discussion. The next section presents that structure and isolates the issues we addressed during and after the workshop.

2. Architecture, Process, Notation, and Traceability

One of the invited talks at WISDOM'99, on user interface design and tool issues, addressed the problems of integrating the user-interface design in the software development lifecycle. According to Srdjan Kovacevic [10], "Currently the software development lifecycle does not take into account specifics of UI design - it neither addresses the usability requirements of interactive applications, nor does it leverage on UI domain knowledge to provide any of the support discussed earlier". Kovacevic identifies three dimensions of integrating UI design into the software development lifecycle: notation, process and architecture (Fig. 2). During the workshop traceability was also raised as another very important issue and was also included as an additional dimension in the framework (Fig. 2).

The following sections present workshop results in terms of the identified dimensions. Section 2.1 discusses the WISDOM'99 meta-architecture, in particular definitions of useful object models and their relationships. It also proposes an architecture for interactive system design. Section 2.2 presents process issues in the light of one organising framework, the WISDOM process, as discussed by Nuno Nunes and João Falcão e Cunha [20] at the workshop. Section 2.3 presents some insights on notation issues and points out future work. Finally, section 2.4 presents a traceability model for interactive systems, a proposal of Marco Toranzo and Jaelson Castro [27] presented and discussed at the workshop.

2.1. The WISDOM'99 Meta-architecture

The WISDOM'99 discussion framework (Figure 2) can also be thought of a meta-architecture for interactive systems. Interactive systems require an architecture that will maximize support of UI domain knowledge and reuse.

In order do discuss the adequacy of this meta-architecture we decided that it was very important to build consensus over the definitions of task model, business model, domain model, interaction model, interactive system model and user interface model. During that process we tried to focus on commonly accepted definitions from both OOSE and HCI fields. Therefore, initial definitions were taken from the Unified Software Development Process (USDP) [8] of the OOSE field, and from the CHI'97 original framework [30], of the HCI field.

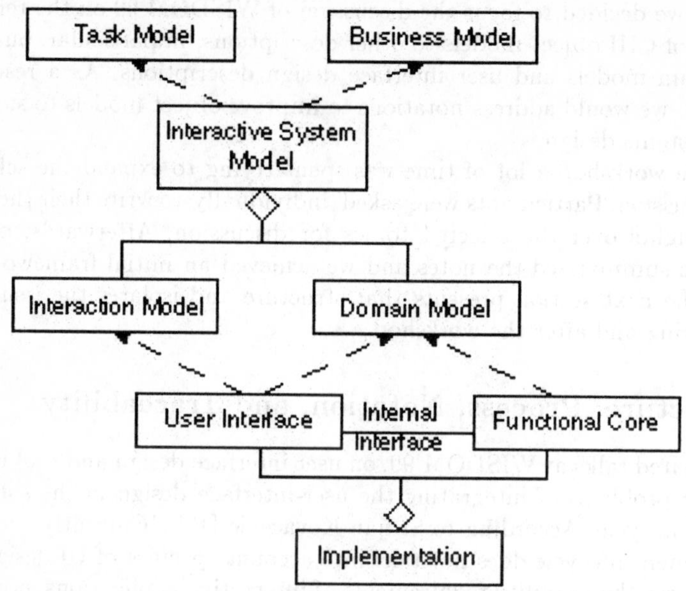

Fig. 2. The WISDOM'99 Discussion framework (adapted from [10] and [30])

Task Models, Business Model, and Domain Model. Task modeling is a central and familiar concept in HCI but seldom used in OOSE. Therefore, we decided to use the CHI'97 definition: "task models describe the activities in which users engage to achieve some goal (...) A task model details the users' goals and the strategies adopted to achieve those goals, in terms of the actions that users perform, the objects involved in those actions and the sequencing of activities". Some confusion might occur when comparing this concept of a tasl model with the concept of a business process model. However task models are abstractions of user behavior while performing tasks with existing or envisioned systems, whereas a business model represents the business from an usage perspective. We concluded that, in this perspective, OOSE doesn't address task analysis, so we decided to include this model in the WISDOM'99 framework (Fig. 2). We also agreed that the task model could influence both the domain model and the interaction model.

A commonly accepted definition of domain model in OOSE is: "A domain model captures the most important types of objects in the context of the system. The domain objects represent "things" that exist or events that transpire in environment in which the system works." [8]. On the HCI field, taking the CHI'97 definition, this model: "(...)specifies user domain semantics. A domain model is composed of types, which model referents and represent the users' world at a sufficient level of detail to perform user interface design. Users may appear as part of the domain model if they are required to be in the model." [30].

The major difference in both definitions was the explicit inclusion of users in the HCI perspective. Mark van Harmelen at WISDOM'99 mentioned that "we should remember that in creating interactive systems we are creating them for users and thus the things which we are capturing in the domain model are things of interest to users". Jean-Claude Tarby reinforced this assumption stating that "generally we think of the domain model as being static but this is false, there is dynamics in this model". Users and dynamics in the domain model lead discussion to the role of the business model and its importance in both fields. The role of the business model was not extensively discussed in the previous workshops on the subject so we started again from the OOSE definition.

The definition of business model from OOSE (USDP) is: "The business process model describes the business processes of a company or organization in terms of its workers, clients and entities they manipulate (...) The business model presents the business from the usage perspective and outlines how it provides value to its users (partners and customers)." [8]. During discussion we agreed that this definition was vague but, in essence, acceptable from both perspectives. There was also consensus that a business model captures the internal operations of a business together with (perforce) interactions with the outside world. An important issue for user-interface design.

Finally we discussed the relationship between both models. Jacobson and colleagues say that "we can think of the domain modeling as a simplified variant of business modeling, where we focus only on the "things", that is, the domain classes or the business entities that the workers need to work with". Even though, in HCI terms, a domain model may include all kinds of user referents that are not germane to the business model, there was general consensus on this assumption. We agreed that it would be useful to introduce the business model in the WISDOM'99 framework, indicating that both the domain model and the interaction model are dependent on the business model (Fig. 2).

Interactive System Model, Interaction Model, and User Interface. Like the task model, the definitions of interaction model and interactive system model only exist in the CHI'97 framework. According to the initial CHI'97 definition: "An interaction model augments the core model providing a specification of the interactive facilities to be used by the users when invoking core functionality in the system". Accordingly, "The interactive system model aggregates the core model and the interaction model. An interactive system model is useful: When using an implementation a user needs, inter alia, to understand both the semantics of the system and the means of interacting with the system".

Although those definitions still apply to the revised framework, the WISDOM'99 model introduces yet another level of abstraction, i.e., the user interface model. The user interface model captures the UI specifics (look and feel, technology dependent, etc.) required to produce an implementation. Therefore we have a clear distinction between an abstract model of interaction (interaction model) and a concrete device dependent specification of that interaction used to produce the system implementation.

Relationships Between Models. Participants at WISDOM'99 agreed that there was a clear advantage to separate the UI from the functional core. Such conceptual (not necessarily physical) separation leverages on UI knowledge in providing design assistance (evaluation, exploration) and run-time services (UI management, help systems, etc.) [10]. This approach should foster multi-UI development over the same functional core.

We considered that an architecture for interactive systems should:

- Support implementation of internal functionality independent of the user interface (core model and user interface model)
- Support the separation of the user interface specifics (presentation, look and feel) from its (conceptual) specification, independent of the type of interaction and technology (interaction model and user interface model)
- Enable automatic user interface implementation from conceptual (abstract) models (user interface and implementation)

In his position paper Marc Evers [6] discusses the conceptual and physical separation between the user interface and the core functionality and how this separation can lead to adaptability problems. He gives the example of semantic feedback as one of the concerns that suffers from such problems and discusses how those concerns can be difficult to adapt.

There was also some argument about the similarity between this proposal and the OO 3-tier architecture. There is clearly a difference. The 3-tier architecture assumes a physical separation between the back-end data management, the business logic and the front end interface. HCI focuses on different UI's that can serve a given application, end user customization, adaptability, etc. For example, for a UI designer, it is important to provide the capability to explore different UIs and evaluate them, with respect to different criteria, including efficiency for a selected set of typical tasks.

2.2. Towards an User-Centered OOSE Process Framework (The WISDOM Process)

One of the workshop position papers describing the Whitewater Interactive System Development with Object Model (WISDOM) [19] proposed a process framework for a user-centered object-oriented process (see Fig. 3) from now on mentioned as the WISDOM process. The WISDOM process is based on the Unified Software Development Process (USDP) framework [8]. USDP is a framework of the Rational Unified Process [11], an iterative, incremental, architecture centric and use case driven process. USDP's 4 iterative phases (inception, elaboration, construction and transition), encompass several process workflows.

The WISDOM process includes the seven following wokflows: User profile, Task analysis, User Interface Principles and Guidelines, Prototyping, User Interface Design, User Interface Implementation and Usability Testing. These WISDOM workflows are summarized below. Fig. 3 above tries to depict the effort that is usually required in each worklow as the actual project time goes by. For other approaches on this subject see also [14].

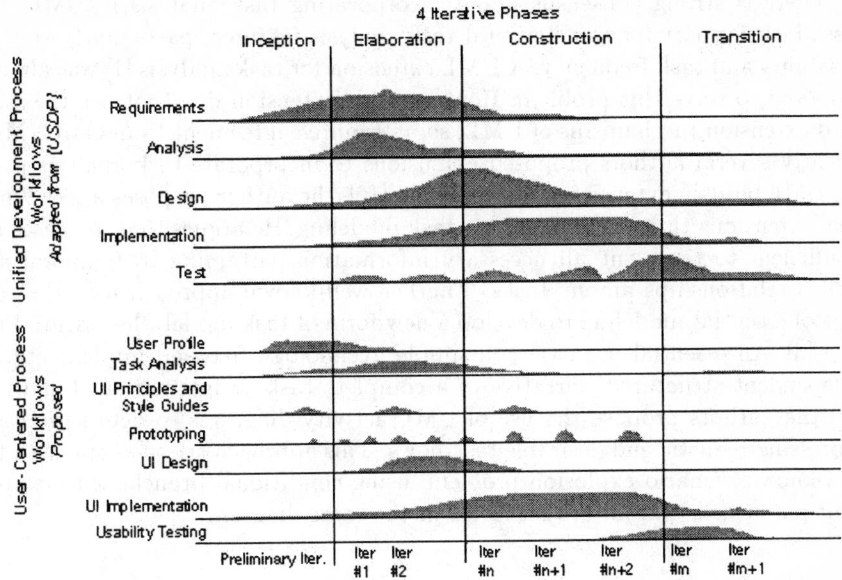

Fig. 3. User Centered Object-Oriented Process Framework

User Profile. User profile analysis concerns the description of the specific user characteristics relevant for interaction design (e.g., special needs, job expertise, computer literacy and expected frequency of use). It also identifies major user groups required for the task analysis workflow. This workflow will drive almost all design decisions, except those related to technical constraints. The effort in this workflow will typically concentrate on the inception and early elaboration phases.

Major techniques used to profile users are questionnaires and interviews. Traditionally, artifacts produced from this workflow are data summaries, analysis and conclusions. More recently the Usage Centered Design approach [3] proposed a User Role Map artifact, actually an extension of the UML that reveals how all the various user roles fit together in defining who will use the system and how it will be used. In such a diagram roles are interrelated in several different ways: by affinity, by classification and by composition.

Task Analysis. Task analysis is the process of learning about users, by observing them in action, and building a user-centered model of their work as they actually perform it [7]. Notice this is quite different from asking users questions outside their typical environments. This workflow will be used to set user interface principles and style guides and drive user interface design. The effort in this workflow starts late in the inception phase, builds up during the elaboration phase and can extend to early construction, if the system boundaries are not stable in the first iterations of this phase.

There is strong consensus about incorporating task analysis in UML. Use cases lack support for some general task analysis features, particularly, decomposability and task frequency. A UML extension for task analysis [1] was already proposed to solve this problem. However, this extension does not use the standard extension mechanisms of UML, so, it requires agreement from OMG. More recently several authors proposed extensions to incorporate task analysis using the UML built-in extension mechanism. In [10], the author proposes a set of minimal extensions that would facilitate task modeling. He argues that use cases are insufficient to represent all necessary information pertaining to temporal and logical relationships among tasks. Another well-known approach uses the concept of essential modeling to develop a new form of task model, the essential use case [3]. An essential use case is a simple, technology free and implementation independent structured narrative of a complete task or interaction. Finally in [21] the authors propose the use of UML activity diagrams to detail use cases expressing realistic and desirable task flows. This approach tries to cope with the well-known scenario explosion problem, using conditional branching to express multiple success and failure scenarios in the same diagram.

User Interface Principles and Guidelines. This workflow concerns gathering, reviewing and adapting relevant user interface design principles, guidelines and standards. Principles, guidelines and standards will ensure coherence and consistency across the user interface, driving the user interface design workflow. The effort in this workflow is divided among the three initial phases. At the inception phase general principles are gathered and reviewed from the literature and consulted from experts. In the elaboration phase those principles are adapted to the specific project information produced in the other workflows, particularly user profile and task analysis. Finally in the construction phase, they are evaluated and refined as a consequence of prototype evaluation. The outputs of this workflow are guidelines and standards documents.

Prototyping. Prototyping is acknowledged to be a major technique in modern software system development. It supports the iterative and incremental nature of the process, enabling the generation, discussion and evaluation of design decisions. Although one can argue that the USDP design and implementation workflows can (and should) inherently support prototyping, the WISDOM process isolates this workflow due its conceptual difference in user interface design. The effort in the prototyping workflow builds up through the phases of inception, elaboration and construction. In the inception phase prototyping is typically used to gather information from users and represent high-level ideas of functional organization and conceptual design. At this stage prototyping is based on low-fi techniques (mock-ups, etc.) and used in conjunction with participatory techniques [16]. In elaboration prototyping is used to validate the user-interface conceptual architecture. At this stage both the overall navigational structure and selected subsets of the system are prototyped and evaluated with the end-users. Hi-fi techniques can be used at this stage, although the participatory nature of the evaluation sessions should limit the fidelity of the prototypes, i.e., it is well acknowledged that users have problems criticizing prototypes that look and feel like real systems. At the construction phase prototyping is mainly used to focus on particular problematic subsets of the system, previously unassessed functionality or users.

User Interface Design. An informal survey in user interface programming [17] concluded that, on average, 48% of the systems programming effort was devoted to the user interface. Respondents estimated that the average time devoted to UI development was 45% on the design phase and 50% on implementation time. The user-centered process framework assumes that roughly half of the effort on the original USDP design and implementation workflows is transposed to the UI design and implementation workflows when developing an interactive system. The goal of this (simple) assumption is only to raise the issue that, since UI design represents a significant part of the total development effort, the development process should conveniently support this workflow. At the notation level several approaches describe mappings between tasks and objects [25] [5]. The translation process depends on the ability of the object modeling language to accommodate additional task information (containment relations, pre & post conditions). Such extensions are already proposed in [10]. Also at the same level different authors proposed the concept of an object view [22] [20] or an interaction space [3]. Although not semantically equivalent, such approaches point out the need for a modeling concept that captures the "interaction points" as the building block of a model driven interactive system architecture.

User Interface Implementation. At the implementation level the fundamental issues are tool support and traceability between conceptual models and the implementation model. Tool support for task analysis is recognized to be insufficient. One approach, described in [13], is to transform task analysis models into UML interaction models and vice versa. This pragmatic approach enables the integration of specialized task modeling tools to industrial strength tools. Also, the interaction point" concept seams to enable a clearer management of traceability between conceptual models, i.e., dependencies can be established between (i) the different "interaction points" that compose the navigational structure of the interface, and (ii) the "interaction points" and the other object descriptions belonging to the functional core. A related approach concerns the definition of user interfaces at an abstract level using a declarative language. That approach [15] proposes an XML (eXtensible Markup Language) vocabulary designed to allow the intent of an interaction with a user to be defined enabling task designers to concentrate on the semantics of the interactions without having to concern themselves with any particular devices to be supported.

Usability Testing. Usability testing aims at identifying problems users will have with the software in all aspects of its use (installing, learning, operating, etc.). Although similar techniques can be used to evaluate prototypes usability testing can only be done when the product reaches the end of the construction phase and in early transition phase. There are different types of techniques that can be used to perform usability testing: formal lab testing, field testing, thinking aloud, walkthrough, inspection, etc. The type of techniques used usually depends on the resources available [18].

2.3. Notation Issues

Bridging the gap between OOSE and HCI also means having a common language to foster collaboration. Both OO and UI designers should work on different views of the same models. Several examples of such need for collaboration are evident when looking to the WISDOM'99 architecture and the WISDOM process. At the architecture level, they all collaborate in developing a domain model, and they all, in the end, work towards producing an implementation model. At the process level, several workflows overlap in time and their outputs feedback interchangeably. The issue is one of focus. While OOSE focus on refining the domain model towards a functional core; HCI focus on complementing the domain model with an interaction model refining both towards the user interface.

It seems obvious that notation must facilitate this collaboration. We need specific constructs to model the user interface, both at the abstract level (interaction model) and at a more concrete level (user interface). Those constructs should appear in specific UI modeling views but they should be closely related to their functional core counterparts. Also we should have some kind of tool interoperability at the semantic level.

As one of the post-workshop activities, participants decided that a good starting point to illustrate notation for interactive system design would be to suggest that every workshop participant worked a simple example. The following paragraph was given to all participants as the problem definition for the Hotel Reservation case study:

"The guest makes a reservation with the Hotel. The Hotel will take as many reservations as it has rooms available. When a guest arrives, he or she is processed by the registration clerk. The clerk will check the details provided by the guest with those that are already recorded. Sometimes guests do not make a reservation before they arrive. Some guests want to stay in nonsmoking rooms. When a guest leaves the Hotel, he or she is again processed by the registration clerk. The clerk checks the details of the staying and prints a bill. The guest pays the bill, leaves the Hotel and the room becomes unoccupied."

Several participants at the workshop worked out with this example. Full versions of proposed solutions to the problem example shown are available at the workshop site (`http://math.uma.pt/wisdom99`). An extensive discussion of that work is out of this report scope, but some references to its outcome will be likely to appear in the mentioned site.

2.4. Towards a Traceability Model of User Interface Design

One of the workshop position paper was [27] that proposed a requirement traceability model. The model does not intend to provide a revolutionary and definitive solution to requirements traceability in user interface design. It addresses some concerns of the CHI community as described in CHI'97 and CHI'98 workshop summary:

- A traceability model that deals with artifacts and activities related with user interface design.
- A traceability model that deals with software change impact analysis impact related with user interface design.
- Traceability to external sources

Requirements traceability is the ability to describe and follow the life of a requirement and its related information within a system, in both forward and backward direction, within/between related social contexts: Environment, organizational, management and development. Requirements and constraints, for example, to develop/maintain a system, can come from these contexts.

The environment concept represents constraints on the universe (bank, government, for example) where the organization is inserted. The organization concept represents an element (with goals and decisions) of the universe. The management concept is used to deal with activities such as management of people, budget and contracts that can be performed by an organization to develop software. The development concept is used to deal with artifacts produced by some object-oriented development process such as Rational Unified Process [11], or OVID (Object, View, and Interaction Design) [22], that provides guidance on user the interface development.

The proposal presented in the position paper introduces a requirements traceability model (Fig. 4) to help identify/retrieve external sources related to object-oriented user interface design (for example diagrams, procedures, etc.). These external sources can be stakeholders (e.g., developers, users, and clients), rationale (project decisions) documents (e.g., books, manuals, e-mail). The relationship between external source and user interface design established by instantiating the UMLRelationship classes (e.g., dependency, aggregation and association) that associate two elements. Through these relationships it is possible to do bi-directional traceability between external source and user interface design elements. Therefore, the traceability model manages change impact between external source and user interface design elements; e.g., from a new requirement (request by some external sources) it is possible to identify the affected user interface design parts. For further details see [28].

In the Figure 4, TrcObject class is a superclass of :

- UIDesign class that represents activities related with user interface design
- Requirement class to register each user's need
- Development class that represents diagrams to visualize your system from different perspectives. Because no complex system can be understand in its entirety from only perspective

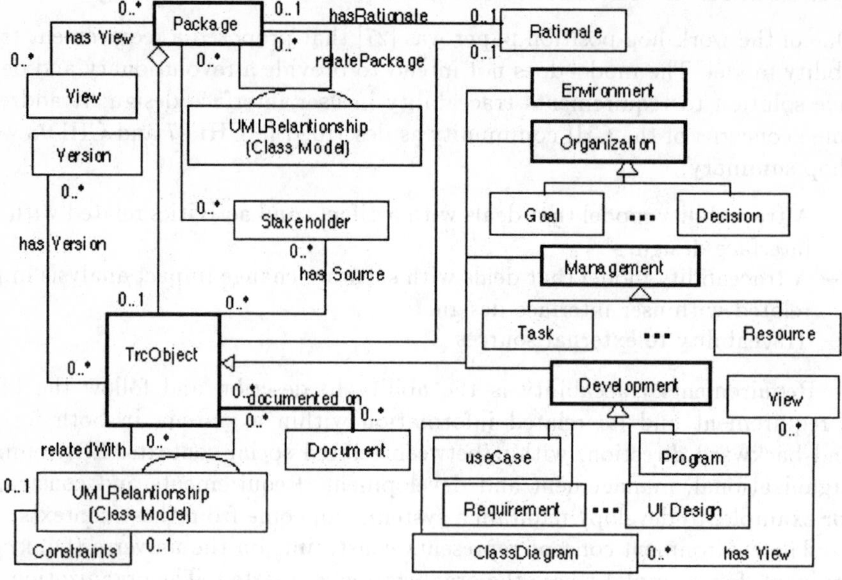

Fig. 4. A Requirements Traceability Model

- ClassDiagram class that represents class diagrams
- Program class that represents programming code
- UseCase class that represents use case diagrams

The recursive relationship (relatedWith) of TrcObject class is inherited by its subclasses, therefore, the instances of these subclasses may be associated among them. This means that an activity of user interface design (UIDesign class) can be related with:

- requirement of the user (Requirement class)
- document (Document class)
- goals of the organization (Goal class)
- class diagram (ClassDiagram class) and view (View class) developed by others stakeholders (Stakeholder class).

Therefore, the model identifies the external sources related with user interface design. This is vital for the maintenance of some systems because it will enable all retrieval of all information about the person that must be interviewed to solve some problems that affect the work.

Other concepts used in the model are rationale, package and version. The rationale concept (Rationale class) is used to capture the "why" or "reason" for the design decision. This can help improve the understanding of a software artifact (e.g., Diagrams, view and user interface design) before some modification is done.

The package concept can be used, for example, to represent a set of related requirements to manage. Consider the following scenario: The Springer organization subcontracts the services of two organizations. The Springer organization provides to each subcontracted organization a set of related requirements (Package class) and a set of constraints (other Package) on user interface design (e.g., formalism, method, standard to use) that both must be met. Using the traceability model, each set of related requirements will be represented and managed as an instance of the Package class.

The version concept is used for adaptation control of some artifacts. A versioned object consists of hierarchy of objects, which captures the version-of relationship between an object and another object derived from the object.

3. Summaries of Position Paper

As another post-workshop activity, authors were asked to write a short summary of their position papers relating them to the workshop topics. Those summaries are presented in the following sections.

3.1. Relationships Between High Level Abstraction Models and User Interface Specification

When the Task's World Meets the Object's World (Jean-Claude Tarby). All models used in object-oriented methods have the same two disadvantages (or advantages?): they are firstly object-driven, and secondly too formal. The consequence is that they occult the user facet of the work by focusing on what the user work and not how he/she works. My paper can be viewed as a complement of object-oriented models. It explains why object-oriented models are sufficient to design an interactive system, and how we can improve this design with the task model by integrating more the user in the design. This integration is made through his/her tasks and his/her habits. The Diane+ method, which is presented in the paper, focused first onto how the user works. Then, we extract the task model and the domain model. This one contains the "user" objects that are what the user believes to use through the system. The object-oriented models occur only after this stage to provide formal aspects of the description. Diane+ is not formal; its role is to "accompany" the object-oriented models to provide them a more human-centered point of view.

Automatic Acquisition of Task Models from Object Oriented Design Specifications: A Case Study (Shijian Lu and Cécile Paris). In this paper, we briefly presented a case study of automatically acquiring task models from object oriented design specification for a commercial software product. In particular, problems encountered and lessons learned. The study demonstrates that the quality of the resulting task model is determined by the quality of the object oriented design model. It has been shown that there were number of problems in the design model used in this study. Attempts are given to draw some guidelines or recommendations to encourage a disciplined approach to system behavior modeling. While this study helps to shed some light on issues related to automatic task model acquisition, it does not suffice to draw a conclusion on how realistic the approach is. More case studies are needed to gain a further understanding of the current practice in industry as well as the practicality of a disciplined approach to system behavior modeling. This paper is for anyone who is interested in the integration between HCI and object oriented system development. In relation to the WISDOM'99, the paper mainly addresses the discussion topic (ii), i.e., The relation of CHI object models to other descriptions, in particular, task models. By showing the semantic linkage between task models and system behavior models, it establishes a bridge to connect HCI with object oriented software development. Apart from further case studies on acquiring task models from system behavior models, it would be interesting to explore the reverse, namely, to acquire system behavior models from task models.

Domain Object Models and User-Interfaces (Michael Thomsen). In object oriented development a considerable amount of time is spent on designing the user interface and on producing the core object model. We have investigated a joint production of these two entities. The user interface supports the users work, and the object model models the users world, so it seems natural that some commonalties must exist. By examining a concrete development project, we have found that many commonalties between the two entities exist. For the simple attributes in the object model, such as integers or texts, a few typical widgets were used in the user interface. For the complex attributes a few more variations were found, but a common pattern was still present, and within grouping of widgets there was a strong coupling to grouping in the object model. Concluding from this study we will argue that a further investigation of the relation between the two entities is needed, and that development projects could benefit from joint work when constructing these. In addition, tool support for a joint production would be helpful.

Some Observations on the Relationships between Tasks Use Cases Scenarios and Requirements Models (E. Kantorowitz). In the described software process the user interfaces are designed in the scenarios and in possible prototypes. The scenarios are written in a natural language that the users understand. This enables the users to check them. These informal scenarios are analyzed and an equivalent formal requirements model, that may be specified in UML, is developed. Experience from student projects show that this process is not trivial. A good understanding of the domain and some common sense are required to develop scenarios with a high level of usability and for following object oriented modeling in UML.

3.2. Methods to Specify Interactive Systems Using OO Notations

A Bridge too Far: The WISDOM Approach (Nuno Nunes and João Falcão e Cunha). Whitewater Interactive System Development with Object Models (WISDOM) is an UML based, lightweight software engineering method, specifically adapted to develop interactive systems. In our position paper we briefly present a proposal for a user-centered object-oriented software engineering process framework, the WISDOM Process (see section 2.2). That framework is used to illustrate the WISDOM method and its impact on the early workflows of the lifecycle (requirements and analysis). We argue and that a UML based method can effectively ensure usability throughout the development lifecycle of interactive systems. The included examples illustrate how this language can be used to perform a form of task analysis, specify the interaction model and create the concrete user interface. It is our belief that the UML, and its built in extension mechanism, under the context of an adequate process, effectively bridge the gap between HCI and OOSE.

The RSI Approach to Use Case Analysis: A ProtoPattern for Structured Use Case Development (Mark Collins-Cope). The RSI approach provides a framework for analyzing and understanding potential use case deliverables and their inter-relationships. The RSI approach also aims to assist in maximizing software re-use - by partitioning functionality into those aspects which are concerned with 'managing the interface' to an actor, and those areas which make up the re-usable core of the system. RSI divides use cases three categories, shown by the UML stereotypes: requirement, service and interface: requirement use cases document business processes for which automated support may be required. They detail the requirements driving the development of a system, but do not define the detail of a system's functionality. interface use cases provide a detailed description of the interfaces presented to the system's actors and association functionality. service use cases provide a detailed description of the underlying functionality a system offers in a manner independent of the needs of any particular interface.

3.3. Traceability between Models in Interactive System Design

A Comprehensive Traceability Model to Support the Design of Interactive Systems (Marco Toranzo and Jaelson Castro). In a development project, traceability is viewed as the problem of maintaining an information system that keeps relevant links between artifacts developed and delivered by the software development process. Based on our definition of requirements traceability (see section 2.4), we have developed a requirements traceability model to CHI community to: Identify/retrieve external source (stakeholders, documents, rationale, for example) related to object-oriented user interface design. Represent software requirements Manage different types of diagrams Associate artifacts (documents, diagrams) and maintain consistency among them. Manage software change impact analysis using the relationships defined among artifacts Separate viewpoints of requirements traceability. Each stakeholder (user, requirements engineer, project manager, software engineer, etc) may have a specific point of view of the development process. Our traceability model contributes to improve the understanding of the importance of requirement traceability in the software development process. It does not intend to provide a definitive solution to requirements traceability in user interface design.

3.4. Architectures and Patterns in Interactive System Development

Adaptability Problems of Architectures for Interactive Software (Marc Evers). Most software architectures for interactive software separate the user interface from the core functionality. This is a conceptual separation, but these concerns are often also physically separated. This separation however can lead to adaptability problems. An example of a concern that suffers from such problems is semantic feedback, which crosses the boundary between user interface and core functionality. In this way, either the separation between user interface and core functionality is compromised or the concern of semantic feedback will be difficult to adapt. These adaptability problems are in our opinion fundamental problems of architectures based on the separation of user interface and core functionality. It is not sufficient to introduce an extra layer or an extra component, because this does not tackle the essence of the problem. We see these problems as being the result of a design trade-off between separation of user interface concerns, (which is what user interface architectures try to do) and concerns like semantic feedback.

Characterizing User Interface Components for Reuse (Richard Cooper and Philip Gray). Components are the emerging standard technique for the re-use of interacting objects in the construction of user interfaces. Components are supplied by vendors on the internet with greater and greater frequency and the designer has an increasingly bewildering range of choice. However, locating the right component for the job is difficult and requires searching through web pages of often inadequate descriptions. What is required a descriptive model for components, which permits a search engine to locate the required description. We are constructing such a model which includes a description of components in terms of the main role (e.g. input, editing or display), their name, the type of data they process and other features such as an image showing the component in action, their price, color and so on. Such a model is analogous to the kind of descriptions provided by component models such as COM or EJB, but our model supports design rather than implementation. Making such model descriptions available is clearly of benefit to the designer for creating a design, but also to the vendors in publicizing their wares. We are currently building a system, which provides the user with the ability to search for components and to store descriptions, which have been found locally.

Designing Synchronous User Interface for Collaborative Applications (Antonio Mendes da Silva Filho and Hans Kurt E. Lisenberg). Synchronous User interface is a medium where all objects being shared on it can be viewed indifferently from the geographical location and its users can interact with each other in real-time. Designing such an interface for users working collaboratively requires dealing with a number of issues. Herein, our concerns lies on the design of control component of Human-Computer Interaction (HCI) and corresponding User Interface (UI) software that implements it. We make use of our approach to interactive system development based on the MPX - Mapping from PAN (Protagonist Action Notation) into Xchart (eXtended Statechart) - and illustrate it by presenting the case study of a collaborative application.

4. Conclusion

The problem of bridging human-computer interaction and software engineering goes way back to the beginning of both disciplines. Like the computer science and software engineering debate, this problem is also one of communication and the obligation of interdisciplinary work. The object-oriented paradigm is opening new perspectives on this problem.

The WISDOM'99 discussion framework builds on existing human-computer interaction work incorporating new contributions from the object-oriented community. This workshop helped discover subtle, but important, differences between concepts commonly used in both disciplines. The framework also helped identify the architecture, process, notation and process dimensions to integrate HCI modeling and OOSE.

The proposed meta-architecture to develop interactive system incorporates important qualities to support adequate user interface design. Besides separating core functionality from the user interface, an important but seldom supported requisite in software architectures. It leverages the separation of user interface specifics (presentation) from its conceptual specification, fostering reuse and automatic generation of multi-user interfaces.

The WISDOM process builds on OOSE best practices and proposes a set of HCI based workflows to support usability throughout the lifecycle. It is well known that usability can only be ensured if supported from early inception to late transition.

Notation issues were not extensively addressed in this paper, as another post-workshop activity some participants worked out a simple example and are now concentrating on results and discussion. Clearly some notation concepts are becoming commonly accepted on object-oriented user interface design. The concept of an object view or interaction space and the related support to the navigational model (or map) are essential to leverage good user interface architectures.

Finally, the proposal of a traceability model for user interface design ties all the other dimensions together. User interface design highly depends on external sources, introducing new requirements for traceability models.

There is still a lot of work to do on this emergent field, "the bridge is (still) too far". The UML "effect" is reaching different areas of software development and clearly user interface design is one of those areas that could highly benefit with a common modeling language and tool interoperability. Object-orientation is not a "silver bullet" and bridges are built from both margins. We certainly need more cross-disciplinary events like WISDOM'99 to help bridge the gap.

References

[1] J. Artim, M. van Harmelen, K. Butler, J. Gulliksen, A. Henderson, S. Kovacevic, S. Lu, S. Overmyer, R. Reaux, D. Roberts, J.-C. Tarby, and K. V. Linden. Incorporating work, process and task analysis into industrial object-oriented systems development. *ACM SIGCHI Bulletin*, (30(4)), 1998.

[2] M. Collins-Cope. The RSI Approach to Use Case Analysis: A ProtoPattern for Structured Use Case Development. In *ECOOP'99 WISDOM'99, http://math.uma.pt/wisdom99*, 1999.

[3] L. Constantine and L. Lockwood. *Software for Use*. Addison-Wesley, 1999.

[4] R. Cooper and P. Gray. Characterising User Interface Components for Reuse. In *ECOOP'99 WISDOM'99, http://math.uma.pt/wisdom99*, 1999.

[5] T. Dayton, A. McFarland, and J. Kramer. Bridging User Needs to Object Oriented GUI Prototype via Task Object Design. In L. Wood, editor, *User Interface Design*. CRC Press, 1998.

[6] M. Evers. Adaptability Problems of Architectures for Interactive Software. In *ECOOP'99 WISDOM'99, http://math.uma.pt/wisdom99*, 1999.

[7] J. Hackos and J. Redish. *User and Task Analysis for Interface Design*. John Wiley and Sons, 1998.

[8] I. Jacobson, G. Booch, and J. Rumbaugh. *The Unified Software Development Process*. Object Technology Series. Addison-Wesley, 1999.

[9] E. Kantorowitz. Some Observations on the Relationships between Tasks Use Cases Scenarios and Requirements Models. In *ECOOP'99 WISDOM'99, http://math.uma.pt/wisdom99*, 1999.

[10] S. Kovacevic. UML and User Interface Modeling. In *Proceedings of the UML'98 Workshop*, 1998.

[11] P. Kruchten. *The Rational Unified Process*. Object Technology Series. Addison-Wesley, 1998.

[12] S. Lu and C. Paris. Automatic Acquisition of Task Models From Object Oriented Design Specifications: A Case Study. In *ECOOP'99 WISDOM'99, http://math.uma.pt/wisdom99*, 1999.

[13] S. Lu, C. Paris, and K. Liden. Towards the Automatic Construction of Task Models from Object-Oriented Diagrams. In *IFIP Working conference on Engineering for HCI*, 1998.

[14] D. Mayhew. *The Usability Engineering Lifecycle*. Series in Interactive Techonologies. Morgan-Kaufmann, 1999.

[15] R. Merrick. Designing User Interfaces in XML. In *IBM Make it Easy Workshop, http://www.ibm.com/easy*. IBM, 1999.

[16] M. Muller and S. Kuhn. Participatory Design. *Communications of the ACM*, (36(3)), 1993.

[17] B. Myers and M. B. Rosson. Survey on User Interface Programming. In *Proceedings CHI'92*. ACM, 1992.

[18] J. Nielsen. *Usability Engineering.* Chestnut Hill, MA: AP Professional, 1993.

[19] N. J. Nunes. A Bridge too far: Can UML finally help bridge the gap? In *Proceedings INTERACT'99*, 1999.

[20] N. J. Nunes and J. F. e Cunha. A Bridge too Far: the WISDOM Approach. In *ECOOP'99 WISDOM'99, http://math.uma.pt/wisdom99*, 1999.

[21] N. J. Nunes and J. F. e Cunha. Detailing Use-Cases with Activity Diagrams and Object Views. In *ECOOP'99 WIHFUCOOM, http://www.crim.ca/ asef-fah/ecoop/*, 1999.

[22] D. Roberts, D. Berry, S. Isensee, and J. Mullaly. *Designing for the user with OVID.* MacMillan, 1998.

[23] A. Silva and H. Lisenberg. Designing Synchronous User Interface for Collaborative Applications. In *ECOOP'99 WISDOM'99, http://math.uma.pt/wisdom99*, 1999.

[24] J.-C. Tarby. When the Task's World meets the Object's World. In *ECOOP'99 WISDOM'99, http://math.uma.pt/wisdom99*, 1999.

[25] J.-C. Tarby and M. Barthet. The Diane+ Method. In *Proceedings CADUI'96*, 1996.

[26] M. Thomsen. Domain Object Models and User-interfaces. In *ECOOP'99 WISDOM'99, http://math.uma.pt/wisdom99*, 1999.

[27] M. Toranzo and J. Castro. A Comprehensive Traceability Model to Support the Design of Interactive Systems. In *ECOOP'99 WISDOM'99, http://math.uma.pt/wisdom99*, 1999.

[28] M. Toranzo and J. Castro. Multiview ++ Environment: Requirement Traceability from the Perspective of different Stakeholder. In *Proceedings of the Second Workshop on Requirement Engineering - WER'99*, pages 198 – 216, 1999.

[29] M. van Harmelen. Object Oriented Modelling and Specification for User Interface Design. In *Proceedings of the EG Workshop on Design, Specification and Verification of Interactive Systems*, pages 199–231. Springer-Verlag, 1996.

[30] M. van Harmelen, J. Artim, K. Butler, A. Henderson, D. Roberts, M. B. Rosson, J.-C. Tarby, and S. Wilson. Object Models in User Interface Design. *ACM SIGCHI Bulletin*, (29(4)), 1997.

Aspect-Oriented Programming

Lodewijk Bergmans[1] and Cristina Videira Lopes[2] (Editors)

[1] University of Twente, The Netherlands
bergmans@cs.utwente.nl

[2] Xerox Palo Alto Research Center, Palo Alto, CA
lopes@parc.xerox.com

http://trese.cs.utwente.nl/aop-ecoop99/

Abstract. Aspect-oriented programming is a promising idea that can improve the quality of software by reduce the problem of code tangling and improving the separation of concerns. At ECOOP'97, the first AOP workshop brought together a number of researchers interested in aspect-orientation. At ECOOP'98, during the second AOP workshop the participants reported on progress in some research topics and raised more issues that were further discussed.
This year, the ideas and concepts of AOP have been spread and adopted more widely, and, accordingly, the workshop received many submissions covering areas from design and application of aspects to design and implementation of aspect languages.

Workshop organisers: Cristina Lopes, Andrew Black, Elizabeth Kendall, Mehmet Aksit, Lodewijk Bergmans

This report received contributions from (in alphabetical order): L. Blair, K. Böllert, S. Clarke, C. Constantinides, Y. Gil, M. D'Hondt, L. Kendall, G. Kiczales, J. Knudsen, R. Lämmel, J. Lamping, K. Mehner, L. Pazzi, J. Pryor, J. Seinturier, M. Skipper, M. Südholt, S. Thompson, I. Welch

1. Introduction

Many systems have properties that do not necessarily align with the system's functional components. Failure handling, persistence, communication, replication, co-ordination, memory management, real-time constraints, etc., are aspects of a system's behaviour that tend to cut-across groups of functional components. While they can be thought about and analysed relatively separately from the basic functionality, programming them using current component-oriented languages results in spreading the aspect code through many components. The source code becomes a tangled mess of instructions for different purposes.

This 'tangling' phenomenon is at the heart of much needless complexity in existing software systems. It increases the dependencies between the functional components. It distracts from what the components are supposed to do. It introduces numerous opportunities for programming errors. It makes the functional

A. Moreira and S. Demeyer (Eds.): ECOOP'99 Workshops, LNCS 1743, pp. 288–313, 1999.

components less reusable. In short, it makes the source code difficult to develop, understand and evolve.

Aspect-oriented programming is a promising idea that could reduce the problem of code tangling, and therefore improve the quality of software. At ECOOP'97, the first AOP workshop brought together a number of researchers interested in aspect-orientation. At ECOOP'98, during the second AOP workshop the participants reported on progress in some research topics and raised more issues that were further discussed.

This year, the ideas and concepts of AOP have been spread and adopted more widely. Accordingly, the workshop received 26 submissions, of which 23 were accepted, covering areas from design and application of aspects to design and implementation of aspect languages.

The program consisted of the following five sessions:

1. An invited talk by John Lamping
2. Applications Session
3. Specification and Design Session
4. Implementation Session
5. Aspect Language Designs Session
6. Wrap-up Session

The first five sessions consisted of a number of presentations followed by discussions. Excerpts of these discussions have been included in this report in the following forms:

!: [Mrs. X] A remark or suggestion made by Mrs. X.

Q: [Mr. Y] A question by Mr.Y to the presenter.

A: An answer, usually by the presenter, if not denoted otherwise.

The last session was a regulated interactive session intended to obtain suggestions from all participants as to what they find important and relevant about AOP.

This workshop report is organised as follows: the following six sections provide a description of each of the sessions described above. Finally, there is a list of participants and their submissions, as well as the collected references.

Note that these excerpts have been reconstructed afterwards from notes that were made, and provide only a short summary of what happened during the workshop. There were some email discussions before the workshop - they can be found in the workshop's web page. Also, for an in-depth view of the works that were submitted, we refer the reader to the collection of workshop papers that can be found in the workshop's web page.

2. Invited Talk (John Lamping)

John Lamping has been working at XEROX PARC on Aspect-Oriented Programming from the very start, he was invited to open the workshop with a talk about his latest insights and ideas. The following is a summary of his talk.

The presentation revolved around the picture in Fig. 1. In object oriented programming, the structure of the basic operations, the messages that objects

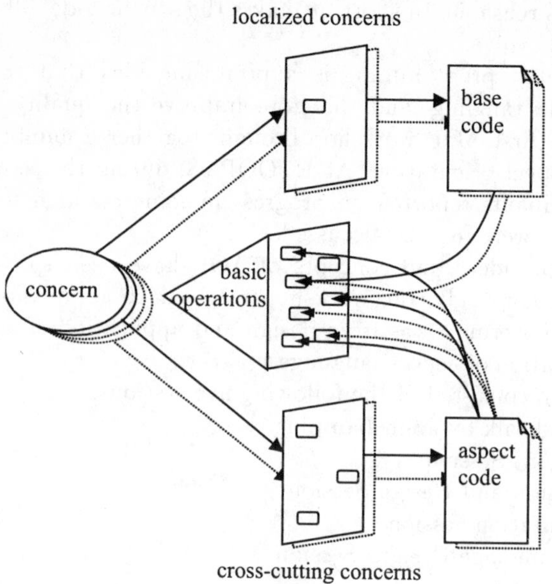

Fig. 1. John Lamping's picture.

can respond to, aligns with the structure of the code, the class files and methods. But in aspect oriented programming the relationship is more subtle, and more interesting.

The designer of an aspect-oriented program identifies the domain and implementation concerns their program must meet, and they also decide on the basic operations the program will be expressed in terms of. For AspectJ, the basic operations are the messages that the program will operate in terms of. These messages play as central a role in AspectJ programs as they do in ordinary OO programs. In particular, the choice of the basic operations determines which concerns will be localised, pertaining to one or a few basic operations, and which will cross-cut the basic operations, pertaining to a number of them. A good choice of basic operations will lead to as many concerns being localised as possible, but aspect oriented programming recognises that it is typically impossible to localise all concerns.

Those concerns that are localised are addressed by base code, while those concerns that cross-cut are addressed by aspect code. Both base code and aspect code contribute to the specification of what should happen when the basic operations are executed.

In summary, the basic operations play a central role in aspect oriented programming, both by determining which concerns cross-cut, and by serving as the common ground where the effect of base and aspect code meets.

Questions and Discussion

!: [Yossi Gil] Design decision about the difference between concerns and base operations are still difficult.
!: [Dominick Lutz] Whatever formalism you adopt, you will always have to make design decisions about how to decompose a system.
Q: [Lodewijk Bergmans] How can you express aspects of other aspects?
A: All aspects can be expressed in terms of the base operations, it is even possible in this way to model aspects of aspects.

3. Applications

This session, about the application of the concepts of AOP to various problems was chaired by Liz Kendall. The presenters of this session were asked beforehand to address the following questions and issues:

- What is the significance of the presented application.
- What about alternative solutions/approaches?
- What are the benefits and drawbacks of AOP solution?
- How has the development of this application progressed your knowledge and understanding of AOP?
- Share your experience with AOP
- How does AOP influence specification and design?
- Will this approach scale to larger applications?
- What is the next step/future work?

3.1. An Aspect Language for Robust Programming (Mario Südholt)

Presentation of the position paper submitted by Pascal Fradet and Mario Südholt

Topics

In this talk a semantically based robustness aspect for numerical programs was presented. The approach provides a specialised aspect language for the specification of the exceptional value domains of component programs. The specifications define program transformations that are used by the weaver to transform the component program into a woven program that provably does not perform calculations based on exceptional values.

Lessons Learned/Conclusions

A very specialised aspect language is useful to describe the robustness aspect as declaratively as possible. In the case of the robustness aspect, statement-level join points are not fine-grained enough. General pattern-based join point definitions have proven to provide adequate flexibility while retaining declarativeness of aspect definitions.

The talk advocated a three-level approach with a clean separation between levels: the aspect language is used to write aspect programs at the user level, the aspect language definition is done at a lower-level (linguistic level which is inaccessible to the user), aspect weaving is done at a generic implementation level supporting tool support.

The approach features a formal (with respect to syntax and semantics) definition of aspects and aspect weavers. By keeping the weaver simple important properties of the woven program can be proven based on the aspect only, i.e. (almost) without knowing the weaver.

Open Issues/Future Work

Since one of the main features of the approach is its formal definition, the question which properties, i.e. aspects, can be integrated must be investigated.

Current work is done in two main areas:

1. Investigating general properties of the formal framework, in particular with respect to the integration of new aspects (properties).
2. Developing a debugging and a security aspect

Questions and Discussion

Q: [Dominick Lutz]: How can you be sure that your pattern matches in the right place(s)

A: The specification allows syntactical patterns of any desired granularity.

3.2. JST: An Object Synchronisation Aspect for Java (Lionel Seinturier)

Presentation of the position paper submitted by Lionel Seinturier

In his talk, Lionel Seinturier presented JST, an aspect weaver for the Java language. JST addresses two aspects: object synchronisation and observation of a distributed CORBA run. The idea is to provide a tool (i.e. a so called aspect weaver) that allows to separate the code related to these two issues from the functional code of a distributed and concurrent CORBA/Java program. The synchronisation aspect is associated to a language with a statechart-like syntax. It wraps base level object and synchronises method calls before delivering them. The join point is the base level class interface. The observation aspect of JST is associated with some annotations of the base level programs. They point out the elements (methods, variables) that need to be traced. The data collected during a distributed run can then be used to perform some post-mortem profiling. This task is based on an extension of the Lamport causality relation.

The extension proposed by Lionel Seinturier adds three sources of order (synchronous method calls, synchronised methods, and read/write dependencies on shared variables) to the two sources (local ordering of events, and asynchronous communications) considered by the Lamport relation. JST is implemented with OpenJava (a compile-time MOP for Java) and ORBacus (a CORBA ORB). A first version of JST can be downloaded from Lionel Seinturier home page at the following URL: http://www-src.lip6.fr/homepages/Lionel.Seinturier/JST

Two conclusions can be drawn from Lionel Seinturier's work. First, reflective languages such as OpenJava provide an useful help in implementing aspect weavers. According to him, a lot of code should have been rewritten if OpenJava hadn't been used for JST. Second, in his opinion, the design of dedicated languages for each aspect leads to a better understanding of the domains involved in the program and of the weaving process. Once the join point between the aspect languages and the base language has been understood, the design of behaviours for each aspect becomes easier.

One of the open issues with AOP lies in the debug process. Indeed, once a program has been woven, the relation between the base level and the aspect level code may not be so clear. Some work still need to be done to address this problem. Finally, according to Lionel Seinturier, another big open issue that remains to be addressed is to know whether AOP scales well and if it can be applied to large scale applications where complex aspects such as fault tolerance, replication or mobility are involved.

Questions and Discussion

Q: [Gregor Kiczales] Can you synchronise multiple instances of multiple classes?

A: [Seinturier] No. This kind of synchronisation has to be done by designing different synchronisation behaviours and associating each behaviour to a particular class.

3.3. Is Domain Knowledge an Aspect? (Maja D'Hondt)

Presentation of the position paper submitted by Maja D'Hondt and Theo D'Hondt

Programs are a combination of domain knowledge and algorithms. Moreover, the real-world example accompanying this talk shows that the first crosscuts the second. The benefits of factoring out domain knowledge are clear: the programming process becomes less complex and both the domain knowledge and the algorithm can evolve independently from one another.

As a first and obvious solution, the presentation pointed to the classical techniques of object-orientation, such as delegation, subclassing and the use of design patterns to factor out domain knowledge. These techniques, however, cannot be applied in all cases. For example, domain knowledge that evolves can sometimes force the addition of a new parameter in the original algorithm. In order to avoid this, this talk focused on aspect-oriented programming as a possible solution.

The exploration and development of a programming environment that supports the separation of domain knowledge from algorithms at coding time, but that weaves the two at compile time or at run time, remains further work. Nevertheless, some initial and successful experiments were mentioned in the talk, consisting of a language symbiosis between Prolog for representing the domain knowledge, and Smalltalk for the implementation of the algorithm.

Questions and Discussion

Q: [Jørgen Knudsen] Why not the OO solution: force the separation through different languages

A: [Theo D'Hondt]: this work is driven by the goal of reusing AI domain knowledge technology and adding it to conventional programming

Q: [Mario Südholt]: if you factor out the heuristics from the algorithm, doesn't that clutter the understanding and optimisation of the algorithm?

A: No, at least in this case rather the reverse, since all optimisations can be expressed as constraints that are derived directly from the domain knowledge.

3.4. Aspect-Oriented Programming for Role Models (Elizabeth A. Kendall)

Presentation of the position paper submitted by Elizabeth A. Kendall

The Role Object with the Decorator pattern has been proposed as the best support for role models in standard object-oriented languages, such as Java. However, the Role Object design has three major drawbacks: object schizophrenia; interface bloat or, alternatively, down-casting; and no support for role composition.

The hybrid approach for AOP-based role model implementation presented by Liz Kendall places role behaviour in a combination of introduce weaves that are added to the core class and advise weaves that are added to the core instances. That is, an aspect both introduces the interface to the core class and then advises or adds the role specific behaviour to the core instance. Further, role relationships and role context reside in the aspect instance to easily support role multiplicity.

Liz Kendall claimed the following benefits of this hybrid approach to role aspects:

- Interface maintenance: The class' own intrinsic interface is not bloated with every potential role. However, the extrinsic behaviour is also accessible without down-casting.
- Object schizophrenia: Most of the role specific behaviour resides in the object; only role relationships and role context reside in the aspect.

She had also investigated Glue Aspects, where roles are represented by objects, and aspects integrate a Core object to the role(s) that it plays. This approach has the following benefits and drawbacks:

- Independent Core and Role hierarchies: Any Core object can play a given Role if the appropriate Glue Aspect is provided. This is the major advantage of this design.
- Interface maintenance: The role specific interfaces are introduced to the Core objects in a modular fashion. This is also true in the hybrid approach.
- Role multiplicity: The glue aspect design provides support for role multiplicity as roles can be indexed by context. This is also true in the hybrid approach.
- Object schizophrenia: The Role and Core objects are independent, so the Glue Aspects have to encode and manage all integration. The hybrid approach is superior in this area, and glue aspects should only be employed when there are only minimal dependencies between Role and Core objects.
- Additional level of components: The major drawback of this design is that it requires three levels of components

The presentation included illustrative examples of these two approaches for AOP-based role model implementation.

3.5. Aspect-Orientated Process Engineering (Simon Thompson)

Presentation of the position paper submitted by Simon Thompson and Brian Odgers

This talk addressed the question of how process knowledge should be structured. The use of Aspect Orientation as an abstraction for capturing and using process knowledge was reported. A description of the method, ASOPE (Aspect Oriented Process Engineering) was given.

The ASOPE system implements a hierarchical planning system that iteratively specialises a plan template stored as an object. The specialisation is done by weaving context specific plan elements, stored as aspects, into the generic plan according to the ownership and execution requirements of the business goal that is to be achieved. This process is illustrated in Fig. 2.

The advantage of using an Aspect Orientated representation was reported to be that the process knowledge developed in one context could be decontextualised and reused in other contexts, and context specific knowledge could be captured and retained for reuse at a local level.

4. Specification and Design

This session was chaired by Crista Lopes. The two first presentations dealt with aspect-based specifications and the two subsequent presentations discussed adding the notion of aspects to the design process and notations.

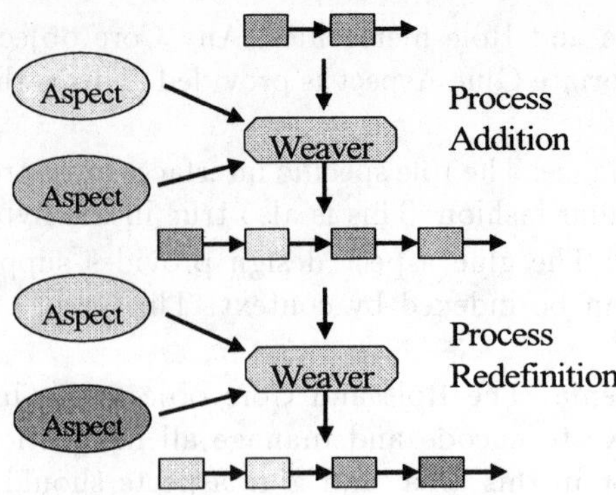

Fig. 2. Picture used in Simon Thompson's presentation. The hierarchical aspect weaving process used to specialise the generic plan.

4.1. A Tool Suite to Support Aspect-Oriented Specification (Lynne Blair)

Presentation of the position paper submitted by Lynne Blair and Gordon Blair

This talk presented an aspect-oriented style for the formal specification of systems, along with a supporting toolkit. The specification of a simple multimedia stream was considered and different aspects were identified, namely functional, non-functional and management aspects. If required, each aspect could be specified in a different formal language, for example using different notations for the functional (base) behaviour and the real-time or stochastic behaviour. Using a common underlying semantic model of timed automata, it was then possible to compose the aspects in order to perform analysis of either the interaction of aspects (c.f. feature interaction) or the overall system behaviour.

Composition in this approach was analogous to aspect-weaving in aspect-oriented programming and the multi-way synchronisation of events (either explicit or implicit) mirrored join-points. The composition process for the multimedia stream example was demonstrated using the Composer toolkit (see Fig. 3). The resulting behaviour was analysed using the tool's simulator and it was shown how temporal logic properties could be proved over the system by model checking.

Importantly, having checked the behaviour of the management aspects (i.e. the monitors and controllers) in the formal world, these aspects have been inserted directly into a running system using a reflective platform. Used this way, the management aspects described in the talk directly and dynamically monitor and control the behaviour of an audio stream.

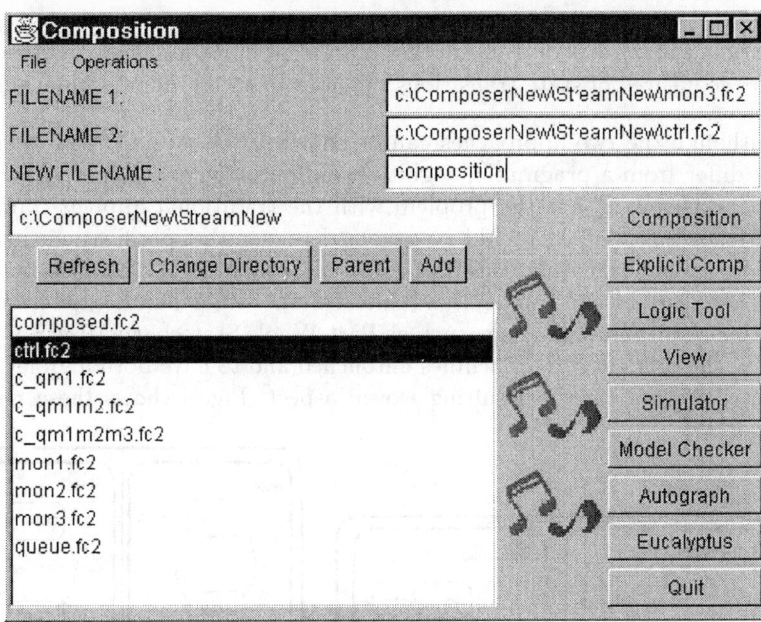

Fig. 3. A screen-dump from the Composer toolkit described and demonstrated by Lynne Blair.

4.2. Explicit Aspect Composition by Part-Whole State Charts (Luca Pazzi)

Presentation of the position paper submitted by Luca Pazzi

Luca Pazzi examined the issue of aspect weaving from two different approaches. As a working hypothesis, aspects were meant as specifications of generic and separable parts of the behaviour of an object. For example joining the aspects "being refillable" and "being breakable" may specify the full behaviour of a bottle, although both aspects are very generic and can be used to characterise any other object that is either refillable or breakable. Aspect specification means finding a suitable mechanism for both aspect specification and composition. The Statecharts formalism [Harel 77] was proposed to: a) specify aspects by separate, self-contained state Statecharts; b) compose aspects by the Statecharts AND composition mechanism.

It was showed that aspect composition could be achieved by two different approaches:

- Implicit weaving: A complex behaviour implicitly results by directly forwarding events from a Statechart to the another.
- Explicit weaving: A complex behaviour is explicitly depicted by a specific state machine whose states are compound states drawn from the Cartesian

product of the sets of states of the component machines, and state transitions are sequences of state transitions taken from the component machines.

Although the two approaches can be shown to be formally equivalent, they really differ from a pragmatic, cognitive and ontological point of view. In fact, it can be observed that the problem with the traditional implicit composition approach is that we have to add exogenous details to the specifications in order to make the global behaviour: this breaks the encapsulation of single aspects making them less reusable and understandable. On the other hand, explicit weaving, adopting a suitable formalism, such as Part-Whole Statecharts [Pazzi 97], allows to leave the original state machines untouched and to have both high level states and events denoting the resulting woven aspect. Fig. 4 shows these respective approaches.

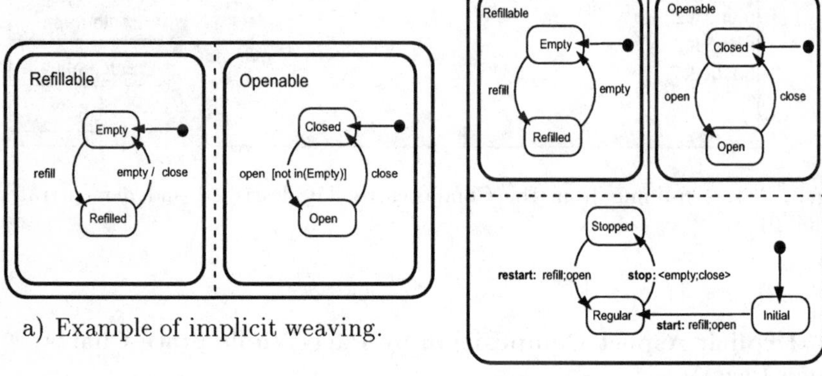

a) Example of implicit weaving.

b) Example of explicit weaving.

Fig. 4. Pictures in Pazzi's presentation.

The implicit weaving of the two aspects "being refillable" and "being openable", by traditional Statecharts AND composition mechanism (denoted by the dotted line). Observe that the synchronisation of the two state machines requires to add exogenous details (underlined features) to the component Statecharts.

The explicit weaving of the two aspects "being refillable" and "being openable", by Part-Whole Statecharts [Pazzi 97]. The global woven aspect is denoted by an explicit state machine (representing the whole behaviour) whose state transitions denote high-level events and map to the lower-level events of the component state machines.

Questions and Discussion

A discussion emerged about implicit vs. explicit and automatic vs. manual join points. It was pointed out that these two are not the same. Implicit vs. explicit has to do with how much information is given to specify the join points. Automatic vs. manual has to do with how the composition is done.

4.3. Separating Concerns Throughout the Development Lifecycle (Siobhán Clarke)

Presentation of the position paper submitted by Siobhán Clarke, William Harrison, Harold Ossher, and Peri Tarr

Siobhán Clarke presented an extension to the notion of separating concerns at just the code level in a position paper called "Separating Concerns throughout the Development Lifecycle". She discussed the need to separate the same concerns across the lifecycle to ease both the initial development, and evolution throughout the software's life. With current object-oriented design methods, designs are caught in the middle of a significant structural misalignment between requirements and code.

This misalignment leads to the scattering of the design and code of individual requirements across multiple classes, and tangling, where individual classes in the design and code may address multiple requirements. Addressing this misalignment problem suggests that it must be possible to reify features within the object-oriented paradigm to permit encapsulation of feature concerns, as specified in the requirements, within designs and code.

In this talk, subject-oriented design was discussed, which is an outgrowth of the subject-oriented programming model. Subject-oriented design supports the decomposition of design models matching requirements specifications, and, is an outgrowth of the work on subject-oriented programming. Subject-oriented programming addressed misalignment and related problems at the code level, and as such, subject-oriented design is the bridge between how requirements are specified and how code can be successfully separated based on features.

The talk further described the subject-oriented design model. A full system design model is divided into design subjects, each of which encapsulates some concern in the object-oriented design. Composition relationships may be specified between design subjects, which specify which design elements in the different subjects correspond, how differences between the specifications of corresponding elements may be reconciled, and how they should be reconciled in a composition process.

4.4. Extending UML with Aspects: Aspect Support in the Design Phase (Junichi Suzuki)

Presentation of the position paper submitted by Junichi Suzuki and Yoshikazu Yamamoto

This talk addressed the aspect support in the design level while it has been focused mainly in the implementation/coding phase. The motivation is that Aspect-Oriented Programming (AOP) has been considered a promising abstraction principle to reduce the problem of code tangling and make software structure clean and configurable. Suzuki proposed an extension to the Unified Modeling Language (UML) to support aspects properly without breaking the existing

UML specification. This allows developers to recognise and understand aspects in the design phase explicitly. This is achieved mainly through the introduction of new stereotypes.

Also, he proposed an XML-based aspect description language, UXF/a, to achieve interchangeability of aspect model information between development tools such as CASE tools and aspect weavers. The goal of the work presented here is to facilitate aspect documentation and learning, and increase aspect reusability and interchangeability.

5. Implementation

This session was prepared by Andrew Black, who could not attend the workshop. In this session there were presented a wide range of approaches towards the implementation of aspects, targeted at different languages (e.g. Smalltalk, Java), and adopting different approaches (e.g. reflection, first class aspects, design pattern/framework based aspects, pre-processor).

5.1. A Reflective Architecture for the Support of Aspect-Oriented Programming in Smalltalk (Jane Pryor)

Presentation of the position paper submitted by Jane Pryor and Natalio Bastán
The presentation described a reflective architecture implemented in Smalltalk that permits the incorporation of aspects to an object-oriented system. The reflective mechanism is supported by the Luthier MOPs framework, where reflection is implemented by means of message interception (by wrapping methods), though other reflection and reification facilities can be added if necessary. The functional objects of the system reside at the base level and the aspects at the meta-level of the architecture. This permits not only a clean separation of concerns, but also permits the dynamic manipulation of aspects in a completely transparent fashion with no modification to the design or implementation of the functional part of the system. An Aspect Manager at the meta-level associates and activates the aspects at run-time, permitting a large degree of flexibility. In particular, cross-cutting is permitted between one or many classes and/or instances of base objects with one or many classes and/or instances of aspects, previously defined by a composition method which associates the aspect/s to the object methods.

In conclusion, this architecture which is now being implemented in Java, has the advantage of dynamic weaving and a very clean separation of the aspect and functional parts of a system. Additionally, the framework that supports it facilitates the incorporation of other facilities, such as the handling of constraints between aspects (the Aspect Manager is easily extended to incorporate additional functionality), and eventually aspects of aspects (through extra meta-levels for example). These considerations and the actual implementation of applications with the incorporation of different types of aspects are the next steps to be taken.

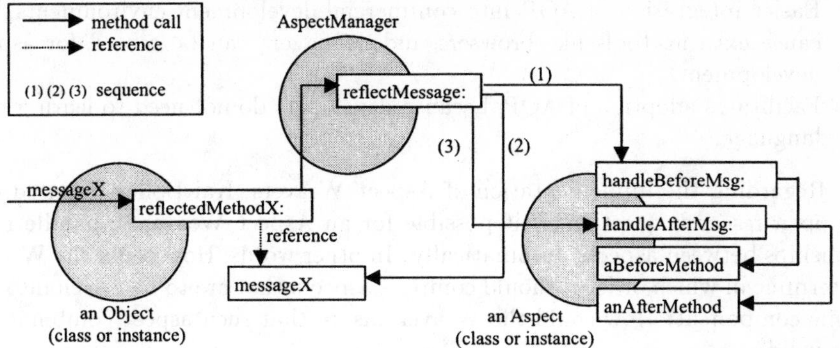

Fig. 5. Picture in Jane Pryor's presentation. Composition Mechanism: relationship among basic objects, the weaver and aspects.

As to the discussion of implementation issues, the pros and cons of static vs. dynamic weaving were mentioned, the problem with the latter mainly being a question of efficiency: for how much longer will this be an issue? In addition, the incorporation of constraints between aspects and the notion of aspects of aspects, should be issues to be considered in future proposals.

Questions and Discussion

Q: [Gregor Kiczales]: why aren't the before/after-method at the base-level?

A: This is possible, but it was not done for separating the aspect definitions from the base level.

5.2. On Weaving Aspects (Kai Böllert)

Presentation of the position paper submitted by Kai Böllert

Today development of aspects is done either in several special aspect languages or in one general-purpose aspect language (e.g., AspectJ). In contrast, Kai Böllert took the position that it may be better to use the same (object-oriented) programming language for writing both components (i.e., classes) and aspects. To illustrate how such an approach could be realised, Böllert showed in his talk the next version of the AOP/ST tool, which adds AOP extensions to the Smalltalk development environment VisualWorks.

The three most important benefits of not writing aspects in one or more special aspect languages are:

1. Significantly reduced implementation effort for AOP extensions, because no aspect language compiler needs to be implemented.

2. Easier integration of AOP into commercial development environments, because existing tools like browsers and debuggers can be reused for aspect development.
3. Facilitates adoption of AOP, because developers do not need to learn a new language.

Regarding the implementation of Aspect Weavers, Kai Böllert pointed out an open research question: is it possible for an Aspect Weaver to handle relationships between aspects automatically? In other words: How could the Weaver determine in which order it should compose aspects that are to be woven into the same component? How could the Weaver ensure that such aspect combinations are valid?

5.3. An Aspect-Oriented Design Framework for Concurrent Systems (Constantinos Constantinides)

Presentation of the position paper submitted by Constantinos Constantinides, Atef Bader, and Tzilla Elrad

The work presented by Constantinides concentrates on the aspectual decomposition of concurrent object-oriented systems. In his presentation, Constantinides categorised aspects as intra-method, intra-object and intra-package according to their hierarchical level of cross-cutting. He also identified certain restrictions imposed by current technologies that use automatic weavers and domain-specific as well as general-purpose aspect languages.

He proposed a design framework where the overall behaviour is made up of the functional behaviour, the aspects of concern and a moderator class that coordinates the interaction between aspects and components while observing the overall semantics.

As aspects can cut across components at every level, the moderator is considered a recurring pattern from intra-method to intra-package. The design framework provides an adaptable model and a component hierarchy using a design pattern, and it allows for an open language where new aspects (specifications) can be added and their semantics can be delivered to the compiler through the moderator. The moderator is a program that extends the language itself.

The framework maintains an aspect bank which is a 2-dimensional composition of the system in terms of aspects and components that can be used to verify the inter-relationships of the aspects and which the moderator will initially consult in order to collect the required aspects.

The goal of the work presented is to achieve separation of concerns and retain this separation without having to produce an intermingled source code. The presenter and his co-authors view weaving as a general mechanism through which one can achieve composition of concerns. As such, the framework performs weaving at compile-time and the intermingled code exists only at the binary level.

Questions and Discussion

Connected to this talk a discussion arose about the use of a manual design pattern approach (as in the presented work) versus automatic weaving.

5.4. Runtime Implementation of Aspects using Kava (Ian Welch)

Presentation of the position paper submitted by Ian Welch and Robert J. Stroud

Kava allows runtime implementation of aspects where aspects are represented by meta-objects. Kava implements runtime behavioural reflection by inserting meta-level interceptions into compiled Java classes. The scope of the runtime meta-object protocol is determined by the particular choice of meta-level interceptions implemented at load-time. The meta-level interceptions switch computation from the base to the meta-level. The meta-level is composed of co-operating meta-objects. Each meta-object can be thought of as an aspect.

Kava falls between the poles of static and dynamic weaving. With static weaving aspects are implemented directly into the base level. This increases the efficiency of the system (no inefficient re-directions) and makes it easier to validate the composed system. However it reduces the runtime adaptability of the system. This can be achieved with dynamic weaving where aspects are kept separate and their binding to the base level can be adjusted at runtime. However, reduces efficiency and makes validation difficult. Kava manages to retain some of the benefits of static weaving (efficiency and easier validation) while retaining some of the benefits of dynamic weaving (adaptability). This is because the meta-level interceptions are static and the meta-level is dynamic.

The separation between meta-level interceptions and the meta-layer eases some of the problems of debugging intertwined aspect and base code. As the aspects are implemented using standalone Java classes these can be developed and debugged before being combined with the base level. What remains an open issue is ensuring that the result of combining aspects and base level results in the intended overall behaviour. This is a problem for formal validation as much as a debugging problem.

The current version of Kava allows interception and redefinition of how methods are received, methods are sent, access to fields and interception of initialisation and finalisation. The authors are working on extending Kava to allow self and non-self method invocations to be distinguished, to support inheritance of meta-objects/aspects and interception of exception raising. More information in: http://www.cs.ncl.ac.uk/people/i.s.welch/home.formal/kava.

Questions and Discussion

Q: [Cristina Lopes] Why not do weaving at load-time as well?
A: Because we also want to do dynamic weaving
!: [Gregor Kiczales/Jane Pryor] Inheriting aspects is difficult and not yet well understood. This appears to be an open issue in general: how to reuse and extend aspects (inside the aspect domain).

Q: [Jane Pryor] why distinguishing between base-level and aspect designers
!: [Cristina Lopes] The moment of weaving seems to depend on the -nature of- the target language. This is reflected by the presentations that addressed different languages such as Smalltalk and Java.
!: [general agreement] The term 'weaving' refers to a general process, which is not (necessarily) tied to e.g. code (pre-)processing, but to the collection of activities that together cause the effective merging of aspect and base level code.

6. Aspect Language Designs

This session was chaired by Crista Lopes. The four presentations in this session dealt with various issues in the definition of aspect languages: respectively about specification of join points, abstractions to improve aspect specifications, aspect-oriented higher-order functional programming, formalisation of aspects (and composition in a more general sense), and finally a presentation about the link between AOP and the existing concept of super-imposition.

6.1. Aspect-Oriented Programming in BETA Using the Fragment System (Jørgen Knudsen)

Presentation of the position paper submitted by Jørgen L. Knudsen

The presentation started out by giving a brief overview of the BETA programming language. The language is a compiled, strong statically typed, object-oriented language, designed to support industrial strengths system development with emphasis on software engineering principles. The first public implementation dates back to approximately 1988.

The talk then turned the focus to the support of aspect-oriented programming in the BETA language as supported by the Mjølner System. The cornerstone to this support is the Fragment System, which is designed to support issues like separate compilation, separation of concerns, information hiding, inter-module dependencies, etc.

The core of the talk was a presentation of several examples of aspects as programmed in BETA using the Fragment System. These examples illustrated the basic concepts of the Fragment System, such as fragments, fragment groups, slot, origin and dependency graph. The principle is, that source code is written in the form of fragments (syntactically legal pieces of BETA code). Fragments that are somehow related are placed in fragment groups (typically files on the file system). In source code, parts may be left unspecified by inserting so-called slots. A slot is the specification of a join point for source code to be specified elsewhere and in the future. Slots and fragments are named and typed (by the syntactic category of the source code). Source code (in the form of fragments) is connected with slots through the origin specification in the fragment groups (origin specifies the name of another fragment group). That is, a fragment is bound to a slot if (and only if) a corresponding slot is found either in the same fragment group, in the fragment group referred to by origin, or in the origin of the origin, etc. The origin specification is one of the ways to construct the dependency graph.

After having presented how to augment classes with new aspects (such as adding a colour aspect to an entire pre-existing class hierarchy of graphical objects, the talk discussed issues like the support for inter-dependent aspects in BETA, and how the Fragment System controls the visibility of aspects.

The final part of the talk was a presentation of the approach to statement aspect weaving. Statement aspect weaving is done using exactly the same mechanisms as described above, namely fragments and slots. This implies that statement join points are specified in the form of slots in the imperative part of the program, implying that statement join points must be anticipated. This allows insertion of statements at any point in the source code, and static specification of statement join points. This approach follows the general design philosophy of aspects in BETA, namely that the location of join points is a deliberate design decision to be made by the designers (following the general principles of predictability of systems, even in the case of extensible systems).

The talk concluded by presenting the workings of the Fragment System Weaver by illustrating how the source code of different aspects are woven into the program source code to give the entire source code of the resulting executable.

Questions and Discussion

Q: [Yossi Gil] Can you use the same fragment in several places?
A: No. (this effectively means that crosscutting of fragments/aspects is not possible)
Q: [Yossi Gil] So it is the same as literate programming?
A: The fragment system uses the same weaving structure, but it is strongly typed.
Q: [Liz Kendall] Can you give examples that illustrate its industrial strength?
A: Apart from the Mjølner System itself, there are no large industrial applications.

6.2. On the Role of Method Families for Aspect-Oriented Programming (Katharina Mehner)

Presentation of the position paper submitted by Katharina Mehner and Annika Wagner

Katharina Mehner presented in her talk a language extension that aims at improving the reusable definition of aspects. The starting point was the observation that the building blocks of current aspect languages such as AspectJ are not properly encapsulated and thus cannot be referred to by a name. Aiming at the reusable definition of aspects, the possibility of factoring out common properties within an aspect and between aspects assigned to classes in an inheritance hierarchy is highly desirable. But it is impossible without a proper encapsulation of their building blocks.

On the other hand, it was proposed in the talk that a solution for making aspect definitions reusable has to fit with the connection technique, i.e. the join points between classes and aspects. Since different methods either of the same class or from super and sub classes show the same behaviour seen under the perspective of an aspect, the building blocks of aspects are defined on a per method basis, either for one method or for a list of methods. Hence methods form the join points.

These requirements are ideally fulfilled with the concept of *method families*, i.e. equivalence classes of methods. A method family consists of its name, a method set and of attached behaviour. For the purpose of reuse method families can be referred to by their name. Thus, a kind of encapsulation of and interface to the building blocks of aspects is achieved, similar to the functional units of classes, the methods. Moreover, the usual set theoretic operations allow for a powerful, semi-automatic extension and restriction mechanism of method families during reuse. It was shown that the concept of method families is applicable to general aspect oriented languages as well as to domain specific languages.

Lessons learned: The main conclusion was, that method families are a useful extension. Moreover, they are a contribution to the question how inheritance or refinement can be carried out for aspects. While at the moment method families are completely part of the aspect language, a future step brought to discussion during the workshop was to make the assignment of sets to the building blocks of aspects part of a connector language between the class code and the aspect code. However, in the opinion of the speaker this cannot lead to more freedom for the connectors as they still have to obey the same concepts for inheritance as before.

6.3. Adaptation of Functional Object Programs (Ralf Lämmel)

Presentation of the position paper submitted by Ralf Lämmel, Günter Riedewald, and Wolfgang Lohmann

The talk was concerned with aspect-oriented higher-order functional programming. Certain operators for program transformation suitable to model aspects were suggested. The program examples were based on functional program modules (i.e. components) implementing language interpreter fragments. Environment propagation, error handling and the introduction of the monadic style were considered as aspects. The approach is based on previous work of Ralf Lämmel, Günter Riedewald et al. on meta-programming and aspect-oriented programming for first-order declarative languages.

In the 1997 ECOOP-AOP workshop Wolfgang De Meuter suggested monads as a contribution to the theoretical foundation for AOP. Ralf Lämmel's talk discussed several limitations and drawbacks of the monadic approach, e.g. the use of a single composed monad versus different conceptual layers of effects, or tangling arising from the monadic style. One important conclusion of the talk was that a more general instance of aspect-oriented programming can be obtained based on a transformation-oriented approach. Monads still provide an important tool in such a setting. The component programmer is no longer required to code in the monadic style, but the monadic style is regarded as a kind of aspect which can be incorporated in the component code by a corresponding transformation. It is clear that such a delayed installation of the monadic style improves flexibility because the installation can pay attention to the actual context, that is to say different layers of effects can be supported and the functions which need to be computed in the different layers can be selected accordingly without overspecification.

The talk mentioned different frameworks to formalise the program transformations, e.g. term rewriting, natural semantics and functional meta-programs. It was supposed that the transformation operators operate on entire functional program modules (i.e. components). This is in contrast to Fradet's and Südholt's approach presented at the 1998 ECOOP-AOP workshop, were an additional weaver applies given transformations until a fixpoint is reached. In other technical papers Ralf Lämmel et al. developed suitable preservation properties for program transformations to facilitate formal reasoning.

The talk concluded with an overview on a kind of operator suite for program transformation that is under development. The operators are meant to model the basic roles in aspect code. There are for example operators addressing data flow issues, the insertion of computations, the installation of sum domains etc. In this sense, the talk also emphasised that program transformations provide a sensible tool even in adapting higher-order functional programming. In contrast, most previous work on program transformations for functional programs was concerned with optimisation issues.

Besides the operator suite the most interesting problem for further investigation is the question how the transformation-based approach can be applied for the common component languages rather than declarative languages.

6.4. Formalising Composition Oriented Programming (Mark Skipper)

Presentation of the position paper submitted by Mark Skipper and Sophia Drossopoulou

Mark presented a snapshot of work in progress to make a formal model of the kind of object-oriented composition mechanisms that underpin AOP and SOP. He motivated the work by pointing out that there exists no way to give an abstract description of the semantics of composition used in current AOP implementations.

He introduced the language Ku: a small imperative OO language with classes methods and attributes. The definition of Ku includes type rules, an operational semantics and a soundness property which cross-checks these against one another. It also includes a composition function that combines collections of classes known as units. Composition attempts to merge classes methods and attributes if they correspond. Merging is undefined for corresponding entities if they do not also match.

Currently correspondence is defined as name equivalence for classes, attributes and methods; matching is defined as signature equivalence for attributes and methods; classes match if all their corresponding attributes and methods also match. This framework allows various hypotheses concerning composition to be formulated and tested. One such hypothesis: that composition preserves type correctness of composed units, was presented and discussed in more detail.

Different kinds of composition can be investigated in the framework by, for example, changing the definitions of correspondence and matching. Mark concluded his presentation with a description of the many directions in which this work can be taken in the future.

6.5. Aspects and Superimpositions (Joseph Gil)

Presentation of the position paper submitted by Shmuel Katz and Joseph Gil

The purpose of this presentation was to draw the attention of the AOP community to an extensive line of research, which started at the eighties, on the topic of superimposition. Joseph (Yossi) Gil, the presenter, pointed out the many similarities between AOP and superimposition, which are both mechanisms for separation of concerns in program design, orthogonal to the usual breakdown into modules. Traditionally, the research on superimposition was motivated and focused on the design of distributed algorithms. Properties such as liveliness, robustness to failures, deadlock prevention, etc., are best dealt with as a superimposition of a generic algorithm that insures them on the main distributed computation algorithm. In contrast, AOP is more general purpose and does not focus in any specific application domain. AOP can however, can, and should be tested and demonstrated against the many examples used in superimposition. On the other hand, there should be work on extending superimposition to other application areas.

Yossi Gil called for researchers working on AOP to build upon some of achievements of the work on superimposition. These include the syntax and language design, as proposed in Katz's 1993 TOPLAS paper which address the problem of join points, the taxonomy of superimposers.

More importantly, superimposition enjoyed the blessings of formal methods, and in particular program verification. There was research to show that the application of a superimposer to any base algorithm is correct, provided that the base algorithm satisfies certain conditions. Just as early work on superimpositions took a macro-like code implementation view of their meaning, aspects have been described in this way. However, it was found more effective to view superimpositions as separate entities, with various ways of combining them with basic systems and with each other, using a binding operator. Treating aspects in this way will also provide a firmer theoretical basis and clearer semantics for this important modularity concept. He stressed that there is a great potential for a similar modular specification and verification techniques in AOP, however, for this to happen, the notion of generic aspects, i.e., aspects that can take parameters must be properly introduced. A group lead by Prof. Katz is currently doing research at the Technion along some of these lines.

Questions and Discussion

Q: [Lodewijk Bergmans]: What are the lessons learned by the superimposition community?

A: At least three lessons have been learned: (a) you can prove properties (b) how to apply parameterised aspects (c) many working examples exist and can be studied.

!: [Mario Südholt] Aspects should be declarative, but proving properties requires a lot of specification and proof effort

!: [Cristina Lopes] We can learn a lot about AOP by looking into work that has been done in the past and that didn't have the word "aspect" in it explicitly.

7. Wrap-Up

Moderator: Gregor Kiczales

The purpose of this session was to revisit key issues from the day, while making sure everyone contributed to the session. The set-up was the following:

> "Imagine N years into the future, when aspects are in widespread use. The dominant aspect language is called Port, and it builds on objects. There are several Port Development Kits (PDKs) and design tools. What properties do Port and PDKs have?"

The discussion was driven by a fixed list of issues that were addressed in the previous sessions (but not all issues made it to this last session!). For each issue, there were quick arguments pro/against, with the constraint that each participant could speak in at most two issues of the list. So participants had to chose their interventions wisely. At the end of each brief discussion there was a vote, to have an idea of the most popular properties of Port. What follows is the summary of the issues that were discussed.

Aspects in the Software Lifecycle

There was a consensus that there would be explicit support for aspects in all phases of the software lifecycle.

Specification Systems

There was a consensus that specification systems with explicit support for aspects should be language independent.

As for the composition of aspect specifications, it was argued that automatic composition (vs. manual composition) would be desirable, but that it was a hard problem. The majority of participants agreed that it would be sufficiently good to reach half-way between automatic and manual composition of aspect specifications.

Re-engineering Support for Aspects

Would there be tools for crosscutting binary COTS software?

The position paper by Welch and Stroud suggested so, by describing one particular technique for weaving aspects at load-time. Other possibilities include using the APIs or using advisory tags. The contra-argument was that aspects should apply only to source code, because they make serious assumptions about the implementation.

At the end, 14 to 3 voted that there would be tools for supporting crosscutting of binary code.

Design Support for Aspects

Will UML of the future support aspects? The consensus was yes. The participants agreed that there needs to standard notation, standard exchange format and mechanisms for automatic code generation.

There was also a consensus that including the concept of aspect into the UML of the future would be crucial for the success of aspects.

Weaving

When will weaving occur? Design-time, coding-time, compile-time, load-time, JIT-time, run-time?

This issue generated quite a bit of discussion. The argument that got approval of the majority of participants was that this issue is not specifically related to aspects, but that it relates to many language features, and that different times are desirable for different features. Another argument was that different weaving times would be desirable or necessary for different design entities.

The votes at the end showed that the most popular weaving time would be fairly static, so at or before compile-time (total of 14 votes). But there would also be more dynamic weaving mechanisms, so at run-time, load-time and JIT-time (total of 8 votes).

Explicit Meta-programming

Several position papers gave different perspectives on this issue. For example, DeVolder, Pryor and Bastán, Lämmel et al., Knudsen, Mehner and Wagner.

The argument for programming aspects at the meta-level was that it makes the distinction clear between objects and aspects. The argument against was that meta-programming is hard.

The votes at the end reflected the division of opinions among the participants. 15 participants voted that Port would be less meta; 10 participants voted that Port would be more meta.

Means of Referring to Join Points

The space for referring to join points ranges from fixed points in the program (a la BETA fragment system) to less fixed, property-driven specifications (e.g. "the public methods of this package"). Other possibilities in between are method identifiers (e.g. "the add(Object) method of class Set"), maybe with a wildcarding mechanism, and using syntactic elements of the programs.

18 participants voted that property-based join point specifications would be more popular, and 3 participants voted that name-based or pre-identified join points would be more popular.

Wrap-Up Summary

To conclude, the following list summarises the properties of Port and its PDKs as estimated/voted upon by the workshop participants:

- Explicit support for aspects in all phases of the software lifecycle
- Specification of aspects is Port-independent; composition of aspect
- Specs is half-manual, half-automatic
- Aspects can affect binary code (important consequences for COTS)
- There is UML-ish support for aspects
- Aspect weaving is mostly static, but Port also supports more dynamic
- Weaving mechanisms that are used less often
- Join points are referred to by property-driven specifications

It should be noted that the approach that was taken to this session, collecting issues and constraining the discussion, was considered rather successful: because of the voting, everybody was involved, and because of the limitation to participate in the discussion, people would wait to make real important points, and the discussion was not dominated by a few people.

8. Participants and Position Papers

The following list shows the participants of the workshop, with their affiliation and e-mail address. If applicable, the position papers and their co-authors are given as well. Persons marked with an asterisk have presented their work during the workshop.

1. Mehmet Aksit, University of Twente, aksit@cs.utwente.nl
2. Lodewijk Bergmans, University of Twente, bergmans@cs.utwente.nl
3. Anders Bjorvand, University of Oslo, torvill@trolldata.no
4. *Lynne Blair, Lancaster University, lb@comp.lancs.ac.uk (with G. Blair), *A tool suite to support aspect-oriented specification*
5. *Kai Böllert, IC&C GmbH, Germany, kaib@acm.org *On weaving aspects*
6. *Siobhán Clarke, Dublin City University, sclarke@compapp.dcu.ie (with H.Ossher, W. Harrisson, P. Tarr) *Separating concerns throughout the development lifecycle*
7. *Constantinos A. Constantinides, Illinois Institute of Technology, conscon@charlie.cns.iit.edu (with Atef Bader & Tzilla Elrad) *An aspect-oriented design framework for concurrent systems*
8. Lutz Dominick, Siemens AG, Germany, Lutz.Dominick@mchp.siemens.de, *Aspect of lifecycle control in a C++ framework*
9. Sophia Drossopoulou, Imperial College of Science, sd@doc.ic.ac.uk (with M. Skipper) *Formalising composition-oriented programming*
10. *Yossi Gil, The Technion, yogi@cs.technion.ac.il (with S. Katz) *Aspects and superimpositions*
11. *Maja D'Hondt, Brussels Free University, mjdhondt@vub.ac.be (with Th. D'Hondt) *Is domain knowledge an aspect?*
12. Theo D'Hondt, Brussels Free University, tjdhondt@vub.ac.be (with M. D'Hondt) *Is domain knowledge an aspect?*
13. *Elizabeth A. Kendall, Royal Melbourne Institute of Technology, kendall@rmit.edu.au, *Aspect-oriented programming for role models*
14. Gregor Kiczales, Xerox PARC, gregor@parc.xerox.com
15. *Jørgen Lindskov Knudsen, University of Aarhus, jlk@daimi.au.dk *Aspect-oriented programming in BETA using the fragment system*
16. *Ralf Lämmel, University of Rostock, rlaemmel@informatik.uni-rostock.de (with G. Riedewald & W. Lohmann) *Adaptation of functional object programs*
17. *John Lamping, Xerox PARC, lamping@parc.xerox.com *The role of base in aspect-oriented programming*
18. Cristina Lopes, Xerox PARC, lopes@parc.xerox.com
19. *Katharina Mehner, University of Paderborn, mehner@uni-paderborn.de (with A. Wagner) *On the role of method families in aspect-oriented programming*
20. *Luca Pazzi, University of Modena, pazzi@unimo.it, Explicit aspect composition by part-whole state charts
21. *Jane Pryor, UNICEN, Argentina, jpryor@exa.unicen.edu.ar (with N. Bastán) *A reflective architecture for the support of AOP in Smalltalk*

22. *Lionel Seinturier, University Paris 6, Lionel.Seinturier@lip6.fr
JST: an object synchronisation aspect for Java
23. *Mark Skipper, Imperial College of Science, mcs@bcs.org.uk
(with S. Drossopoulou) *Formalising composition-oriented programming*
24. *Mario Südholt, Ecole des Mines de Nantes, Mario.Sudholt@emn.fr
(with P. Fradet) *An aspect language for robust programming*
25. *Junichi Suzuki, Keio University, suzuki@yy.cs.keio.ac.jp
(with Y. Yamamoto) *Extending UML with aspects: aspect support in the design phase*
26. *Simon Thompson, BT Labs, Simon.2.Thompson@bt.com
(with B. Odgers) *Aspect-oriented process engineering*
27. *Ian Welch, University of Newcastle upon Tyne, i.s.welch@ncl.ac.uk
(with R. Stroud) *Load-time application of aspects to Java COTS software*
28. Edward D. Willink, Racal Research Limited, UK, Ed.Willink@rrl.co.uk
(with V. Muchnick) *Weaving a way past the C++ One Definition Rule*

References

[Bougé 88] L. Bougé and N. Francez. *A compositional approach to superimposition.* In ACM SIGACT-SIGPLAN Symposium on Principles of Programming Languages, pages 240–249, Jan 1988.
[Harel 77] D. Harel. *Statecharts: A visual formalism for complex systems. Science of Computer Programming,* **8**:231–274, 1987.
[Katz 93] S. Katz. *A superimposition control construct for distributed systems.*, ACM Trans. on Programming Languages and Systems, 15:337–356, April 1993.
[Pazzi 97] L. Pazzi. *Extending StateCharts for representing parts and wholes.*, In Proceedings of the EuroMicro-97 Conference, Budapest, 1997.

Semantics of Objects As Processes (SOAP)*

Uwe Nestmann[1] and António Ravara[2]

[1] BRICS***, Aalborg University, Denmark
uwe@cs.auc.dk
[2] IST, Technical University of Lisbon, Portugal
amar@math.ist.utl.pt

1. Introduction

One of the most popular programming paradigms today is that of object-oriented programming. With the growing popularity of the language C++ and the advent of Java as the language of choice for the World Wide Web, object-oriented programs have taken center stage. Consequently, the past decade has seen an exponentially increasing interest within the programming language research community for providing a firm semantic basis for object-oriented constructs.

Recently, there has been growing interest in studying the behavioral properties of object-oriented programs using concepts and ideas from the world of concurrent process calculi, in particular calculi with some notion of mobility. Not only do such calculi, as the well-known π-calculus by Milner, Parrow and Walker [26], have features like references and scoping in common with object-oriented languages; they also provide one with a rich vocabulary of reasoning techniques firmly grounded in structural operational semantics and static typing.

The process calculus view has therefore proven to be advantageous in many ways for semantics and verification issues. On the one hand, the use of encodings of object-oriented languages into existing typed mobile process calculi enables formal reasoning about the correctness of programs; on the other hand, using standard techniques from concurrency theory in the setting of calculi for objects may help in reasoning about objects, e.g. by finding appropriate and mathematically tractable notions of behavioral equivalences. Encodings may also help clarify the overlap and differences of objects and processes, and suggest how to integrate them best in languages with both.

The aim of the SOAP workshops is to bring together researchers working mainly in this area, but in related fields as well, where other process models or calculi are used as a basis for the semantics of objects.

Historical Remarks

The origin of the SOAP workshops may be found in the early *Fränkische OOrientierungstage 1993*, organized by Uwe Nestmann and Terry Stroup, where a

* http://www.cs.auc.dk/soap99/

*** Basic Research in Computer Science, Centre of the Danish National Research Foundation

A. Moreira and S. Demeyer (Eds.): ECOOP'99 Workshops, LNCS 1743, pp. 314–325, 1999.

programming tutorial by Benjamin Pierce [35] on objects in the π-calculus-based programming language Pict [36] was followed by an invited workshop on the semantics of objects as processes. The first open workshop, SOAP '98, organized by Hans Hüttel and Uwe Nestmann, then took place as a satellite event to ICALP'98 in Aalborg, Denmark. The proceedings can be downloaded from http://www.brics.dk/NS/98/Ref/BRICS-NS-98-Ref/, more information is accessible through the workshop web page at http://www.cs.auc.dk/soap99/.

Brief Summary of SOAP'99

For the '99 edition of SOAP, taking place as a satellite workshop of ECOOP '99, among nine submitted abstracts five were recommended by the programme committee (Hans Hüttel, Josva Kleist, Uwe Nestmann, and António Ravara) based on a formal refereeing process, and are summarized below. The proceedings can be downloaded via http://www.brics.dk/NS/99/Ref/BRICS-NS-99-Ref/, also accessible through http://www.cs.auc.dk/soap99/.

We would like to thank the organizers of ECOOP '99, in particular Ana Maria Moreira, for helping us logistically to set up the SOAP workshop, we thank BRICS, in particular Uffe Engberg Nielsen, for the publication of these proceedings, and we thank Massimo Merro and Silvano Dal-Zilio for their assistance in the refereeing process.

According to the specific topics of the accepted contributions, the workshop programme is composed of two complementary thematic building blocks.

The first block was addressing the motto 'objects *as* processes' literally in that objects are represented as a derived concept within a framework of processes; we welcomed Oscar Nierstrasz, Markus Lumpe, and Jean-Guy Schneider as invited speakers to present the work they have been accomplishing in this area—starting out from a mobile process calculus—and to let us learn about their conclusions. This session was rounded up by a verification approach using a temporal logic as a target setting for, in this case, UML-style objects.

The second building block, divided into a session on behavioral subtyping and another one on behavioral typing, is seen as an adaptation of the process-theoretic viewpoint to some object-oriented framework. While the typed λ-calculus is a firm ground to study typing for object-oriented languages, the typing of concurrent objects poses particular problems due to synchronization constraints. A static notion of typing is not powerful enough to capture dynamic properties of objects' behavior, like non-uniform service availability. Concurrency theory inspires dynamic notions of typing and subtyping, and this block of SOAP'99 exemplified the state of the art in the field.

The rest of this report contains brief summaries of workshop presentations (where the presenting speaker is indicated by a *), preceded by short overviews of the fields, and followed by concluding remarks and a list of selected references.

2. Objects as Processes

Background: An Annotated Bibliographic Overview

Rather soon after the development of process algebras, basically triggered by pioneering work of Tony Hoare [15] and Robin Milner [25], and enabled by first attempts to capture the semantics of parallel object-oriented programming within the POOL-family [3] of languages, Frits Vaandrager [46] started out to give a first explicit study on the semantics of objects as processes, where he encoded a variant of POOL into the process algebra ACP [4]. An encoding in this context usually simply means a translation of some high-level (object) syntax into some lower-level (process) syntax. An encoding is usually considered 'good', if it is compositional and exhibits some preservation and reflection properties concerning operational and behavioral relations of the languages or calculi involved.

Although some basic principles of concurrent objects could be clearly expressed in Vaandrager's approach by means of concurrent processes, several aspects of object-oriented programming, like the persistent identities of objects and certain inheritance features, were not modeled in a natural way. It needed another landmark invention, the π-calculus [26], to get a more suitable and, as it turns out, quite appropriate process model for objects. David Walker took over and extended Vaandrager's initial work, now targeting at the π-calculus [49]. Moreover, together with Xinxin Liu and Anna Philippou, in a series of papers, they investigated the possibilities of using the process-algebraic semantics for reasoning about concurrent object-oriented programs [22, 23, 24, 32, 33, 34], some of it in order to solve a tricky program transformation problem proposed by Cliff Jones [19, 20]. Related to this line of research, Xiaogang Zhang and John Potter provided some more understanding of class-based object-oriented programs using π-calculus [51]. These developments have not only been of theoretical nature, but gave also rise to implementations that closely follow the pencil-and-paper encodings, like Benjamin Pierce and David Turner exemplified in their Pict compiler [36].

Another strand of research has been opened up by the advent of the object calculus (OC) by Martín Abadi and Luca Cardelli [1], who provide a minimal model of typed objects. Again, the study of encodings has been the main tool for SOAP-investigations. Hans Hüttel and Josva Kleist gave a first encoding of the untyped object calculus into the π-calculus [17]. Davide Sangiorgi gave a different one for the typed object calculus [45], and extended this work together with Josva Kleist to the imperative object calculus [21]. Hans Hüttel, Josva Kleist, Massimo Merro and Uwe Nestmann extended this work to mobile objects [18].

There have also been other approaches to internalize object-oriented notions as primitives within process calculi. Here, we just list Oscar Nierstrasz' higher-order object calculus [31], Kohei Honda and Mario Tokoro's ν-calculus [16], Vasco Vasconcelos' TyCO [47], and Gérard Boudol's Blue Calculus [6]. Two further object calculi can be viewed either as extensions of OC with concurrency, or as extensions of process calculi with objects: one by Paolo Di Blasio and Kathleen Fisher [13] and another one by Andrew Gordon and Paul Hankin [14].

At SOAP '99, we also had presentations on how to represent objects within the framework of Petri Nets (see Section 3). In the remainder of the current section, however, we summarize the three presentations on objects as strongly typed name-passing processes, and one presentation on objects as cTLA agents.

Piccola — A Small Composition Language (Oscar Nierstrasz)

Although object-oriented languages are well-suited to implementing software components, they fail to shine in the construction of component-based applications, largely because object-oriented design tends to obscure a component-based architecture. We propose to tackle this problem by clearly separating component implementation and composition. Piccola is a small "composition language" that embodies the paradigm of "applications = components + scripts." Piccola models components and composition abstractions by means of a unifying foundation of communicating concurrent agents. Flexibility and extensibility are obtained by modeling both interfaces to components and the contexts in which they live by extensible records, or "forms". We illustrate the realization of an architectural style in Piccola and show how external components may be adapted and composed according to the style. We show how separating components from their composition can improve maintainability.

The πL-Calculus A Formal Foundation for Software Composition (Markus Lumpe)

In this talk, we present a formal language for software composition that is based on the π-calculus. More precisely, we present the πL-calculus, a variant of the π-calculus, in which agents communicate by passing extensible, labeled records, or so-called "forms", rather than tuples. This approach makes it much easier to model compositional abstractions than it is possible in the plain π-calculus, since the contents of communications are now independent of positions, agents are more naturally polymorphic since communication forms can be easily extended, and environmental arguments can be passed implicitly. The πL-calculus is developed in three stages: (i) we analyze whether the π-calculus is suitable to model composition abstractions, (ii) driven by the insights we got using the π-calculus, we define a new calculus that has better support for software composition (e.g., provides support for inherently extensible software construction), and (iii), we define a first-order type system with subtype polymorphism that allows us to statically check an agent system in order to prevent the occurrences of runtime errors.

Object Models in the πL-Calculus (Jean-Guy Schneider)

The development of concurrent object-based programming languages has suffered from the lack of any generally accepted formal foundation for defining their semantics, although several formal models have been proposed. Most of these models define objects and object-oriented abstractions as primitives, but they either do not incorporate important features found in object-based programming languages (e.g., they lack inheritance), hard-wire the underlying inheritance model, or integrate concepts in a non-orthogonal way. As an approach to overcome the problems of existing models, we present a (meta-level) framework for object models in the πL-calculus. We show that common object-oriented programming abstractions such as instance variables and methods, different method dispatch strategies as well as class features are most easily modeled when class meta-objects are explicitly reified as first class entities. We illustrate that various concepts which are typically merged (or confused) in object-oriented programming languages can be expressed in a more natural way by making a clear separation between functional elements (i.e. methods) and their compositions (i.e. inheritance). Furthermore, we show that the same concepts can also be applied for modeling mixins, mixin application, and mixin composition.

Composing Object-Oriented Specifications and Verifications with cTLA (Günter Graw*, Peter Herrmann, and Heiko Krumm)

In order to support formally correctness preserving refinement steps of object-oriented system designs, we refer at one hand to the practically well-accepted Unified Modelling Language (UML) and at the other hand to Leslie Lamport's Temporal Logic of Actions (TLA) which supports concise and precise notions of properties of dynamic behaviors and corresponding proof techniques. We apply cTLA which is an extension of TLA and supports the modular definition of process types. Moreover, in cTLA process composition has the character of superposition which facilitates the modular transformation of UML diagrams to corresponding formal cTLA process system definitions and their structured verification. We exemplify transformation and formal verification. Furthermore, we outline the application of this method for the establishment of domain-specific specification frameworks which can directly support the UML-based correct design of OO-systems.

3. Behavioral Typing and Subtyping

Background: An Annotated Bibliographic Overview

Behavioral typing and behavioral subtyping are notions of (respectively) typing and subtyping for concurrent object-oriented programming, which take into account dynamic aspects of objects' behavior. In the beginning of the 90's, Nierstrasz argued that typing concurrent objects poses particular problems due to the non-uniform methods availability, since by synchronization constraints, the availability of a method depends upon the internal state of the object (which reflects the state of the system) [30]. Therefore, a static notion of typing, like interfaces-as-types, is not powerful enough to capture dynamic properties of the behavior of concurrent objects. Hence, Nierstrasz proposed the use of a regular language as types for active objects, to characterize the traces of menus offered by the objects. He also proposed a notion of subtyping, *request substitutability*, which is based on a generalization of the *principle of substitutability* by Wegner and Zdonick [50], according to the extension relation of Brinksma et. all [7]. It is a transition relation, close to the failures model.

Several researchers are working on this track, developing object-based process calculi and static typing disciplines which cope with non-uniform objects.

Jean-Louis Colaço and others [8, 9, 10, 11] propose a calculus of actors and a type system that aims at the detection of "orphan messages" (messages that may never be accepted in some actor's execution path, either because the requested service is not in the actor's interface, or due to dynamic changes in an actor's interface). Types are interface-like, with multiplicities (thus, without dynamic information), and the type system requires some complex operations on a lattice of types. A set-constraints algorithm does the type inference.

Elie Najm and Abdelkrim Nimour [27, 29, 28] propose several versions of a calculus of objects featuring dynamically changing interfaces and distinguishing private and public objects' interfaces. For each version of the calculus, they develop a typing system handling dynamic method offers in private interfaces, and guaranteeing some liveness properties. Types are sets of deterministic guarded parametric equations, equipped with a transition relation, and represent infinite state systems. They define an equivalence relation, a compatibility relation, and a subtyping relation on types, based on the simulation and on the bisimulation relations.

Franz Puntigam [38, 39, 40, 41] defines a calculus of concurrent objects, a process-algebra of types (with the expressiveness of a non-regular language), and a type system which guarantees that all messages that are sent to an object are accepted; sequencing of messages is enforced to achieve the purpose.

Gérard Boudol proposes a dynamic type system for the blue calculus (a variant of the π-calculus directly incorporating the λ-calculus) [5]. The types are functional, in the style of Curry-Church simple types, and incorporate Hennessy-Milner logic with recursion (thus, with modalities, interpreted as resources of names). Processes inhabit the types, and this approach captures some causality in the usage of names in a process, ensuring that messages to a name will meet a corresponding offer. Well-typed processes behave correctly, this correct behavior being preserved under computation.

In the context of the lazy λ-calculus [2], Laurent Dami proposes a liberal approach to potential errors [12]. He argues that the common notion of erroneous term is over-restrictive: some programs, in spite of having error terms inside them, do not actually generate a run-time error when executed. Since there is a family of programming languages based on the lazy λ-calculus, Dami proposes a lazy approach to errors—a term is considered erroneous if and only if it always generates an error after a finite number of interactions with its context.

It seems quite natural to have a liberal approach to potential errors in the context of non-uniform concurrent objects. António Ravara and others claim that it allows a more flexible and behavior-oriented style of programming, and moreover, detects some deadlocks [44, 43, 42]. The type system they propose accepts all processes that 'traditional' systems [48] do, except for those that do not conform to the restriction that only the output-capability of names can be transmitted, and furthermore, rejects some deadlocked processes.

In the next section we summarize the four talks in this second building block—two on behavioral subtyping in the context of petri-nets and two on behavioral typing of non-uniform object calculi.

A Practical Approach to Behavioural Inheritance in the Context of Coloured Petri Nets (Charles Lakos and Glenn Lewis*)

There are a number of proposals for substitutability in the context of concurrent object-oriented systems. it is unclear whether these proposals are overly constrained for practical application.

In the context of colored petri nets, we propose a set of three incremental modifications which lie somewhere between weak an strong substitutability. The constraints that we impose can be checked statically and they have the property that if the refinement is *at least as live as* the abstraction, then strong substitutability holds. (This property *cannot* be checked statically.) An examination of case studies in the literature suggests that the above forms of refinement are applicable in practice.

While the above proposals were formulated in the context of colored petri nets, it turns out that if the colored petri nets are transformed into the corresponding (elementary) petri nets, then the three forms of refinement correspond to recognized net morphisms. The formal definition for these morphisms can be found elsewhere, as can the proofs that the composition of refinements is a refinement.

Current work is investigating the extent to which analysis techniques can take advantage of the structure implicit in the above incremental modifications in producing more efficient analysis.

Behavioural Types in CoOperative Objects (Nabil Hameurlain and Christophe Sibertin-Blanc)

Behavioral typing and subtyping has proved to be a very useful concept for the support of incremental reuse in the area of object-oriented (O-O) languages.

With the emergence of formalisms integrating the O-O approach and Petri nets, the question arises how behavioral subtyping may be supported by such formalisms. We present a formal framework for the definition of behavioral typing in CoOperative Objects, a concurrent Object Oriented language, based upon Client/Server Petri nets. This framework is based upon the preorder and equivalence relations which are considered in the study of concurrent systems, allowing to define various subtyping relations.

A Concurrent Object Calculus with Types that Express Sequences (Christof Peter* and Franz Puntigam)

Sequencing of messages specified by types of objects is desirable especially in concurrent systems. Types in popular concurrent object calculi cannot support sequencing of messages. We present a calculus that supports sequencing of messages and compare it to the calculus of Vasconcelos and Honda. Type safety in our calculus does not allow a certain kind of nondeterminism supported by other calculi.

Explicit Behavioral Typing for Object Interfaces (Elie Najm and Abdelkrim Nimour*)

In this paper we describe an approach for typing objects with non-uniform service availability. We define behavioral types for object interfaces based on labeled transition systems that specify the succession of available methods (services) at an interface. Each transition label is a method signature. In addition, each interface has to be declared public or private. A private object interface has only one client at a time and offers non-uniform services depending on the "protocol" the client and the server have agreed on. On the other hand, a public interface can have multiple clients at the same time and is required to perform the same services for all its potential clients: the services on a public interface are uniform.

4. Open Discussion

The last workshop session consisted of an open "round-table" discussion on the topics of the workshop: objects as processes and behavioral types. We summarize briefly the individual subjects:

- If one successfully studies objects as processes, why not also extend this to general forms of "component", and look for more general notions of plugging of objects/components?
- What is the border between types and programs, or type systems and process calculi, respectively? Should type declarations be added explicitly? What should be typed? Names or processes?

- What do we do with untypable, i.e., ill-typed programs? Can we provide simple fixes automatically? Can we provide over- or underestimates, or should we simply generate warnings?
- What is the best notion of error? Or, do we have to have many different ones for different application domains?
- What is the "real" problem domain for behavioral types? Non-uniform Objects? Protocol specification?
- What would be a good means for comparing the many systems for behavioral types? By encodings into some generic foundational system? By case studies?

Although we could not find an agreement on the individual questions raised above, we agreed at least on the fact that more work needs to be done and seems to be worth being carried out.

Participants: Gérard Boudol, Ilaria Castellani, Mauro Gaspari, Günter Graw, Glenn Lewis, Markus Lumpe, Uwe Nestmann, Oscar Nierstrasz, Abdelkrim Nimour, Christof Peter, António Ravara, Arend Rensink, Jean-Guy Schneider.

5. Conclusion

The summaries of workshop contributions presented, and summarized above, show that the field of object-oriented programming can substantially profit from both the representation of objects as processes as well as from the borrowing of process-theoretic concepts for adaptation to object-oriented settings.

References

[1] Martín Abadi and Luca Cardelli. *A Theory of Objects.* Monographs in Computer Science. Springer-Verlag, 1996.

[2] Samson Abramsky. The lazy lambda-calculus. In *Research Topics in Functional Programming*, pages 65–117. Addison Wesley, 1990.

[3] Pierre America. Issues in the design of a parallel object-oriented language. *Formal Aspects of Computing*, 1(4):366–411, 1989.

[4] Jos Baeten and Peter Weijland. *Process Algebra*, volume 18 of *Cambridge Tracts in Computer Science.* Cambridge University Press, 1990.

[5] Gérard Boudol. Typing the use of resources in a concurrent calculus. In *Asian Computing Science Conference*, volume 1345 of *lncs*, pages 239–253. sv, 1997.

[6] Gérard Boudol. The π-calculus in direct style. *Higher-Order and Symbolic Computation*, 11:177–208, 1998. Previously published in the *Proceedings of POPL '97*, pages 228–241.

[7] Ed Brinksma, Giuseppe Scollo, and Chris Steenbergen. LOTOS specifications, their implementations and their tests. *Protocol Specification, Testing and Verification VI, (IFIP)*, pages 349–360, 1987.

[8] Jean-Louis Colaço, Mark Pantel, and Patrick Sallé. CAP: an actor dedicated process calculus. In *Workshop Reader of the 10th European Conference on Object-Oriented Programming (ECOOP'96).* Dpunkt Verlag, 1996.

[9] Jean-Louis Colaço, Mark Pantel, and Patrick Sallé. A set constraint-based analyses of actors. In *2nd IFIP Workshop on Formal Methods for Open Object-based Distributed Systems (FMOODS'97).* Chapman & Hall, 1997.

[10] Jean-Louis Colaço, Mark Pantel, and Patrick Sallé. From set-based to multiset-based analysis: a practical approach. In *4th Workshop on Set Constraints and Constraint-based Program Analysis*, 1998. Satellite event of the *4th International Conference on Principles and Practice of Constraint Programming (CP'98)*.

[11] Jean-Louis Colaço, Mark Pantel, Fabien Dagnat, and P. Sallé. Static safety analyses for non-uniform service availability in actors. In *4th IFIP Workshop on Formal Methods for Open Object-based Distributed Systems (FMOODS'99)*. Kluwer, 1999.

[12] Laurent Dami. Labelled reductions, runtime errors and operational subsumption. In *24th International Colloquium on Automata, Languages and Programming (ICALP'97)*, volume 1256 of *Lecture Notes in Computer Science*, pages 782–793. Springer-Verlag, 1997.

[13] Paolo Di Blasio and Kathleen Fisher. A concurrent object calculus. In Ugo Montanari and Vladimiro Sassone, editors, *Proceedings of CONCUR '96*, volume 1119 of *Lecture Notes in Computer Science*, pages 655–670. Springer-Verlag, 1996. An extended version appeared as Stanford University Technical Note STAN-CS-TN-96-36, 1996.

[14] Andrew D. Gordon and Paul D. Hankin. A concurrent object calculus: Reduction and typing. In Uwe Nestmann and Benjamin C. Pierce, editors, *Proceedings of HLCL '98*, volume 16.3 of *Electronic Notes in Theoretical Computer Science*. Elsevier Science Publishers, 1998.

[15] Charles A. R. Hoare. Communicating sequential processes. *Communications of the ACM*, 21(8):666–677, 1978.

[16] Kohei Honda and Mario Tokoro. An object calculus for asynchronous communication. In Pièrre America, editor, *Proceedings of ECOOP '91*, volume 512 of *Lecture Notes in Computer Science*, pages 133–147. Springer-Verlag, July 1991.

[17] Hans Hüttel and Josva Kleist. Objects as mobile processes. Research Series RS-96-38, BRICS, October 1996. Presented at MFPS '96.

[18] Hans Hüttel, Josva Kleist, Massimo Merro, and Uwe Nestmann. Migration = cloning ; aliasing (preliminary version). In *Informal Proceedings of the Sixth International Workshop on Foundations of Object-Oriented Languages (FOOL 6, San Antonio, Texas, USA)*. Sponsored by ACM/SIGPLAN, 1999.

[19] Cliff Jones. Constraining interference in an object-based design method. In Marie-Claude Gaudel and Jean-Pierre Jouannaud, editors, *Proceedings of TAPSOFT '93*, volume 668 of *Lecture Notes in Computer Science*, pages 136–150. Springer-Verlag, 1993.

[20] Cliff Jones. Accomodating Interference in the Formal Design of Concurrent Object-Based Programs. *Formal Methods in System Design*, 8(2):105–122, 1996. To appear.

[21] Josva Kleist and Davide Sangiorgi. Imperative objects and mobile processes. In David Gries and Willem-Paul de Roever, editors, *Proceedings of PROCOMET '98*, pages 285–303. International Federation for Information Processing (IFIP), Chapman & Hall, 1998.

[22] Xinxin Liu and David Walker. Confluence of processes and systems of objects. In Peter D. Mosses, Mogens Nielsen, and Michael I. Schwarzbach, editors, *Proceedings of TAPSOFT '95*, volume 915 of *Lecture Notes in Computer Science*, pages 217–231. Springer-Verlag, 1995. Presented in the CAAP-section. Available as University of Warwick Research Report CS-RR-272, October 1994.

[23] Xinxin Liu and David Walker. Partial confluence of processes and systems of objects. *Theoretical Computer Science*, 1998.

[24] Xinxin Liu and David Walker. Concurrent objects as mobile processes. In Plotkin et al. [37]. To appear.

[25] Robin Milner. *A Calculus of Communicating Systems.* Springer-Verlag, 1980. LNCS 92.

[26] Robin Milner, Joachim Parrow, and David Walker. A calculus of mobile processes, part I/II. *Information and Computation*, 100:1–77, September 1992.

[27] Elie Najm, Abdelkrim Nimour, and Jean-Bernard Stefani. A calculus of object bindings. In *2nd IFIP Workshop on Formal Methods for Open Object-based Distributed Systems (FMOODS'97).* Chapman & Hall, 1997.

[28] Elie Najm, Abdelkrim Nimour, and Jean-Bernard Stefani. Guaranteeing liveness in an object calculus through behavioral typing. In *IFIP Joint International Conference Formal Description Techniques For Distributed Systems and Communication Protocols & Protocol Specification, Testing, and Verification (FORTE/PSTV'99).* Kluwer, 1999.

[29] Elie Najm, Abdelkrim Nimour, and Jean-Bernard Stefani. Infinite types for distributed objects interfaces. In *4th IFIP Workshop on Formal Methods for Open Object-based Distributed Systems (FMOODS'99).* Kluwer, 1999.

[30] O. Nierstrasz. Regular types for active objects. In *Object-Oriented Software Composition*, pages 99–121. Prentice Hall, 1995.

[31] Oscar Nierstrasz. Towards an object calculus. In M[ario] Tokoro, O[scar] Nierstrasz, and P[eter] Wegner, editors, *Object-Based Concurrent Computing 1991*, volume 612 of *Lecture Notes in Computer Science*, pages 1–20. Springer-Verlag, 1992.

[32] Anna Philippou. *Reasoning about Systems with Evolving Structure.* PhD thesis, University of Warwick, December 1996.

[33] Anna Philippou and David Walker. On confluence in the π-calculus. In Pierpaolo Degano, Roberto Gorrieri, and Alberto Marchetti-Spaccamela, editors, *Proceedings of ICALP '97*, volume 1256 of *Lecture Notes in Computer Science*, pages 314–324. Springer-Verlag, 1997.

[34] Anna Philippou and David Walker. On transformations of concurrent object programs. *Theoretical Computer Science*, 195(2):259–289, 1998. An extended abstract appeared in *Proceedings of CONCUR '96*, LNCS 1119: 131–146.

[35] Benjamin C. Pierce. Fränkische OOrientierungstage 1993 (Rothenbühl, Fränkische Schweiz, Germany). Tutorial on programming in the π-calculus, 1993.

[36] Benjamin C. Pierce and David N. Turner. Pict: A programming language based on the pi-calculus. In Plotkin et al. [37]. To appear.

[37] Gordon Plotkin, Colin Stirling, and Mads Tofte, editors. *Proof, Language and Interaction: Essays in Honour of Robin Milner.* MIT Press, 1999. To appear.

[38] Franz Puntigam. Types for active objects based on trace semantics. In *1st IFIP Workshop on Formal Methods for Open Object-based Distributed Systems (FMOODS'96)*, pages 5–20. Chapman & Hall, 1996.

[39] Franz Puntigam. Coordination requirements expressed in types for active objects. In *11th European Conference on Object-Oriented Programming (ECOOP'97)*, number 1241 in lncs, pages 367–388. sv, 1997.

[40] Franz Puntigam. Coordination requirements expressed in types for active objects. In *4th International Euro-Par Conference*, number 1470 in lncs, pages 720–727. sv, 1998.

[41] Franz Puntigam. Non-regular process types. In *5th International Euro-Par Conference*, number 1685 in lncs, pages 1334–1343. sv, 1999.

[42] António Ravara and Luís Lopes. Programming and implementation issues in non-unifom TyCO. Technical report, Department of Computer Science, Faculty of

Sciences, University of Porto, 4150 Porto, Portugal, 1999. Presented at the *Workshop on Object-Oriented Specification Techniques for Distributed Systems and Behaviours (OOSDS'99)*. Satellite event of the *1st Conference on Principles, Logics and Implementations of high-level programming languages (PLI'99)*. Web page: http://www.tec.informatik.uni-rostock.de/IuK/congr/oosds99/program.htm.

[43] António Ravara, Pedro Resende, and Vasco T. Vasconcelos. An algebra of behavioural types. Technical report, Section of Computer Science, Department of Mathematics, Instituto Superior Técnico, 1049-001 Lisboa, Portugal, 1999. Preliminary version presented at the *1st Workshop on Semantics of Objects as Processes (SOAP'98)*. Satellite event of the *25th International Colloquium on Automata, Languages and Programming (ICALP'98)*. Web page: http://www.cs.auc.dk/soap99/index98.html.

[44] António Ravara and Vasco T. Vasconcelos. Behavioural types for a calculus of concurrent objects. In *3th International Euro-Par Conference*, number 1300 in lncs, pages 554–561. sv, 1997. Full version available as DM-IST Research Report 06/97.

[45] Davide Sangiorgi. An interpretation of typed objects into typed π-calculus. *Information and Computation*, 143(1):34–73, 1998. Earlier version published as Rapport de Recherche RR-3000, INRIA Sophia-Antipolis, August 1996.

[46] Frits Vaandrager. Process algebra semantics for POOL. Report CS-R862, Centre for Mathematics and Computer Science, Amsterdam, August 1986.

[47] Vasco T. Vasconcelos. *A process-calculus approach to typed concurrent objects.* PhD thesis, Keio University, 1994.

[48] Vasco T. Vasconcelos and Mario Tokoro. A typing system for a calculus of objects. In *1st International Symposium on Object Technologies for Advanced Software*, volume 742 of *lncs*, pages 460–474. sv, 1993.

[49] David Walker. Objects in the π-calculus. *Information and Computation*, 116(2):253–271, 1995.

[50] Peter Wegner and Stanley B. Zdonik. Inheritance as an incremental modification mechanism or what like is and isn't like. In *2nd European Conference on Object-Oriented Programming (ECOOP'88)*, number 322 in lncs, pages 55–77. sv, 1988.

[51] Xiaogang Zhang and John Potter. Class-based models in the pi-calculus. In Christine Mingins, Roger Duke, and Bertrand Meyer, editors, *Proceeding of The 25th International Conference in Technology of Object-Oriented Languages and Systems (TOOLS Pacific '97, Melbourne, Australia)*, pages 219–231, November 1997.

Quantitative Approaches in Object-Oriented Software Engineering

Fernando Brito e Abreu[1], Horst Zuse[2], Houari Sahraoui[3], and Walcelio Melo[4]

[1] Faculdade de Ciências e Tecnologia / INESC, Portugal
fba@di.fct.unl.pt - http://www.fct.unl.pt
[2] Technische Universitat Berlin, Germany
zuse@cs.tu-berlin.de - http://www.tu-berlin.de
[3] Centre de Recherche Informatique de Montréal , Canada
hsahraou@crim.ca - http://www.crim.ca
[4] Oracle, Brazil
wmelo@acm.org

Abstract. This full-day workshop was organized in four sessions. The first three were thematic technical sessions dedicated to the presentation of the recent research results of participants. Seven, out of eleven accepted submissions were orally presented during these three sessions. The first session also included a metrics collection tool demonstration. The themes of the sessions were, respectively, "Metrics Definition and Collection", "Quality Assessment" and "Metrics Validation". The last session was dedicated to the discussion of a set of topics selected by the participants.

1. Introduction

Quantitative Methods in the Object Oriented (OO) field is an active research area. This workshop aimed to shed some light on recent research results and future directions that might interest not only the academic community but also industry. The latter is eagerly launching software process improvement initiatives but is often insecure on how to assess the corresponding results both at the product and process levels. Measures of software structural attributes have been extensively used to help software managers, customers and users to characterize, assess, and improve the quality of software products. Many large software companies have intensively adopted software measures to increase their understanding of how and how much software product internal attributes affect the overall software quality. Estimation models have successfully been used to perform risk analysis, to assess software maintain-ability and error-proneness, mainly on what we call today "legacy technology". Also, large software companies have taken advantage of software measures to built up useful cost models and delivery schedules. By doing so, they have been able to improve their software development processes by producing realistic deadlines and allocating adequate resources. OO paradigm provides powerful design mechanisms which have not been fully or adequately quantified by the existing software product measures. Much work is yet to be done to investigate analytically or empirically the relationship between OO

A. Moreira and S. Demeyer (Eds.): ECOOP'99 Workshops, LNCS 1743, pp. 326–337, 1999.

design mechanisms, e.g., inheritance, polymorphism, encapsulation, usage etc., and different aspects of software quality, e.g., modularity, modifiability, understandability or extensibility. Emerging concepts and technologies, such as OO frameworks, OO Analysis/Design Patterns, Web technology and Component-based development, take advantage of OO design mechanisms. To understand their pros and cons we must be able to assess the quality of the base technology on which they are built upon.

Several workshops on similar topics have occurred in previous years, such as the following:

- "Object-Oriented Product Metrics for Software Quality Assessment" - ECOOP'98
- "Object-Oriented Design Quality" - OOPSLA'97
- "Object-Oriented Product Metrics" - OOPSLA'96
- "Quantitative Methods for Object-Oriented Systems Development" - ECOOP'95
- "OO Process and Metrics for Effort Estimation" - OOPSLA'95
- "Pragmatic and Theoretical Directions in OO Software Metrics" - OOPSLA'94

This workshop took place on the 15th June 1999 at the Faculty of Sciences of the Lisbon University. The workshop started by the mutual presentation of participants. All organizers except Walcelio Melo attended the workshop. Authors of all submissions selected for oral presentation were present, so no changes had to be operated. The workshop organic details were explained to participants and then the technical sessions begun.

The structure of this report mirrors the actual workshop program layout. The workshop was organized into 3 technical sessions and a roundtable discussion on elected topics. The technical sessions were thematic:

- Session 1 - Metrics Definition and Collection
- Session 2 - Quality Assessment
- Session 3 - Metrics Validation

The complete set of accepted submissions is available online at:
http://www.esw.inesc.pt/ftp/pub/esw/mood/ecoop99

2. Technical Presentations

In this section we will present an abstracted version of the presentations done during the three technical sessions.

2.1. Session 1 - Metrics Definition and Collection

This session included three communications and a metrics collection tool demonstration.

2.1.1. Modeling and Measuring Object-Oriented Software Attributes with Proximity Structures (Geert Poels and Guido Dedene)

Geert Poels from the Department of Applied Economic Sciences of the Catholic University of Leuven, in Belgium, presented this communication.

The authors advocated an approach to model software attributes with proximity structures. These are empirical relational structures that describe the concept of dissimilarity or conceptual distance. Measurement theory is used to formally validate software measures as measures of distance.

Their "distance-based" approach was presented as a constructive five-step measurement procedure that hides the complexity of the underlying measurement theoretic constructs from the user. Special attention was paid to an intuitive hierarchy of assumptions on which the constructive procedure is based. They also gave a brief overview of some results regarding the distance-based measurement of object-oriented enterprise models.

The distance-based approach presents an alternative way of modelling and measuring software attributes. On the one hand, the approach has firm measurement theoretic foundations. On the other hand, the complexity of the measurement theoretic constructs involved is largely hidden from the user by means of a constructive, five-step procedure. They paid special attention to the assumptions underlying the approach as they determine its successful use. They found proximity structures especially useful in the context of object-oriented enterprise modelling measurement. They do acknowledge, however, that further experiences with their approach are needed to draw definite conclusions about its usefulness for (object-oriented) software measurement in general. Further research must also focus on the relations between alternative models of software attributes (e.g., proximity structures versus belief structures), their underlying assumptions, and their implications regarding uniqueness and meaningfulness of measurement scales.

2.1.2. The GOODLY Design Language for MOOD2 Metrics Collection (Fernando Brito e Abreu, Luis Ochoa, and Miguel Goulão)

Fernando Brito e Abreu from the Faculty of Sciences and Technology of the Lisbon New University and INESC, both in Portugal, presented the GOODLY language that is being used by his team in the production of a new generation of the MOODKIT tools that allow the MOOD2 metrics extraction. The MOOD2 design metrics set is an extension of the original MOOD set. A detailed definition of the MOOD2 set is available as an INESC internal report. The GOODLY language, whose syntax and semantics were briefly described, allows specifying the design of systems built according to the Object Oriented paradigm. This language, whose features are fully described in the paper submitted to this workshop, allows expressing the most relevant OO design information, such as the class structure with corresponding inheritance relations, class parameterization, uses relationships, message exchanges and information hiding. The presentation also described the architectural evolution of MOODKIT, along with its rationale. It was evident how the GOODLY design language played a fundamental role in this effort.

Miguel Goulão then made a presentation of the MOODKIT G2 tool. This tool, in its current version, allows parsing Eiffel and Smalltalk code (C++ and Java are also sought), as well as object models expressed in OMT and UML (using the ParadigmPlus tool), to produce GOODLY code. The tool has a linking facility for identification of missing components and besides generating the MOOD2 metrics, it also produces a hypertext version of GOODLY code (HT-GOODLY) with traceability features. Miguel showed how a large software system specification expressed in GOODLY could be navigated with a normal browser supporting frames. The software industry interest on the MOOD metrics set was evidenced by the availability of several tools that support the collection of this metric set, such as Cantata++, a tool for C++ and Ada95 projects (http://www.iplbath.com/tools/) and Krakatau, a tool for Java and C++ projects (http://www.power-soft.co.uk/english/kr/).

Fernando ended the presentation with a call for cooperation to other research teams in the OO metrics area. His team is specially interested in finding partners with process data that can be used along with OO product metrics for building validation experiments. The web site of the MOOD project can be used for browsing a large set of systems expressed in HT-GOODLY, to see the original code from which they were generated or to get papers produced within the MOOD team. (http://www.esw.inesc.pt/ftp/pub/esw/mood)

2.1.3. Software Metrics and Object-Oriented Systems (Horst Zuse)

Next presentation, after the morning coffee break, was from Horst Zuse of the Technical University of Berlin, Germany.

He focused on the validation of software measures in order to predict an external variable. Such external variables can be costs of maintenance, time to repair a module, etc. Validation of software measures is a very important task, but not an easy one. Mostly, correlation coefficients or regression analysis for the validation of software measures are used. He pointed out that measures for the objected-oriented paradigm and imperative languages are very differently related to the prediction of maintenance effort.

2.1.4. Demo of a Tool for OO Metrics Collection (Brian Henderson-Sellers)

Brian Henderson-Sellers from the School of Computing Sciences of the University of Technology in Sydney, Australia, presented a tool for OO metrics collection. This tool, named "IT 903 Metrics Tool" was developed by a group of five students (Peter Bonifacio, John Cain, Mimi Cheong, Goran Duspara and Tracey Richards) from the Master of Information Technology at Swinburne University of Technology, Australia. The available user manual indicated that the last version was 1.1 and its revision date was from November 1998.

According to the authors this tool runs on Windows 95, requires a 80386 processor or above, 8 Mbytes of RAM, 10 Mb of hard disk space and a standard file archiving utility such as, for example, WinZip, for installation purposes. The tool uses activeX technology for displaying charts. The tool's main features are:

- extraction of around 30 distinct OO metrics from source code in Java
- comparison among projects or different versions of the same project
- metrics collection at four distinct abstraction levels: method, class, package (module / subsystem) or system
- definition of two warning levels for each metric; these levels are used, for instance, to select values to display
- metrics display in several graphical display formats (area charts, horizontal and vertical bars, line, mark, pie and fit to curve charts)
- several report options
- metrics data export facility

The tool had an appealing interface and seemed to be user friendly. The origin of the supported metrics was not identified, although, among others, we could distinguish the set proposed by Chidamber and Kemerer from the Sloan School of Management at the MIT. Brian informed the audience that to try this tool one should contact their authors, since it is the Swinburne University of Technology policy that students keep the copyright of their academic assignments' outcome.

2.2. Session 2 - Quality Assessment

After the lunch break we restarted the workshop with session 2, which included two communications.

2.2.1. Towards the Measurement of Reuse by Inheritance in Legacy Systems (Radu Marinescu)

Next presentation was done by Radu Marinescu from the Faculty of Automatics and Computer Science / "Politehnica" University of Timisoara, Romenia.

He argued that the possibility of using object-oriented metrics to support the re-engineering of legacy systems is still put under question. Radu believes that the cause of this fact does not lie in an intrinsic incapacity of metrics to help in re-engineering, but in applying metrics that are inadequate for this purpose. The use of metrics that take full advantage of the information available for a legacy system, instead of using simple, high-level design metrics, increases the chances of successfully applying metrics to re-engineering. The paper presents guidelines for defining such metrics and proposes a multi-layered system of metrics that measures the real reuse of a base class in its descendants. It also reports the first results and conclusions of applying these metrics on three legacy systems. The author believes that the future use of such systems of metrics will offer a systematic and flexible manner of dealing with metrics, increasing the scope of their usability.

2.2.2. Using Metrics for Refactoring (Houari A. Sahraoui, T. Miceli, and R. Godin)

Houari A. Sahraoui from the Computer Science Center of Montreal (CRIM) and the University of Montreal in Canada, presented the following communication.

The authors proposed a technique that aims at detecting and correcting design flaws. This technique uses quality estimation models which are based on the correlation between quality characteristics (e.g. maintainability) and quantitative attributes of software (metrics) and software transformations. The idea behind this work is to relate potential transformations with symptomatic situations. To do that, a four-step

process is proposed. First, a set of transformations that can be applied to improve the quality of a system is chosen. Then, a set of metrics is selected under the basis that they can be good indicators of design anomalies. Third, a study of the impact of the transformations on the metrics in term of variation is done. Finally rules are designed to correct the anomalies using these variations.

The speaker mentioned that the approach was applied to C++ classes. In the majority of the cases, the suggested transformations were adopted. The authors recognize that even if the first results were very satisfactory, the limited number of the studied transformations does not allow to measure in a precise way the impact of the technique. The attendees agreed that further experiences are needed to draw a definite conclusion.

2.3. Session 3 - Metrics Validation

The last technical session, with two additional papers, started after the afternoon coffee break.

2.3.1. An Hypothesis-Based Evaluation of an Object-Oriented Inheritance Metric (Steve Counsell, P. Newson, and K. Mannock)

Next speaker was Steve Counsell from the Department of Computer Science at the Birkbeck College, University of London in the United Kingdom.

He started by observing that various Object-Oriented (OO) metrics have been proposed to capture features of a systems' inheritance hierarchy. Some of these metrics appear more useful than others. In this communication the authors used a single inheritance metric - the Number Of Descendants per class (NOD) to highlight a relationship with the number of friends found in five C++ Systems. Classes containing friends in each of the five systems were found to have considerably less descendants than other classes, indicating that to obtain the benefits of extra functionality, friends will tend to be found in classes deep in an inheritance hierarchy. Their analysis highlights the importance of choosing an inheritance metric that allows hypotheses of these sort to be tested. As a result they compared the applicability of the NOD metric with two other frequently used inheritance metrics.

2.3.2. Validation of Metrics for Object-Relational Databases (Coral Calero, Mario Piattini, Francisco Ruiz, and Macario Polo)

The last speaker was Mario Piattini from the ALARCOS Group at E.S. Informática / U.C.L.M., Ciudad Real in Spain. He presented a work in the databases area which, he argued, the metrics community has neglected. Nowadays a new generation of object-relational databases is coming out. These database systems will have a big impact. They propose a set of metrics for object-relational database systems, characterizing them in a well known formal metric framework.

3. Discussion

The participants selected cooperatively a set of topics for discussion. The selection process included a voting process based on individual scientific interest. The discussion around those topics then took place, ordered by decreasing votes obtained. The topics discussed and the ideas, or even questions, that emerged about them, were the following:

Many New Metrics Continue to be Proposed Every Year in the Literature. Isn't It Time to Start Reducing the Set?

- Horst Zuse observed that more than three hundred OO metrics have already been proposed.
- Reducing sets implies that authors reach an agreement. Under which assumptions?
- Most proposed metrics are static! Don't we need dynamic ones?

Which Are the Most Relevant Obstacles to Metrics Validation?

- Scarce availability of process data.
- No public repository (this rises the question of how could it be managed so that some non-disclosure problems could be withdrawn).
- Need for standard data sets with different recognized variations.

How Can We Use Existing Metrics to Predict Software Quality Attributes?

- As pointed out in the talk of Horst Zuse, the prediction of external variables, like effort, is still a difficult task. The calculation of correlation or the use of regression analysis is only one way to do it and it is not sufficient.
- Statistical based validations with significant samples must be carried on.
- A quality model for software is needed here. The ISO9126 model can be a good starting point. However, there has been a very slow progress within the

ISO JTC1/SC7 towards choosing appropriate metrics to quantify the proposed quality characteristics. Horst Zuse claimed that the reference model itself took 6 years to be published.

What about Metrics in the OO Databases Field?

- We need to define new metrics for Object-Relational Databases.
- Can existing OO metrics be applied to OO database schemes?
- We need to consider both the schema level (DDL) and the manipulation one (DML)

How to "Sell" Metrics to Industry?

- Industry must be convinced that every euro/dollar spent on quality has a return.
- We need product metrics standards, even if not "perfect"!
- Lack of validation is still an obstacle.
- Software industry is reasonably well convinced to use metrics to increase software quality.
- Introduction of a metrics programme is the most difficult task.

Which "Niches" for Research?

- Bridging design-patterns (qualitative) with OO metrics (quantitative) research work.
- Metrics for Use-cases
- Metrics for components technology
- Metrics for dynamic OO design modelling

4. Other Accepted Submissions

The following papers were accepted but not presented orally:

Representation of High Level Models for Reuse (Soliman M. Algeri and Ian Finch)

This paper presents the reuse engineering paradigm of the conceptual framework for reuse(CFR). The framework consists of reuse management and reuse engineering. The reuse engineering paradigm describes a chain of activity that addresses reuse-related software development. The reuse engineering paradigm consists of three processes: model creation, model management, and model utilization. Reuse initially started at the low level (code reuse), but current research is interested in the broader picture of a high level reuse (design and requirement). In the mean time, attention has been paid to the model creation process of high level models (such as use cases and design patterns) and less on the model management and model utilization processes. Their research interest is focused on the model management process. This management process consists of three processes: acquisition, representation, and retrieval of the domain models. The work presented in their paper focused on the representation of high level models such as use cases and design patterns. The objective was to facilitate the production of a complete system design (a design instance) by integrating both models. The use case model and design patterns have been chosen because both are in line with the object-oriented paradigm.

Measuring the Impact of Migration to an Object Oriented Paradigm (David John Leigh, Colin J. Theaker, Neil Blackwood, and Robert Mason)

This paper describes the practical application of metric measurements to an evolving project. The initial implementation in a C-based non OO environment has been assessed using a number of techniques. The migration to a Java-based OO implementation is then discussed.

Towards Techniques for Improved OO Design Inspections (Forrest Shull, Guilherme H. Travassos, and Victor Basili)

This paper is about OO Design Inspections. Software inspections aim to guarantee that a particular software artifact is complete, consistent, unambiguous, and correct enough to effectively support further system development. For instance, inspections have been used to improve the quality of a systems design and code. Typically, inspections require individuals to review a particular artifact, then meet as a team to discuss and record defects, which are then sent to the document's author to be corrected. The position paper discussed some issues regarding the definition and application of reading techniques that can be used to read requirements, use-cases and design artifacts within a domain in order to identify defects among them.

Combining Metrics, Principles, and Guidelines for Object Oriented Design Complexity Reduction (Guilherme H. Travassos and Renata da Silva Andrade)

In their paper, Guilherme Travassos and Renata Andrade argue that the need for large and more complex software systems is ever increasing. The object-oriented paradigm is one of the options that developers have to develop complex software systems, providing them with flexibility to decide about software design and architecture. But, associated to OO software construction, structural complexity is still an issue that must be addressed. This position paper describes results of a work that identified object-oriented standards, guidelines and metrics that can be combined to help developers to observe and reduce OO design structural complexity.

Annex. Participants List with Contacts

Geert Poels (`Geert.Poels@econ.kuleuven.ac.be`)
Department of Applied Economic Sciences, Katholieke Universiteit Leuven, Belgium.

Guido Dedene (`Guido.Dedene@econ.kuleuven.ac.be`)
Department of Applied Economic Sciences, Katholieke Universiteit Leuven, Belgium.

Radu Marinescu (`radum@cs.utt.ro` / `marinesc@fzi.de`)
Faculty of Automatics and Computer Science, "Politehnica" University of Timisoara, Romenia.

Coral Calero (`ccalero@inf-cr.uclm.es`)
Grupo ALARCOS. E.S. Informática. U.C.L.M., Ciudad Real, Spain.

Mario Piattini (`mpiattin@inf-cr.uclm.es`)
Grupo ALARCOS. E.S. Informática. U.C.L.M., Ciudad Real, Spain.

Francisco Ruiz (`fruiz@inf-cr.uclm.es`)
Grupo ALARCOS. E.S. Informática. U.C.L.M., Ciudad Real, Spain.

Macario Polo (`mpolo@inf-cr.uclm.es`)
Grupo ALARCOS. E.S. Informática. U.C.L.M., Ciudad Real, Spain.

Horst Zuse (`zuse@tubvm.cs.tu-berlin.de`)
Technische Universitat Berlin, Germany.

Houari A. Sahraoui (`hsahraou@crim.ca`)
Centre de Recherche de Informatique du Montréal (CRIM)
University of Québec, Canada.

T. Miceli
University of Québec, Canada.

R. Godin
University of Québec, Canada.

Fernando Brito e Abreu (fba@di.fct.unl.pt / fba@inesc.pt)
Faculdade de Ciências e Tecnologia / Universidade Nova de Lisboa, Portugal.
INESC, Portugal.

Luis Ochoa (luis.ochoa@link.pt)
Link, Portugal.

Miguel Goulão (miguel.goulao@inesc.pt)
Faculdade de Ciências e Tecnologia / Universidade Nova de Lisboa, Portugal.
INESC, Portugal.

Steve Counsell (steve@dcs.bbk.ac.uk)
Department of Computer Science, Birkbeck College, University of London, United Kingdom.

P. Newson
Department of Computer Science, Birkbeck College, University of London, United Kingdom.

K. Mannock
Department of Computer Science, Birkbeck College, University of London, United Kingdom.

Soliman M. Algeri (algeri@csc.liv.ac.uk)
Department of Computer Science, University of Liverpool, United Kingdom.

Ian Finch (ian@connect.org.uk)
Department of Computer Science, University of Liverpool, United Kingdom

David John Leigh (D.J.Leigh@soc.staffs.ac.uk)
Staffordshire University, Stafford, United Kingdom

Colin J Theaker (C.J.Theaker@soc.staffs.ac.uk)
Staffordshire University, Stafford, United Kingdom

Neil Blackwood (nb@terrafix.co.uk)
Terrafix Limited, Stoke-on-Trent, United Kingdom

Robert Mason (R.Mason@terrafix.co.uk)
Terrafix Limited, Stoke-on-Trent, United Kingdom

Forrest Shull (fshull@cs.umd.edu)
Experimental Software Engineering Group, Department of Computer Science, University of Maryland, USA

Guilherme H. Travassos (travasso@cs.umd.edu / ght@cos.ufrj.br)
Experimental Software Engineering Group, Department of Computer Science, University of Maryland, USA
Computer Science and System Engineering Department, Federal University of Rio de Janeiro, Brasil

Victor Basili (basili@cs.umd.edu)
Experimental Software Engineering Group, Department of Computer Science, University of Maryland, USA

Renata da Silva Andrade (randrade@cos.ufrj.br)
Computer Science and System Engineering Department, Federal University of Rio de Janeiro, Brasil

Introducing OO Design and Programming with Special Emphasis on Concrete Examples

Erzsébet Angster[1], Joseph Bergin[2], and László Böszörményi[3]

[1] Dennis Gábor College, H-1115 Budapest, Etele út 68, Hungary
angster@okk.szamalk.hu
[2] Pace University, Computer Science, One Pace Plaza, NY 10038, USA
berginf@pace.edu
[3] Universität Klagenfurt, A-9020 Klagenfurt, Universitätstraße 65-67, Austria
laszlo@ifi.uni-klu.ac.at

Abstract. Our report consists of six parts. In the first section we give the workshop announcement, in which there are seven predefined questions. We will try to answer these questions throughout the report. The workshop discussion was dominated by the following: Top-down or bottom-up? How much structured programming should we teach (if any) before the first OO course? In sections 2, 3, and 4, the three workshop leaders present their teaching concepts. In section 5 all the presenters make their contribution based on the predefined questions. Everybody gives a pointer to the URL of his/her presented paper. Finally, in section 6 we try to summarize the workshop results. Three of the presenters (Böszörményi, Bergin and Abreu) presented the extreme points-of-view on which the debate mostly concentrated.

1. Introduction

The main question of the workshop was: *how should we introduce object-orientation*, if one of the goals is to provide students with the ability to build well-designed object-oriented systems? We insisted that every participant would provide a number of examples in order to make the discussion really concrete and practical. Most participants addressed the problem of teaching computer majors at a university. There was, however, one contribution about teaching computers to *excellent* management students and two contributions about courses at a college with partly distance learning students. One teacher was from the USA, the others were from Europe: Austria(2), Germany(1), Hungary(2), Lithuania(1), and Portugal(2). The workshop was very interesting, but there was not much consensus, and we had too little time to discuss the different approaches.

1.1. Workshop Announcement

Teaching and learning design and programming is hard. If one of the goals is to provide students with the ability to build well-designed object-oriented systems, then doing it „right" may be even more demanding. The shift to any new

A. Moreira and S. Demeyer (Eds.): ECOOP'99 Workshops, LNCS 1743, pp. 338–361, 1999.

programming style can take years. Teachers must learn new things, use different tools, interpret the hype, and risk failure. All too often, teachers must accomplish this on their own or with only minimal support. Teachers manage the changes and have good ideas. Some of these ideas are abstract. Some are concrete.

The goal of this one-day workshop is to discuss how teachers teach and students learn object-oriented design and programming, and especially, how concrete examples can help the learning process. One question is when and how it is best to introduce the concepts. Workshop presenters will briefly explain a concrete example and show how they introduce object-oriented programming and design while discussing successes and failures. Besides the course data - topics, preliminary knowledge, and so on - the concrete example must contain the problem specification and a solution that we would expect from students to produce, or preferably, actual student solutions.

Workshop participant's material will be put on the web prior to the workshop. Participants are expected to read submissions before the workshop in order to make workshop time more profitable. Participants will have the opportunity to not only obtain new ideas, but to also offer suggestions for enhancing and improving the exercises.

The material to be issued by the workshop participants is the following:

- Title of the course
- Preliminary knowledge
- Lecture time, laboratory time
- Learning and practice time at home
- Topics of the course (15-20 subtitles)
- List of all materials (books, handouts, web information, exercises etc.) given to students. These materials must be shown on the workshop.
- A concrete exercise specification as the students get it. Answer the following: When (after which topic) is this exercise assigned? What are the execution conditions? How is the exercise evaluated?
- The complete solution of the problem given in the previous point. The solution must be exactly the one, to which we give the maximum points when evaluating.

Questions to be Answered on the Workshop:

- How to teach: top-down or bottom-up? (This question arose in the workshop)
- How much structured programming should we teach (if any) before the first OO course? (Control structures; Writing procedures and functions, parameter passing; arrays; data structures, structured programming, algorithms such as ... etc)
- How much design should we have to teach in the first OO course?
- Which OO concepts should be introduced, and in which order?
- What environment/language do we need to use?
- How should we teach the user interface (screen handling, using windows, etc.)?
- What kind of problems do we have to teach (data manipulation, algorithms, implementation problems, etc.)?

1.2. Workshop Participants

Workshop leaders: Erzsébet Angster, Joe Bergin, László Böszörményi

Presenters: Fernando Brito e Abreu, Miguel Goulão, Beáta Kelemen, Doris Schmedding, Christoph Steindl, Raimundas Vaitkevitcius

2. Introduction of OO with Bottom-Up Approach, Structured First (László Böszörményi)

2.1. Software Engineering Questions

Object-orientation is certainly a new paradigm, it has, however, its long historical development. It did not arise from the sea (like Venus), but on the top of a number of existing concepts. It arose first in the context of *programming languages* (Simula-67) and it took a few decades until it has reappeared in a number of programming languages (Smalltalk, C++, Eiffel, Oberon, Modula-3, Sather, Java etc.). In the second wave a number of object-oriented *design methods* (MVC, Booch, OMT etc.) arose as well. Object-oriented *databases* still have great difficulty being accepted by the market, database technology seems to be stabilized at the compromise solution of object-relational databases. Remarkably, there is very little good *theory* about object-orientation (a positive example is the work of Cardelli and Abadi[1]).

Object-orientation is certainly not the best paradigm for all kinds of software development. Although there are some efforts to develop object-oriented operating systems, compilers and network protocols (just to tell a few example), in these fields the procedural approach is still more widely used. Especially important is the procedural approach in cases where performance is an issue, as object-orientation is not for free. Mixed approaches - object-oriented design and procedural implementation - are of course also possible.

Object-orientation has some concepts that are difficult to understand, and that are therefore often misunderstood. E.g. inheritance and dynamic binding are often sources of unexpected design and/or programming errors. This is partly of course a problem of education. On the other hand, we have good reasons to assume that object-oriented programming in C++ or Java is not the last word in the history of programming. This means that even if object-orientation is the best paradigm today, it will not necessarily remain that forever. A good university education should consider this possibility by concentrating on fundamental concepts and capabilities, instead of exhaustive training in one certain approach.

Structured programming in the sixties has made people first aware that programming must become from an ,,art" a scientific discipline. As opposed to object-orientation, structured programming provided from the very beginning a sound theory (by Dijkstra, Hoare, Dahl, Wirth etc.). Maybe the most important point in this theory is that verification should be done on a very small-scaled basis, and large programs should be composed from verified basic components, with the help of composition rules, that guarantee that verification constraints are not violated by composition. This enables us to build large, correct systems.

Object-orientation relies on this principle, it is a fulfillment of it, however, not the only possible one. Object-orientation relies on a number of notions that are older than object-orientation itself, such as modularization, information hiding, encapsulation, overloading, polymorphism etc. From these observations follows that the conceptual framework of structured programming is more fundamental than that of object-orientation, and the latter can hardly be understood fully, without the previous one. Moreover, it is not unlikely that in ten years object-orientation is substituted by a better paradigm, but the theory and the tools of structured programming seem to have a much higher persistence.

2.2. Didactical Questions

The question whether we should start with object-orientation just at the beginning can be reformulated in a more general form: Should we start teaching top-down or bottom-up? Should we start with the principles of *programming in the large* and come from those to small program portions (top-down) or should we start with *programming in the small* and come gradually to always larger problems? It is clear that the top-down approach suggests to start with object-orientation just at the beginning, the bottom-up approach suggests the opposite of that. Let's take a closer look at both approaches.

- Top-down approach: The motto of this approach is: *First use, next understand, then implement* [5], or *first read, next modify, then create* [2]. The idea is that the students get a non-trivial, pre- fabricated software environment, containing of a number of components, some of them possibly very simple. The student first has to understand the system as a whole and he/she is introduced into more and more details. To put it in another way, he/she gets a big ,,box" recursively containing a number of smaller ,,boxes" which are opened incrementally.
- Bottom-up approach: The motto of this approach is: *First understand, next implement, then use.* Note that this is the way we construct new things: we cannot start with reading or using, because what is new, must be first invented (understood). The student constructs small ,,boxes", which can be built together into always larger ones [4].

Well, on this level of investigation both approaches seem to be meaningful and useful. How can we select among them?

The advantage of the top-down approach is that there is no gap between programming in the small and in the large. Software engineering principles of large, i.e. ,,real" software systems are emphasized just from the beginning. Moreover, the students develop their programs in a non-trivial environment, which is more realistic and often more motivating as well (e.g. ,,fancy" features, such as advanced graphics may be made available very soon).

The disadvantage of this approach is that at the beginning the student is confronted with a large number of concepts and software, he/she cannot understand fully. An argument against this observation could be that a full understanding is not necessary if a *proper abstraction* is available. This is certainly true - however, it is very difficult for beginners to build these abstractions. If they fail in that, then they are sailing with an unsafe boat over a windy ocean of half-understood notions. A second disadvantage can be - it need not be - that some students never understand some fundamental notions (e.g. they never understand properly what is a procedure and what is the difference between a procedure and a method).

The advantage of the bottom-up approach lies in the fact that we start with the fundamental notions. These are not easy either, e.g. the notion of a procedure, of modes of parameter passing, of encapsulation and information hiding etc. are difficult enough. They are, however, orthogonal to the notion of objects and classes, and can and should be understood per se. This approach is also much nearer to the historical way computer science made. This is an extremely important argument. First, because thus the students understand deeply that computer science has developed in a complex process and is still under development. Second, because it is easier to understand basic notions first and the more complex ones later, than the other way around.

The disadvantage of the bottom-up approach is the ,,paradigm-switch" students have to do from programming in the small to programming in the large. This takes certainly some time and could be regarded as lost time. However, we must not forget that this is certainly not the last paradigm-switch in the life-carrier of our students. Looking at the explosive development of software technology, we can be quite sure that our students will have in 20-30 years quite different problems and methods as we have. Therefore, it seems to be a good idea to make such a paradigm-switch quite intentionally, not in an uncontrolled way as many people are forced to do so in practical life, but with academic support. This ensures also that students really understand the special problems of programming in the large and they do not continue to use their small-scale methods in the development of large systems. Altogether, this may need some more time than the top-down approach, however, this time is well invested.

As already mentioned, in the actual context top-down means: start with object-orientation, bottom-up means: start with structured programming. It seems to be a valid argument for starting with object-orientation that advanced topics always go downstream in the curriculum, pushing old topics entirely off at the beginning. Thus, nowadays, we generally do not start programming with assembly, but with a higher level language, we do not start databases with the network, but with the relational model etc. This is true. However, we generally do not start programming with formal specification or databases with deductive databases. ,,Modernization" in the educational process has some very natural limits: students must be able to understand what we teach them. Considering introductory courses, we require even more: they have to prepare understanding of courses that build on the top of these. This gives also an answer regarding the evaluation of an introductory course: it cannot be evaluated in itself, only in the context of an entire curriculum.

Another related question is the selection of the programming language. Languages that are strongly object-oriented (such as Smalltalk, Eiffel and Java) are well-suited for the top-down approach, but not for the other one. Rather conventional languages (such as Oberon, Modula-3, Ada) leave more freedom to choose any of the both methods [6]. Java is now very fashionable. It is however, not ideal for beginners, some of its didactical shortages are listed in [3].

The question of whether we should start with programming or rather with specification and design methods is a quite complex one. Principally it sounds better to say, we start with design methods and programming comes later when we already know how to design. On the other hand, this seems to not work as a didactic concept. Students have extreme difficulties with design methods until they have some solid basis in programming. Abstraction is fine, but to be able to abstract one has to have quite an exact imagination about the details we abstract away. It is extremely difficult to explain somebody on an abstract level what is a table, if he/she has never seen a table. And even if the explanation is good, the experience of having seen a table remains an indispensable experience.

2.3. Philosophic Questions

Even if there is a consensus about the ,,best paradigm", it remains a question whether universities should try to teach final wisdom, or they should rather try to prepare students to be able to make their proper selections. Taking a rather historical approach in the curriculum and letting the students go through some paradigm switches consciously, makes the students aware that in computer science absolute truths are very rare. Rather, it is a discipline based on human effort, requiring good engineers, who are able to understand, to invent, to abstract and to select. To educate students to have these capabilities is exactly the aim of a good academic education. This can be achieved surely both with the top- down and with the bottom-up approach. However, the latter seems to be better in that.

In any case, we should be aware, whether we make our didactical decisions under political pressure (of the industry) or we consider first of all the long-term interests of our students.
Workshop paper:
http://colossus.itec.uni-klu.ac.at/~laszlo/papers/ecoop99/submission.htm

3. Introduction of OO with Java, Objects First (Joseph Bergin)

I am going to discuss some ideas for teaching Java in the first courses and thoroughly integrating object oriented ideas into the course. This is based on a number of pedagogical patterns that I, and others, have developed over the past couple of years. While most of the patterns I will mention were written up by myself, very little of the pedagogy is mine alone. Patterns, in fact, are a way to capture good practice, in this case pedagogical practice. Patterns are discovered in good practice, not invented. Many of these are in use in other institutions and some of these patterns have been given rigorous review in a patterns workshop.

Most of the patterns discussed here can be found in either
http://csis.pace.edu˜bergin/PedPat1.2.html or
http://csis.pace.edu˜bergin/fivepedpat.html.

When I mention a pattern by name it will appear in italics.

The most important pattern here is *Early Bird* . According to this pattern a course should be arranged so that the most important topic is taught as early as possible. First, if possible. For example, in a Calculus course, limits are taught first and then the derivative. The derivative is the key concept, but it is difficult to teach (standard analysis anyway) without the limit first. When teaching OT (Object Technology) the most important topic is polymorphic runtime method dispatch. This is a relatively deep topic (like the derivative), and it needs to be approached with some care. If you try to put off teaching this until late in the course you do the students a disservice as it is fundamental to both the ideas of what object-orientation is all about, and also because this concept fundamentally affects how you approach program design.

Simply put, polymorphic dispatch means that an object is always in control of the code it executes. No specific code execution is ever imposed on an object. In imperative programming, when a function is called, some piece of code (the client) is asking another piece of code (the server) to perform a service. Since function calls are all resolved at compile time, you can look at the text of the program and determine precisely which code will be executed. Therefore we can say that the client is in control since the programmer that writes the client code chooses the specific implementation of the server code to be executed.

In an object-oriented program, however, the client can have no such knowledge. This is because a reference variable can refer to any object in the class with which the variable was declared, or any subclass. Since the subclasses can override methods, when a client sends a message to ,,an object" using a variable referring to the object, the client has no specific knowledge in general of the particular class of the server object. This means that the client does not know (and can not know) which code will be executed when it sends a message. The client can not know because the method dispatch is only ever done at run time using the real type of the object, not the type of the reference that points to it.

The implication of this in practice is that the focus of design in an OO program is on the servers. Each server must be implemented in such a way that it ,,does the right thing" (maintains its invariants and performs the appropriate transformations), according to its own type. The client that sends it a message will need to trust that the code executed is the ,,right" code for that kind of object.

Indeed, in the real world, this is precisely the situation we have when we as a person go to a professional for service. When I go to a doctor, I am the client and the doctor is the server. I make service requests of the doctor, who will carry out some appropriate process, perhaps unknown to me, to fulfill the service. I do not direct the specific actions of the doctor and to do so would be foolish.

That is why we encapsulate behavior in the server, so that the server can be responsible for the correct performance of the service.

Since the focus of design is on the servers and their services, an OO program looks very different from a non-OO program. OO is not an incremental add on to procedural/ imperative programming. It is a completely different kind of undertaking.

Then the question arises on HOW to teach this topic. The answer is not to reveal the inner workings of an OO run- time system that implements it. It is actually much easier than that. If the instructor always proceeds by doing design from the standpoint of the objects performing services, and focuses on the objects and their responsibilities, then the stage will be set. If the students at the very beginning see examples of programs with several different kinds of interacting objects, and the instructor uses a *Consistent Metaphor* to describe what is going on, the students will naturally get the right idea. One appropriate metaphor is to think of the objects as if they were people. When you ask a person to do something for you, that person carries out the request using his or her own process. When you send a message to an object that object executes its own code. The object is in control, and the code is owned by the object.

One of my key examples when teaching this is to talk about the process of the professor asking the students to do a piece of homework. In this case the professor becomes a ,,homework client" and the student is a ,,homework server." The client can only make a request, and each server (all of the same generic type–student, but with various subtypes) interprets the message in light of precisely what kind of student they are AND their current ,,state" of being. Therefore, the professor gets back a wide range of results from the various student ,,servers."

I also formalize the notion of client-server relationships when I discuss message passing. And note that the client server relationship imposes a ,,role" on each partner for only a single ,,transaction". What is this moment a server, may next moment become a client of another object, which often happens when a server, having received a request, requires help of another object in carrying out its own service.

When discussing the execution of the program, I don't talk about the cpu executing code. I talk about the objects executing their own code. A message is just asking an object to execute one of its methods for me and I trust it (actually its implementor) that the code it executes will faithfully carry out the service that I've requested. When the students have more sophistication, I deepen this idea a bit. When a message is sent from one object to another, the executing object has a cpu (or it couldn't be executing). When it sends the message, it sends the cpu along with it, so the server object then has a cpu on which to execute its method. The client gives up the cpu and must therefore wait until the server completes the request, at which me the cpu will come back from the server to the client. In the interim, the server may have made additional requests of other objects, passing the cpu on with those requests, but eventually getting it back. Note that this metaphor extends nicely to a multi-threaded environment in which there are several (virtual) cpu's and also helps explain why bad things can happen when two cpu's arrive at the same object at the same time.

Teaching objects in such a way that it is clear that the object is in control (owns its own code, executes its own code...) means that polymorphic dispatch becomes the only thing that will enter students' heads when they think about the execution model. A static model won't even occur to them. However, when sufficient groundwork has been laid (inheritance and overriding methods) I do make it explicit and name it ,,The Fundamental Polymorphism Principle": Every message sent is interpreted in the context of the object executing the code.

If this polymorphic dispatch rule were not the case, then hierarchies would be completely unworkable. The client code would need to somehow keep track of the specific type of each object. This is harder in practice than it sounds. Suppose you have a stack of A's. If B's are A's, the stack can hold B's as well. If the client were in control, you would need to keep track of which object had which type so that the client could assure that each object, when removed from the stack, executed the right code when asked to y(). But with polymorphic dispatch, the client doesn't need to know, since the server knows its own code.

Because of all of this, an OO program is a web of interacting objects and these objects are designed relatively independently of one another. The dependence is only at the service interfaces. This has two beneficial results. One is that the focus of design is clear, and can proceed in relatively small units. The other is that an object-oriented program in operation (web of server-client) LOOKS like a data flow diagram that is a standard systems analysis documentation technique. The implication of this is that there is much less of a cusp in OT between analysis/design on one hand and implementation on the other. The one flows smoothly into the other. The opportunity for educators in this is that you now can do analysis and design in a programming course without it detracting from the main task. Furthermore, if OT is employed with certain design patterns, the maintenance cycle is eased and rationalized as well.

Starting the Course

I think the introductory course should start with a few days of talking about objects and what they are. Careful here. I didn't say Classes. Objects. This can be done before ever opening the course textbook. Objects have behavior, they have responsibilities, they interact with one another (client/server discussion here). They know things (eventually their state) and they can do things (eventually their methods.) There is another pedagogical pattern, *Student Design Sprint*, that can be used in the classroom as a team exercise to give the students experience in finding objects and doing simple design. Students can document their object interactions with simple diagrams and with CRC cards. These simple diagrams can use a visual syntax taken from OO modeling tools, though in a simplified form. One simple design sprint exercise is to design a coffee machine. A good design requires about six classes and one or two of them are instantiated several times.

I think that the design of this coffee machine is probably about the limit of what could be expected of students at the beginning of the program. But note that it has the following interesting(and critical) features. First, there are several kinds of objects and they interact, and second, at least one of the object types is instantiated more than once. I think both of these are critical to teaching object think. So this example has about the minimum complexity of a real system. See the paper at http://csis.pace.edu˜bergin/papers/OOAD.html for a description of a *Student Design Sprint* to develop the coffee machine.

Another important pattern, not in the papers cited, is *Readers-Writers.* The basic idea here is that students can read and learn from artifacts more complex than they can build. So at this stage, the professor can show some more complex designs and have students examine and discuss them. Some can be good, and some can be less good. You can give them a *Fixer-Upper*, which is any artifact that has an intentional flaw (or flaws), but is otherwise well designed. The exercise can be to find and fix the flaw. This can be a team or individual exercise and can be done in class or as homework.

Notice that classes haven't been discussed at all yet, but that is the next topic. The question arises, how do you implement objects in a software system, and the answer is to use classes. At this point you want to get students to begin looking at (not writing) classes. Instead of a bottom up approach in which you try to teach the (many) details in some more or less logical order, you can try the *Larger Than Life* pattern. Give them a very well designed and implemented program that is too big for them to understand at this point. It will have several classes, each with a few methods and a few instance variables. It doesn't need to be overly complex, but it should be something like the coffee machine above or maybe a little less. It is a Reader-Writer, of course and it could be a Fixer-Upper. If it is the latter, then it has a few syntax errors, one or two run-time errors, and a fairly simple intent (logic) error. They are to fix it. The compiler can help them with syntax errors, of course.

In any case, the class discussion about the *Larger Than Life* program should proceed from the top down– from overall design to low-level detail. Look at the classes as descriptions of objects. Look at the method names and parameters as descriptions of responsibilities/ behaviors. In the initial discussion avoid questions about assignments, initializations, and if statements. We are primarily interested in having them look at the overall plan of the program and how it relates to our object design. The input parameters describe information sent from the client to the server, and the return value type represents information returned by the client at the end of the fulfillment of the request. The types of these help specify the nature of the client/server contract.

At this point in the course, all member variables should be private (some say they should ALWAYS be private) and almost all member functions should be public. Your examples should be simple enough that private member functions aren't yet needed and you don't need to talk about ,,helper functions" yet.

The next important pedagogical pattern to consider is *Spiral.* Here we try to teach only enough of a complex topic to get the students to be able to solve interesting problems. We teach a number of topics to no great depth and get them started. Then we cycle around again, teaching more complete versions of the topics taught earlier, as well as adding first cycle level discussions of additional topics. In the current instance, you can introduce integer variables, simple assignment statements, simple boolean expressions (not variables) and simple if statements. With classes, methods, and just these few tools, very complex problems may be explored. So, if your *Larger Than Life* is carefully chosen, you will be able to answer the questions about it in a reasonable amount of time, and yet the students have seen (and run, and modified, perhaps) a real example.

The third element of the course, after objects and then classes, is this first cycle on programming in the small with if and assign. You don't need loops, but if you want to, do just a simple while, with only simple tests. You don't need a lot of operators, or primitive data, though you might want to introduce strings so that you can produce some outputs on standard out.

Assurance time. I know that using something like a *Larger Than Life* (especially if it is also a *Fixer- Upper*) is scary to many educators used to teaching with a more bottom up style. I have used these techniques and they really work. You do have to guide the discussion, however. You can probably point out a few dangers in this technique, and so could I. However, the danger in the bottom up method is that the students are bored for too long doing things of no particular interest and they only get to see how ,,real" programs are put together after a long and painful apprenticeship. Nothing is more boring than a chapter on all of the variations of selection (if, if-else, switch, break,...) when you don't have enough overall tools to write interesting programs.
Workshop paper: http://csis.pace.edu˜bergin/PedPat1.2.html

4. Introduction of Programming with Bottom-Up Approach, Early OO (Erzsébet Angster)

There are two important viewpoints we have to take into consideration before beginning any teaching. First, we have *to set up the main goal*, i. e. what we want to reach with the students, or, which is the same, what we want to teach in the complex entirety. Second, we have *to reach the predefined goal in the shortest possible time*, so that both the students and the teacher could be happy. The main goal today is to provide students with the ability to build well-designed object-oriented systems, but it is also important to provide them with the ability to change the paradigm when the time comes. I think that on this workshop some antagonisms and problems were originated from the different goals. But let us assume that the main goal is to suit the today's requirements to build OO software on a high level. To define the goal, we have to determine the material, which fulfills these requirements. On another workshop it would be an interesting job to assemble such a material (topics list). To reach our goal (teach the material) is mainly a didactical question. The teaching time is more or less restricted on any course, besides material is undoubtedly large, so doing it "right" is an extremely demanding job. The following questions have great importance in the problem of teaching OO.

How to Teach: Top-Down or Bottom-Up? I think that the most important thing is to teach in a *"step by step, based on patterns"* style, in which students, even the slower-witted ones, can follow the course/book with enthusiasm and with not too much unnecessary energy and despairs. My personal experience is, that it is easier to do with a *mainly bottom-up style*, extending it by pointing ahead discussions at some places. So, the student is continuously aware of what he/she will achieve, but can understand every step one by one and continuously gets a real sense of achievement. With a bottom-up style it is possible to write running programs from the very beginning, so that the student can look and feel the result of his/her development process. It does not mean however, that you have to code everything. It is possible to fully understand a model on the design level. A good practice is to play the model with the students. This way you can teach the model of a coffee machine, the container object or even the event-driven programming. It is also important, of course, to teach always the 'good' style, otherwise the investment time cannot be a minimum.

How Much Structured Programming Should We Teach (If Any) Before the First OO Course? Every program consists of algorithms working on either primitive or complex data or objects. Therefore we have to teach to understand and construct data types and algorithms. Since this is the first step to understand any programming, it is possible to teach structured style first. It is very important, however, not to teach too much of the structured style. If we do it, enthusiastic and demanding students would make large structured style libraries. It is dangerous, since this will be their mother style and the paradigm shift will be very hard for them. If we teach only some structured programming (even in an OO language), the learning process can be easy, and if we introduce the OO early, the paradigm shift problem does not occur. It is also good to begin with OO, but it is important not to show too much, later explained concepts. For example, if we use Java as the first programming language, there are many things to explain before writing the first program: without explaining the concepts of class, method, class method, visibility etc., the line *public static void main (String args [])* is quite disturbing for a beginner. If we begin with an OO language, after introducing the simple OO concepts we can teach the simple algorithms in a single class, then we can continue with more and more difficult OO concepts.

How Much Design Should We Have to Teach in the First OO Course? Everything should be done parallel with design from the beginning. It is important that the student thinks on a design level, so that the design can be his/her mother tongue. It is possible to teach collaboration and class diagrams from the very beginning, even before any programming.

Which OO Concepts Should Be Introduced, and in Which Order? For a short time, you can teach design on a certain level without programming. When writing programs, the order is the following: first using objects, then creating one class, writing methods, using it. After it we can connect the objects and classes (association), and reuse the classes by inheritance. At the beginning we have to teach only a very small part of any class library. My opinion is that establishing the collaboration diagram before or parallel with the class diagrams is very important. The collaboration diagram is the projection of the program, which is closer to the reality. So the student can see the programs structure more easily.

What Environment/Language Do We Need to Use? This is a difficult question. There is no good OO language we can begin with. A good teaching language and its class library must be very simple. Java is difficult, since one cannot even input and output data in a simple way. This problem can be solved with an instructor's package, but this is quite an uncomfortable way. Another problem with Java is, that in many cases the concepts are not clear enough for beginners: for instance the array as an object is not easily explainable.

How Should We Teach the User Interface (Screen Handling, Using Windows,etc.)? To write interesting and good-looking programs is indispensable to the successful learning process. The problem is, that the GUI libraries are too complex for a beginner (particularly the event driven control), so we have to begin programming with simple input and output. However, as mentioned in the previous point, this is not an easy question.

What Kind of Problems Do We Have to Teach (Data Manipulation, Algorithms, Implementation Problems, etc.)? Software becomes more and more sophisticated. Since a programmer's talent and capacity does not increase in a significant extent, the abstraction level must increase continuously. Since today it is impossible to write programs without strong modeling, modeling is on the first place to teach. Hence, we have to teach more modeling, and less algorithms and data structures then before. It is important however to teach an algorithmic thinking and the characteristic features of a good algorithm. We have to teach the basic algorithms such as sorting and searching on a basic level.

The following workshop paper shows an OO course after learning two semesters of structured programming. Our college plans to change the curriculum, so that we begin programming with OO.
Workshop paper: http://www.gdf.hu/angster/ecoop99w21/ae.htm

5. Participants Contributions to the Predefined Questions, and Their Concrete Examples

In his section each workshop presenter gives his/her contribution based on the predefined questions in short. They were also asked to touch upon the questions:

What have I learned on the workshop? and *What were the most important discrepancies?* After the questions the URL of the concrete examples, which he/she presented on the workshop, is given.

5.1. Top-Down Approach, Strong Design (Fernando Brito e Abreu and Miguel Goulão)

How Much Structured Programming Should We Teach (If Any) Before the First OO Course? There were two non-consensual approaches presented during the workshop:

- Structured programming should be taught first, with some focus on basic algorithms and data structures. This should then be followed by the introduction of abstract data types. OO would then be presented as the result of a historical evolution of the way people design and implement the software systems. Ideally, the first programming courses should be designed to make the transition as smooth as possible, so that the basic OO concepts would be introduced as a logic evolution of the previous approaches to cope with their problems. The approaches described by *Steindl, Vaitkevitcius, Kelemen, Böszörményi and Angster* assume that the students took a previous procedural programming course.
- OO should be taught from the start. An argument for favouring this approach is the paradigm shift problems programmers suffer when changing from a procedural approach towards an object-oriented one. For most interesting problems, the conceptual gap between the OO approach and the problem formulation is smaller than its procedural counterpart. The reuse of didactical-purposed components created or adapted by the lecturing team, widens the possibility of development of more challenging and interesting problems for the students. The first language / paradigm learnt makes the most lasting influence. Therefore, we should teach first the one that we think is the best. Agreeing with this approach were the submissions of Schmedding (although the described course was not the first OOP course in her student's curricula), Bergin and Abreu.

Students should be exposed to the different paradigms (including others such as functional and logic programming). This helps them to be able to choose the paradigm that helps them most to deal with a given problem. If there is not enough time to cover all those paradigms, then the focus should be turned towards the one that is more likely to be useful, in most real-life problems (OO).

How Much Design Should We Have to Teach in the First OO Course? With the creation of UML most courses are changing to use it for design. All the attendants agreed that there is no point in overwhelming the students with all the aspect of it, therefore, only a relatively small subset should be used. The class diagrams form the minimal subset, although many approaches to this problem also include interaction diagrams. The students should be exposed to some fairly simple design patterns (e.g. the Iterator), so that they could at least understand them, although not necessarily be able to implement them.

Which OO Concepts Should Be Introduced, and in Which Order? Object, object state, object identity, class, instantiation, encapsulation, information hiding, message passing, associations, inheritance, polymorphism, generalisation, specialisation, composition, reuse, modularity, design patterns?

What Environments Do We Need to Use? The usage of visual programming environments that incorporate compiling and debugging facilities, as well as syntax highlighting, helps students focusing on the more essential aspects of good design and programming principles. The usage of some sort of design tool is also recommended, although there is no consensus about the best one, for pedagogical purposes.

What Language Should We Adopt? Many prefer to use languages that are better suited for pedagogic purposes (such as Modula-3, Object-Oriented Pascal, Oberon and Smalltalk). C++ is regarded as a very complex language for educational purposes, at least for inexperienced students. Java seems to be a good compromise between market needs and pedagogical ones. When it comes to choosing a pure OO language or a hybrid one, courses that start by a procedural approach tend to use one of the latter group. Another position on this subject supports the usage of different languages so that the students do not confuse the concepts of OO with their implementation in a specific language. The student's curricula are a constraint to the latter approach. If only a few programming courses are taken, the usage of several programming languages is not feasible. Regardless of the programming language and environment, all agreed that the main emphasis should be on the underlying concepts, not on implementation issues.

How Should We Teach the User Interface (Screen Handling, Using Windows, etc.)? In a first course, exposing the students to the petty details of user interfaces is counter-productive. User interfaces should be as simple as possible for the students to use. While some simply do not use GUI's, others use components libraries that enable students to use graphical interfaces without increasing the overall complexity of the problems given to the students. If such libraries are available and were developed with pedagogical purposes, then they are a good alternative to just using ASCII interfaces, as they might increase the student's enthusiasm.

What Kind of Problems Do We have to Teach (Data Manipulation, Algorithms, Implementation Problems, etc.)? The problems should have a strong design orientation, while teaching OO programming, especially during the earlier phases of the courses. More complex algorithms, usage and implementation of complex data structures such as binary trees, linked lists, etc, are normally explored further on a follow-up course. If the students start by learning a procedural approach, their algorithmic abilities are strengthened during that course, thus allowing for more complex problems (in what algorithms are concerned) in the OO course.

If, on the other hand, students start by learning the OO paradigm, the problems should evolve in a spiral way. In other words, by reusing components, students would be exposed to increasingly detailed problems and solutions.

There were different approaches to the dichotomy between programming in the small, versus programming in the large. While all agreed that, at some point, the students should be motivated to build their software in a way that is suitable for programming in the large, the opinion about the moment of introducing these concepts varied. The approaches that introduce OO programming from the start tend to introduce this earlier, through the idea of reusing components built by someone else. Other approaches start from building the small components and then showing bottom-up how they can be built for larger projects.
Workshop paper:
http://www.esw.inesc.pt/ftp/pub/esw/mood/ecoop99/workshop21

5.2. Laying the Foundations Is Essential (Beáta Kelemen)

How to Teach: Top-Down or Bottom-Up? 2000 years ago Democritos introduced the idea of atoms: he supposed that these small particles make up the whole world. It was a viable idea then, and I think it is still a good approach today. Teaching using the bottom-up method means starting at the smallest particles and building up the students' knowledge from these small atoms until they are ready to piece the puzzle together and write complex programs using the appropriate small blocks.

Why should our students be ready to write huge, complicated OO programs at the end of the first semester? An architect student is not expected to be able to design a skyscraper in the first year: they have to learn the basics of architecture first: laws of physics, the usage of the different kinds of bricks and other building materials, the theory of statics, forces etc. I have learnt - and I think any serious system designer would agree on this - that writing a correct, efficient, extendible, maintainable program is as hard as drawing up a plan for a complex building. So I do not want to see my students developing fancy programs just to make them enjoy programming during the lessons when they still have problems with the fundamentals. It is possible to write some OOP programs using window techniques without understanding the basics - but what is the point in them? Compare it to a plan of a bridge which was designed without applying the laws of statics: it might be nice, it might even stand - but the question is for how long? Students who start writing full-blown OOP applications without enough practice regarding the fundamentals will soon feel a kind of uncertainty and this can seriously hinder their work and advancement in OOP.

How Much Structured Programming Should We Teach (If Any) Before the First OO Course? I think understanding even the easiest OO program („HelloWorld") needs such a big amount of programming knowledge that forces the teacher to start long explanations. To avoid overwhelming the students at this point it is essential to start with a short introduction of structured programming at the very beginning of the course. This should contain only the basics (writing max. 60-80 line-long programs) and should not take too much time, and this way the students do not have to face the so-called paradigm shift.

How Much Design Should We Have to Teach in the First OO Course? We start the OO course with designing and we go on with coding only later keeping the emphasis on the design part as well. Even the shortest program is not prepared without any design in our course.

Which OO Concepts Should Be Introduced, and in Which Order? Object, class, Instantiation, Message, Responsibility, Encapsulation, Information hiding, Associations, Generalization, Specialization, Inheritance, Visibility, Polymorphism, Dynamic binding, Virtual methods, Containers, Object stereotypes.

What Environment/Language Do We Need to Use? You can choose from several environments and languages, but in my opinion, it is important to find an easy-to-use IDE to make the best use of the students' time during the lessons. That is why I do not agree to use the pure Java Development Kit, for example. I do not think that students get so accustomed to an environment that they are not able to change to another one later if they have to.

How Should We Teach the User Interface (Screen Handling, Using Windows, etc.)? No matter how tempting it is to use the GUI, I do not advise that. It is much more beneficial to start with simple screen handling and not to confuse the students with the background process of event handling.
Workshop paper:
http://www.gdf.hu/angster/ecoop99w21/kb.htm

5.3. Objects First, Modeling Is Important (Dorris Schmedding)

The question if to start the education with imperative concepts and then switch to object orientation or to start with object oriented concepts at the very beginning gave the most rise to controversy.

Objects First. For a long time, object oriented programming was considered an advanced subject that was taught late in the curriculum. To avoid the problem of paradigm shift object orientation should be introduced at the beginning of the education. Learning to program in an object oriented style seems to be very difficult after becoming familiar with the procedural style. We know that experienced programmers need about a year for the paradigm shift from procedural to object oriented. On the other hand, inexperienced students do not seem to have any difficulty to understand object oriented concepts if they learn them first. That leads to the assumption that the shift causes the problem, not the object oriented concepts.

If we do not use a pure object oriented language students experienced in programming with a procedural language are not encouraged to change their style. They can write programs for a long time believing them object oriented while missing all important concepts. If we teach object orientation we must do objects first and should use a pure object oriented language.

Modeling Is Important. The object oriented paradigm shapes our whole way of thinking how to map a realistic problem into a program. It determines in fundamental ways the structure of even a simple program. To support this new way of thinking we have to integrate the modeling of a system in our first lessons. We should not only use class diagrams to demonstrate the static structure of a program but also the dynamic model to analyze the dynamic behavior of the system, how the objects interact and exchange messages.

Graphical User Interfaces Are Difficult. State of the art is the use of a framework to realize the graphical user interface. The user causes events triggering the execution of actions developed by the programmer. The sequence of the execution of the actions is determined by the global event loop. The programmer does not have to be concerned with managing this loop. On one hand this is helpful for the programmer on the other hand this is very difficult to understand for the beginners. Although graphical user interfaces are classical object oriented topics I would teach them only at the end of the education in object orientation.

The Role of Exercises to a Course. The theory of learning distinguishes different levels of knowledge. After having heard a lecture the students should understand the object oriented concepts. Normally our courses are combinations of lectures and exercises. After having done the exercises every week successfully the students should be able to use the object oriented concepts. The description of the tasks contain exact instructions which of the new learned concepts have to be used. This kind of training is necessary in this phase of learning to become familiar with the new concepts.

Laboratories to Consolidate the Knowledge. But our final aim must be to make the students able to decide which of the object oriented concepts is most suitable to solve a realistic complex problem. Small examples come to their limits if you want to discuss different design alternatives. For example a model with a small number of classes doesn't offer the opportunity to connect the classes differently. Moreover it is difficult to present the process of design in a lecture.

In Dortmund we established the "Software-Praktikum" to consolidate the students' knowledge of object oriented software development and to show the benefits of object orientation. The students solve complex problems in form of projects in a team using an object oriented analysis and design method and the object oriented programming language BETA. The descriptions of the given problems are formulated vaguely so that different solutions are possible. The students discuss the advantages and disadvantages of different realizations. Some decisions may be wrong but lead to valuable experiences. Students learn the difficult development of complex software only by doing it themselves.
Workshop paper:
http://ls10-www.cs.uni-dortmund.de˜schmeddi/

5.4. OO Is Programming in the Large (Christoph Steindl)

The discussion at the workshop made it clear that there is no single best way to teach object-oriented programming. The question whether we teach object-orientation top-down or bottom-up cannot be answered in isolation. We must take into account the whole curriculum, the overall goals as well as on the previous knowledge of the students. For the situation that we have at the Johannes Kepler University in Linz, we think that a bottom-up approach is best for our students.

We believe that OOP is ,,programming in the large" and should be preceded by courses on ,,programming in the small". OOP is a ,,packaging" technique that helps one to deliver the services of a program in small packages (i.e. classes) with a well-defined interface. Before one can build a package, however, one has to know how to build its contents. This is a non-trivial task, and it doesn't have much to do with OOP.

Programming in the small (i.e. building the package contents) has to teach the following concepts: Algorithmic thinking, type concept, control structures, together with assertions and invariants, visibility and life times of variables, parameter passing concepts, recursion, dynamic data structures and pointer handling, program decomposition techniques (e.g. stepwise refinement, divide and conquer, etc.).

Programming in the large (i.e. OOP) then adds to this mainly the following concepts:

- Data abstraction. The students should learn how to structure a program into classes so that the complexity of the program is reduced and the readability and maintainability are increased. Concepts that are to be understood are information hiding, interfaces, coupling and cohesion, and programming by contract.
- Extensibility. The students should learn how to extend prefabricated classes and to adapt them to their needs. They should understand the power of frameworks, and learn how to use them, how to design them and how to

document them. Concepts that are to be learned are inheritance, dynamic binding, abstract classes, frameworks, and programming by difference.

From this comparison we conclude that it is not a good idea to teach OOP to programming novices. They would have to learn both the concepts of OOP and the more fundamental programming concepts at the same time. The result is confusion. We don't deny that it is possible to start programming in an OO language (e.g. in Smalltalk), but we don't think that it is good from a pedagogical point of view. Good examples for data abstraction and extensibility cannot be taught with toy examples. In order to convince the students of the power of OOP we need to present large and realistic case studies. This is only possible after the students already know a little bit about programming.

The following list gives an overview of the topics of the course:

1. Introduction: Basic idea of OOP, object-oriented thinking, information hiding, data abstraction, inheritance, dynamic binding, terminology, history
2. Programming by Contract
3. Object-Oriented Design
4. UML Notation: Object model, dynamic model and functional model
5. Class Libraries and Frameworks
6. Design Patterns: Creational, structural and behavioral patterns
7. Components
8. Smalltalk and C++
9. Implementation of Object-Oriented Languages

Our OOP course has a special emphasis on design patterns. Patterns are an ideal vehicle for teaching. Starting from a convincing example, we can extract the reusable concept behind it. Students will remember the example and therefore also the concept behind it. By collecting several such examples the students acquire expert experience, which would otherwise take years to learn.

Our course is oriented on concepts and not on a particular programming language. All the concepts such as data abstraction, inheritance, dynamic binding, UML modeling, frameworks, design patterns are taught in a general form (mostly with a graphical notation). Currently we us Oberon-2 as a programming language because the students already were exposed to it in the previous semesters. In the future we plan to switch to Java because the introductory programming courses will also use Java. We only use programming environments that are freely available.

Orthogonal to problem of a bottom-up or top-down approach are pedagogical issues: Joe Bergin pointed us to the work about pedagogical patterns (http://www-lifia.info.unlp.edu.ar/ppp/) which provides many ideas to make the learning process easier and more effective for the students.

Workshop paper:
http://www.ssw.uni-linz.ac.at/Research/Papers/Ste99c.html

5.5. Concepts First, Design Later (Raimundas Vaitkevitcius)

What Have I Learned on the Workshop? The existence of the top-down approach in teaching OO. ,,Historical" approach in teaching programming (László Böszörményi).

What Were the Most Important Discrepancies? Between top-down and bottom-up approaches.

How to Teach: Top-Down or Bottom-Up? My approach is based on the following basic principles:

1. Concepts first, design later.
2. Start from simple things and move to advanced and complicated ones.
3. Learning should be interesting for students, teaching should be interesting for teachers.

The bottom-up approach corresponds the first two principles better than the top-down one. However, the top-down approach is also needed. After the workshop, I am inclined to use some combination of these two approaches.

How Much Structured Programming Should We Teach (If Any) Before the First OO Course? There are at least two other alternatives: functional programming and logic programming (some would say ,,constraint programming"). It is easier to write small programs, therefore we should start from writing small programs. For such programs, OO advantages are not essential. Besides, we have often no choice. Most of my students start programming already in their secondary schools. Their first languages are Pascal, Basic, Logo. It is also possible to start teaching programming directly from OO. There should be situations in which this approach is the best or close to the best. I do not believe in the existence of the one ,,right" way that would be the best in all situations and for all students.

How Much Design Should We Have to Teach in the First OO Course? If we have only one semester, we cannot give too much time for teaching design. However, design cannot be ignored also in the first OO (or programming in general) course. We cannot teach OO-concepts without programming. And we cannot program without design. Even very small programs should be designed, at least in our brains, before we write them. Think first, code later. However, these designs should not necessarily be laid down on paper or saved in files. We have to speak about design issues since the beginning, we can use simple design tools, give students simple examples. Advanced design should be taught in the second OO-course.

Which OO Concepts Should Be Introduced, and in Which Order? Objects and messages; classes and methods; instances; encapsulation; inheritance and polymorphism; instance variables and class variables, aggregation.

What Environment/Language Do We Need to Use? It depends on many circumstances. Personally, I would prefer a two semester course with two (very) different languages.

How Should We Teach the User Interface (Screen Handling, Using Windows, etc.)? At the beginning, we could use some simple interface means of some standard library. Important is to choose an appropriate language and class library, so that the programming of the user interface would be easy for beginners.

What Kind of Problems Do We have to Teach (Data Manipulation, Algorithms, Implementation Problems, etc.)? We can start from simple data and existing objects' manipulation algorithms. Then we can teach how to create and use new objects. New methods. New classes. Using inheritance. Aggregation. Then students can design and implement simple applications (some 5 new classes). If we have time and students work in teams, we can also develop and implement relatively big projects (some 20-50 classes).
Workshop paper: http://www.vdu.lt/staff/informatics/Vaitkev.htm

6. Summary (Erzsébet Angster)

Teaching and learning OO is neither trivial, nor easy. Not even the list of themes we have to teach is obvious. There is not a general agreement on which are the more suitable teaching concepts, languages, software, and course text books.

In the workshop we learned eight teaching methods, of which some were quite different. It turned out to be a good idea to show concrete exercises, since it is much easier to discuss anything through examples. As I remember from other conference workshops with similar themes, big debates originated always from concrete examples. One can speak about teaching top-down generally, but if you realize that it means the design of a complete home-heating system on the first lecture for novices, you might be suspicious.

Originally we wanted to discuss the six predefined questions throughout the workshop, but we could not carry out this plan for two reasons. First, the time turned out to be short, second, Böszörményi and Bergin represented two extreme approaches, and much time passed in the spirit of their debate. There were two presenters (Abreu, Bergin), who had very special top-down OO approaches, and in connection with these concepts, an extra question arose: *How to teach: top-down or bottom-up?* After all, there were two main questions the discussion mostly went on:

6.1. How to Teach: Top-Down or Bottom-Up?

There were completely different opinions on this subject. Most of the presenters represented the bottom-up approach, while Abreu and Bergin propagated the top-down concept. Abreu's approach was quite noteworthy: he makes a class diagram of an airline company information system in the first semester. Students learn the UML and Delphi with a simple user interface (Read and Write statements), and they are able to translate design to code and vice versa. Bergin leaves a lot of things open to see the whole picture first. Böszörményi represents a historical approach, which is obviously a bottom-up one. Steindl teaches 'programming in the small' first (structured), before 'programming in the large' (OO). Angster argued that the real question is not whether a bottom-up or top-down approach should be followed. It is much more important that the topics are introduced step by step, not leaving too many loose ends in the knowledge. The bottom-up approach fits better for this concept.

6.2. How Much Structured Programming Should We Teach (If Any) Before the First OO Course?

This was the most controversial issue on the workshop and there was no consensus at the end of the workshop. The following questions arose during the discussion:

- Do we have enough time to reach our goal, namely to give the students the ability to build OO software?
- Isn't OO design and programming too difficult for a beginner?
- Do we have to teach the structured and other programming methods besides OO?
- Isn't the paradigm shift too painful later? Must it be painful?
- What will be the student's mother language?

Abreu, Bergin, and Schmedding teach OO from the very beginning. They say that the way of looking at software first is determinant for the future. Furthermore, beginning with structured programming, the paradigm shift is painful, and we have not enough time for building real OO systems.

Böszörményi teaches in a traditional and historical way - he adds Object-Orientation on the top of the structured programming in a bottom-up style, introducing the OO concepts smoothly and continuously.

Angster, Kelemen, Steindl and Vaitkevitcius teach structured programming first, OO later. They say that students have to understand simple things first, then they can deal with the more and more complicated problems. In addition, learning the simple basics of data types and algorithm construction helps the understanding of the OO concepts. They agreed however, that in case of learning too much structured programming, the paradigm shift problem occurs.

Although the other predefined questions were also important, we had no time to discuss them. The presenters gave their view in their contribution. Everybody agreed on the importance of giving the students the ability of building good software and changing the paradigm. Hence, if we have enough time, it is advisable to teach the different kinds of programming methods, such as structured, functional, logic, etc. Everybody agreed also, that the programming environment, the class libraries, and the user interface must be simple for novices. However, it is also important to engage the student's attention by giving as interesting problems and solutions as possible.

I can state that we have all learnt a lot on the workshop. Of course many extra questions arose and many questions remained opened. But I hope that in the future we can continue exchanging our thoughts, teaching experiences and our concrete examples.

References

[1] Martin Abadi and Luca Cardelli. *A Theory of Objects.* Springer Verlag, Heidelberg, 1996.

[2] Owen Astrachan and David Reed. Aaa and cs1: The applied apprenticeship approach to cs. In *SIGCSE'95*, 1995.

[3] Laszlo Boeszoermenyi. Why java is not my favorite first-course language. *Software - Concepts & Tools*, 1998.

[4] Laszlo Boeszoermenyi and Carsten Weich. *Programming in Modula-3 - An Introduction in Programming with Style.* Springer Verlag, Heidelberg, 1996.

[5] Thoman Hilburn. A top-down approach to teaching an introductory computer science course. In *SIGCSE'93*, 1993.

[6] Roland Mittermeir and Laszlo Boeszoermenyi. Choosing modula-3 as "mother tongue". In *Joint Modular Programming Languages*, 1997.

Panel Session: Object Technology and Systematic Reuse

Sholom Cohen

Software Engineering Institute, Carnegie Mellon University
sgc@sei.cmu.edu - http://www.sei.cmu.edu/plp/

Abstract. The continuous demand for software of ever-increasing complexity will change our current approach to software development. In the future, the creation of software will apply increasing levels of automation to the development process. The application of componentware will become commonplace and development will move from the back office to the application user's workstation. All of these developments point to an essential increase in the many forms of software reuse. This panel brought together experts in object technology and reuse to explore issues relating to object technology and the impact it has on systematic software reuse.

1. Motivation

Object technology has long been proffered as the solution to software reuse, but it still has not delivered the "knock out punch." Object technology recognizes the need for examining groups of related applications but does not provide direct, formal guidance for that examination. In addition, products of analysis of single systems differ from those needed for multiple systems; inheritance, polymorphism, and encapsulation are not sufficient to address the requirements for systematic reuse [6]. Patterns give us support across applications, but it is generally up to the analyst to recognize the appropriateness of a pattern for solving the problem at hand. The concept of frameworks begins to address a multi-system perspective. For a family of related problems, frameworks embody an abstract design in the form of a set of classes. They may be created through evolution over development of several related systems [7]. Other framework development approaches recommend an a priori examination of future needs [2].

Anecdotal evidence of the application of object technology suggests that reuse of these products is not so straightforward [5]. Survey results seem to confirm this view [4]. Object-oriented approaches do not automatically produce a reusable product. Objects developed with a single system in mind do not accommodate the types of variation needed for future reuse. Without serious consideration of their potential use in other systems as well as the context for that use, the products cannot be directly applied via reuse.

In addition to considering future systems, there must also be an explicit goal of mapping variability analysis results into design for reuse [3]. This should be

A. Moreira and S. Demeyer (Eds.): ECOOP'99 Workshops, LNCS 1743, pp. 362–370, 1999.

coupled with established and enforced criteria for reusability as a desired software quality attribute. Taken together, the consideration of future systems during analysis and the capture of variability analysis in design will enable systematic reuse.

2. Issues

The panel members discussed object technology and systematic reuse by addressing the following issues:

- What are the barriers to reuse of object-oriented products?
- Why does the use of object-oriented methods or languages not guarantee an object- oriented product?
- Are there object-oriented analysis methods that may be applied to reuse? Are they too sketchy from a process perspective?
- How can we create object-oriented products that are automatically reusable in other situations, that is, designed for a variety of uses and contexts?
- What is the difference between reusability (a product quality) and reuse (a development activity)?

In addition to this list of technical issues, the panel also discussed organizational issues:

- How do we obtain sufficient interaction between the developers and the stakeholders for future applications?
- How may we best look beyond the current development: eliminating the single- system mentality?
- If object technology cannot directly tackle these issues, what aspects of OO development approaches can obtain sufficient involvement and break the single- system mentality?

Presentations were ordered to indicate the breadth of interest in the topic, from general to specific:

- Challenges to OO reuse - Krzysztof Czarnecki
- Contributions of object technology to a product line framework - Linda Northrop
- Architectures and object technology - Philippe Lalanda
- Frameworks from domain knowledge and the knowledge domain - Mehmet Aksit
- Implementation: Know-It-All - Greg Butler

The following sections provide highlights from the panelists position papers and presentations.

2.1. Krzysztof Czarnecki. Daimler Chrysler AG Research and Technology, Germany.

Object-oriented concepts and techniques such as abstraction, encapsulation, polymorphism, inheritance, OO design patterns, and OO frameworks are indisputably helpful in the development of reusable software. Unfortunately, the use of object- oriented technology alone does not guarantee successful development of reusable software. In particular, most OOA/D methods focus on engineering single systems rather than families of systems. These methods offer little support for:

- development for and with reuse
- domain scoping (where domain is the set of existing and potential systems)
- differentiating between variability within one application (versioning) and variability between several applications (product lines)
- implementation-independent means for modeling variability

Various object technology approaches offer partial remedies. Taken to an extreme, the application of similar methods for construction automobiles might offer the following:

- design patterns: "front wheel drive"
- frameworks: "We've got the car body, you supply the rest"
- components: "We deliver the parts, you assemble"

There are also problems in the area of implementing reusable models. Certain kinds of features, particularly in the area of distribution, concurrency, persistency, and security, are difficult to parameterize since the corresponding code is usually spread through many classes. This problem is being addressed in the new area of Aspect- Oriented Programming. Another problem is the binding of reusable libraries to specific programming languages. The development of Java only proves how difficult it is to protect investment in reusable software in the long run. The problem can be addressed by representing reusable models at the domain level (rather than the level of a general purpose programming language) and using a customizable generation process in other to generate executables for different target platforms. This approach is best exemplified by the Intentional Programming system from Microsoft Research.

A system family approach includes domain engineering and application engineering. Domain engineering applies the following:

- analysis to scope a problem and identify common and variable features and feature dependencies
- design to create a common architecture
- implementation to create reusable components, domain-specific languages, or configuration generators

Application engineering produces customized systems using the results of the analysis, design, and implementation.

All these concepts discussed above can be used together to effectively facilitate the development of reusable software. Indeed, this has been the driving force behind the collaborative work of Ulrich Eisenecker and myself on Generative Programming. The technological development outlined above is aimed at enabling sustainable improvement, deep specialization, and broad interoperability of reusable software. To accomplish these goals, software engineering must accept several "theses"

- *A component is always a part of a well-defined production process.* Criteria such as binary format, interoperability, language independence, etc., are always relative to the product process.
- *Transition to interchangeable components won't happen instantly.* The need for cultural change includes customers, consultants and vendors accepting solutions based on standard componentry rather than individualized solutions.
- *If you can assemble the components manually, you can also automate the process using a generator.* However, additional cost is involved in automation (just as for other reusable assets).
- *Standard architectures and components* and industrial-quality metaprogramming environments based on the idea of *active libraries* will help reach the break-even point.

These factors are capable of totally transforming the software industry and making software reuse a matter of survival.

2.2. Linda Northrop. Software Engineering Institute/CMU, EUA

Object technology has since its introduction been heralded as the vehicle to achieve reuse in software development. Certainly there is potential with the abstraction it affords. However the widely advertised reuse potential and payoff have never been realized. In order for reuse to be truly beneficial it needs to be systematic and strategic; that is, something truly significant needs to be reused and there needs to be a real system perspective to the reuse.

Reuse occurs across systems with similar functionality or similar needs. The reuse leverages the commonality and addresses the variability that distinguishes the individual systems. As Fred Brooks so eloquently states in his seminal article, *No Silver Bullet*, the decisions that are made to build software solutions are the most difficult and hence costly part of software development. It is in the embodiment of these decisions that it pays to reuse and such reuse is planned not accidental. Analysis of these decisions must be a planned part of the analysis stage of software development.

Current object-oriented methods fail to adequately analyze families of similar systems to capture common decisions and points of variation. Earlier domain analysis techniques were targeted to achieve such an ambition but lacked the abstraction power of the object concept. Marrying use cases and object abstraction with these earlier domain analysis techniques holds great promise in achieving systematic reuse.

However, improved analysis techniques alone will not achieve systematic reuse. We achieve what might be called: plug and *no* play. There must be a real systems approach to the development process. Recent modifications to object-oriented methods have included more system flavor, however, most of the methods still lack any real sense of system engineering. In order to achieve the systematic reuse that provides big payoffs sound system building approaches must be coupled with the current methods and language constructs.

In addition, there must be a realization that the greatest reuse approaches don't assure use of the resulting assets. There is a notion of: *build it and they will come*. Give potential users of assets all the variability they could ever use, provide libraries of components, and assure them of significant savings. The reality is that limiting variability, targeting solutions, and understanding the business needs of the specific organization are the real ends that systematic reuse should address. For one organization the goal of cost savings may be paramount; for others, meeting time-to-market outweighs incremental cost savings.

Product lines are a way to address these needs. A product line should be built as a product family using common assets. Rather than focus on components or libraries, the product line focuses on the decisions that are the essence of product development. A reference architecture, a domain model, a production plan all offer developers guidance in the key product decisions that are the essence of development and that can be leveraged across multiple systems.

The Product Line Framework of the SEI [1] is intended to guide organizations making the transition to a product line approach for software development. The framework address needs of developers, technical managers, and business planners through a set of practice areas. Where the product line architecture addresses technical decisions, the framework also covers management decisions and guidelines. The framework captures actual product line experience and will, in the future, describe scenarios for applying a product line approach.

2.3. Philippe Lalanda. Schneider Research Center, France

A software product-line is a collection of products sharing a common set of features that address the specific needs of a given business area. In a product-line context, products are built from reusable software artifacts, called reusable assets, which are managed at the product-line level. Core assets concern every software artifact that can be reused, including requirements, software components, software architecture, test cases, budget estimation, development structures, etc. These reusable assets have to be generic enough to be appropriate for several products in the product-line, and specific enough to be reusable in a straightforward manner and then provide a real added value.

One of the major core assets is a software architecture, called a product-line architecture, which is shared by all the products in a product-line. A product-line architecture is a generic, adaptable architecture that applies to a set of products grouped into a product-line and from which the software architecture of each product can be derived. The architecture brings the minimal level of similarity between products that is mandatory to build shareable assets. Variabilities are architectural features that may vary from one product to another. The purpose of specifying variabilities is to prepare the architecture for adaptations and to lead software engineers to the hot spots of the architecture, that is the architectural places that need to be adapted. Encapsulating variability guides software engineers and prevents them from changing structures that must be preserved.

Given our agreement that architecture is key, what issues must be addressed. The issues may be grouped into three categories:

1. techniques for exploring and defining the architecture
2. representation
3. implementation of systems in the product line using the architecture

Object technology can be used here. There are specific areas within object technology that will address systematic reuse:

- Patterns are a key factor in any design approach. For product lines, they represent areas of commonality within and across architectures.
- UML will become the standard for representation and for support of traceability. While not ideal in its current form, the broad base of support for UML offers an opportunity for refinement in the area of architecture representation.
- Frameworks provide the necessary flexibility to support system development for product line members.

The appropriate use of object technology both to domain and application engineering can make reuse happen in a systematic approach.

2.4. Mehmet Aksit. Centre for Telematics and Information Technology, The Netherlands

Although a considerable number of successful object-oriented frameworks (or applications) have been developed during the last decade, designing high-quality frameworks is still a difficult task. Generally, it is assumed that finding the correct abstractions is very hard, and therefore a successful framework can only be developed through a number of iterative (software) development efforts. Accordingly, existing framework development practices span a considerable amount of refinement time, and it is worthwhile to shorten this effort.

To this end, we aim to define explicit models for the knowledge domains that are related to a framework. The absence of such models may be the main reason for the currently experienced extensive refinement effort. The key factor here is the difference between what you have (reflected either in assets or legacy systems) and what you need (the new system). If the difference is great, then the refinement effort will be great. The goal of systematic reuse should be to address the difference by minimizing the needed extensions or additions to what you have.

Current practice within most object-oriented organizations is base development on customer requirements. There is obviously nothing wrong here, they represent what you (or the customer) need. The OO organization develops use cases, classes, and prototypes. The result are components to accomplish individual functions and the hope that these components will be applicable elsewhere.

An alternative starting point is the creation of reusable models from knowledge domains, not from use cases and specifications. These models derive from experience and guide our understanding of customer need. Again, the issue stated in Linda Northrop's talk comes up, "they plug but do they play?" Components derived from knowledge domains are build to play together, where components derived from individual systems are not. An example of incompatibility may be in the area of synchronization. Synchronization and consistency cannot be added on later; they must be an architectural qualities derived from the knowledge domain.

2.5. Greg Butler. Concordia University, Canada

Object technology has, traditionally, provided its primary support to design and code. Commonality and variability are addressed via the class hierarchy, with patterns to address recognized areas of reuse. Evolution is not pre-planned; rather, it is addressed through refactoring and extension.

Object-oriented frameworks offer a concrete reusable architecture for a family of applications. Methodologies for the development of a framework have been suggested that use domain analysis, software evolution, and design patterns. However, the problem is identifying the required flexibility for the family of applications and designing mechanisms that provide this flexibility. Furthermore, the evolution of the framework must be considered, especially as all frameworks seem to mature from initial versions through to a stable platform. Frameworks and other models need alignment *and* synchronized refactoring.

A framework for database and knowledge-based systems, called Know-It-All, supports models for a family of applications. The intent is to align the following elements:

- a use case model of requirements including variation points
- an architectural design including hotspots, facades, abstract classes and aggregates
- a design/class diagram including design patterns, roles, abstract classes, and the template and hook method
- code including inheritance, polymorphism, hooks, templates and reflection

Architecture is an essential and encompassing issue. The architecture must fit functional and non-functional requirements, other constraints, and, to address multiple systems, flexibility for variation. Refactoring approaches can be applied for experimentation with possible architectures.

3. Questions and Answers

Question: These approaches seem more suited to large organizations that can share development costs across multiple developments. What does a small start up company do?

Answer: (Northrop) Product line approaches are not all or nothing. Investment can be made to advance toward a true product line approach. Some start-ups have actually been built around a niche-market that they can target with highly tailorable systems.

Question: OO has not worked in our company. Can we base our reuse approach on unproven methods?

Answer: (Czarnecki) Many organizations think that using an object oriented language means they are using object technology. In fact, some object oriented languages may be an impediment to use of object technology. Object technology reflects a change in the way we think, not just in the language we use. Rather than assume that OO did not work, examine the unlying approach to see where object technology may be applied. (Northrop) Most organizations pursing product line approaches are using object technology. Their use of OO includes use cases and frameworks. But remember that most OO methods are still weak in the area of process support and that UML is still not completely supportive. The issue should be reducing risk and improving predictability, not use of a language. (Lalanda) Most companies start with the recognition or identification of a computing "platform" for their products. OO technology offers the approach not the answer.

Question: What is the experience in measuring the results of reuse?

Answer: (Northrop) Software metrics are not generally there for single system development and for reuse and product lines there are many outstanding issues. Case studies show some critical factors, but much research is needed. Areas include: the results of specific approaches, levels of commonality exploited, and how to make sound investment decisions. The work of Barry Boehm in this area is probably the most promising.

References

[1] Paul Clements and Linda Northrop. *Product Line Framework, Version 2.* Software Engineering Institute, Pittsburgh, 1999. See: http://www.sei.cmu.edu/activities/plp/framework.html.

[2] Sholom Cohen. Object technology, architectures, and domain analysis - what's the connection? - is there a connection. In *Workshop on Institutionalization of Software Reuse (1997)*, pages cohen–1 – cohen–4, 1997. See: http://www.cis.ohio-state.edu/ weide/WISR8/WG-object.html.

[3] J. Coplien, D. Hoffman, and D. Weiss. Commonlaity and Variability in Software Engineering. *IEEE Software*, 15(6):37–45, November/December 1998.

[4] R. G. Fichman and C. F. Kemerer. Object Technology and Reuse: Lessons from Early Adopters. *IEEE Software*, 14(5):47–59, September/October 1997.

[5] Martin Griss. Panel on object technology and reuse. In *Third International Conference on Software Reuse (1994)*, page 194, Rio De Janeiro, 1994. IEEE Computer Society.

[6] Martin Griss, John Favaro, and Massimo d'Alessandro. Integrating feature modeling with the rseb. In *Fifth International Conference on Software Reuse (1998)*, pages 76–85, Victoria, British Columbia, Canada, 1998. IEEE Computer Society.

[7] Don Roberts and Ralph Johnson. Evolving frameworks: A pattern language for developing object-oriented frameworks. See: http://st-www.cs.uiuc.edu/users/droberts/evolve.html.

Poster Session

Carlos Baquero

Dep. de Informática - Universidade do Minho, Portugal,
cbm@di.uminho.pt - http://www.di.uminho.pt/~cbm/

Abstract. Report on the poster exhibition that took place at ECOOP'99.

1. Introduction

The poster session complemented the specialized work-groups of ECOOP workshops and presented an exhibition of abstracts covering a broad range of object orientation topics.

This report gathers contributions from seven posters that were on display at the exhibition during the conference period. These posters covered fresh research projects, presented new tools for object oriented analysis and programming, and included as well applications of object technology.

2. The Oberon Program Slicing Tool (Christoph Steindl)

Program slicing [46] is a program analysis technique that reduces programs to those statements that are relevant for a particular computation. These statements may influence a statement S either because they decide whether S is executed (*control dependence*) or because they define a variable that is used by S (*data dependence*).

Object-oriented programming languages allow one to write programs that are more flexible, reusable and maintainable. However, the concepts of inheritance, dynamic binding and polymorphism represent new challenges for static analysis.

The Oberon Program Slicing Tool[1] [42, 43] is a fully operational program slicer for static backward slicing of Oberon-2 [30] programs. It integrates state-of-the-art algorithms and applies them to a strongly-typed object-oriented programming language. It extends them to support intermodular slicing of object-oriented programs. Control and data flow analysis considers inheritance, dynamic binding and polymorphism, as well as side-effects of functions, short-circuit evaluation of Boolean expressions and aliases due to reference parameters and pointers. The algorithm for alias analysis is fast but effective by taking into account information about the type of variables and the place of their declaration. The result of static analysis is visualized with active text elements. The programmer

[1] The Oberon Program Slicing Tool can be downloaded (including all source and documentation) via http://www.ssw.uni-linz.ac.at/Research/Projects/ProgramSlicing/

A. Moreira and S. Demeyer (Eds.): ECOOP'99 Workshops, LNCS 1743, pp. 371–383, 1999.

can restrict the sets of possible aliases and call destinations via user interaction. These restrictions are then used to compute more precise control and data flow information. In this way, the programmer can limit the effects of aliases and dynamic binding and bring in his knowledge about the program into the analysis.

3. Aspect-Oriented Programming in Smalltalk (Kai Böllert)

The implementation of technical requirements like persistence, failure handling, communication, or process synchronization often cuts across a whole software system instead of being well localized in a few modules. If a cleaner separation of a system's functionality and its technical concerns could be achieved, software components would be easier to understand, better to maintain, and more flexible to reuse [20].

Aspect-Oriented Programming (AOP) introduces aspect modules to capture technical concerns separately from the functionality. For example, one aspect module might describe how to make a stock portfolio persistent, while a second one defines the synchronization strategy for concurrent access to the portfolio. Aspect modules (aspects, for short) are written in special aspect description languages. Common to all of these languages is that they cannot be processed by today's programming language compilers. Until that changes, aspects and functionality modules have to be merged before a compiler can take over to produce the executable program. The process of merging is called weaving; the tool required is named Aspect Weaver [23].

Integrating AOP into the various programming languages and development environments is a challenging task. In particular, a cross-referencing mechanism is desirable that shows developers which functionality is affected by which aspects. Two of such integration approaches are AspectJ and AOP/ST. AspectJ [3] provides a general-purpose aspect language for Java and has been applied, for instance, to build a web-based learning environment [22]. AOP/ST [4] originated from a project to reengineer the server part of an industrial system management application written in VisualWorks/Smalltalk. During the project two technical concerns, process synchronization and tracing, were reimplemented in the form of aspects by using specifically designed aspect languages. In addition, an Aspect Weaver was developed, which is able to adapt aspects in a deployed software release. This feature is mainly used to customize tracing aspects at deployment sites to track down the cause of malfunctions [9].

Shown on the poster was the design of an entirely new version of AOP/ST, which integrates itself more seamlessly into the VisualWorks environment by substituting special aspect languages with pure Smalltalk. Aspects are now implemented as ordinary Smalltalk classes, i.e. an aspect's behavior is defined by the methods in the corresponding aspect class. To specify where to weave aspect behavior, so-called pragmas need to be inserted into aspect methods. For example, assume an aspect method with the pragma <weave: Rectangle method: #area>.

When the Aspect Weaver processes this method, it recognizes the pragma and merges the aspect method with the area method of the Rectangle class. Furthermore, Smalltalk's cross-referencing mechanism searches pragmas for references to classes and methods. Hence, putting weave instructions into pragmas has the advantage that browsing all references to a class also finds the aspect methods that affect this class.

To sum up, the new AOP/ST version enables programmers to develop aspects using the same language and the same tools that they already use to develop a system's functionality. This may help programmers to learn and adopt AOP faster. Moreover, aspect modules benefit from Smalltalk's expressiveness and are not limited to the constructs provided by special aspect languages.

4. Java Type System with Exceptions (Sophia Drossopoulou et al.)

We develop a proof of type soundness for a substantial subset of the Java language. The distinguishing feature of this work is the study of types for exception handling in the Java setting.

Consider the following example in Java:

```
class Worry extends Exception {}

class Illness extends Worry {
    int severity;
    Illness treat() throws Worry {
        if (...) throw new Worry();
        else return this;         }
    Illness cure() { severity = -10; return this; }
}

class Person {
    int age;
    Illness diagnose() { return new Illness(); }
    void act() throws Worry {
            try { if (...) throw diagnose().treat();
                   else age=age+1;
            } catch( Illness e) { e.cure(); }       }
}
```

Assume that the variable peter points to a Person object. The term peter.act() may execute normally (*i.e.* either no exception is thrown, or the Illness exception is thrown and caught), or it may execute abnormally (*i.e.* the Worry exception is thrown).

Therefore, we distinguish between *normal execution* where any exception thrown is also handled and *abnormal execution* where an exception is thrown and not handled.

Correspondingly, we distinguish normal and abnormal types. *Normal types* describe the possible outcomes of normal execution. *Abnormal types* describe the possible outcomes of abnormal execution. A normal type is a class, an interface, or a primitive type. An abnormal type is a set of subclasses of the predefined `Exception` class. The type of a term consists of both its normal and abnormal types: $\mathtt{T} \parallel \{\mathtt{E}_1, \ldots, \mathtt{E}_n\}$.

For example, the type of the term `peter.act()` is **void** $\parallel$ {`Worry`}. Also, the type of `peter.diagnose().cure()` is `Illness` $\parallel \emptyset$, whereas the type of `peter.diagnose().treat()` is `Illness` $\parallel$ {`Worry`}.

A type *widens* to another type if the normal component of the first is identical or a subclass or subinterface of the latter or a class that implements the latter, and if any class of the abnormal component of the first has a superclass in the set of classes of the abnormal component of the latter, *i.e.*

$$\frac{\mathtt{T} = \mathtt{T'} \quad \text{or} \quad \mathtt{T}\ \textit{subclass}\ \mathtt{T'} \quad \text{or} \quad \mathtt{T}\ \textit{subinterface}\ \mathtt{T'} \quad \text{or} \quad \mathtt{T}\ \textit{implements}\ \mathtt{T'} \qquad \forall \mathtt{i} \in \{\mathtt{1...n}\}\ \exists \mathtt{j} \in \{\mathtt{1...m}\}\ \ \mathtt{E_i}\ \textit{subclass}\ \mathtt{E'_j}}{\mathtt{T} \parallel \{\mathtt{E}_1, \ldots, \mathtt{E}_n\}\ \ \textit{widens}\ \ \mathtt{T'} \parallel \{\mathtt{E'}_1, \ldots, \mathtt{E'}_m\}}$$

So, the type `Person` $\parallel$ {`Illness`} widens to the type `Person` $\parallel$ {`Worry`}, and the type `Illness` $\parallel \emptyset$ widens to the type `Worry` $\parallel$ {`Exception`}.

With this set-up we prove a subject reduction theorem. In our example subject reduction states that `peter.act()` will either execute normally, or it will throw and not catch an exception of a subclass of `Worry`; in all cases the states will remain consistent with the program and the environment.

Thus, the meaning of the subject reduction theorem which includes exceptions is stronger than usual: it guarantees that normal execution of a term returns a value of a type compatible with the normal type of the term, whereas its abnormal execution throws an exception compatible with the abnormal type of the term.

5. Using Patterns into the Conception of a Medical KBS (Marie Beurton-Aimar et al.)

Our purpose is to present some problems linked to the design of medical diagnostic systems. Medical Knowledge Based Systems must be able to store information, to search for a specific disease, to consult validated clinical tables, and to compare the results for several diseases. This suggests the production of strongly inter-connected process modules, sharing a common base of information [6]. The design of an abstract model of the knowledge base makes possible this sharing and allows to specify diagnostic processes regardless the data implementation. Object-oriented methods of analysis are powerful tools to realize this task. Nevertheless, significant elements remain hidden during the stage of first analysis. Conception of software requires the definition of objects which do not exist as full entities in a human cognitive system, such as algorithm models linked to data structures, or description of generic behaviours. Patterns proceed from these expectations, giving a new approach of the modeled domain and providing some specific solutions to problems of design.

LADRI (Logiciel d'Aide au Diagnostic en Rhumatology Inflammatoire) is a software for diagnosis in Rheumatology developed at the Bordeaux Medical University [5] for which we have used three patterns (issued from [16]) present at different levels in the object model. The patterns **Composite** and **State** are used for the management of medical signs. The pattern **Iterator** defines generic class of treatments. **Composite** is introduced to structure both the patient and diseases descriptions. This application must take into account diseases described from simple signs and aggregations of signs. Using **Composite** allows to consider an aggregation of objects like a primitive object. It makes possible to implement all the signs into a single way. It offers an unique access to these objects whatever their internal structure.

In a disease description, a value for each sign is assigned. It means the weight of this sign for the diagnosis. But usually, this value also codes implicitly the concept of presence or absence of a sign (with a negative value for absence). **State** represents explicitly the different possible states of a sign. It keeps their independent from the specific type of value. In this way, this pattern reduces the complexity of systems to share the disease description between several treatments which have their own type of value.

The pattern **Iterator** concerns a generic task performed by all reasoning methods. The diagnostic task is mainly an enumeration of all patient signs observed, to compare them with signs belonging to the descriptions of pathologies. This task is involved whatever the structure of these definitions or the applied operations in the reasoning module. The introduction of **Iterator** gives up a generic access to the element independently from the data structures. **Iterator** allows a communication between data modules and treatment modules through a generic interface. Moreover, for all treatments, it factorizes in a single object the traversal of the descriptions. These three patterns have caught a part of the essence of medical diagnostic system which is not obvious after the analysis of the domain even if it is an object analysis. They draw an architecture mainly relevant to software concerns. This architecture is then overlapped with the conceptual model issued from the object analysis. Medical informatics is relevant from Artificial Intelligence domain. The use of such tools come from software engineering area are not really a normal practice in Artificial Intelligence community but many voices in medical informatics [18, 19, 32, 31] claim the integration of such technics to solve the problems of maintenance and complexity in medical applications.

6. Validation of Object Oriented Models Using Animation (Ian Oliver et al.)

The combination of graphical notations for object-oriented modeling and formal methods has resulted in notations suitable for precise modelling. However, current validation techniques for these so called second generation OO modelling techniques are either limited or non-existent.

Prototyping has been shown to be a valuable validation technique during analysis and design [41]. This technique, however, can suffer from the semantic-gap between the model and the prototypical executable code being too great for useful feedback between the code and model. There does exist a technique known as animation where the model can be executed (in some sense) without the need from the writing of prototypical code [47, 44, 7, 13]. Using animation we can investigate the behavioural properties of a model without resorting to writing prototypical code and, therefore, provide almost instant and direct feedback to the analyst/designer and/or domain expert.

Because animation has required a precisely specified model, current animation tools are based around formal specification languages such as Z [14], VDM [21], and B [2]. Work on the usefulness of animation has shown it to be valuable in refining the specification and removing potential ambiguities and errors at a much earlier stage. The disadvantage is that the formal methods, animation has been applied to, are primarily mathematical in nature and 'non-expert unfriendly.'

The Unified Modelling Language (UML) [33] is a graphical OO modelling notation with a co-existing textual specification language known as the Object Constraint Language (OCL) [45]. The OCL - based upon Z - is written using a 'non-expert friendly' English-like syntax and integrates completely with the UML.

Using the UML's object diagrams and the OCL's action contract specifications, the analysis/designer can describe the behavioural properties of a model. Animation of these constructs can provide instant, visual feedback on the effects of that specification. In conjunction with relating these constructs to the UML class diagram and associated invariants, this can provide a way of validating and refining models without resorting to writing prototype code at a much earlier stage in the software process [36, 34].

This poster presented ongoing work to provide a method [35] and framework to facilitate the animation of object oriented models specified using UML/OCL.

7. The BLOOM Model Revisited: An Evolution Proposal (Alberto Abelló et al.)

The growing need to share information among several autonomous and heterogeneous data sources has become an active research area. A possible solution is providing integrated access through a *Federated Information System* (FIS). In order to provide integrated access, it is necessary to overcome semantic heterogeneities, and represent related concepts [39]. This is accomplished through an integration process in which a *Canonical Data Model* (CDM) plays a central role.

Once argued the desirable characteristics of a suitable CDM (see Subsection 7.1), the BLOOM model (BarceLona Object Oriented Model) was progressively defined [11, 12, 17]. Recently, we have revised the BLOOM model giving rise to BLOOM99. We discuss the change reasons and the main innovations that BLOOM99 includes in Subsection 7.2.

7.1. Motivation for the BLOOM91 Model

In our project for a FIS we focused on tightly coupled federations and we adopted a schema architecture based upon the 5-level reference architecture by Sheth & Larson [40]. Therefore, we needed a CDM and we looked for one.

We took the position that the CDM needs a high degree of *representation ability*, because the difficult process of *schema integration* requires as much *semantics* as possible. The representation ability of a model consists of two factors: *Expressiveness* and *Semantic Relativism*.

In [38] we developed a *framework of suitable characteristics* of a data model to be adequate as the CDM of a FIS. After analyzing existing data models according to this framework without finding someone which satisfy all characteristics, we designed the first version of BLOOM, now referred to as BLOOM91 [12], that contributes to:

- the generalization/specialization dimension by offering four different kinds of specialization, and the tagged of the specializations by means of a criterion.
- the aggregation dimension by considering existence dependencies among objects; depending on the semantic strength of these dependencies, composed objects appear.

7.2. From BLOOM91 to BLOOM99

The necessity of revising the BLOOM model outcropped during the design process of the directory of the FIS. The directory is the core of our FIS architecture and it must contain the different schema levels as well as the mappings among them [37]. Therefore, the model had to be fixed in order to store this information in a structured manner. This revision consisted on:

- the aggregation and generalization metaclasses have been combined into a single metaclass hierarchy by generalizing them in the *All_nexus* metaclass. In addition, the *All_classes*, and *All_characteristics* metaclasses also appeared to be able to classify everything in a BLOOM schema.
- considering the collection as a concrete case of composition where the aggregate object is composed by a set of elements of just one class.
- generalization of the coverage and disjointness properties to any kind of existence dependency.
- improving the classification of some concepts in the model to better understand them, splitting metaclass specializations by new criteria.
- orthogonal specializations have been found and moved up in the metaclass hierarchy to simplify it and avoid generating unnecessary mixing metaclasses.
- representation of the aggregation dimension in the metaclass schema in order to know what information to store in the directory about every metaclass.

Our objective is making BLOOM99 operative on a centralized DBMS as well as a FIS. For this reason we are working on: a *Graphical User Interface Tool* and a *precompiler for BLOOM99* [1].

This set of tools makes BLOOM99 operative on a centralized DBMS (object oriented or relational). However, the real interest of BLOOM99 is to be used as a CDM of a FIS. In order to accomplish this goal, we are working on a *Semantic Enrichment Tool* and a *Graphical Integration Workbench.*

8. The COAST Object Database System (Sven-Eric Lautemann et al.)

The[2] possibility to update the schema of an existing database is a highly required feature in many environments. The *Complex Object And Schema Transformation* (COAST) project focuses on the design and implementation of a schema evolution support system using the versioning concept both at the instance and at the schema level of object-oriented database management systems (OODBMS) to provide a high degree of flexibility.

In ordinary systems two elements depend heavily on the database schema, and, therefore, prevent schema changes in many cases: The database which is stored according to the types specified in the schema, and the set of application programs on top of the schema which require certain properties from the instances. The basic idea of the schema versioning mechanism [15, 24] is to keep the old schema and database state as a version to allow continuous operation of existing application programs. This decouples the schema from existing instances and applications, and allows arbitrary schema updates at any time.

At the schema level, a general update taxonomy provides primitives to modify a schema. However, instead of overriding the previous state when classes are created, modified, or deleted, a new schema version is *derived* while the old one can be continuously used.

At the instance level, each schema version *sv* has its *Instance Access Scope* ($IAS(sv)$) which contains the objects accessible to applications of *sv*. To allow cooperation of applications of different schema versions objects are propagated between the IASs of different schema versions by various types of class specific (default and user-defined) conversion functions [25]. Their (re-)execution is triggered by object creations, modifications, and deletions and can be specified by propagation flags [26]. This allows cooperation of applications of different schema versions.

At the physical layer, the propagation of instances is done in a deferred fashion, i.e. objects are propagated only when necessary to save both time and space. However, the propagation mechanisms preserve *time-equivalence*, i.e. at the logical level the behaviour is equivalent to an immediate propagation.

---

[2] authors: Sven-Eric Lautemann, Sabbas Apostolidis, Alexander Doll, Jan Haase
affiliation: University of Frankfurt / Main, Department of Computer Science (20). D-60054 Frankfurt / Main, Germany, lautemann@coast.uni-frankfurt.de, http://www.coast.uni-frankfurt.de/

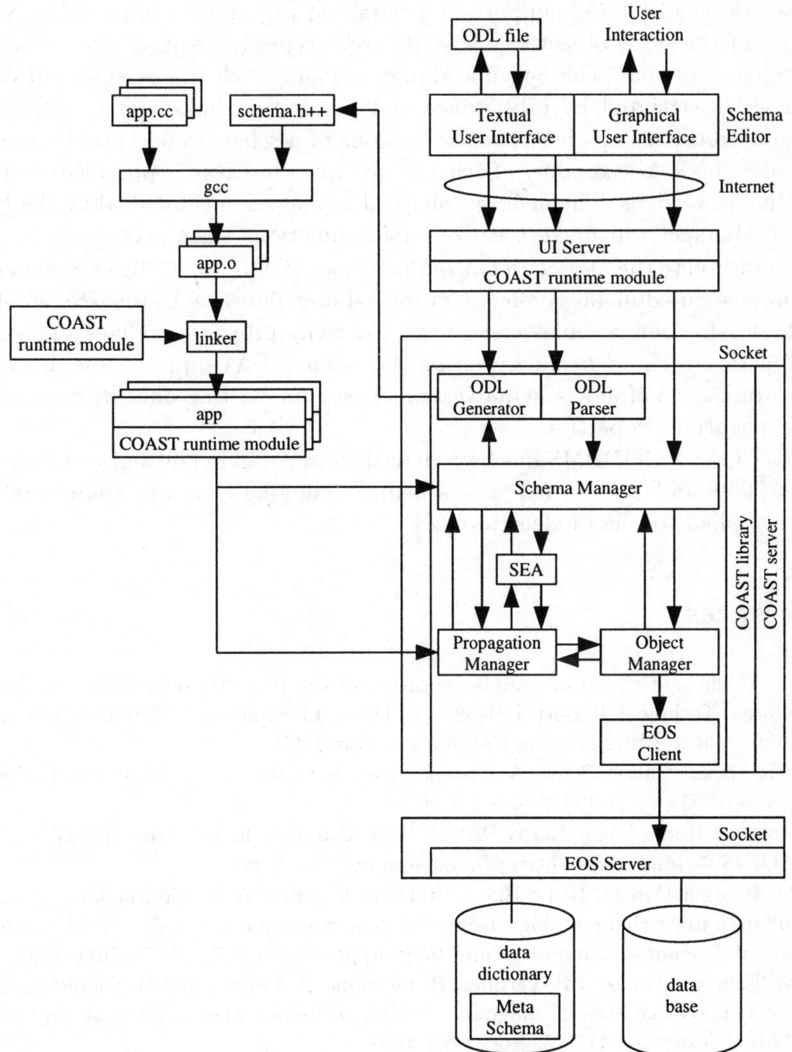

Fig. 1. The COAST Architecture.

The architecture of the COAST prototype (see Figure 1) is similar to those of both other prototypes and of commercial OODBMSs. It consists of a database engine and a user interface.

The database engine contains an Object Manager and a Schema Manager which extend the functionality offered by other systems. The Object Manager is based on EOS [8] and supports a generalized object versioning model where versions of the same object can have different types as required by the schema versioning approach. The Schema Manager handles schema versions consisting of classes interrelated by inheritance and association links and maintains the derivation relationships between the versions of a schema and between the versions of a class. A taxonomy of schema update primitives is provided to derive new schema versions. The deferred physical propagation is handled by the Propagation Manager which executes conversion functions when necessary.

In addition to the *Object Definition Language* (ODL) the COAST Schema Editor (implemented in Java) offers a graphical user interface to the *Schema Manager* to develop new schema versions and to specify propagation flags and conversion functions. The *Schema Evolution Assistant* (SEA) supports the derivation and optimization of new schema versions based on existing ones with respect to the propagation properties.

The COAST OODBMS has been described in detail in [29] and was presented at CeBIT'98 and '99 [10, 28]. The schema versioning concepts are general and can be applied to role models, too [27].

References

[1] A. Abelló and F. Saltor. Implementation of the BLOOM data model on ObjectStore. Technical Report LSI-99-7-T, Dept. Llenguatges i Sistemes Informàtics (Universitat Politècnica de Catalunya), May 1999.

[2] J-R Abrial. *The B-Book - Assigning programs to Meanings.* Cambridge University Press, 1995. 0-521-49619-5.

[3] AspectJ Home Page. Xerox PARC, Palo Alto, CA. http://aspectj.org/.

[4] AOP/ST Home Page. http://home.foni.net/ boellert/.

[5] M. Beurton-Aimar, B. Le Blanc, and J.P. Vernhes. A decision-making system in inflammatory rheumatology using different reasoning methods. *IJCA - International Journal of Computers and their Applications*, 6(2):73–77, June 1999.

[6] M. Beurton-Aimar, J.P. Vernhes, B. Le Blanc, J. Dehais, and R. Salamon. Creating a knowledge base for diagnosis making in rheumatology. *Revue du rhumatisme édition française*, 11:762, November 1997.

[7] J. C. Bicarregui, A. J. J. Dick, B. M. Matthews, and E. Woods. Making the most of formal specification through animation, testing and proof. *Science of Computer Programming*, 29:55–80, June 1997.

[8] Alexandros Biliris and Euthimios Panagos. *EOS User's Guide.* AT&T Bell Laboratories, Murray Hill, NJ 07974, October 1994. Release 2.2, 51 pages.

[9] Kai Böllert. *Aspect-Oriented Programming, Case Study: System Management Application.* Graduation thesis, Fachhochschule Flensburg, 1998. http://home.foni.net/ boellert/thesis.pdf.

[10] Frank Buddrus and Sven-Eric Lautemann. Internet, Java, Datenbanken. In *Kooperationspartner in Forschung und Innovation*, pages 11–12. Hessisches Ministerium für Wissenschaft und Kunst, March 1998. CeBIT Messebroschüre.
[11] M. Castellanos, Th. Kudrass, F. Saltor, and M. García-Solaco. Interdatabase Existence Dependencies: A Metaclass Approach. In *Proceedings of the 3rd International Conference on Parallel and Distributed Information Systems (PDIS'94, Austin, 1994)*, pages 213–216. IEEE-CS Press, 1994.
[12] M. Castellanos, F. Saltor, and M. García-Solaco. A Canonical Model for the Interoperability among Object-Oriented and Relational Databases. In Ozsu, Dayal, and Valduriez, editors, *Distributed Object Management (Proceedings, International Workshop on Distributed Object Management, IWDOM, Edmonton, Canada, 1992)*, pages 309–314. Morgan Kaufmann, 1994.
[13] M Costa, J Cunningham, and J Booth. Logical animation. In *Proceedings of the International Conference on Software Engineering*, 1990.
[14] Antoni Diller. *Z - An Introduction to Formal Methods.* John Wiley & Sons, Chichester, 2nd edition, 1994. 0-471-93973-0.
[15] Fabrizio Ferrandina and Sven-Eric Lautemann. An Integrated Approach to Schema Evolution in Object Databases. In Dilip Patel, Yuan Sun, and Shushma Patel, editors, *Proc. of the 3rd Int'l Conf. on Object Oriented Information Systems (OOIS)*, pages 280–294, London, United Kingdom, December 1996. Springer-Verlag.
[16] E. Gamma, R. Helm, R. Johnson, and J. Vlissides. *Design Patterns Elements of Reusable Object-Oriented Software.* Addison Wesley, 1994.
[17] M. García-Solaco, F. Saltor, and M. Castellanos. Semantic Heterogeneity in Multidatabases. In Bukhres and Elmagarmid, editors, *Object Oriented Multidatabases.* Prentice-Hall, 1995. Invited chapter.
[18] D. A. Giuse and R. A. Miller. Potholes in the road to professionalism in medical informatics. *Methods of Information in Medicine*, 34:434–440, 1995.
[19] H. A. Heathfield and J. Wyatt. The road to professionalism in medical informatics: A proposal for debate. *Methods of Information in Medicine*, 34:426–433, 1995.
[20] Walter Hürsch and Cristina V. Lopes. Separation of concerns. Technical Report NU-CCS-95-03, Northeastern University, Boston, MA, February 1995.
[21] Cliff B Jones. *Systematic Software Development using VDM.* International Series in Computer Science. Prentice Hall, 2nd edition, 1990. 0-13-880733-7.
[22] Mik A. Kersten and Gail C. Murphy. Atlas: A case study in building a web-based learning environment using Aspect-Oriented Programming. Technical Report TR-99-04, Department of Computer Science, University of British Columbia, Vancouver, April 1999.
[23] Gregor Kiczales, John Lamping, Anurag Mendhekar, Chris Maeda, Cristina Lopes, Jean-Marc Loingtier, and John Irwin. Aspect-Oriented Programming. Technical Report SPL97-008 P9710042, Xerox PARC, Palo Alto, CA, February 1997.
[24] Sven-Eric Lautemann. An Introduction to Schema Versioning in OODBMS. In Roland R. Wagner and C. Helmut Thoma, editors, *Proc. of the 7th Int'l Conf. on Database and Expert Systems Applications (DEXA)*, pages 132–139, Zurich, Switzerland, September 1996. IEEE Computer Society Press. Workshop Proceedings.
[25] Sven-Eric Lautemann. A Propagation Mechanism for Populated Schema Versions. In Keith Jeffrey and Elke A. Rundensteiner, editors, *Proc. of the 13th Int'l Conf. on Data Engineering (ICDE)*, pages 67–78, Birmingham, U.K., April 1997. IEEE, IEEE Computer Society Press.

[26] Sven-Eric Lautemann. Schema Versions in Object-Oriented Database Systems. In Rodney Topor and Katsumi Tanaka, editors, *Proc. of the 5th Int'l Conf. on Database Systems for Advanced Applications (DASFAA)*, pages 323–332, Melbourne, Australia, April 1997. World Scientific. In Advanced Database Research and Development Series, Vol. 6.

[27] Sven-Eric Lautemann. Change Management with Roles. In Arbee L. P. Chen and Frederick H. Lochovsky, editors, *Proc. of the 6th Int'l Conf. on Database Systems for Advanced Applications (DASFAA)*, pages 291–300, Hsinchu, Taiwan, ROC, April 1999. IEEE.

[28] Sven-Eric Lautemann. Dynamische Schemaänderungen mit COAST. In *Kooperationspartner in Forschung und Innovation*, pages 17–18. Hessisches Ministerium für Wissenschaft und Kunst, March 1999. CeBIT Messebroschüre.

[29] Sven-Eric Lautemann, Patricia Eigner, and Christian Wöhrle. The COAST Project: Design and Implementation. In François Bry, Raghu Ramakrishnan, and Kotagiri. Ramamohanarao, editors, *Proc. of the 5th Int'l Conf. on Deductive and Object-Oriented Databases (DOOD)*, pages 229–246, Montreux, Switzerland, December 1997. Springer-Verlag. Lecture Notes in Computer Science No. 1341.

[30] Hanspeter Mössenböck and Niklaus Wirth. The Programming Language Oberon-2. *Structured Programming*, 12(4), 1991.

[31] M. A. Musen and E. A. Barnett. The road to professionalism in medical informatics: the role of training. *Methods of Information in Medicine*, 35:148–151, 1996.

[32] M. A. Musen and A. Th. Scheilber. Architectures for intelligent systems based on reusable components. *Artificial Intelligence in Medecine*, 7:189–199, 1995.

[33] Object Management Group. *OMG Unified Modelling Language Specification (draft)*, version 1.3r9 edition, January 1999. http://www.rational.com/uml.

[34] Ian Oliver. *Animating of Object Oriented Conceptual Models.* PhD thesis, University of Kent at Canterbury, 1999. in preparation.

[35] Ian Oliver. "executing" the OCL. PhDOOS'99 at ECOOP'99, Lisbon, Portugal, June 1999.

[36] Ian Oliver and Stuart Kent. Validation of object oriented models using animation. In *Proceedings of the 25th EuroMicro Conference, Milan, Italy.* IEEE Press, September 1999.

[37] E. Rodríguez, M. Oliva, F. Saltor, and B. Campderrich. On Schema and Functional Architectures for Multilevel Secure and Multiuser Model Federated DB Systems. In S. et al. Conrad, editor, *Proceedings of International CAiSE'97 Workshop on Engineering Federated Database Systems (EFDBS'97)*, pages 93–104, Barcelona, Catalonia, Jun 1997. Otto-von-Guericke-Universität Magdeburg, Fakultät für Informatik.

[38] F. Saltor, M. Castellanos, and M. García-Solaco. Suitability of Data Models as Canonical Models for Federated DBs. *ACM SIGMOD Record (special refereed issue: A. Sheth (guest ed.): Semantic Issues in Multidatabase Systems, December 1991)*, 20(4):44–48, 1991.

[39] F. Saltor and E. Rodríguez. On Semantic Issues in Federated Information Systems (Extended abstract). In S. Conrad, W. Hasselbring, and G. Saake, editors, *Proceedings of the 2nd Workshop on Engineering Federated Information Systems (EFIS'99)*, pages 1–4, Kühlungsborn, Germany, May 1999. Infix-Verlag.

[40] A.P. Sheth and J. Larson. Federated Database Systems for Managing Distributed, Heterogeneous, and Autonomous Databases. *ACM Computing Surveys*, 22(3):183–236, September 1990.

[41] Ian Sommerville. *Software Engineering.* Addison Wesley, 4th edition, 1992. 0-201-56529-3.

[42] Christoph Steindl. Intermodular Slicing of Object-Oriented Programs. In *Proceedings of CC'98, Lecture Notes in Computer Science No. 1383*, 1998.

[43] Christoph Steindl. *Program Slicing for Object-Oriented Programming Languages.* PhD thesis, Johannes Kepler University Linz, 1999.

[44] Leon Sterling, Paolo Cianarini, and Todd Turnidge. On the animation of non executable specification by prolog. *International Journal of Software Engineering and Knowledge Engineering*, 6(1):63–87, 1996.

[45] Jos Warmer and Anneke Kleppe. *The Object Constraint Language - Precise Modeling with UML.* Object Technology Series. Addison Wesley, 1999. 0-201-37940-6.

[46] Mark Weiser. Program Slicing. *IEEE Trans. Software Engineering*, 10(4), 1984.

[47] Margaret M West and Barry M Eaglestone. Software development: two approches to animation of Z specifications using prolog. *Software Engineering Journal*, 7(4):264–276, July 1992.

Author Index

Lecture Notes in Computer Science

For information about Vols. 1–1677
please contact your bookseller or Springer-Verlag

Vol. 1678: M.H. Böhlen, C.S. Jensen, M.O. Scholl (Eds.), Spatio-Temporal Database Management. Proceedings, 1999. X, 243 pages. 1999.

Vol. 1679: C. Taylor, A. Colchester (Eds.), Medical Image Computing and Computer-Assisted Intervention – MICCAI'99. Proceedings, 1999. XXI, 1240 pages. 1999.

Vol. 1680: D. Dams, R. Gerth, S. Leue, M. Massink (Eds.), Theoretical and Practical Aspects of SPIN Model Checking. Proceedings, 1999. X, 277 pages. 1999.

Vol. 1681: D. A. Forsyth, J. L. Mundy, V. di Gesú, R. Cipolla (Eds.), Shape, Contour and Grouping in Computer Vision. VIII, 347 pages. 1999.

Vol. 1682: M. Nielsen, P. Johansen, O.F. Olsen, J. Weickert (Eds.), Scale-Space Theories in Computer Vision. Proceedings, 1999. XII, 532 pages. 1999.

Vol. 1683: J. Flum, M. Rodríguez-Artalejo (Eds.), Computer Science Logic. Proceedings, 1999. XI, 580 pages. 1999.

Vol. 1684: G. Ciobanu, G. Păun (Eds.), Fundamentals of Computation Theory. Proceedings, 1999. XI, 570 pages. 1999.

Vol. 1685: P. Amestoy, P. Berger, M. Daydé, I. Duff, V. Frayssé, L. Giraud, D. Ruiz (Eds.), Euro-Par'99. Parallel Processing. Proceedings, 1999. XXXII, 1503 pages. 1999.

Vol. 1686: H.E. Bal, B. Belkhouche, L. Cardelli (Eds.), Internet Programming Languages. Proceedings, 1998. IX, 143 pages. 1999.

Vol. 1687: O. Nierstrasz, M. Lemoine (Eds.), Software Engineering – ESEC/FSE '99. Proceedings, 1999. XII, 529 pages. 1999.

Vol. 1688: P. Bouquet, L. Serafini, P. Brézillon, M. Benerecetti, F. Castellani (Eds.), Modeling and Using Context. Proceedings, 1999. XII, 528 pages. 1999. (Subseries LNAI).

Vol. 1689: F. Solina, A. Leonardis (Eds.), Computer Analysis of Images and Patterns. Proceedings, 1999. XIV, 650 pages. 1999.

Vol. 1690: Y. Bertot, G. Dowek, A. Hirschowitz, C. Paulin, L. Théry (Eds.), Theorem Proving in Higher Order Logics. Proceedings, 1999. VIII, 359 pages. 1999.

Vol. 1691: J. Eder, I. Rozman, T. Welzer (Eds.), Advances in Databases and Information Systems. Proceedings, 1999. XIII, 383 pages. 1999.

Vol. 1692: V. Matoušek, P. Mautner, J. Ocelíková, P. Sojka (Eds.), Text, Speech and Dialogue. Proceedings, 1999. XI, 396 pages. 1999. (Subseries LNAI).

Vol. 1693: P. Jayanti (Ed.), Distributed Computing. Proceedings, 1999. X, 357 pages. 1999.

Vol. 1694: A. Cortesi, G. Filé (Eds.), Static Analysis. Proceedings, 1999. VIII, 357 pages. 1999.

Vol. 1695: P. Barahona, J.J. Alferes (Eds.), Progress in Artificial Intelligence. Proceedings, 1999. XI, 385 pages. 1999. (Subseries LNAI).

Vol. 1696: S. Abiteboul, A.-M. Vercoustre (Eds.), Research and Advanced Technology for Digital Libraries. Proceedings, 1999. XII, 497 pages. 1999.

Vol. 1697: J. Dongarra, E. Luque, T. Margalef (Eds.), Recent Advances in Parallel Virtual Machine and Message Passing Interface. Proceedings, 1999. XVII, 551 pages. 1999.

Vol. 1698: M. Felici, K. Kanoun, A. Pasquini (Eds.), Computer Safety, Reliability and Security. Proceedings, 1999. XVIII, 482 pages. 1999.

Vol. 1699: S. Albayrak (Ed.), Intelligent Agents for Telecommunication Applications. Proceedings, 1999. IX, 191 pages. 1999. (Subseries LNAI).

Vol. 1700: R. Stadler, B. Stiller (Eds.), Active Technologies for Network and Service Management. Proceedings, 1999. XII, 299 pages. 1999.

Vol. 1701: W. Burgard, T. Christaller, A.B. Cremers (Eds.), KI-99: Advances in Artificial Intelligence. Proceedings, 1999. XI, 311 pages. 1999. (Subseries LNAI).

Vol. 1702: G. Nadathur (Ed.), Principles and Practice of Declarative Programming. Proceedings, 1999. X, 434 pages. 1999.

Vol. 1703: L. Pierre, T. Kropf (Eds.), Correct Hardware Design and Verification Methods. Proceedings, 1999. XI, 366 pages. 1999.

Vol. 1704: Jan M. Żytkow, J. Rauch (Eds.), Principles of Data Mining and Knowledge Discovery. Proceedings, 1999. XIV, 593 pages. 1999. (Subseries LNAI).

Vol. 1705: H. Ganzinger, D. McAllester, A. Voronkov (Eds.), Logic for Programming and Automated Reasoning. Proceedings, 1999. XII, 397 pages. 1999. (Subseries LNAI).

Vol. 1706: J. Hatcliff, T. Æ. Mogensen, P. Thiemann (Eds.), Partial Evaluation – Practice and Theory. 1998. IX, 433 pages. 1999.

Vol. 1707: H.-W. Gellersen (Ed.), Handheld and Ubiquitous Computing. Proceedings, 1999. XII, 390 pages. 1999.

Vol. 1708: J.M. Wing, J. Woodcock, J. Davies (Eds.), FM'99 – Formal Methods. Proceedings Vol. I, 1999. XVIII, 937 pages. 1999.

Vol. 1709: J.M. Wing, J. Woodcock, J. Davies (Eds.), FM'99 – Formal Methods. Proceedings Vol. II, 1999. XVIII, 937 pages. 1999.

Vol. 1710: E.-R. Olderog, B. Steffen (Eds.), Correct System Design. XIV, 417 pages. 1999.

Vol. 1711: N. Zhong, A. Skowron, S. Ohsuga (Eds.), New Directions in Rough Sets, Data Mining, and Granular-Soft Computing. Proceedings, 1999. XIV, 558 pages. 1999. (Subseries LNAI).

Vol. 1712: H. Boley, A Tight, Practical Integration of Relations and Functions. XI, 169 pages. 1999. (Subseries LNAI).

Vol. 1713: J. Jaffar (Ed.), Principles and Practice of Constraint Programming – CP'99. Proceedings, 1999. XII, 493 pages. 1999.

Vol. 1714: M.T. Pazienza (Eds.), Information Extraction. IX, 165 pages. 1999. (Subseries LNAI).

Vol. 1715: P. Perner, M. Petrou (Eds.), Machine Learning and Data Mining in Pattern Recognition. Proceedings, 1999. VIII, 217 pages. 1999. (Subseries LNAI).

Vol. 1716: K.Y. Lam, E. Okamoto, C. Xing (Eds.), Advances in Cryptology – ASIACRYPT'99. Proceedings, 1999. XI, 414 pages. 1999.

Vol. 1717: Ç. K. Koç, C. Paar (Eds.), Cryptographic Hardware and Embedded Systems. Proceedings, 1999. XI, 353 pages. 1999.

Vol. 1718: M. Diaz, P. Owezarski, P. Sénac (Eds.), Interactive Distributed Multimedia Systems and Telecommunication Services. Proceedings, 1999. XI, 386 pages. 1999.

Vol. 1719: M. Fossorier, H. Imai, S. Lin, A. Poli (Eds.), Applied Algebra, Algebraic Algorithms and Error-Correcting Codes. Proceedings, 1999. XIII, 510 pages. 1999.

Vol. 1720: O. Watanabe, T. Yokomori (Eds.), Algorithmic Learning Theory. Proceedings, 1999. XI, 365 pages. 1999. (Subseries LNAI).

Vol. 1721: S. Arikawa, K. Furukawa (Eds.), Discovery Science. Proceedings, 1999. XI, 374 pages. 1999. (Subseries LNAI).

Vol. 1722: A. Middeldorp, T. Sato (Eds.), Functional and Logic Programming. Proceedings, 1999. X, 369 pages. 1999.

Vol. 1723: R. France, B. Rumpe (Eds.), UML'99 – The Unified Modeling Language. XVII, 724 pages. 1999.

Vol. 1724: H. I. Christensen, H. Bunke, H. Noltemeier (Eds.), Sensor Based Intelligent Robots. Proceedings, 1998. VIII, 327 pages. 1999 (Subseries LNAI).

Vol. 1725: J. Pavelka, G. Tel, M. Bartošek (Eds.), SOFSEM'99: Theory and Practice of Informatics. Proceedings, 1999. XIII, 498 pages. 1999.

Vol. 1726: V. Varadharajan, Y. Mu (Eds.), Information and Communication Security. Proceedings, 1999. XI, 325 pages. 1999.

Vol. 1727: P.P. Chen, D.W. Embley, J. Kouloumdjian, S.W. Liddle, J.F. Roddick (Eds.), Advances in Conceptual Modeling. Proceedings, 1999. XI, 389 pages. 1999.

Vol. 1728: J. Akoka, M. Bouzeghoub, I. Comyn-Wattiau, E. Métais (Eds.), Conceptual Modeling – ER '99. Proceedings, 1999. XIV, 540 pages. 1999.

Vol. 1729: M. Mambo, Y. Zheng (Eds.), Information Security. Proceedings, 1999. IX, 277 pages. 1999.

Vol. 1730: M. Gelfond, N. Leone, G. Pfeifer (Eds.), Logic Programming and Nonmonotonic Reasoning. Proceedings, 1999. XI, 391 pages. 1999. (Subseries LNAI).

Vol. 1731: J. Kratochvíl (Ed.), Graph Drawing. Proceedings, 1999. XIII, 422 pages. 1999.

Vol. 1732: S. Matsuoka, R.R. Oldehoeft, M. Tholburn (Eds.), Computing in Object-Oriented Parallel Environments. Proceedings, 1999. VIII, 205 pages. 1999.

Vol. 1733: H. Nakashima, C. Zhang (Eds.), Approaches to Intelligent Agents. Proceedings, 1999. XII, 241 pages. 1999. (Subseries LNAI).

Vol. 1734: H. Hellwagner, A. Reinefeld (Eds.), SCI: Scalable Coherent Interface. XXI, 490 pages. 1999.

Vol. 1564: M. Vazirgiannis, Interactive Multimedia Documents. XIII, 161 pages. 1999.

Vol. 1591: D.J. Duke, I. Herman, M.S. Marshall, PREMO: A Framework for Multimedia Middleware. XII, 254 pages. 1999.

Vol. 1624: J. A. Padget (Ed.), Collaboration between Human and Artificial Societies. XIV, 301 pages. 1999. (Subseries LNAI).

Vol. 1635: X. Tu, Artificial Animals for Computer Animation. XIV, 172 pages. 1999.

Vol. 1646: B. Westfechtel, Models and Tools for Managing Development Processes. XIV, 418 pages. 1999.

Vol. 1735: J.W. Amtrup, Incremental Speech Translation. XV, 200 pages. 1999. (Subseries LNAI).

Vol. 1736: L. Rizzo, S. Fdida (Eds.): Networked Group Communication. Proceedings, 1999. XIII, 339 pages. 1999.

Vol. 1737: P. Agouris, A. Stefanidis (Eds.), Integrated Spatial Databases. Proceedings, 1999. X, 317 pages. 1999.

Vol. 1738: C. Pandu Rangan, V. Raman, R. Ramanujam (Eds.), Foundations of Software Technology and Theoretical Computer Science. Proceedings, 1999. XII, 452 pages. 1999.

Vol. 1740: R. Baumgart (Ed.): Secure Networking – CQRE [Secure] '99. Proceedings, 1999. IX, 261 pages. 1999.

Vol. 1741: A. Aggarwal, C. Pandu Rangan (Eds.), Algorithms and Computation. Proceedings, 1999. XIII, 448 pages. 1999.

Vol. 1742: P.S. Thiagarajan, R. Yap (Eds.), Advances in Computing Science – ASIAN'99. Proceedings, 1999. XI, 397 pages. 1999.

Vol. 1743: A. Moreira, S. Demeyer (Eds.), Object-Oriented Technology. Proceedings, 1999. XVII, 389 pages. 1999.

Vol. 1744: S. Staab, Extracting Degree Information from Texts. X; 187 pages. 1999. (Subseries LNAI).

Vol. 1745: P. Banerjee, V.K. Prasanna, B.P. Sinha (Eds.), High Performance Computing – HiPC'99. Proceedings, 1999. XXII, 412 pages. 1999.

Vol. 1746: M. Walker (Ed.), Cryptography and Coding. Proceedings, 1999. IX, 313 pages. 1999.

Vol. 1747: N. Foo (Ed.), Adavanced Topics in Artificial Intelligence. Proceedings, 1999. XV, 500 pages. 1999. (Subseries LNAI).

Vol. 1748: H.V. Leong, W.-C. Lee, B. Li, L. Yin (Eds.), Mobile Data Access. Proceedings, 1999. X, 245 pages. 1999.

Vol. 1749: L. C.-K. Hui, D.L. Lee (Eds.), Internet Applications. Proceedings, 1999. XX, 518 pages. 1999.

Vol. 1750: D.E. Knuth, MMIXware. VIII, 550 pages. 1999.